The Social Construction of
Sexuality and Perversion

The Social Construction of Sexuality and Perversion

Deconstructing Sadomasochism

Andrea Beckmann
University of Lincoln, UK

First published 2009 by
PALGRAVE MACMILLAN

Palgrave Macmillan in the UK is an imprint of Macmillan Publishers Limited, registered in England, company number 785998, of Houndmills, Basingstoke, Hampshire RG21 6XS.

Palgrave Macmillan in the US is a division of St Martin's Press LLC, 175 Fifth Avenue, New York, NY 10010.

Palgrave Macmillan is the global academic imprint of the above companies and has companies and representatives throughout the world.

Palgrave® and Macmillan® are registered trademarks in the United States, the United Kingdom, Europe and other countries.

ISBN: 978-0-230-52210-7

This book is printed on paper suitable for recycling and made from fully managed and sustained forest sources. Logging, pulping and manufacturing processes are expected to conform to the environmental regulations of the country of origin.

A catalogue record for this book is available from the British Library.

A catalog record for this book is available from the Library of Congress.

10 9 8 7 6 5 4 3 2 1
18 17 16 15 14 13 12 11 10 09

Printed and bound in Great Britain by
CPI Antony Rowe, Chippenham and Eastbourne

To Wolfgang, Gundula, Amélie Rosa,
Bob (the late Professor Robert L. Morris)
and BM for very different reasons

Contents

Acknowledgements

In trying to give an account of myself as the author of this work, I wish to acknowledge many who incited my 'self's' reflexivity as,

> ...one person's discourse leads another person into self-reflection. The self does not simply begin to examine itself through the forms of rationality at hand. Those [...] are delivered through discourse, in the form of an address, and they arrive as an incitement, a form of seduction, an imposition or demand from outside to which one yields. (Butler 2005: 125)

This work could never have been conducted without the inspiring openness and willingness to share 'life[his]stories' that I found during my time in London amongst the many practitioners of consensual 'SM' I met.

Thank you all so very, very much!

The reader of this work might, on occasion, find linguistic traces of my German roots that I fondly associate with my time at Hamburg University. The above-mentioned incitement to critical 'self' and 'truth' explorations was certainly not only offered in Hamburg but also provided for in the context of the former 'Centre for Criminology and the Social and Philosophical Study of Law' (CCSPSL) at Edinburgh University, during both my Erasmus study programme as well as during the research for my PhD. I also want to especially acknowledge the incredibly warm, helpful and deeply informed supervision of my work by the late Prof. Robert L. Morris. A very big thank you to Prof. Jackie Tombs for all her support and enduring friendship. It is not less important to mention the 'seduction' that is the 'European Group for the Study of Deviance and Social Control' and the friendship and comradeship that I share there with so many lovely and committed people. Amongst these people, Louk (the late Prof. Louk Hulsman) is missed by us all. I further like to thank Del for a beautiful friendship 'beyond' all boundaries and a shared political vision.

Last but not least, I want to thank my supportive colleagues at Lincoln, the team at Newgen Imaging Systems (P) Ltd., Chennai, India and, indeed, my poor, still healing, shattered heel-bone, for giving me the, however painful, time to finally write this book or, as Prof. Jeffrey Weeks might put it, the "'Blue Angel'...".

1
Introduction

This book aims to deconstruct the social construction of 'Sadomasochism', revealing it to be a mystification of social reality via insights into the 'lived realities' of consensual 'SM' practitioners obtained through ethnographic research of the author. It moves beyond the de-familiarization of the social constructions of 'sexuality' and 'Sadomasochism' and exposes their functional relationships to power.

While the substantive focus of this work is on the social construction of 'Sadomasochism' as well as the 'lived realities' of consensual 'SM', there are broader relevancies of this topic in relation to the knowledges concerning our own 'lived bodies'. This book therefore provides a critical and engaged contribution to contemporary debates about the 'body' (e.g. Blackman and Walkerdine 2001; Brennan 2004; Butler 1990/1993/2004/2005; Diprose 2002; Falk 1994; Featherstone 1993; Murphy 1997; Shilling 1993/2003/2008; Turner 1996/2008; Welton 1998 etc.) and 'sexualities' (e.g. Beasley 2005; Califia 1988/2001; Califia and Sweeney 1996; Foucault 1990; Grosz and Probyn 1995; Jeffreys 1991/1993/2003; Weeks 2003 etc.). In particular, the last sections of the book can be read as a contribution to the debates surrounding the notions of 'New Intimacies' and/or the 'postmodernization of intimacy' (Giddens 1990/1991; Plummer 1995/1999 in: Browning et al. 1999/2003; Weeks et al. 2001) within late modern times.

The 'bodily practices' (Mauss 1979) of consensual 'SM' can be related to a variety of broader socio-cultural phenomena and meanings (e.g. Beckmann 2001a,b/2004/2005; Langdridge and Butt 2004; Langdridge and Barker 2007; Taylor 1997; Taylor and Ussher 2001). The book's contemporary relevance not only derives from the fact that an earlier article (2001) by the author received many positive email-responses of practitioners of consensual 'SM' internationally and led to many invitations to guest-lecture at diverse universities, but also because it has been frequently cited by other academics and was called 'groundbreaking' (Langdridge and Butt 2004) as it was not only one of the first academic pieces of work that depathologized consensual 'SM' but further as it was based on qualitative, ethnographic research

1

that has been rarely conducted within this context. As this part of my work generated such positive responses it seemed appropriate to shed light on this social research project in its full complexity.

Sawicki's (1991) notion of a 'politics of difference' included the important suggestion to see differences as resources and in my opinion this piece of work, based on reflections of field-experiences and 'subjugated knowledges', illustrates that the 'bodily practices' of consensual 'SM' and their practitioners have a lot of resources to offer that stand in stark contrast to the reductionism of decontextualized commodified 'kink' that is marketed in consumer society.

While it is evident that elements of 'SM' and of fetish culture have become part of capitalist consumerism and thus of mainstream society, it is important to acknowledge that this development has obviously impacted on the ways in which the 'bodily practices' of consensual 'SM' are 'lived out' and interpreted. Capitalism's proliferatory imperative led to the commodification and proliferation of representations of 'sex' as well as 'kinky sex' (see also Beckmann 2001).

Saner (2008) confirms as well that there occurred a 'mainstreaming' of 'sadomasochist' representations in the media as well as of BDSM [Bondage Discipline, Dominance and Submission, SadoMasochism] behaviour forms. Despite the positive side-effects of greater access to tools, outfits, clubs, and so on, that were triggered by this (s)exploitation of 'kink' for commercial benefits, this trend cannot in itself be interpreted as representing a greater understanding or openness for the whole variety of these 'bodily practices' as they remain selectively criminalized and as in contrast to the mainstream commodified ' "SM" as package' "a large number of the erotic practices of the Kink community are not genitally focused; some don't even involve the body. The importance of headspace, the inner experience of sexual encounters, which is so important to Kinky sex, is barely recognized." (Dominguez 1994: 63). Thus, the important existential, interrelational and political dimensions of consensual 'SM' play are totally absent from public representation.

These, however, as will be seen especially in Chapter 3, do not only provide an example of an *ars erotica* but further provide examples of the application of 'sexual ethics' that in contemporary times, according to Plummer who refers to Weeks (1995) and Seidman (1997), should be: "...bound to meanings, contexts, recognition of diversities, respect, the importance of consent, responsibility and the consequences of acts" (Plummer in Browning et al. 1999: 442).

The crucial importance of education in relation to 'sexual ethics' is confirmed by recent findings of the Sex Education Forum (Bell 2007) that found that commodified 'sexualized bodies' and stereotypically 'gendered' porn have seemingly replaced other forms of education in terms of 'sexualities' and relationships in contemporary Britain. The findings of a new survey of British teenagers conducted in 2008 confirmed these concerns and revealed: "...when it actually comes to sex education [people, *sic*] have no idea about sexually transmitted infections; they are not particularly clued-up about contraception; they have no idea about what they'd do if they got pregnant."..."They're massively overexposed to pornography on the internet, in magazines and over their mobile phones. That's where they're getting their sex education from" (Hill 2008: 10). The consequences of such problematic learning resources become evident when one considers that sexism, 'sexual' exploitation and gender stereotyping appears to be an increasing problem within UK schools (Curtis 2008: 17) that problematically gets related to "...misogynistic attitudes linked to gang culture" (Curtis 2008: 17). Upon critical reflection (see also Chapters 4 and 5) this destructive attitude is not isolated to a specific group in UK society but has become part of mainstream consumer culture's 'conditions of domination' without being acknowledged as such. In contrast to these problematic sources consensual 'SM' emphasizes and facilitates negotiation, empathy and communication which clearly are existentially important, not only to allow for 'safe sex' or prevent pregnancies but most crucial of all, in order to establish a context for genuinely consensual pleasure.

The highly publicized case of Mr Mosley's engagements with the now 'normalized' commodified world of 'SM' in 2008 (e.g. Pidd 2008) should remind us that the indirect and selective criminalization of consensual 'SM' 'body practices' that began with the *R. v. Brown-case* ([1993] 2 WLR 556; [1993] 2 All ER 75; 1994] 1 AC 212) and the following decision of the European Court of Human Rights in Strasbourg ([1997] Cr App Rep 44) have as yet still to be revoked; thus, the case this book makes is as relevant as ever, as: "Crime has no ontological reality. Crime is not the *object* but the *product* of criminal policy. Criminalization is one of the many ways to construct social reality" (Hulsman 1986: 71 – emphasis in original). It therefore follows that the attribution of 'negative labels' (such as 'criminal') depends on the intervention of official agencies of social control and negotiation processes that are decisive in terms of the success of applying these 'labels'. The 'criminal status' is negotiated during organizational processes and is therefore deeply influenced by power relationships. In the context of Mr Mosley's case, McSmith stated in *The Independent* on 25 July 2008 that: "The implication of yesterday's judgment by Mr. Justice Eady is that people who have sexual habits others might find bizarre or unpalatable have the same right to privacy as anyone else" (McSmith 2008: 8) This observation and the findings of the ethnographic research presented in this book definitely challenge the legitimacy of upholding the existing law.

As argued in Chapter 3 the 'conditions of domination' set up by conventional society mentioned by Chancer (1994) are, in the context of consensual 'SM' practice, replaced by negotiated and consensually agreed upon 'limits'. Thus consensual 'SM' 'body practice' does not even qualify as violence or as being a stabilizing factor for societal power relationships which was/is an accusation voiced against consensual 'SM' by some feminist scholars (see Chapter 2).

This section of my work introduces the central concepts that are touched upon, the approaches which I adopt throughout and guides the reader through the subsequent chapters of this critical criminological work. My definition of 'critical criminology' is not only a necessarily inter- or multidisciplinary one but also one that is based on a perspective that acknowledges the injustice of contemporary social order (de Haan 1992) and that sees dominant ideologies and discourses as having the potential of limiting human creativity and expression, thus as establishing 'conditions of domination' (Foucault, e.g. in: Kritzman 1990; Lotringer 1996). 'Critical criminology', as critique of ideology as proposed by Hess (1986), is the underlying framework of this book and thus a central focus will be the deconstruction of mystifications of social reality and their relationship to experienced realities as well as their functional relationship to formations of power. Practitioners of consensual 'body practices' labelled 'Sadomasochism' continue to be in danger of being prosecuted once their enacted 'plays' ('scenes') leave woundings that are not 'trifling or transient'.

Modernity did not only effect a redistribution of violence (Bauman 1992) but also led to a limiting of legitimate pleasures: "Bodily pleasure was reduced to genital, sexual pleasure" (Stratton 1996: 166). As consensual 'SM' (in contrast to commodified 'kink'; see Beckmann 2001) aims at the production of pleasure through the empathetic 'play' with 'lived bodies' which, as will be shown, is not limited to 'sexual pleasure', I consider the term 'body practice' and/or 'bodily practices' to be a more adequate term in order to describe this social phenomenon. Apart from using Mauss' (1979) notion of 'bodily practice' (and/or 'body techniques'), I will also make use of Merleau-Ponty's (1968) concept of 'lived body' which overcomes the 'enlightened dualism' of body/mind that 'haunts' much of the traditional readings on 'sexualities' as well as much of feminist and deconstructionist accounts. The existential phenomenology of Merleau-Ponty offers, with the concept of the 'lived body', insight into the realms of 'lived experience' which centres around 'being-in-the-world' and intentionality. In "The Visible and the Invisible" (1968), Merleau-Ponty points out that speech is a manifestation of intentionality which is the defining quality of human beings' 'transcendence'. Thus, the concept of the 'lived body' provides space for the potential in human beings to change, to construct their own versions of 'reality' and meaning, and does not discredit them by rendering them subordinate to biological, psychological and/or sociological determinants.

It is further crucial to acknowledge and investigate the interrelationships between 'lived body' and the realm of politics as:

The modern sociological debate about whether the body is natural [outside the city] or socially constructed (under the realm of political sovereignty) has unfortunately become disconnected from the political. If the sociology of the body is to have an important future role in shaping sociological debate, it needs to embrace the relationship between the political and the corporeal as a major research focus. (Turner 2008: 1)

While the interdisciplinary approach of this book is shaped by my academic and professional background as a former social pedagogue and lecturing critical criminologist, this work certainly contributes to this central sociological research focus. My criminological approach defines the phenomenon of 'Sadomasochism' as a construction of reality rather than a reality in itself (e.g. as positivistic orientated approaches would suggest). Based on this premise, the reconstruction of the development of this 'social censure' (Sumner 1990) can only be undertaken through an understanding of its socio-political and discursive contexts.

Social censures combine with forms of power and economy to provide the distinct features of specific practices of domination and 'social control'. These ideologies help to explain and to mystify the routine targeting of the practices of surveillance and control: explain, because their surrounding discourse tells us something about the specific complaint; and mystify; because censures are often expressed in universalistic language which appeals to general moral principles. (Sumner 1990: 201)

The social censure of 'Sadomasochism' is part of what Foucault (1990) termed the 'deployment of sexuality'. In Foucault's view, power did not and does not operate through means of repression only but may be even more effective (because less obvious) through productive power relations which occur and operate throughout the social body. In 'History of Sexuality', Foucault (1990) shows how the authoritative character of medical, psychiatric and governmental experts' discourses and practices worked to constitute subjects and therefore became an important tool to operate social control. This 'sexual technology' was constituted at the beginning of the nineteenth century as a 'scientia sexualis' and, as Foucault suggests, probably every culture constitutes knowledges about 'sexuality'. This Western 'sexual technology' stands in contrast to an *ars erotica* that, according to Foucault, was constituted in ancient China and was aimed at an intensification of pleasure, whereas the Western *scientia sexualis* did not share this aim but "... rather that of causing relations of power to function in the finest and most intricate elements of the body and its conduct. Sexuality is linked to truth, not because it would be an access to truth, but because truth permits access to sexuality and permits its subjugation as an object" (Foucault in Lotringer 1996: 166/167).

As the processes of the ascription of the label 'Sadomasochism', embedded within this 'scientia sexualis', are aimed at (re)producing socio-political power relationships, it is evident that it is important to analyse the inter-relatedness of certain ideas about 'Sadomasochism' and its binary construction of 'natural sexuality' that is cast as 'normality'.

This book will necessarily defamiliarize the social constructions of 'sexuality' and 'Sadomasochism' in order to expose the operations of the discourses (religion, medicine, law, psychology etc.) that aim at the objectification, determination and de-authorization of the so constructed 'Other'. Chapter 2 deconstructs modern, reductionistic concepts that are elements of the social construction of 'Sadomasochism' in order to provide a more authentic understanding of the operation of such organizing categories.

This book does not engage in the project of constructing a 'grand theory'. Instead it is committed to a critical exploration of significant concepts that serve as normativizing injunctions which function as limits to human beings' experiences of 'lived body'. The critical analysis of culturally institutionalized conceptions of 'sexuality' as well as their contemporary representations and meanings, but also of 'body' and 'pain', are in this context crucial, as these appear to be the major elements on which the 'social censure' of 'Sadomasochism' is based. The assessment of these concepts was also a central aspect of the 'reflexivity' of the process of social research, as the information gained in the 'field' pointed towards a need to focus more specifically on those normative and reductionistic concepts that appear to be 'destabilized' in many of the 'bodily practices' of consensual 'SM'. As these institutionalized and often still individually and collectively internalized concepts remain powerful (e.g. as they continue to be major tools of subjection within expert discourses and practices, and are still evident in for example many of my students' understandings of themselves and others) the sections within Chapter 2 are necessarily extensive. Such approaches do not tap into the realities of the 'life-world' and thus often join the league of traditional scientific 'disembodied' approaches that ultimately refer to generalizing, often moralizing concepts of 'truth' that create an 'Other'. Shilling's work (1993) emphasizes and illustrates the importance of understandings of the 'body' as always being in "a process of becoming" (Shilling 1993: 5) and pointed to the need to explore and interpret the 'body' as a "phenomenon that is simultaneously biological and social" (Shilling 1993: 100). Amongst others, the concept of 'social flesh' that was coined by Carol Lee Bacchi and Chris Beasley (2000/2002) and that was further explored within the context of 'inter-sex' corporeality by Grabham (2007) goes some way to remedy this lack.

The sections on 'body', 'sexuality' and 'pain' reveal instabilities of 'naturalized' and thus depoliticizing concepts, through the strategy of deconstruction. As all human beings are, to more or lesser degrees, caught up in these 'normalizing' schemes of representation and regulation which result in social inclusion and exclusion, it is crucially important to open up channels that allow for the reflection of meanings, and thus create a distance from identifications with pre-given meanings. This was also a task that

I had to first engage myself with, in order to be 'open enough' for the experiences of my fieldwork.

As obviously not all sources of this complex undertaking can be taken into consideration, this book should not be read as being engaged with the traditional strategy of scholarship which desperately tries to produce integrity. In sympathy with a lot of recent feminist writers, I embrace the notion of the 'fragmentary' which, perhaps because of the renewed interest in the works of Friedrich Nietzsche, has gained acceptance within the academic world: ".. feminists must explore the meaning of the diversity of sexual practices to those who practice them, to resurrect the 'subjugated knowledge' of sexuality elided within dominant culture" (Sawicki 1991: 31).

Chapter 3 will introduce the reader to the empirical world of consensual 'SM' I encountered in London. I will account for my research design and methodology and my sample-generation as the social stigma that was/is attached to the label and practice of consensual 'Sadomasochism' as well as the selective criminalization of some practices which effectively turned practitioners of consensual 'SM' into a 'hidden population'. In this context there were no predefined sociometric criteria that would have enabled me to selectively include or exclude people from the sample. For some, the sample obtained could be considered to be 'unrepresentative' but "...one is still sampling with reference to the social structure, though this time in an *implicit* manner" (Lee 1993: 66 emphasis in original).

The presentation of the accounts of my subjects presented in Chapter 3 were mainly shaped by the accumulation of data on specific topics, rather than through directive questions that would have guided my respondents' answers. The main points of emphasis detailed in these accounts seem to have had relevance for most of my interviewees and, to this extent, this ensures a certain degree of representativeness. An important aim of my work is to give the usually silenced or media-sensationalistically distorted voices the space to articulate themselves: "...an experience is neither – true or false; it is always a fiction, something constructed, which exists only after it has been made, not before; it isn't something that is 'true', but it has been a reality" (Foucault in Halperin 1995: 222). In order to account for the diverse realities of the usually 'unheard', distorted and/ or de-authorized voices the sections of Chapter 3 make up a substantial part of this book and thus aim to redress the ordinarily existing profound imbalance in terms of space given to 'subjugated knowledges' in contrast to concepts of 'truth'.

Within Chapter 4, I attempt to illustrate both the impact of the social censure of 'Sadomasochism' on individual perceptions of practitioners of these 'bodily practices' and the use that the maintenance of this 'social censure' (Sumner 1990) seems to continue to have for society. The project of deconstruction does not exhaust itself in the deconstruction of concepts, but also engages in the exposure of, for example, socially-legitimized power relationships which are in many ways contradicted by the realities of consensual 'SM'. 'Sadomasochism' as a social construction serves, for example, to keep existing and sedimented socio-political 'conditions of domination' unchallenged as their immanent inequality is projected onto practitioners of consensual 'SM'. This distortion and 'mystification of reality' is accounted for by an exploration of the inherently unequal structures and relationships of power within capitalist-consumer society which are then compared to the 'lived realities' of consensual 'SM'. Following the demonstration of the 'non-consensual sadomasochistic dynamic' (Chancer 1994) that pervades Western patriarchal, ethnocentric, capitalist-consumer cultures, the effects and aims of institutionalized and legitimized pain-distribution are discussed.

On the basis of the knowledge presented in Chapters 2 and 3, examples of state-authorized exertion of violence within the context of 'conditions of domination' are contrasted with the role and use of 'pain' in the 'bodily practices' of consensual 'SM'. As consensual 'SM' is frequently publicly misrepresented as 'torture' and, further, as one of Lord Templeman's comments within his ruling on the 'Spanner' case were that this "... cruelty was uncivilised" (*Times Law Reports* 12.3.93: 42), the exposure of the contradictions within the social construction of 'Sadomasochism' in Chapter 4 concludes with a discussion of the practice of torture and its origins in the alleged 'birthplace' of 'civilization', ancient Greece.

Chapter 5 continues with the problematization of fundamental social constructions of modernity. The socio-political operations of the constructed dualisms of 'civilization' and 'wilderness' are explored and their relation to both the social construction of 'Sadomasochism' as well as the 'bodily practices' of consensual 'SM' are revealed. In this chapter I therefore aim to provide a deeper understanding of the mechanisms of inclusion and exclusion that operate on various interacting discursive and societal levels that produce and maintain the social construction of 'Sadomasochism'. The 'violence of rationality', in contrast to consensual 'SM' as well as the selective permissiveness of generating harmful 'conditions of domination' and of 'risk taking' within consumer culture, are therefore discussed. This book addresses the apparent hypocrisy that is existing between the way in which elective (normative) cosmetic surgery is represented and legislated and how 'bodily practices' that involve similar "... bloody natures ..." (Jones 2008: 186) such as consensual 'SM' are demonized and selectively criminalized.

The focus here is to point to several 'flip-points' of constructed meaning that the social construction of 'Sadomasochism' helps to keep hidden via its function as 'Other'. The project of deconstruction aims to expose: "... the problems which reside in the endeavor to keep meaning pure, to say 'just this' and not 'that', because 'just this' always depends on 'that' which it is not" (Naffine 1997: 89). Through the examination of the consensual 'bodily practices' of 'SM' in their specific historical context which is characterized by, for example, an increasing 'normalization' of invasive 'body projects' (such as cosmetic surgery, botox, etc.), the 'sexualization' and commodification of younger and younger 'bodies', Chapter 5 will further attempt to define the potential social meanings that the 'bodily practice' of consensual 'SM' has in the context of contemporary consumer and technological cultures: "Indeed, the rational 'enframing' of people and nature associated with technological culture in the West not only erodes meaning from human life, expelling the spiritual and sacred from its borders. It also creates the conditions in which it is possible for other cultural forms of belief to challenge its principles from outside and within its parameters" (Shilling 2008: 166).

Chapter 6 also deals, in a more complex fashion, with one of the thus indicated potential broader social meanings of these 'bodily practices' – a meaning which is located in the longing for 'transcendental states' and/ or religious, spiritual experiences through consensual 'SM'. This chapter is also based on empirical research as the results of a self-completion questionnaire on 'transcendental states' through consensual 'SM' will be presented. In adaptation of Jana Sawicki's (1991) understanding of Foucault's politics, which are based on the assumption that differences cannot always be bridged but do not make effective resistance impossible, I employ her terminology of calling the politics that inform my work the 'politics of difference'. My work thus aims at providing a space for the articulation of different opinions and life-experiences of people whose voices often are only to be heard in distorted fashions or silenced and partake in the 'arena of struggle' labelled 'Sadomasochism'.

"Only an examination of concrete, historical situations can determine whether resistance is taking place or the body being 'rewritten' or dualisms being 'transcended'" (Bordo in Welton 1998: 92). Another purpose of this piece of work therefore consisted of establishing the potential of consensual 'SM' as a 'practice of resistance'. "On the basis of specific theoretical analyses of particular struggles, one can make generalizations, identify patterns in relations of power and thereby identify the relative effectiveness or ineffectiveness, safety or danger of particular practices" (Sawicki 1991: 32). Chapter 7 will thus elaborate on alternative readings of consensual 'SM' which will include the possibility to interpret these 'bodily practices' as 'practices of freedom' and also a discussion of the ethics of consensual 'SM' in their relation to Foucault's notion of 'care of the self' (1990 and 1992; also in: Rabinow 1997). As: "one escaped from a domination of truth not by playing a game that was totally different from the game of truth, but by playing the same game differently or playing another game, another hand, with other trump cards" (Foucault in Lotringer 1996: 444).

On the premises outlined above my critical criminological project could also be understood as an attempt to engage in the struggle for a relational and contextual 'justice' for 'lived bodies'. It is highly disturbing that consensual 'SM' is still classified as pathological within the Diagnostic and Statistical Manual of Mental Disorders of the American Psychiatric Association DSM-IV-TR (APA 2000). This continuing stigmatization and the semi-criminalization of consensual 'SM' only serve to restrict consensual 'SM' education and facilitate the continuing existence of stereotypes, associated blackmailing and/or the production of decontextualized media-spectacles.

As stated before, the 'subjugated knowledges' of consensual 'SM' can be helpful in terms of generating a 'sexual ethics' not only in terms of highlighting and illustrating the importance of negotiating 'consent' (see also Beckmann 2004 in Cowling and Reynolds 2004) but also in terms of Barker's (in Langdridge and Barker 2007) training/education and challenge to the still widespread stereotypes and myths about consensual 'SM' and the continued predominance of unreflected 'normative heterosexuality'.

This book is also a reflection of my professional and personal development, triggered by the experiences in the empirical field and by the many encounters with my interviewees. During the four years I spent researching for and writing my PhD thesis on which this book is based, I was thus able to further my understanding of my own 'embodied self' in various aspects as: "...it is only through an engaged encounter with the Other, with the otherness of the Other, that one comes to a more informed, textured understanding of the traditions to which 'we' belong. It is in our genuine encounters with what is other and alien (even in ourselves) that we can further our own self-understanding" (Bernstein 1990: 66/67).

2
Deconstructing 'Normalizing' Concepts

This chapter attempts to describe the 'historical field' within which the social construction of 'Sadomasochism' was and remains possible and describes the major conceptual frameworks of order that underlie the emergence and enforce the permanence of the label of 'Sadomasochism'. The different sections of this chapter introduce the reader to the theoretical, conceptual and analytical tools that are used throughout.

This work follows Plummer's (1975) suggestion that it is crucial to examine our assumptions about 'sexuality' as human 'sexuality' is primarily a matter of symbolism. Therefore the deconstruction of the concepts of 'body', 'sexuality' and 'pain' which play central roles in the operation and constitution of the social construction of 'Sadomasochism' are of crucial importance. It will become evident that only in their deconstructed states do they allow for a less prejudiced access into the 'lived realities' of consensual 'SM'.

The strategy of deconstruction, despite having limits, serves to reveal instabilities of meaning through pointing to the social constructedness of concepts like, for example, 'body'. This contrasts with the depoliticizing and claimed 'naturalness' of these social constructions.

> Deconstruction is an intervention into the workings of language designed to reveal the limits of concepts we often treat as unproblematic and so use unthinkingly. Delimitation of meaning is revealed to be an effect of exclusion. That is, concepts establish their limits by differentiating themselves from that which they are not (as 'man' defines himself against 'woman'), and, as a consequence, concepts are never autonomous and self-contained. (Naffine 1997: 89)

The notion of the 'historical field' (Foucault in Miller 1994) is of crucial relevance as human beings never stand outside of the schemes of representation with their implicit exclusion and inclusion-mechanisms. The specific 'historical field' thus shapes the 'self'– construction and – perception of human beings as well as their possibilities of transgression and/or their 'transcendence', a concept which is further explored within Chapter 6. Although the 'bodily practices' of consensual 'SM' can be read as acts of transgression and thus enable the human being to experience the power of the 'Dionysian' (Nietzsche 1954, 1967), James Miller clarified the crucial importance and meaning of the 'historical field' in Foucault's work: "...no act of transgression can escape its origins in a historical field that, in crucial part, motivates, defines – and insofar as the object of transgression is to tap the untamed energy of transcendence – (de)forms it" (Miller 1994: 115).

2.1 'Bodies'

> Body-sense is experienced as an ever-renewed gift of culture.
>
> (Illich 1976: 135)

From a Foucauldian perspective modernity has been characterized by the deployment of 'biopower' that relies on the premise that the most effective access to the subject is via its 'body', insinuated within this body's 'naturally' given imperatives. Metaphors of 'body' thus serve to lay down the meanings 'body' is made to bear. In 'The Body Social' (1993), Anthony Synnott examined constructions of the 'body' and noted the cultural variability of these and, parallel to that, the diversity of sociological and anthropological approaches which all seem to construct matching 'sociologies of the body'.

Synnott's definition of a sociology of the body is therefore broad and entails:

> ... the study of the self as embodied, and of the various attributes, organs, processes and senses that constitute our being embodied; it is the study of the body as a symbolic system and a semiotic process; it is the phenomenology of the body, i.e. the subjectively and culturally created meanings of the body; it is the study of the lifelong socialisation and political control of the self in and with and through the body until death; it is also the anthropology, history and psychology of the body... (Synnott 1993: 262/263)

Given the diversity of potential readings and interpretations of the 'body', there are multiple possibilities to understand and perceive one's and other 'bodies' and this has important consequences for the 'body-experience' and consequently one's relation to one's body. In 'The Body and Society' (1996/2008), Bryan S. Turner gives a detailed overview of the most recent approaches on the 'body' within contemporary debates. The range of these approaches is wide as it covers a variety of understandings reaching from foundationalism to social constructionism and can be seen as being in contrast to the limited meanings of 'body' in contemporary consumer cultures as illustrated below.

The anthropological perspective offers a view of the 'body' as 'a set of social practices'. The 'body' is within this contextual framework seen as "... a potentiality which is realised and actualised through a variety of socially regulated activities or practices" (Turner 1996: 24). Exponents of this stream of thought are Goffman (1967) within the framework of symbolic inter- actionism and Mauss who adopted an anthropological approach (1979) as well as Garfinkel (1967) from an ethno-methodological perspective. The notion of 'body as social practice' underlines the importance given to every- day life-practices.

The notion of 'bodily practices' and/or 'body techniques' is derived from the anthropological perspective of Marcel Mauss (1979) who defined them as: " ... physio-psycho-sociological assemblages of series of actions. These actions are more or less habitual and more or less ancient in the life of the individual and the history of the society ... Cases of invention, of laying down principles, are rare" (Mauss 1979: 120/121). These 'bod- ily practices' are usually assembled for and by social authorities and can be classified according to their efficiency. In the context of consensual 'SM' new 'bodily practices' were (are) being invented in order to prod- uce pleasurable sensations (Chapter 3) which were not assembled by any social authority. In the case of 'bodily practices' that do have a historical background like, for example, whipping, the innovation that the 'bodily practices' of consensual 'SM' do represent can be located on the levels of meaning and consequences for the 'lived bodies', as well as in the rever- sal of its formerly 'disciplinarian' function in the service of the powers of domination.

A similar, more historical view of the 'body' is to be found in other theor- ies of social constructionism. In this theoretical context the 'body' is seen as a system of signs representing and expressing relations of power. The con- cept of 'body' is detected as shaped and changed through changing societal power relations. According to Turner, this approach is the " ... characteristic epistemological approach of feminist views on the body", which focuses its criticism on the fact that " ... the fashion industry and consumerism construct an ideal type of the female body which cannot be achieved by real women and that pornographic images of women in the fashion industry underpin and support the basic patriarchal power relations which continue to control men and women" (Turner 1996: 27). As I consider consensual 'SM' as hav- ing the potential to be a 'practice of resistance', located not only within the innovative 'body practices' but also within the use of the traditional modes of 'power' (discourses as well as 'body practices') itself, my work will often refer to Judith Butler's (1990, 1993, 2004, 2005) work. Inspired by Foucault's works, Butler suggests the performative disruption of the 'order of things' as possible resistance. She points out that 'gender' as well as 'sexuality' only emerge through repetitive performances and, thus, through the course of time: "... produce the appearance of substance, of a natural sort of being"

(Butler 1990: 33). Butler's account of subversion is focused in effect on the disruption of these continuous and 'naturalized performances'. Dissident sexual acts which either undermine and/or transcend the traditional dualism of male (active) and female (passive) have the potential of disruption. The weakening of the dominating heterosexual and reproductive discourses by performances of diverse 'genders' and 'sexualities' will, according to Butler, reveal the constructed 'nature' of 'gendered sexuality' and the 'sexualized gendered body'. Halperin also views freedom and resistance as being contained in power itself. For him potential counter-practices lie in 'creative appropriation and resignification', 'appropriation and theatricalization' as well as in 'exposure and demystification' (Halperin 1995).

2.1.2   The lack of the 'lived body' and the reproduction of modern binarisms

Turner's (1996/2008) general criticism of deconstructionist approaches is the 'disappearance of the lived body' which is similar to Murphy's critique of many feminist accounts. Although the use of the term 'woman' served feminist politics in law to expose the disabling fiction of 'woman' which is frequently applied in legal cases to naturalize men and women's social roles (gender), Murphy insists that many feminist accounts contain "...overly-Cartesian resonances" (Murphy 1997: 39). In other words, many feminist accounts (e.g. de Beauvoir 1974; Gilligan 1983; MacKinnon 1987) have the tendency to leave the binarism of mind/body intact and thus portray the 'female body' as essentially less detached, fragile etc., therefore apparently accepting these ascribed patriarchal assumptions. The sex/gender binarism has to be overcome as we still seem to accept, partly as a result of this, the 'existence' of two 'genders'. It is therefore crucial to challenge the 'naturalization' of differences on the basis of modern assumptions which is still taking place as evidenced for example, in my experience of teaching and learning about my students' understandings of 'body', 'gender' and 'sexuality' (Beckmann, forthcoming).

The introduction of the notion of 'transcendence' in Michel Foucault's later work (e.g. 1990 and 1992) breaks with his earlier expressed 'nihilistic' or rather hopeless outlook on the possibilities for an escape of the 'techniques of domination' by the human being. As the criminological approach adopted here, not only on the topic of the social construction of 'Sadomasochism', is, not only ideology-critical, but also motivated by the search for ways to overcome internalized 'social censures', Foucault's hopes for the 'transcendence' of inscribed categories of for example, 'sexuality' through a new 'politics of the self' and the practice of consensual 'SM' are a central concern of this work. Thus, I do not agree with Turner's and others' critiques of Foucault's work as characterized by a lack of the 'lived body'. My reading of Foucault's later work entails a potential for fundamental transformations located in the 'body' through 'bodily practices' of consensual 'SM'. Boyne's reading of Foucault seems to reflect a similar understanding of his last works as a break with Foucault's former nihilism. Boyne suggests that the later works of the French philosopher: "... do begin to present a countervision to the experience of modern culture. Like some contemporary Descartes, Foucault offers the possibility, especially in *The Use of Pleasure*, that there are political resources within the self that have remained untapped and forgotten for millennia" (Boyne 1990: 166). For Foucault, the 'self' is a strategic possibility which in contrast to being regulated by morality, ought to be regulated by the voluntary care of each individual as a political principle. This transformative capability matches the notion of 'lived body' and in particular Merleau-Ponty's understanding of 'peak-experiences' in this context (which is a central topic of Chapter 6).

"Truly embodied or spontaneous action presupposes *insight*, the ability to fuse theory and praxis... Self-awareness has to be accompanied by a change in the way one relates to oneself and the world, it has to herald a change in the meaning of one's existence" (Spurling 1977: 133). The notion of 'lived body' adopted here is therefore able to account for transformations and change as well as emotional experiences in a far more non-deterministic manner than even postmodern notions of the 'body' are. For example the notion of 'body as sign' (Derrida 1978; Irigaray 1993; Kristeva 1982; Lacan 1998) is in great danger of ignoring and/or denying "... experimental and affective dimensions of social practice and social relations" (Turner 1996: 28). The ambiguity of 'bodily existence' and its fundamental interdependence with its environment are too important to ignore if the aim is to reach a more authentic understanding of human development. As: "... What distinguishes the human body is that it can transform itself in the process of transforming and being transformed by the material bodies which surround it. Being self-transformative the body is always a kind of 'surplus', something over and above its existence at any moment for itself or others" (Segal 1994: 161).

This understanding of 'body' is also characteristic for the so-called 'affective turn' in theories of 'body'. Shilling's work (1993/2003) understands the 'body' as always being in "a process of becoming" (Shilling 1993: 5), pointing to the need to interpret the 'body' as a "phenomenon that is simultaneously biological and social" (Shilling 1993: 100). Important in the context of 'rationalized', technologized consumer society is Howes (2005) notion of 'skin knowledge' that describes forms of knowledge that have been substituted and covered over by mechanized ways of knowing ('electronic skins') that place the sensing 'body' into the background. In contrast to this trend, consensual 'SM' practices clearly emphasize the sensing 'body'.

Bigwood (1998) noted the immanent value of Foucault's maintenance of a sort of 'natural body' as this directs us to the 'lived body' of Merleau-Ponty (Bigwood in Welton 1998: 112). In order to appreciate the concept of 'lived body' as well as other concepts of the 'body' which do account for its interaction with the world, several notions of 'body' that are prevalent in consumer societies will be introduced as they will be contrasted to the productive use and understanding of 'bodies' within the context of consensual 'SM' 'body practice'.

2.1.3   Dimensions of 'body' in consumer culture

The traditional image of 'body' that emerged within the era of the Enlightenment is still present in contemporary capitalist-consumer society and now serves the purposes of the market. The 'body' in this conceptualization, rooted in Descartes' philosophical visions of 'body as machine', serves as a tool for the construction of fantasies of eternal possession, power and desire. As a site of inscription the 'body' gets used and shaped in order to conform to impossible ideals.

Within the context of consumer culture 'unruly bodies' (Foucault), 'grotesque bodies' (Bakthin 1968) are 'bad bodies' which show the external signs of a management gone wrong and therefore are interpreted as internal failures of the agent, instead of being regarded as different and valid choices and expressions or reflections of the diversity of human beings. In the context of increasing uses of biometrics, in which the 'body' is once again (as in traditions of positivism in general as well as in practices of torture in specific) constructed as the ultimate bearer of 'truth', Agamben (2004) stated thus that in contemporary times 'bodies' become marked by 'biopolitical tatoos' distinguishing 'good' and 'bad' citizens.

In my opinion the rising engagement with consensual 'SM' 'bodily practices', in contrast to its commodification, should not be viewed as passive reactions to historical, social and cultural changes but as a productive effort which reflects the contradictory position of human beings in late modern capitalist-consumer societies on the macro level. On the micro level, consensual 'SM' can be read as reflecting also the tensions within individuals in their social lives between control and indulgence, as represented by notions of the 'closed' and the 'open' body. Modern anthropology, since Mary Douglas (1966), views the 'body' as a system of signs, as a bearer of social and symbolic meaning. In this perspective the 'body' is understood as an "... important source of metaphors about the organisation and disorganisation of society. Thus, disorganized bodies express social disorganization" (Turner 1996: 26). Falk illustrates this understanding of 'bodies' well in stating that the characteristic transformation in modern society is a shift from collective rituals of eating to privatized meals. Falk transformed Tõennie's concept of Gemeinschaft/Gesellschaft distinction into a theory of body/self/society: "... such that the communal bonds of the ritual meal are eventually replaced by the privatized forms of consumption in modern society, but this historical transformation is also one from the open body/

closed self to the closed body/open self of modern society" (Turner in Falk 1994: xv). The notion of 'in a body' expresses the idea that the 'body' is complete in its wholeness and does not need or require other 'bodies' for its own completion. The crossing of bodily boundaries (e.g. the practical function of the 'Master', 'Dominatrix' or 'top' in consensual 'SM') and the opening up of one's body for other 'bodies' (e.g. the 'slave', 'submissive' or 'bottom'-space-possibility) are considered to be taboo. "Controlling the boundaries at an individual level implies a strengthened control over the flows in and out of the body. The body becomes more 'closed' in its relationship to the objects and subjects of the outside world" (Falk 1994: 25). In contrast to, for example, mainstream society's members reinforced attempts to hide blood, sweat, urine etc. from sight and even self-perception, the attitude of consensual 'SM' practitioners to these bodily fluids is less paranoid and on occasions a reason for pride (as will be shown in Chapter 3). In recent times, however, cosmetic surgery TV programmes do show 'bloodiness' though:

> ...this opening of the time and space between before/after has, counter-intuitively, contributed to cosmetic surgery becoming increasingly mainstream and fashionable. The simple explanation for this is that gruesome scenes desensitize and initiate a surgical-virgin audience. Surgery becomes an everyday media event. In this sense television is a cultural anaesthetic through which we experience virtual surgery, making that small step to real surgery a little bit easier. But the connection is more complex: it is to do with showing *labour revealed* within a very specific framework. When painful recovery periods, embarrassing consultations and vulnerable, anaesthetized subjects are displayed, cosmetic surgery becomes associated with hard work and sacrifice. (Jones 2008: 53)

This neatly fits in with a fostered mainstream consumer ideology whereby the lifting of body-boundaries in consumer society is legitimized for 'good reasons' (e.g. operations, sports, war, reproduction technology, etc.) and in consensual 'SM' the reasons and limits for these boundary- manipulations are self-defined and negotiated. The possibility to set bodily limits, the experience of being inside and outside of one's body as well as the 'work' on new limits of the individual body, could, in my opinion, be understood as an active attempt of re-gaining or achieving an affective, more authentic feeling of body-sense which for many people within consumerism is made impossible through the alienation and depersonalization of 'bodies' that are merely images and simulations. Langdridge stated that consensual 'SM' "...offers up a highly refined version of [...] moments of intersubjectivity, where the particularity of such experiences is raised to a fine art" (Langdridge in Langdridge and Barker 2007: 95).

2.1.4   The body as 'project'

> The body constructed by consumer culture represents the inter-
> section of two contradictory regimes: a form of cultural produc-
> tion articulated in terms of penology (a coercive panopticon geared
> toward the production of docile bodies) and, paradoxically, a form
> of cultural production articulated in terms of a culture of the self as
> the manifestation of individual agency.
>
> (Radner 2008: 98)

The notion of the 'body as project' is, according to Turner (1996/2008),
closely associated with contemporary consumerism. Here the 'body' is
transformed into the site of 'hedonistic practices' which permanently seeks
to fulfil ever new desires. "The transformation of medical technology has
made possible the construction of the human body as a personal project
through cosmetic surgery, organ transplants, and transsexual surgery. In
addition there is the whole panoply of dieting regimes, health farms, sports
science and nutritional science which are focused on the development of
the aesthetic thin body. Modern sensibility and subjectivity are focused on
the body as a representation of the self, such that the body is in contemporary society a mirror of the soul" (Turner in Falk 1994: xii).

This relationship between body and soul originates in Hegel's philosophy
which saw in the body, particularly in the face, a manifestation of the soul,
of the inner 'truth' of the person. "In the twentieth century, the twin beliefs
that the face (and the body) mirror the soul, and that beauty and goodness
are one, and are reflected in the face, still persist as they did in the past"
(Synnott 1993: 92).

Within this context, the decision and realization of individual 'body
projects' is limited as individual choice is pre-structured *but not determined*
by social class, 'gender', 'race' and 'age' etc. and the means that are on offer
or rather marketed for the individual socio-political categories of human
beings. In recourse to Shilling (1993), Turner points out that the 'body as
project' notion implies that the body becomes a tool, a means of expression
of needs and belonging through 'self-construction'. The empirical parts of
my research point to the same notion of 'body as project' as being valid for
practitioners of consensual 'SM' as well in terms of the 'lived body's' function as an affirmation of 'self'-hood. Examples of legitimated 'body projects'
are to be found in surplus as cosmetic surgery, transplant technology and
genetic engineering are constantly setting new limits for their extensions.
It appears thus that the recent advances in medical science have reinforced
traditional mechanistic and materialistic constructions of the 'body' within
mainstream consumer society as the 'body bionic' becomes a valid alternative for 'bodies' that can afford it. As the dependency of 'bodies' on
machines increases, borderlines decrease: "Finally, the humans/machines
may be 'unplugged' or 'switched off'. The line between human and machine

is blurred, so is the fine line between life and death. The brain-dead can be kept alive" (Synnott 1993: 34). Through transplants and xenografts (transplantations across species), 'chosen bodies' involving either the new reproductive technologies as well as 'gender transformation'– surgery and the engineering of the 'body' by means of gene therapy, cloning etc., the biomedical model of the 'body' constantly becomes reinvoked.

In consumer societies human beings live under the imperative to manage their 'bodies'. The notion of 'choosing one's body' as well as the continuing inspection and disciplining of the 'flesh' via botox and cosmetic surgery etc. according to commodified 'body-images' of normalization are perceived as signifying the moral and social worth of persons. In commenting on Boots' move to offer Botox fixes on the high street Boseley suggested already in 2002 that: "The enormous popularity of Botox and its move to high street accessibility has potential social implications, increasing the pressure on women and men (...) to make themselves look younger" (Boseley 2002: 7).

Jones (2008) explores the pressures on 'body' further in her book 'Skintight' in which she demonstrates how the phenomenon of cosmetic surgery is globally growing at a fast pace. This trend has important implications locally and personally: "As cosmetic surgery becomes popular and commonplace it is necessary to look at how concepts of 'normal' are negotiated and renegotiated within makeover culture" (Jones 2008: 6).

All these phenomena point to the need for an 'ethics of the body', however, there is little to no evidence of governmental encouragement to openly and publicly debate such crucial realms outside crude market-concerns. While the 'bodily practices' of consensual 'SM' also involve representations, manipulations and interventions of and into the 'body', they do foster and allow for the 'experience of the body' within interactive 'body' practices or 'body games'. It is further possible to relate the insubjective experience of consensual 'SM' practice to Diprose's (2002) notion of 'corporeal generosity' as 'intercorporeal generosity' which implies a concept of 'freedom' which is relational as it is based on the 'capacity' of 'lived body' (Merleau-Ponty's notion of 'tolerance') to give and receive corporeality from the other.

2.1.5 Limits to the commodification of 'bodies'(?)

In her book 'Contested Commodities', Margaret Radin (1996) discussed the market rhetoric of 'uncontested commodification'. From this perspective: "..., all things desired or valued-from personal attributes to good government-are commodities" (Radin 1996: 2). This simplistic and reductionistic view on life that is characteristic to discourses of market rhetoric is destructive to personhood.

Radin suggests a standpoint of 'incommensurability' as an alternative to the notion of 'commensurability' that parallels logically the market rhetoric of 'uncontested commodification'.

The notion of 'incommensurability' supports Radin's aspirations for non-commodification and market-inalienability in order to prevent further and/or total commodification. In order to arrive at a more flexible and positive understanding of personhood than traditional approaches, Radin introduces apart from the traditional composing concepts of freedom and identity, the notion of contextuality which matches the notion of the 'lived body'. As conceptions of 'freedom' and 'identity' are not detachable from enabling/disabling contexts, the context for example, social structure allowing for human flourishing or not, becomes the central issue. Law in Radin's eyes does not only reflect but shapes culture and consequently: "...the law indeed influences how we understand ourselves and our values..." (Radin 1996: 203). The impact of law becomes crucially important in an often very existential sense in the context of consensual 'SM' as we shall see later. Commodification expresses and creates alienation and therefore in Marx's view not only institutions but people themselves have to change in order to be able to live 'uncommodified lives'. Marx's notion of 'commodity fetishism' which denotes human subjection to commodities implies the projection of power and action onto consumerable commodities which transform human social interactions as well as concepts of 'self'.

> Today, in the age of the complete domination of the commodity form over all aspects of life, what remains of the subdued, senseless promise of happiness that we received in the darkness sheathed in Dim stockings? Never has the human body-above all the female body – been so massively manipulated as today and, so to speak, imagined from top to bottom by the techniques of advertising and commodity production. (Agamben 2007: 48.9 pp)

2.1.6   "The consuming body – disenchanted 'body-images'"

Synnott noted that diverse cultures 'produce' and shape diverse bodies through their varying constructions of the human body and that therefore every physical body is eminently social. The consequences of these historically changing social constructions of the body are of an existential nature: "Any construction of the body, however, is also a construction of the self as embodied; and as such, influences not only how the body is treated but also how life is lived" (Synnott 1993: 37).

Weber had already pointed out that the power of eroticism would develop a tense relationship with religions that focused on salvation. In 'The Sociology of Religion' (1948) Weber presents a view of eroticism and sexuality that a priori excludes faith in ascetics as well as mystical quests. Sexuality and eroticism were according to Weber seen as the animalistic antithesis to rational organization and self-control. Once again the dualism-game of nature/culture, body/mind and reason/madness is unfolded. The restriction of 'bodily drives' (e.g. via abstinence/diets etc.) was undertaken in order to gain spiritual salvation and material profit. Consumer society's demands shifted the meaning and purpose of 'bodily restrictions' and started to exploit images of the constructed 'sexualized body' in order to create new markets. "Whereas traditional forms of diet subordinated desire in the interest of the salvation of the soul, in contemporary consumer society the diet assumes an entirely different meaning and focus, namely as an elaboration or amplification of sexuality" (Turner in Falk 1994: xii).

The 'consuming self' of contemporary society is a representational being, permanently engaged in the 'body/self'-project. The 'self' in consumer societies is in danger of being reduced to the 'body-image' presented as "... it is the body-image that plays the determining role in the evaluation of the self in the public arena" (Turner in Falk 1994: xiii). As will be shown in Chapter 3, within the consensual 'SM'-Scene in London this relationship appeared to be reversed, the individual abilities of 'tops' and 'bottoms' were compared and other notions of 'body-image' in relationship to 'self' became relevant. The dominance-display of most 'tops' depended more on emotional and cognitive powers as well as technological skill and empathy than on physical attributes of the 'body'. The same holds true for the 'submissive body', its physical representations do not have the fatal relevance they have in the power plays of 'normal' society, the 'bottom's' most crucial attribute is the optional willingness to receive pain and/or physical sensations in general.

Stratton (1996) suggested another reading of the reconstruction of the modern experience of the 'body'. The formation of the nation-state with its increase in 'biopower' and thus experienced reach into individual 'lived bodies' of the power of the phallic Father formed the basis of what Stratton termed 'cultural fetishism'(Stratton 1996: 25). The expression of male power was located in the penis which never matched the 'mythical phallus of the state'. Stratton proposes that the resulting preoccupation with the male genital and his mythological analogy represented in the 'phallic' state: "... was translated into a male fetishisation of the body of the pubescent girl. It was this fetishisation which began the general eroticisation of the life-world and led to a cultural, male-determined, reconstruction of the preferred female body as phallicised" (Stratton 1996: 25). For Stratton then, the institutionalization of the difference between cultural phallus (state/Father) and the individual male body's penis established 'cultural fetishism'. The concerns and complexes that many men have with regards to the physical dimensions of their erect penises ('heteros' as well as 'gays') is thus an expression of this socially constructed 'lack of phallic power'. "The male experience of inadequacy is projected on to the female body which is produced as the key phallic fetish" (Stratton 1996: 25). For Stratton both 'bodies', 'male' as well as 'female', became spectacularized in the course of modernity although different sources can be made responsible for this development. "Where the female body was spectacularised as the effect of cultural fetishism, the male body was placed on display for men as a expansionary attempt to create a new male consumer market" (Stratton 1996: 180). The result of this consumer targeting expansion is that now all 'bodies' are constructed as sites of lack. In contemporary consumer societies incomplete and/or inadequate 'bodies' of both 'sexes' are thus continuously attempting to make up for these constructed lacks through fetishistic consumption and 'bodily practices' of normalization. "Men, and men's bodies, are as much caught up within the structure of cultural fetishism as are women, and women's bodies" (Stratton 1996: 236).

The structure of 'cultural fetishism' with its signifier of 'desirable body' embedded in capitalist consumerism thus subjects all 'bodies' in order to sell commodities. "The increasing packaging of men's bodies in the media – it is now common to see men's bodies displayed in advertising in ways that were conceivable only for women's bodies a generation ago – coupled with increased economic anxiety (which leads us to focus on the things we can control, like how we look), has led to a dramatic shift in men's ideas about their bodies" (Kimmel 2004: 235). The recently coined pathologizing and decontextualizing category of 'muscle Dysmorphia' which is meant to describe a belief suffered by increasing numbers of men that one's 'body' is too small and insufficiently muscular, clearly demonstrates the harmfulness generated by the capitalist commodification of 'bodies' that is further explored in Chapter 5.

The practice of consensual 'SM' is in various aspects 'transgressive' in relation to valued organizing categories of the 'body' not only in terms of a rejection of the ideals of Western 'cultural fetishism' but in particular the extension of the 'legitimate body-spaces' of the 'sexual' and, as will be discussed in Chapter 3, an actual prolonging of the time 'normally' invested in 'play'-activities that involve 'body-experiences'. This stands again in sharp contrast to an increasingly hectic consumption of 'bodies' in the 'sexual' and relational realm of mainstream society that is characterized by fast consumption practices such as 'speed dating'. Such 'lived realities' obviously suit the market-driven spirit of capitalist societies that promote individualism and mobility.

2.1.7   'Experiencing bodies', 'body usage' and the 'lived body'

Synnott's 'The Body Social' (1993), underlines the limitations and the reductionism of biomedical models of the body. He refers to Emily Martin's research 'The Woman in the Body' which empirically showed that "...how women think and feel about their bodies is totally at odds with the assumptions made about women embodied in the medical texts by medical science" (Synnott 1993: 231).

The post-Freudian psychoanalyst D.W. Winnicott (1971), already proposed that the concept of experience was/is mostly lacking in modern culture as well as in traditional psychoanalysis. These therefore selective and reductionistic perspectives on human life miss out on one crucially important part of the people's lives, the "...intermediate area of experiencing, to which inner reality and external life both contribute. It is an area that is not challenged because no claim is made on its behalf except that it shall exist as a resting-place for the individual engaged in the perpetual human task of keeping inner and outer reality separate yet interrelated" (Winnicott in Jones 1991: 57). Between the inner and outer reality of human 'life/body' lies interaction which is the basis of the intermediate area of 'experience', "...a product of the *experiences of the individual person...in the* environment" (ibid.). This emphasis on experience Winnicott shares with Jaspers and Maslow (see Chapter 6) as well as with Foucault. Michel Foucault was convinced that human beings can only look for 'truth' through experience. His hopes considering the 'transcendence' of human beings fixation with 'sexdesire' lay in an authentic return to 'bodies' and 'pleasures' in experience. Foucault thus saw in consensual 'SM' the possibility of a 'laboratory of life'.

As Arthur Frank's (in Turner 1996) constructive modification of Turner's 'model of the geometry of bodies' also focuses more on the experiential level of 'body in action', it therefore seems a more adequate tool for the analysis of the 'body'. Frank distinguishes four ideal types of body usage which according to Synnott should be either seen as points of a continuum or as intermediate categories that exist and overlap. His argumentation is based on the observation that people within different life situations and, contexts need to make use of all the four types of 'body usage' through the course of their lives.

In Frank's typology the *first ideal type of body usage* is the disciplined body with the ideal- typical body of the ascetic as its collective representation. Regimentation is the mode of action for this type of 'disciplined body usage' which aims for the 'control over body'. As elaborated on in Chapter 3, the experiences of consensual 'SM'-practitioners clearly show 'disciplined body usage' on both play-partners sides ('bottom'/'top'). Whereas the 'bottom', 'submissive' or 'slave' aims for the internal control of body reactions towards sensations from the 'outside', the aim of the 'top', 'dom' or 'master' is the control of her/his external 'body' in order to be able to for example, precisely place and measure the strokes given with a whiplash (see Chapter 3) as this allows for enhanced experience on the side of the 'bottom's' body. Although both 'bodies' are disciplined, the ideal type of body usage of regimentation appears to be more of a constant experience for 'bottoms'.

The *second ideal type of body usage* in Frank's model is the mirroring body with the matching ideal-typical body of the consumer. The problem for the 'body' is desire and its mode of activity is consumption. The model for this type of 'mirroring body usage' is the department store as opposed to the model of the 'disciplined body usage' which is the 'rationalization of the monastic order'.

The practice of consensual 'SM' does not encourage consumption as the traditional notion of the concept of 'sexuality'-practice might suggest as it is based on another type of 'body usage' which is Frank's fourth ideal type of the 'communicative body' as will be clearly shown in Chapter 3.

The *third ideal type of body usage* Frank termed the 'dominating body' with its ideal-typical body of the warrior. Even though the mode of action of 'dominating body usage' is force in order to solve the body's problem of other-relatedness and might therefore be seen as the style of body usage as applied by 'tops' this turns out to be true only on a representational level (as seen in Chapter 3). As the model for its mode of action is force with the ultimate model of warfare, it might become already obvious that consensual 'SM' by definition excludes total domination through negotiated consensus and, as we shall see later, through the 'bottom'-power tool of the 'safeword' or 'safe-gesture'.

The *fourth ideal type of body usage* Frank suggests is the 'communicative body'. Through the course of my fieldwork in London I learned that 'communicative body usage' appears to be the most crucial form of body usage in consensual 'SM' especially within the new 'Scene'. The medium of activity for the 'communicative body usage' is recognition in order to regulate the body's problem of self-relatedness with the ideal-typical body of for example, parent, lover and friend. The model for the mode of activity of recognition are for example, shared narratives, caring for others and communal rituals. As Chapter 3 will illustrate, both (or all as varying people might 'play') 'play-partners' within consensual 'SM' ideally engage in 'communicative body usage'.

According to Frank, the 'essential quality' of this last type of 'communicative body usage' is that 'it' is in the process of creating itself. As opposed to the 'mirroring' and the 'dominating' style of body usage, the 'communicative body usage' crucially dependents on authentic recognition of oneself as well as the 'Other' and therefore has to be based on and derived from potentially changing body experience and practice. The 'communicative style of body usage' as constantly applied and worked on in consensual 'SM' is thus a creative process.

The concept of 'body usage' is certainly a helpful analytical tool in the context of this research but needs to be supplemented with an appropriate concept of 'body'. In order to gain an understanding of the 'body practice' or 'body usage' in the context of consensual 'SM' a concept of 'body' which moves beyond the realms of biologism and sociologism appears crucial. According to Turner the focus of sociological enquiries of the body has "... to concentrate on corporeality or bodiliness as the experientiality of the body" (Turner in Falk 1994: xii).

Welton made use of the distinction of phenomenology between 'physical body' (objective characterization of 'body', e.g. anatomy, neurology) and 'lived body' (experiential characterization of 'body'). The notion of the 'lived body' describes: "... certain structures of our body in terms appropriate to the way we *are* and *have* a body... the way it is involved with human environments" (Welton 1998: 2). In the context of the consensual 'body practice' of 'SM' the concept of the 'lived body' which will be explored more in what is to follow, is of substantial advantage when it comes to the understanding of the actual experiences of the practitioners. Abstract biological (especially conceptions of pain, 'bodily harm' etc. applied in legal cases) and/or sociological approaches cannot capture this dimension of the 'body'. Welton stated: "... we have a form of constitution that cannot be contained by the dyad of subject and object... it is situated *beneath* that difference as it serves as the silent background to focused intentional acts, different forms of action, and even our most intimate kinds of interaction" (Welton 1998: 3). Instead of passivity the 'lived body' or 'living body' of Merleau-Ponty's phenomenological approach is characterized by a unique sensitivity that makes 'it' experience environments with an openness that is fundamental to 'its' 'sentience'. Bigwood describes this as: "Existence realises itself in the body because of this incarnate communion with the world" (Bigwood in Welton 1998: 105). This concept of 'body' allows a view of 'bodies' as being in active participation with their life-worlds and does not degrade the human body into a passive existence. Another advantage of the concept of the 'lived body' is 'its' flexibility, the 'phenomenological body' "... is not fixed but continually emerges anew out of an ever changing weave of relations to earth and sky, things, tasks, and other bodies". The living world, "... is an ever-present horizon latent in all our experiences" (Bigwood in Welton 1998: 105).

The 'lived body' participates in the 'incarnate constitution of sensory experience' and thus this concept gives far more room to the experience of 'bodily sensations' which appears to me to be especially crucial in attempts to understand and appreciate the 'bodily practice' of consensual 'SM'. Merleau-Ponty's 'lived body' locates sensation not merely in the mind but in experience which changes the relationship of 'body' towards the environment. Bigwood refers to Heidegger's notion of 'world-earth-home' and explains: "The sympathetic relation of our sentient body with the sensible world-earth-home, then, is primarily a *preçognitive* one. Experience shows that as living bodies we are sensibly attuned to, and harmonized with, our surroundings through a 'latent knowledge' that is present before any effort of our cognition ..." (Bigwood in Welton 1998: 105/106).

The concept of the 'lived body' thus appears to allow us to go beyond the dreaded dualisms of body/mind and inner (subject)/outer (world) as this conceptualization gives the 'body' significance and makes it possible to understand that 'lived body' has a way of 'ordering things' on 'its' own through: "... a noncognitive apprehension of immanent meanings in the sensible field" (Bigwood in Welton 1998: 106). This conception also matches Howes' (2005) notion of 'skin knowledge' that underlines the importance of tactile forms of knowing that 'atune' human beings in order to be open to be affected by others and their context.

2.2   The 'sexualized body' and the social construction of 'sexuality' and 'perversion'

After a short exploration of notions of 'body', the following section aims to give an insight into the 'sexualization of the body' and its importance for understanding the data presented on consensual 'SM' in Chapter 3. The problematization of the status and seeming 'nature' of the human body which I elaborated upon in 2.1 already indicated that there appears to be no possibility to represent the 'body' in an objective or neutral way due to 'its' ties with the invisible network of historical socio-political and culturally generalized conventions. The same seems to hold true for the realm of 'sexuality'.

2.2.1   The creation of an 'objective reality of sexuality'

Plummer (1975), suggested an interactionist perspective in order to understand how a 'natural' order of 'sexuality' is constructed and reinforced on a multitude of levels. For example, societal institutions like family and gender tend to provide routine patterns of 'sexuality' that are deeply influenced by the statements of the legal and normative systems of society which produce 'truths' about 'normal', 'natural', 'safe' and, nowadays, 'representational commodified sexuality'. On the cognitive level of the individual, selective imagery, belief systems, language and legitimations serve as justification of the status quo and make 'sexuality' appear as 'normal', 'natural' etc. The interactionist perspective on the 'nature' of sexual meanings suggests, according to Plummer, that no act is in itself sexual but that instead: "Sexuality is a social construction learnt in interaction with others" (Plummer 1975: 30). The crucial point is that the realm of the 'sexual' is not given but defined as socio-culturally constructed meanings affect and shape what we define as our 'sexuality', 'sexuality' itself becomes a cultural variable.

The constructed meanings of 'sexuality' (e.g. utilitarian, erotic, romantic, consumerist) organize 'sexual lives' as they narrow the possibility of the development of others. The notion of 'Sexuality as objective reality' therefore denotes that individuals are born into 'pre-existing sexual worlds', composed of institutions and backed up by their legitimations which thus get apprehended as objective reality. Plummer suggests that the so constructed 'sexual world' possesses the properties of 'social facts' in a Durkheimian sense in that they are external, coercive and in the fact that this 'sexual world' possesses moral authority and historicity. (Plummer 1975: 47/48). The still widespread belief in a 'natural sexuality', triggered by bodily drives and serving the purpose of procreation, misses out the very distinctive characteristic of humans' 'lived bodies' which is to aim for transcendence and humans capability to use symbols and their (humans') dependency on them. Therefore human 'sexuality' is *unnatural* and deeply connected with the symbols surrounding the 'sexual sphere'.

"Sexuality's biological base is always experienced culturally, through a translation" (Ross and Rapp in Snitow et al. 1983: 51). As 'sexual behaviour' is 'scripted behaviour', which means behaviour that has developed after interactive learning of individual as well as social 'scripts', the notions of 'natural' and 'deviant sexual drives' become crude simplifications of complex processes.

2.2.2 Traditional definitions of 'sexuality'

Foucault's 'The History of Sexuality – Vol. 1' (1990) serves as a basis for the reconstruction of the background to the evolution of meanings of 'sexuality' for individuals in contemporary Western societies which will be illustrated further by the data obtained in the empirical world (Chapter 3). In Foucault's perspective modern 'sexuality' was and is manufactured within a three-dimensional technological constellation, consisting of discourse, knowledge and power. This production of 'sexuality' is culturally and historically specific but becomes a signifier of 'truth'.

The notion of 'sexuality', which Michel Foucault dates back to the beginning of the sixteenth century, implied more than the well known repression of sexuality, but a general change within the economy of discourses on 'sexuality' and an increase and sophistication of the 'polymorphous techniques of power'. "All these negative elements-defenses, censorships, denials-which the repressive hypothesis groups together in one great central mechanism destined to say no, are doubtless only component parts that have a local and tactical role to play in a transformation into discourse, a technology of power, and a will to knowledge that are far from being reducible to the former" (Foucault 1990: 12).

In commenting on Foucault's departure from the long held 'repression hypothesis' of 'sexuality', Rudi Visker (1995) noted that the more recent phenomenon of 'sexuality' and its dimensions, is: *"...produced* by a power which has found in the 'will to knowledge' an instrument which makes its operations acceptable, but also an 'effect' which situates them in a broader field: the regime of 'power-knowledge-pleasure', which has set the discourse on human sexuality in train and continues to keep it in being" (Visker 1995: 77). Under the premise that 'sexuality' is seen as a social construction its study, and the study of 'its perversions', can neither be ahistorical nor can it focus on 'disembodied sexual acts' which is the case in traditional approaches on these interconnected topics. The social embeddedness of 'sexuality' implies that: "Social processes shape the availability and selection of 'sexual' partners, the transmission of 'sexual' knowledge, the definition of taboos, and the connection of taboo to erotic excitement" (Ross and Rapp in Snitow et al. 1983: 51).

'Sexuality' is therefore a product of and shaped by social power relations, its conditions and values, whereby the categorization and following
hierarchization of 'sexualities' become part of a political ordering of 'lived
bodies' and thus, the structuring of human lives ('biopower'). The marginalization of socially censured acts prevents the questioning of the constructed
norm. The nearly institutionalized understanding of 'sexuality' by means
of psychiatric as well as psychoanalytical knowledge, semi-knowledge or
lay-knowledge is problematic, as it also serves as a tool to medicalize 'sexuality'. 'Sexuality', as already indicated, acquires a meaning of potential risk
from its very beginnings and the adaptation of the technique of inquisitor-
ial confession by modern 'technologies of the self' aimed at control over its
potential risks.

2.2.3   The origins of 'sex' as the code of pleasure and the emergence of the concept of 'libido'

Given that the form and content of the social meanings of 'sexuality' that
emerge, and, in consequence, determine and affect our understanding of
'sexuality' and the way in which we engage in 'sexual' relationships and
practices, are valid only within a specific given culture and epoch, my argument is that they should be considered from an interactionist perspective as
cultural variables. It appears to be evident though, that rather than understanding 'sexuality' as an ambiguous category, a majority of individuals
within the empirical field still understand 'sexuality' and their own 'sexuality' as a universal and absolute category (see Chapter 3).

Foucault suggested pre-Christian roots to this notion of a necessity to combine sex and sexuality and proposed political motivations for the Christian
adaptation of this double- construction that allowed Christianity to integrate
itself into the state structures of the Roman empire, yet for a costly price as:
"Sex then became the 'code' of pleasure" (Foucault in Lotringer 1996: 112).

The patterns of 'sexual behaviour' which still prevail within discourses
and institutions and thus consequently shaped/shape the 'gendered and
sexualized body' Foucault traced back to paganism as well as to Hellenistic
and Latin ethics. At the very heart of the philosophical patterns of sexual
behaviour in the Western world lies a complex system that fundamentally
connects 'sexuality', subjectivity and truth obligation. Foucault pointed out
that before this specific pattern became the dominant one, it was in competition with other alternatives, but "this pattern soon became predominant
because it was related to a social transformation involving the disintegration of the city-states, the development of the imperial bureaucracy, and the
increasing influence of the provincial middle class" (Foucault in Rabinow
1997: 179). The effects of these socio-political and philosophical shifts were/
are striking as through the linking of 'sexuality', subjectivity and truth
human beings developed a completely new relationship to themselves, and,
in turn, to others. Foucault offered historical illustrations of these processes.

He suggested that opposed to pagan ethics, like for example, Artemidorus that there had occurred through the influence of Christianity, a shift in the focus, from penetration to erection and: "As a result, it is not the problem of a relationship to other people but the problem of the relationship of oneself to oneself, or, more precisely, the relationship between one's will and involuntary assertions" (Foucault in Rabinow 1997: 181).

Foucault further pointed out that starting with Augustine the 'real' libidinization of sex had begun. Augustine termed the principle of autonomous movements of the sexual organs 'libido', which was seen as an internal component of the will and not the manifestation of petty desires. Libido was constructed to be understood as "... the result of one's will when it goes beyond the limits God originally set for it" (Foucault in Rabinow 1997: 182).

The spiritual struggle in Christianity required constant hermeneutics of oneself in order to locate among the movements of the soul which of these movements was derived from the 'libido'. "The task is at first indefinite, since libido and will can never be substantially dissociated from one another. And this task is not only an issue of mastership but also a question of the diagnosis of truth and illusion" (Foucault in Rabinow 1997: 182). Based on these historical, cultural, philosophical and socio-political premises the struggle for 'truth' continued and expanded within the realm of 'sexuality'.

2.2.4 The 'sexualized body' and its dependency on 'gender'

"Sexuality, like mental illness, is linked to a wider morality. People become more innocent and more guilty. Sex for Foucault was a means of access to the life of the body and the life of the species' " (Brake 1982: 27).

The social construction of 'sexuality' served in Foucault's view as a strategical access-tool to the individual body operating through the 'discipline of the body' and, on the side of the population, operating in the form of 'bio-politics'. The 'body' thus is structured through social constructions of 'sexuality' based on a concept of 'libido' which in turn shape the representations of 'gendered sexual bodies'. The necessities of external self-presentation (Goffman 1967) of 'appropriate bodies' are intimately linked to the social constructions of 'gender' and 'sexuality' and are given a crucial relevance in the 'panopticon' (Foucault 1975) of day-to-day interaction. "I think that people still consider and are invited to consider, that sexual desire is able to reveal what is their deep identity. Sexuality is not *the* secret but it is still a symptom, a manifestation of what is the most secret in our individuality" (Foucault in Kritzman 1990: 11).

The social construction of 'gender' with its culturally and specific significances, is, at its core, a 'sexual' construction that has strong impact on the lived experiences of human beings.

Butler (.) argues against the notion of an essential or natural basis for gender identity, stating that gender is the effect of a performance. This is not,... suggesting that gender is a 'custom or role that can be put on or off at will' but rather that a stylized repetition of acts produces gender as either male or female. For Butler there is no essential or authentic gender that prompts performance, rather performativity produces the gender just as it purports to represent it; *Because gender is not a fact, the various acts of gender create the idea of gender, and without these acts, there would be no gender at all* (Butler 1990: 140). (Raisborough 2002: 283)

Sadly the performative 'nature' of the 'genders' has still not become part of common sense and so, in order to 'pass' as a 'man' (Garfinkel 1967), given the framework of the social construction of 'masculinity', a 'dominating type of body usage' (Frank in Featherstone et al. 1991) is frequently still considered to be 'normal' and 'natural'. At the very heart of the thus shaped socio-cultural expectations towards men are modes of dominating 'Macho-display' which imply 'male' body usages of penetration, invasion, and, on a psychological level, assertiveness. The parallel social construction of 'femininity' promotes a 'mirroring type of body usage' (Frank ibid.) which implies notions of passivity, submission and continuous self-observation. These 'engendered' power imbalances are a crucial part of the 'sexual culture' of mainstream society that through continuous reinforcement and internalization become 'naturalized' and thus represent 'hidden power relations'.

Although recent years have seen a change in the public sphere concerning 'equality of the sexes' as for example, representations of 'masculinity' and 'femininity' have become more fluid and the traditional exclusively 'female' traits now also find acceptance in conceptions of the 'new masculinity', fluid 'masculinities' and/or notions like the 'new man' (caring, childrearing, use of cosmetic products, 'male bodies' in advertisements and strip-shows), the impact of the traditional 'sexual culture' is too powerful and thus still: "... expresses contempt for and the objectification of what is female... and glorification of what is male. ... It sees sexual 'normality' and identity only in the context of male domination of a woman" (Bleier 1984: 175).

Kimmel remarked that 'masculinity' continues to be a "... far more rigid [...] role construction than femininity, and how that rigidity is also part of the coercive mechanisms of gender role socialization" (Kimmel 2004: 132).

While violence can be regarded as synonymous with power (Galbraith 1983; Green and Ward 2004), it is crucial to be aware that there are no essential links between misogyny and 'masculinity'; "rather, masculinity seems bound to misogyny structurally in the context of patriarchy and male privilege" (Halberstam 1998: 255).

As the 'sex' of an individual is, within the social construction of 'gender', intimately linked with 'sexual performance' and set within a patriarchal, capitalist context, the possibilities for 'communicative body usage' (Frank in Featherstone et al. 1991) are, in my opinion, extremely limited for *all human beings*. The official legal, medical, psychiatric and psychological discourses on 'sexuality' traditionally and even the 'pornofication' of the cultural landscape (Attwood 2005) now still reinforce predominantly patriarchal relationships on an ideological and 'sexual' level and constitute big business in the UK as well as in the USA.

Jane Juffer argued in *More Dirty Looks:*

> Pornography consumption, it would seem, is becoming a 'normal' practice in the US, an accepted part of home entertainment, a domestic technology). This normalization stems from different factors such as new media technologies like satellite TV, DVDs, and the internet which further domesticate porn beyond the 80s explosion of the video market. Other factors include sizable economic investment by major media players (at least $10 billion, with General Motors, AT&T, Time Warner and Rupert Murdoch's News Corp making huge profits through DirecTV, broadband cable services, hotel room casts, on demand) and accompanying corporate assertions that justify pornography through an ideology of 'the self-regulated individual defined by consumer choice'. (Juffer in Church Gibson 2004: 45)

The mainstreaming of representations of 'sexual' activity and a proliferation of hard-core pornography propelled by the mass media as well as the intense availability of porn online could have generated a queering of 'porn':

> ...with a greater diversity and variety reflecting the greater range of people producing their own material rather than simply having to accept the standard product of the male dominated porn industry. Yet, whatever novel forms may appear on the margins, the fact remains that the bulk of cyberporn continues to conform to long established patterns and categories...., the options available on most websites are in fact restricted and highly codified. (Hardy 2008: 62)

Alike the discourses of Ellis and Freud such limiting and reductionist representations in the context of 'hetero-porn' still frequently: "...describe and explain the sexual mastery and superiority of man and the penis over woman and the vagina, whether we view the penis as real or symbolic. They make woman's acceptance of that sexual mastery and its extension (penetration) into the rest of her life as synonymous with her normality" (Bleier 1984: 182).

While Hearn's (2008) interpretation of consensual 'SM' as 'sexual' violence is not in agreement with the findings of this research, Hearn's insights into the broader arena and evolution of public representations of 'sexualities' are useful. In Hearn's view the "...pervasive dominance of various masculine heterosexualities, as well as the associations of some of those heterosexualities with invocations of violence" (Hearn 2008: 38) are likely to continue and are reflected in the bulk of mainstream porn, Paasonen et al. (2007) problematize the use and repetition of heterosexual, patriarchal stereotypes of 'sex' in 'porn' as well as its lack of emotional, relational contents in favour of technicalities.

As representations are frequently taken for reality and expectations are oriented towards the 'sexual representation of bodies', alienation sets in and prevents communication.

> Researchers working in the new field of 'porn studies' (Gibson 2000; Williams 2004) now tend to take it as axiomatic that pornography functions to blur the distinction between representation and reality. Indeed the latter category itself has been called into question and redefined as the world that is *not just representation* (Gaines 2004). It is widely recognized that porn has the power to move the body and to structure desire in new ways. (Hardy 2008: 63)

If the 'pornofication' of society continues alongside the aforementioned limiting, reductionistic social constructions, 'lived bodies' are existing under 'gendered' and 'sexualized' conditions of domination that shape also the field of possible transgressions. "While the process of logging-on and tracking down gratifying images and sexual fantasies, may be experienced by the individual consumer as an exploration of deeply personal preferences, taken as a whole the overall effect of cyberporn can be seen as the highly efficient commercial homogenization of desire" (Hardy 2008: 62).

2.2.5   The domination of a 'natural'/'normal' genital fixation

As the so-called 'normal sexuality' of human beings ['heterosexuality'] is often referred to as 'natural sexuality', I consider a small excursion into biology to be an 'enlightening' introduction into the following section on 'perversions'.

> Sex is the great force which sustains life. Moreover, every creature seems to exist solely for the purpose of reproduction and there are few animals that outlive their period of sexual usefulness. In fact, humans are the only animals that survive after their reproductive days are over and they are the only species with an unlimited capacity to enjoy sex at any time of the year. Having greater imagination and communicative skills, humans use hundreds of different sexual positions whereas most wild creatures enjoy just one. So when someone tells you are behaving like an animal having sex they are actually wrong. Contrary to popular myth, animals cannot fornicate at the drop of a hat but are subject to very strict laws. Thus, it is only when humans begin restricting their sexuality with moral codes that they do in fact behave like animals. (Windybank 1992: 2)

Practices that are labelled 'abnormal' or 'unnatural' actually often occur within the animal world and thus in 'nature'. Windybank introduced several species that include 'SM' elements in their mating rituals, for example, wild horses, cats and especially the Roman and the African snail, as well as ocean creatures like cephalopods (squids, cuttlefish and octopuses). "Sadomasochistic tendencies are part of the natural reproductive cycle which nature has established for the perpetuation of many species" (Windybank 1992: 208). As illustrated through this short excursion into biology even animals do have diverse 'sexual behaviours' which could be labelled 'SM'. This fact underlines the immanent problematic of the impact of constructed meanings in the field of 'sexuality'. Plummer (1975) pointed out that the fundamental concern of an interactionist approach on 'sexuality' is the problematic and socially constructed nature of sexual meanings. The basically 'open-ended' conception of human beings leaves them only in marginal restriction by their biological constitution. "Our biology does not possess intrinsic meanings in its own right. These arise through interpretative, interactive procedures" (Brake 1982: 25).

To illustrate the limited understanding and the genital fixation inherent in 'heterosexually normative' discourses on 'sexuality', Scharfetter's 'General Psychopathology' (1980), and its definition of 'normal sexual development' is revealing: "If sexual consciousness and sexual feelings are to develop normally, it is essential for a child to have a healthy psychosocial environment in which to mature, including the relationship with the mother and the rest of the family, especially brothers and sisters, as well as with playmates of both sexes" (Scharfetter 1980: 254).

'Normal sexuality' seems to be dependent on 'healthy' psychosocial circumstances which are defined by the normative model of the nuclear family.

Freud's concept of 'sexuality' is of central importance in this context because of its significance for the construction of 'sexual deviations'. The basis of 'sexuality' for Freud, lies in the existence of the libido. During the clearly marked libido development stages instances of fixation, regression or conditioning may arrest it at one stage and perversions may develop. The psychoanalytical schema of psychosexual development therefore shows ten stages of normal 'sexual' development and parallel to this it provides a perversion to be avoided for every 'normal' stage.

Even though Scharfetter underlines the relativity of the definition of 'normal sexuality' and that the traditional dogmatic approaches of Krafft-Ebing and others have given way to more open understandings of 'sexuality', he does not offer a less dogmatic view of 'mature sexuality': "Mating or coitus (copulation, cohabitation) is central to the sexual behaviour of the sexually mature individual. Coital behaviour may be defined as *normal when* it *takes place with a partner of the opposite sex in such a way that there is a possibility of fertilization, and that neither partner suffers from it or is damaged by it*" (Scharfetter 1980: 257).

Foucault considered both psychology in general and psychoanalysis in particular as problematic. His critique of the scientific ideal of psychology is based on his opposition towards "...both to the universalizing strategy by which psychology seeks to reinforce the plausibility of an object independent of its constitution and also to the independence thesis itself. The object which psychology believes it 'discovered' not only arose historically, but is also dependent on that discovery in a way which excludes a realist interpretation" (Visker 1995: 19).

In her account of psychoanalytical explanations of the development of 'sexuality', Dianne Chisholm (1995) is concerned with Laplanche and Lacan. Lacan follows Laplanche's conceptualization and elaborates on his 'sublimation is satisfaction of the drive without repression' notion but also links sublimation in a negative evaluative manner to the 'castrated body'. "The body that finds illusory satisfaction in the symbolic sublimation of desire is a castrated body; the lips of speech do not close on the real object of desire, but on a sublimated substitute, a desexualized token of loving" (Lacan in Chisholm in Grosz and Probyn 1995: 29).

This modified, contemporary version of psychoanalysis offered by Lacan to my mind only repeats Freud's reductionist understanding and lack of appreciation for sublimation. Although I am aware of the impact of Lacan's work on some feminists work on consensual 'SM', I consider it not to be sufficiently sensitive to the diversity of meanings of the body found within Western cultures in general and thus too limiting. I further consider Lacan's work to be unable to account for the fluidity and flexibility of 'bodies' and 'sexualities' of the empirical world as it is deeply phallocentric.

Hans Loewald (in Jones 1991) who modified and complemented Freud's work as well, has a far more positive view of sublimation. In his opinion sublimation represents a real transformation of instincts and he characterizes sublimation as a process during which diverse spheres of mental activity are being created while these are still in touch with their primary source (instinct/drive). Within 'Contemporary psychoanalysis' Loewald's approach allows for a much more open and dynamic understanding of the spheres of 'id' and 'ego', instinct and reason, in which both are not separate compartments but interconnected. Loewald fortunately also breaks with Freud's normative developmental theory which only allowed a perspective of linear progress from 'childishness' to adulthood which was very much influenced by the notion of progress.

For Loewald the teleological hermeneutic of mental life as well as a more flexible (backward and forward) view of intra-dynamic processes make an understanding of sublimation as a process in which basic instincts are rendered useful possible. In Loewald's 'cycle of sublimation' 'id' as well as 'ego' are capable of being a source of neurosis and/or reason. If 'id' is also the source of reason, Loewald concludes, it also must have a 'rationality' of its own by which dichotomies are transcended and a unity is apprehended.

The possibility of 'transcendence', is, again, intimately connected to 'corporeality' as James W. Jones noted: "...there is no escaping the confines of human experience, even when speaking of the transcendent. The experience of the transcendent always begins from, or occurs in conjunction with, some human experience" (Jones 1991: 125).

Given that my argument is that 'sexuality' is to be understood as a social construction, its study can neither be ahistorical, nor can it focus on 'disembodied' sexual acts displaced from their context of 'lived experience', which was the case in traditional approaches on 'sexuality' or 'perversions'. This is clearly demonstrated within the empirical data presented in large sections of both Chapter 3 and Chapter 6.

2.2.6 'Perversions'

As Foucault argued so convincingly discourses are not neutral forces but solidifying and organizing forces with ambivalent effects. He argued that along with the notion of 'sexuality' the construction of 'peripheral sexualities' began through the development of extensive discourses within the eighteenth and nineteenth century, which according to Foucault's 'History of Sexuality' (Vol. 1) (1990), signified the emergence of the 'unnatural'. This special and separate dimension of 'sexuality' was from then on dealt with not only by means of law and penalty, but because of the new and entirely different embedding within scientific discourses, by the power mechanisms of medicine and regimentation.

The discourses that emerged from the 'unnatural' dimension of 'sexuality' let to scrutiny and were followed by the 'appearance' of formerly unnoticed 'essentially different' individual 'sexualities'. These 'unnatural sexualities' were thought of, or rather constructed, as autonomous and defining characteristics of individuals. The confession of a 'perversion' became a confession on one's person, whose identity was determined by a 'nature' that medicine had defined. The species of the 'perverts' was 'born'.

Consequently several diverse fields of knowledge were constructed in order to deal with the different members of the new species. These 'knowledges' established rules and norms that were a mixture of traditional as well as 'new' regulations and conventions. As these specified 'knowledges' were themselves 'backed up' by religious, pedagogical, medical and juridical institutions and their discourses, their impact was invasive to the individual. "...an 'experience' came to be constituted in modern Western societies, an experience that caused individuals to recognize themselves as subjects of a 'sexuality', which was accessible to very diverse fields of knowledge and linked to a system of rules and constraints" (Foucault 1985 Vol. 2: 4).

For Foucault the notion of a mere repression of some constructed 'original of sexuality' is not the most striking feature of this power relationship but: "...the effect of power lies not in doing violence to an as yet intact, virginal 'matter', but in seducing it. Foucault discovers subjectivity – a 'matter' which can be seduced" (Visker 1995: 81). Merleau-Ponty's concept of 'lived body' or 'living body' matches this notion as it is understood as an 'intending entity' which is "...bound up with, and directed toward, an experienced world. It is a being in relationship to that which is other: other people, other things, an environment" (Leder in Welton 1998: 123).

The 'seductive' discourse of science in the realm of the thus constructed 'perversions' is again based on the 'relational distance' that 'sexual' behaviour has in relation to 'normal coitus', the established norm of 'heterosexuality'. For example:

> *Non-coital sexual behaviour on the part of sexually mature individuals may be called abnormal only when it is practiced not just as an introduction to or accompaniment of coitus but, despite opportunities for coitus, the exclusive or preferred form of behaviour.* Then only can we speak of *sexual deviations.* The further such behaviour is removed from normal coital behaviour, the more immature it is, the more rigid its performance, the more passionate dependence there is on it, the more justifiable it is to use the *term perversion.* (Scharfetter 1980: 257)

This genitalia and coitus fixed social construction of 'natural sexuality' that demarcates 'normal' and 'abnormal' from 'perverted' 'sexualities' shows how notions of 'abnormality' and 'perversion' are utilized to establish divisions between human beings. "Sexuality is one dimension of interpersonal relationships. All sexual disturbances should be regarded as signs of disturbed relationships reaching far beyond the narrow sexual field" (ibid.: 257). Under the wide range of what Scharfetter (1980) terms 'pathologies' of sexual behaviour or 'sex disorders', classifications are constructed although these dividing categories often overlap. 'Abnormal sex object', 'abnormal sexual practices', 'abnormal sexual identity', 'abnormal intensity of sex drive' and 'disorders of potency', clearly demarcate the outer framework of the constructed 'normal sexuality'.

Scharfetter more or less keeps to the concept of 'perversion' defined by Freud, who in 'Three Essays on the Theory of Sexuality' wrote: "Perversions are sexual activities which either (a) extend, in an anatomical sense, beyond the regions of the body that are designed for sexual union, or (b) linger over the intermediate relations to the sexual object which should normally be traversed rapidly on the path towards the final sexual aim" (Freud in Apter 1991: 17).

In the 'sexual world' of the psychoanalytical and causal-genetic model of 'perversion', repression might lead to the dominance of a partial drive which over time becomes fixated as a 'perversion'. The postulate of a 'normal' but transitional stage in human 'sexual development' which is termed 'polymorphous perverse' serves only to degrade other 'sexual' interests as immature.

"...", the fluctuating boundaries of what constitutes 'abnormal' sexual behaviour indicate a social rather than a medical basis for defining sexual deviance. Nevertheless, some sexual interests are considered psychologically as well as socially dysfunctional" (Blackburn 1995: 280/281). In the DSM-IV-TR of the American Psychiatric Association which is still widely used the pathologizing category 'paraphilia' is however applied to 'sexual sadism' and 'sexual masochism'. Even though the DSM-IV-TR acknowledged the existence of the vast and growing commercial market that has developed around 'paraphilic pornography' and 'paraphernalia', and although research has shown that paraphilias are probably widespread as part of 'sexual games' in couples (either in the form of fantasies or acted out), the symptoms of psychopathology are still looked for within the framework of the construction of 'sexual deviance'. While alternatives to the current paraphilia category have been proposed (Moser 2001) and while the DSM paraphilia section does not reflect the current state of scientific knowledge (Moser and Kleinplatz 2005 in Langdrigde and Barker 2007) it remains in place.

2.3   The 'perversion' of 'Sadomasochism' – supplementing the social construction of 'normal' 'heterosexuality'

'Sadomasochism' is a by-product of the complex processes that accompanied the construction of the modern form of 'sexuality' itself. As the construction of modern 'sexuality' is connected to the 'truth'– production process through discourses by legitimized experts 'Sadomasochism' had to be constructed alongside other 'peripheral sexualities' (Foucault 1990) in order to serve the functional requirements of reason. The 'sadomasochist' is therefore a mere supplement, functioning to define and stabilize the 'heterosexual' and his/her identity.

> ..., the very logic of supplementarity entails the unmarked term's dependence on the marked term: the unmarked term needs the marked term in order to generate itself as unmarked. In that sense the marked term turns out to be structurally and logically prior to the unmarked one. (In the case of heterosexuality and homosexuality, the marked term's priority to the unmarked term is not only structural or logical but historical as well: the invention of the term and concept of heterosexuality – which was originally the name of a perversion [what we now call bisexuality] and only gradually came to occupy its familiar place as the polar opposite of homosexuality.) (Halperin 1995: 45)

Through the constitution of consensual 'SM' as well as other unlegitimized 'sexualities' as objects of expert knowledge, so-called 'normal' 'heterosexuality' automatically reached the privileged position of subjectivity, representing the condition of knowing. This strategical positioning of 'heterosexuality' allows it never to become an object of knowledge itself. The incoherencies of 'heterosexuality' therefore never became the focus of expert discourses. As part of the collection of 'peripheral sexualities' which were ranging within the separate dimension of 'unnatural sexualities', 'Sadomasochism' had to be dealt with not only by means of law and penalty but also by the power mechanisms of medicine and regimentation. Even though the affirmation of the social constructedness of 'sexual pleasure' has become more customary as Wilkinson and Kitzinger suggested in 'Heterosexuality' (1993), the elements of this social construction are rarely specified. In focusing on the social construction of (hetero) sexual pleasure they state that "...one of the clearest arguments to emerge from many of the contributions is the equation of heterosexual sex with the expression of power and powerlessness – 'sex' as male domination and female submission" (Wilkinson and Kitzinger 1993: 16). As this seems to be the blueprint of the traditional definition of 'normal' 'sexuality' and the point of departure of many aetiological approaches on 'Sadomasochism' it is not surprising that the 'dominant moral order' requires this categorization. Sadly but unsurprisingly these patriarchal stereotypes also continue to shape wider socio-cultural mores (e.g. representations of 'sex' in mainstream advertising and in hetero-porn etc.).

2.3.1   The origins of the term 'Sadomasochism'

The social construction of 'Sadomasochism', derived its terminology from the novels of de Sade and von Sacher-Masoch. Leopold von Sacher-Masoch published his famous book 'Venus in Furs' in 1870 and was deeply disturbed when Krafft-Ebing used his name in order to name a 'perversion'. The content of this novel deals with the imbalance of power between the 'sexes' which is due to societal conditions, as von Sacher-Masoch lets his protagonist announce: "Goethe's words, 'Be the anvil or be the hammer' are never more true than when applied to the relations between man and woman. ...Woman's power lies in the passion she can arouse in a man and which she will exploit to her own advantage unless he remains always on his guard. Man has only one choice: to be a slave or to be a tyrant" (von Sacher-Masoch in Deleuze 1989: 150).

This account of gender-relations is obviously deeply informed by drive-theories which were quite common at the time when this novel was published. The view of the power of the woman also reflects very traditional and Christian ideas about the danger 'females' pose to 'male' reason through the merely uncontrollable power of the 'sex drive'. It should be remarked though that von Masoch deeply rejected the existing power inequalities between men and women and that 'Venus in Furs' deals, in contrast to de Sade's works, with consensual 'body practices'. The later developed 'scientific' assumption of a dialectical unity of 'Sadism' and 'Masochism' that was perpetuated by the discourses of sexology became part of the 'technologies of subjection'.

Deleuze (1989) criticizes this concept of a 'sadomasochistic entity', which, originating in Krafft-Ebing, Havelock Ellis and Fere, became the basis of psychiatric understanding. Freud who reformulated 'Sadomasochism', suggested that there was an 'identity of experience' of 'Sadomasochism' which would operate in one and the same individual that involved opposing instincts and drives.

"Sadomasochism is one of these misbegotten names, a semiological howler", Deleuze noted and at a another stage he stated that to "... assume that there is an underlying common 'substance' which explains in advance all evolutions and transformations is surely to proceed by abstraction" (Deleuze 1989: 134 and 45). To my mind this statement holds true for most of the theories of consensual 'Sadomasochism' that are about to follow, in which abstractions always outweigh and thus ignore the diversities of real-life experience. Psychiatric, psychological and sexological theories which work with socially constructed personages, with differences which are as well socially constructed, thus have no meaning independent of the cultural discourses that created them in the first place. 'Scientific' accounts as well as other social constructions that distort by controlling the conditions under which the 'Other' is known and lives, are not only alternative accounts and do not offer 'genuine understanding'. As monologic formulations do not leave space for other equally valid discourses and thus do make the participation of 'experiencing bodies' impossible, they are bound to become tools of subjection. Sampson laid out the foundation of dialogic argumentation in favour of monologic accounts which urge to match theory with reality. It is: "... its emphasis on the idea that people's lives are characterized by the ongoing conversations and dialogues they carry out in the course of their everyday activities, and therefore that *the most important thing about people is not what is contained within them, but what transpires between them.*"

(Sampson 1993: 20) This is definitely one of the major lacks of the approaches to 'Sadomasochism' that are about to follow.

2.3.2 Traditional approaches on 'Sadomasochism'

Any approach that views 'Sadomasochism' as well as the other categories of perversion and/or 'sexual disorder' not as social constructions, thus evoking notions of 'natural impulses' and 'normal desires' are depolitizing, and thus stabilizing tools for the societal status quo. As Sawicki states: "... the naturalistic recourse to an innocent or malevolent desire is inadequate" (Sawicki in Diamond and Quinby 1988: 180). Within the framework of the traditional and naturalistic understandings of 'sexuality' several approaches on the phenomenon of Sadomasochism' shaped the discourses and, following that, general beliefs about this variation of erotic pleasure.

The 'Psychopathia Sexualis' published in 1886 and written by Richard von Krafft-Ebing, a Professor of Neurology, serves even today as a basis for many definitions and meanings given to 'sexuality' as well as 'perversions'. Krafft-Ebing's a priori understanding of the source of 'perversions' was a belief in inherited 'deviant' sexual traits, which he illustrated with bizarre case studies. His focus on the manifestations of 'sadism' and 'masochism' was then combined with the morals and 'sexual ideals' of his time and could only result in a misunderstanding of 'sadism' and 'masochism' as substitutes for 'natural sexuality'. Even though Krafft-Ebing considered the possibility that there could be a link or rather a continuum that reached from 'normal', heterosexual 'horseplay' to 'sadism', which he never elaborated on, he still defined 'sadism' as the 'experience of sexual pleasurable sensations (including orgasm) produced by acts of cruelty, bodily punishment inflicted on one's own person or when witnessed'. Although this definition would also cover 'masochism' as he stated that a 'sadist' could also gain sexual pleasure by infliction of pain on his/her own body, he created the theoretical construct of 'masochism'. The creation of the associate of 'sadism' probably stemmed from the stereotypical belief that sadism was a pathological form of the 'natural heterosexual relationship' and as women were meant to be, and therefore seen as, passive, 'sadism' had to represent a pathological intensification of the 'male sexual character'.

As 'sadism' was envisioned as active, represented by the stereotype of the 'man', 'masochism' had to be a predominantly 'feminine' characteristic or a sign of impotence. Following the establishment of the core-manifestations of 'Sadomasochism' as a possibly symbiotic form of 'sexual pathology' Krafft-Ebing constructed a typology of these 'perversions', which resulted in a further sub-categorization of three forms of 'sadomasochism'. He distinguished a 'mental'/'psychic' form, which was defined as being grounded in fantasies with following masturbation. The 'symbolic' form which was not focused on actual pain but humiliation/domination and that did not have to involve orgasm. The last form, the 'physical' form involved the inflicting or receiving of pain that could involve orgasm but without necessity.

As Krafft-Ebing's theories are completely determined by Victorian morals and stereotypes, which are treated as 'truths' instead of being reflected upon, their use is more than questionable as they only reinforce stereotypes of 'masculinity' and 'femininity' and generate the image of inherited pathologies of 'perverse individuals' that are in need of treatment.

Havelock Ellis's 'Studies in the Psychology of Sex' (1896–1928), were also deeply influenced by the socio-cultural beliefs of his time. As Krafft-Ebing before him, he also considered a connection between love, sexual arousal and anger and fear, which explained 'sexual horseplay' between 'normal' couples. Ellis theory on 'sadism' and 'masochism' derived from a general theory of arousal that considered all states of arousal as physiologically undistinguishable. Based on the concept of a 'natural sex drive', Ellis concluded that 'Sadomasochism' derived from a 'weak sex drive' and that this deficiency of an 'unhealthy organism' was overcome by the use of anger or fear transformed into sexual energy.

Freud's theories on 'sadism' in males and 'masochism' in females again evoked the stereotypical 'heterosexual' dichotomy between the allegedly 'male aggression' and 'female passivity' rooted in the 'sexual instincts'. In 'A Child Is being Beaten'(1919), Freud tried to integrate seemingly common 'beating fantasies' into his concept of childhood 'sexuality' by suggesting that there potentially exists a 'beating fantasy process' of three phases in which disassociation processes on the side of the child lead it to develop a 'regressive replacement' for forbidden erotic relationships. Apart from again labelling everything that does not 'fit' his model of 'sexual' progress towards 'genital sexuality' as 'regression', this attempt to explain the 'masochism' was not even by Freud himself considered to be 'enlightening'.

"... legal categories of exclusion usually do have their medical or clinical correlatives. What is deceptive is that legal terms, for a number of reasons, are rather stable and constant, whereas clinical categories are relatively unstable and have changed rapidly" (Foucault in Lotringer 1996: 83). Shifts in the meaning of 'Sadomasochism' were bound to occur as the theories so far did not bring about any 'real' understanding of the 'nature' of the socially constructed 'sadists' and 'masochists'. It wasn't long after the publication of Krafft-Ebing's work that the terms 'sadism' and 'masochism' became diffused throughout psychiatric and psychoanalytic circles, and in everyday life. But the popularized connotations of sadism and masochism were not necessarily related to sexuality. As early as 1920 Freud noted that the term masochism was used to refer both to self-injurious behaviour and the erotic attachment to pain. An analogous diffusion of the term sadism occurred, as its meaning also expanded to refer to cruelty or the derivation of pleasure from inflicting pain on another, with or without an erotic component (Linden in Linden et al. 1982).

Freud's construction of a 'death instinct' in 'Beyond the Pleasure Principle' later tried to explain variations of 'masochism' (from erotigen to moral) along the axes and struggles between the 'life-instinct' and the 'death-instinct', thus localizing once again 'deficiencies' within the individual.

2.3.3   More recent theories on 'masochism'

The impact of ethnological findings such as Malinowski's (1963) as well as Mead's (1962) works and the first systematic and statistical research on 'sexual behaviour' conducted by Kinsey (1948/1953), has slightly changed the perspective on 'sexuality', less dogmatic but not less judgmental approaches on 'sexual pathology' and 'sex disorders' emerged. Even though these seemingly acknowledge the dependence of 'sexuality' on its socio-cultural and historical context, the centrality of coitus and the classification of other forms of 'sexual' behaviour as 'sexual deviations' and/or 'perversions' lingered on as well as the tendency to characterize 'sexual deviants'. For example, in Scharfetter's 'General Pathology', published in 1980, 'sadism' and 'masochism' still serve as sub categories within the classification of 'sexual pathology'.

Sadism (synonyms: active algolagnis, love of torture) is sexual stimulation and gratification derived from the infliction of pain. No reliable data exist on the frequency of sadism, which appears to occur predominantly in men. ... Sadism is principally of forensic significance since it can lead to injury to the sex objects or even to murder... The sexual sadist can express his feelings towards his fellows only by cruelty. He is dangerous only to those whom he would love if he were normal. He is usually impotent and can release his sexual tension only by sadistic acts (Scharfetter 1980: 267/268)

The definition of 'masochism' and the characterization of the 'masochist' is not any less judgmental and Scharfetter's explorations also gain another category of distinction here: 'gender'.

Masochism (synonym: passive algolagnia) i.e. sexual stimulation and gratification from suffering pain, may be heterosexual or homosexual or take the form of automasochism. *Masochism in the male.* Methods: torture, sometimes self-inflicted, by beating, chaining, strangulation, electric shock, tying a cord round the penis. It can lead to injury and even to self-inflicted fatalities. ... *Masochism in the female.* This can also be heterosexual or homosexual or can take the form of automasochism. The methods are similar to those employed by the male. In automasochism objects may be introduced into the genitals, into the urinary passage (masochistic urethralism), into the bladder or into the rectum (masochistic analism). Surgical intervention may be called for. (Scharfetter 1980: 269)

The interpretations that Scharfetter offered for the 'genesis' of 'hetero' and 'homosexual sadism and masochism' are psychoanalytical in origin. They are thus based on the belief in ideal intra familiar relations that did not develop in the perfectly 'normalizing' manner as they should have and they also suppose 'abnormal' fixations on libidonal stages of 'normal sexual development'.

A Jungian perspective on 'masochism' is offered by Cowan (1982), who understands 'masochism' as a metaphor conveying the suffering and passion of the soul (psyche). Masochism, here understood as an experience of shadow, connects the individual and the collective unconscious. For Cowan the sense of worship and submission for the god that 'moves in' 'masochism' are crucial because: "When masochism is literal only, it is pathological" (Cowan 1982: 26). This very spiritual interpretation of 'masochism' which is embodied in the figure of Dionysos, 'the patron god of masochism' (Cowan 1982: 125), still pathologizes the experiences of 'lived bodies' though, in Cowan's view masochism can impede the individuation process and is "...an operation of negatives" (ibid.).

The psychoanalyst Karen Homey offers an explanation of 'masochism' as a defensive strategy against fears of intrinsic weakness and insignificance. In contrast to Christian martyrs, the primacy in masochism is not guilt but the achievement of Dionysian oblivion as: "...abandoning oneself to excessive suffering may serve as an opiate against pain" (Horney 1937: 265).

The notion of the search for a 'Dionysian' loss of self in ecstatic states that Cowan suggested to be the most important motivation in masochism is developed here as well. Although Chapter 6 will also deal with the topic of consensual 'SM'-'bodily practice' as a spiritual exercise, my reading of this 'bodily practice' and its practitioners does not assume a lack of control and/ or despair as given as the data of my fieldwork did not validate any of these stereotypes.

Baumeister's (1991) psychological interpretation of 'masochism' is a more positive one, although it presupposes a wish to escape the 'self' on the side of the individual practitioner. Here 'masochism' is seen as a form of self-forgetting. 'Masochism' functions as a tool to get rid of the burden of the modern 'self' through the escape from identity into the body. 'Masochism' in this view becomes a healing device against a 'culturally constructed constraint': "Sexual masochism, despite its somewhat unsavoury reputation and deliberate bizarreness, appears to be neither helpful nor harmful. Most people who engage in it don't end up injured or sick. Nor does it make them better people. It simply provides an effective escape that is treasured by a certain majority" (Baumeister 1991: 17). The 'bodily practice' of consensual 'SM' is in this perspective is a form of 'escapism' based on a dualistic notion of human beings as the 'body' is seen as a refuge for the exhausted mind.

The marginalization and pathologization of the socially censured 'bodily practices' of consensual 'SM' prevents the questioning of the norm of 'heterosexuality'.

2.3.4   'Redefining' a social construction(?)

In Gosselin and Wilson's view, consensual 'SM' is a "...mutually agreed sexual relationship of unbalanced power" (Gosselin and Wilson in Howells 1984: 92) and not reducible to a defined set of behaviours. Therefore a new definition was championed which describes consensual 'SM' as: "A relationship giving rise to the sexual interaction of two or more people via a ritual whose outward appearance involves coercion, pain, restriction or suffering of some kind but which has been agreed upon, tacitly or overtly, between the parties concerned and may in reality involve none of these constraints" (Gosselin and Wilson in Howells 1984: 93). Although the new definition offered in this account is far more open and less deterministic, the social construction of 'Sadomasochism' is left intact, and, as will be shown in Chapter 3, the fact that not all consensual 'SM'- encounters involve 'sexual interaction' is left out. Gosselin and Wilson also pointed out that studies that tried to detect and discover genetic factors and/or brain malfunctions in order to explain 'Sadomasochism' have been fruitless and that empirical studies on 'sadomasochism' are relatively rare. It is important to point to the fact that recent years generated some non-pathologising work on consensual 'SM' (Beckmann 2001/2001a; Beckmann in Cowling and Reynolds 2004; Beckmann in King and Watson 2004; Langdridge and Barker 2007; Langdridge and Butt 2004; Taylor 1997 and Taylor and Ussher 2001) which, however, has not been absorbed into commonsense notions and that certainly did not lead to a revoking of the semi-criminalization and/or pathologization of consensual 'SM'.

2.3.5   Empirical studies

The discipline of sexology operates still mainly with the presumption of a 'natural sexuality' and as it is focusing on individual expressions of its subject, it misses out on the crucial inter relatedness of the individual and society as expressed in the concept of 'lived body'. As Carole S. Vance points out this leads to: "...intellectual isolation and theoretical impoverishment [which] can be seen in most sex research journals. Thus, as sex is isolated and privatized within the couple, the study of sexuality is encapsulated within 'sexology'. The theoretical position of most sex researchers, evident (though implicit) in their work, is functional and ahistorical" (in: Snitow et al. 1983: 377). An example of sexological work and an individualistic approach on 'Sadomasochism', in this case focusing on the 'paraphilia' of masochism, is the book 'The armed robbery orgasm' by Ronald W. Keyes and well known sexologist John Money (1993). In this book, which consists mainly of an autobiography of Keyes, who was involved in a 'sadomasochistic' relationship that included robberies, John Money, even though he seems to be aware of the problems of stigmatization and the not determined but ongoing processes of human development, still applies the label of 'paraphilia' and focuses on the individual and his attempts to achieve 'sexological health': "the sexologist and he will form an alliance against the paraphilia. (...) Their joint strategy will include selective use of pharmacologic substances in dosages and for periods of time specific to individual efficacy... Without a true understanding of the nature and phenomenology of the paraphilias, ascertainment of the where, when, and how of paraphilias, and of how persistently they become patterned in the brain and the mind, will not be possible" (Money and Keyes 1993: 11 and 13). The social constructedness of 'sexuality' and its 'perversions' is definitely not the focus here.

The study of the German sexologist Andreas Spengler, called: 'Manifest Sadomasochism of Males...' (1977) focused on male practitioners of consensual 'SM' that were either placing contact adverts for these 'bodily practices' and/or that were members of a 'SM'-club. The sexual preferences within the gained sample spread nearly evenly into 38 per cent of gay interest, 31 per cent of bi- and 30 per cent of heterosexual-preference. The majority of Spengler's subjects were in between 30–40 and most of them were better educated and paid which might be the reason for their cooperation and not an indication of the average socio-economical background of most male consensual 'SM'ers. Secrecy about these 'bodily practices' appeared to be a general feature, two thirds of the sample admitted that even their closest relatives and friends did not know about their practices which once again highlights the impact of the social censure of 'SM'. The occurrence of comparatively high divorce rates that Spengler found to be characteristic (16 per cent in heteros, 12 per cent in bisexuals and 5 per cent in gays) might also rather be interpreted as an effect of the 'social censure' (Sumner 1990). It was harder for heterosexual players to find partners than for the bisexuals and gays that enjoyed consensual 'SM'. The frequency of their 'bodily practices' was relatively low as only 20 per cent 'played' once a week by average. Compulsion or dependency on 'SM' rituals which was suggested by many of the theories on consensual 'SM', thus does not seem to be a valid suggestion as most of the sample (parallel to mine) also practiced other sexual variations. As only 16 per cent of the sample played exclusively the role of the 'Master' or 'slave', a fixation on one position was found to be as rare as extremely painful 'play'. The importance of fetish dress was pronounced only by half of the sample. Ninety per cent of the sample never consulted professional help as they were not worried or disturbed by their practices. The social stigma though that accompanies the label 'Sadomasochism' was felt to be a problem and is reflected by the fact that those ten percent of the sample who did feel bad about their practices were the least integrated into the 'SM'-subculture.

In 1983 Kamel and Weinberg's study on 'Sadomasochism' which was conducted in America was published. This sociological research found that self-identified consensual 'SM'-practitioners had a preference to stay in the company of each other rather than trying to 'play' with people who did not share their specific interests. In order to avoid offending the straight population and also in order to informally control the safety of 'play', they preferred to be within their 'SM'-community which parallels much of my findings. As the gay 'SM'-subculture appeared to be more organized and therefore more effective in enforcing or rather reinforcing self-imposed restraints of consensual 'SM' than their hetero-counterparts, Kamel suggested that the lack of these systems of informal control through the subculture is less effective for heteros and therefore more often leads to negative images of consensual 'SM' as violent and non-consensual within the media and consequently, amongst the public.

A survey conducted by Gosselin and Wilson (1980 in Howells 1984) on 'sexually variant males' ('fetishists', 'sadomasochists' and 'transvestites') found overlapping sexual preferences and activities within these three groups. A majority of these men enjoyed impersonal sex objects and a preference for 'playing' the 'submissive' role during sexual activities. As 'fetishism' does appear to overlap more with 'sadomasochism' and 'transvestism', than does 'sadomasochism' with 'transvestism' the researchers came to the following thesis: "Thus fetishism would appear more basic or 'prototypic'-sadomasochism and transvestism could be interpreted as alternative directions for the fetishistic impulse to travel" (Gosselin and Wilson in Howells 1984: 100). As will be shown in Chapter 3, the 'fetishistic impulses' do not always seem as determining as suggested here. The notion of 'fetishistic impulses' that are characteristic to individuals gains another dimension when Gosselin and Wilson sum up the results of the Eysenck Personality Questionnaire. In comparison to a control group of 'normal' males, the sample group consisting of 'fetishists', 'sadomasochists' and 'transvestites' showed a tendency towards 'neuroticism' and introversion even though not far from the average in society. "Analysis of individual items indicated that they were inclined to be shy, lonely, sensitive and depressed, and less likely to enjoy telling jokes. All of this suggests some difficulty in social interaction, whether as a cause or effect of the sexual pattern" (Gosselin and Wilson in Howells 1984: 100). The 'social stigma' that leads many practitioners into depression and/or isolation might be worth exploring in this context.

Against a widespread scientific belief, Gosselin and Wilson found no correlation between the three sexual variants and frequency of corporal punishment. Like in the studies mentioned above they found 'normal' socio-economic backgrounds and middle age to be quite characteristic for all three groups. These findings parallel the data I collected in London. The concluding thoughts of Gosselin and Wilson in my opinion reflect the still prevalent dogmatic ignorance within scientific as well as public discourses about consensual 'SM' as well as other 'sexual deviations'. "Fetishism, sadomasochism and related sexual behaviours remain something of a mystery to the scientist as well as the layman. Since the sex drive has clearly evolved for reproductive purposes, and these behaviours are comparatively non-reproductive, it is reasonable to think in terms of something 'going wrong' in the course of development" (Gosselin and Wilson in Howells 1984: 105/106).

Within these very rare empirical researches of consensual 'SM' the principle of the 'sexual politics of truth' remain. Legitimized 'sexual identities' still instantly have an assumed ontologically privileged position in comparison with unlegitimized ones, whereas the claiming of an unlegitimized 'sexual identity' regularly implies an instant disqualification within mainstream society. However, similar to my findings (2001a,b) Cross and Matheson's (2006) findings confirm that there is no evidence of escapism, psychpathology and/or other forms of 'psychopathology' amongst consensual 'SM'ers.

2.3.6 Consensual 'SM'– 'body practice' – a site of power struggles

Consensual 'SM' has, maybe as one effect of the media attention it attracted, become a site of power-struggles in contemporary discourses. Some of the positions taken, mainly in sociologically and/or feminist oriented approaches will be discussed in what is about to follow.

In recent years a few 'libertarian' approaches towards consensual 'SM' appeared. Although I do not employ the same political position, the criminological work of Bill Thompson (1994) which is written against the criminalization of consensual 'SM', thus became a resource used throughout my thesis. Like Thompson, Ian Young argues that 'SM' is 'natural' as all human beings have needs for aggression as well as submission. He then, on the basis of the sophistication involved in consensual 'SM', claims that therefore consensual 'SM' is to be regarded as a more 'evolved form' of 'sexuality' (Young in Jeffreys 1993: 222). These approaches are countered by exponents like John Rechy who condemn consensual 'SM' on the basis of its alleged 'destructiveness'. In Rechy's view, the: "... proliferation of sadomasochism is the major threat to gay freedom" (Rechy in Jeffreys 1993: 223).

Feminist readings of consensual 'SM' can be distinguished from each other in a similar manner, as evident from the positions taken during the heat of the feminist 'sex wars'. It is important to be aware that there continue to be different positions taken, from the stance that consensual 'SM' helps women to assert agency (Ardill and O'Sullivan 2005) to a rejection of consensual 'SM' as being emblematic of patriarchal (and 'queer' replication thereof) 'sexual' oppression of women (Jeffreys 2003; Superson 2005). Similarly, 'radical feminism' or 'cultural feminism' (Echols in Vance 1984) can be characterized as moralistic dogmatism that operates with a monolithical view of power as possessed by 'males' and centralized within 'male institutions'. Exponents of this stream of ideology can further be distinguished by the employment of natural, biological determinism (e.g. Rich 1986) which features notions of essentialism in terms of 'male' and 'female' 'sexuality' and by the employment of sociological determinism (e.g. Dworkin 1987; Linden et al. 1982). Such feminisms thus ignore the diversity of experiences of 'lived bodies' in contemporary society and promote a destructive identity politics which re-inscribes passivity and powerlessness onto women's bodies.

One of the most polemical accounts of consensual 'SM' was presented by Sheila Jeffreys (1993) who locates the origins of 'Sadomasochism' (her term) in 'masculine' and particularly gay 'male sexual practices'. She accuses gay men who practice consensual 'SM' of not theorizing about it and accuses the 'sexual radical' position of Jeffrey Weeks to be prejudiced and protective towards "... the sacred absolutes of the male gay sexual agenda" (Jeffreys in Jackson and Scott 1996: 239). These unfounded claims Jeffreys then tries to support through accusing gay men in general of 'worshipping masculinity' and 'self-hatred' which in her view led to the development of gay consensual 'SM'. Although she points to the fact that the traditional social construction of 'heterosexuality' is 'an S/M romance', she does not realize the potential for resistance within these 'bodily practices' despite her statement that: "Through the exaggeration of the characteristics of gender roles, the naked, eroticized power dynamic which fuels heterosexuality is laid bare" (Jeffreys in Jackson and Scott 1996: 241). This perspective appears to suggest that the knowledge of the social constructedness of 'gender'-roles etc. is only a property of 'feminist expertise' that cannot be known or experimentally explored and thus learned by the practitioners of consensual 'SM' themselves, particularly not when they happen to be gay. For Jeffreys this amounts to the ideological preference of lesbian 'SM' based on the socially constructed powerlessness of 'females': "Lesbians cannot ingest ruling-class power by serving as bottoms since no women have that power" (ibid.: 243). This obviously very much represents an essentialist understanding of 'gender' and 'sexual identity'.

"In order to map a disciplinary grid of social order the subject of discipline must be fixed" (Stanley 1995: 94). This appears to be the basis of 'radical' feminist accounts on consensual 'SM' which engage in the external labelling and sometimes selective classification of human beings, in turn rendering 'lived bodies' and their activities static, denying their potential for agency and thus providing a basis for an increase in social control in the future. In Mandy Merck's critical explorations of "the feminist ethics of lesbian s/m" (1993), the claim for 'truth' on both sides of the debates around the 'bodily practices' of consensual 'SM' are exposed. The concern for 'political correctness' which was portrayed by Ruby Rich as the 'casus belli' of the 'Sex Wars' within feminism still appears to be the primary focus of most 'moral feminists'. In Merck's account of three 'psychologies of lesbian s/m' located in the works of Adams, Creet and Modleski show their lack of acknowledgement for the position of the 'sadist'.

Parveen Adams's Freudian feminist account 'On Female Bondage' (1989 in Brennan 1989) selects 'lesbian sadomasochism' out of the wide range of potentially transgressive consensual 'SM'-'bodily practices' and appoints this variation to be the new type of 'transgressive sexuality'. Based on selected readings of lesbian feminist consensual 'SM' narratives edited by Pat Califia, Adams suggests that the lesbian variation of these 'bodily practices' represents a practice that uniquely splits 'gender' from 'sexuality'. The lack of compulsion and the turn away from genital fixation Adams attests, to my mind very reductionist, only to consensual 'SM'-play between women. Lynne Segal also mentions the unexplained limitations of Adams's account: "But existing as it does in an unspecified relation to 'external reality', what is it that restricts this transgressive play with phallic signification to lesbian s/m practices?" (Segal 1994: 164).

Adam's psychoanalytical account Merck (1993) thus describes as being 'formal'. In an evaluation of the account that Creet provides of consensual 'SM' Merck notes her emphasis on the notion of 'guilt'. Within a Freudian framework based on the cultural repression of instincts this treatment of the 'bodily practices' becomes to Merck a 'moral' one. Although Merck does not categorize Modleski's account which focuses on the 'dominatrix' function of preparing her daughter for the "...travails of patriarchy,..." I am tempted to label it 'adaptive'. These feminist accounts of consensual 'SM' so far presented, do not account for the full variety of possibilities offered by the 'bodily practices' of consensual 'SM' and have a tendency to favour a priori woman to woman encounters as well as leaving out any further elaboration on the 'dominating' part. Much of feminist argumentation thus seems to ground itself: "...in an epistemology of subordination, a reverse hierarchy through which the subject claims superior knowledge (and moral standing) by virtue of her oppressed identity" (Merck 1993: 263).

Instances of this 'discourse of truth' can be localized in the often absolutist investment of maternity with morality and in the general tendency of radical feminism to engage in a 'valorization of the victim' (Merck 1993) which in effect widened the scope for yet another system of power/knowledge that subjects and invests 'bodies'.

It appears to hold true that 'moral feminism' indulges in this 'will to power' by authorizing themselves at the costs of human beings that lack the socio-political and moral credentials derived from 'victimization' as an essential prerogative for 'truth'.

Janice O. Raymond (1989) views lesbian 'S&M' as well as 'butch-femme' as 'male-power modes of sexuality' and traces the rising interest and engagement in these practices back to 'the liberalism of lesbian lifestyle' which in her opinion makes these expressions of 'sexuality' 'sexy' for women. Tolerance towards 'such acts' is not indicated as Raymond suggests but the creation of a 'lesbian sexuality' that is rooted in 'lesbian imagination' as opposed to 'lesbian fantasies'. This value-laden account could be read as re-inscribing 'deviancy' onto the 'bodies' of fellow lesbians who instead of constantly surveilling their own 'bodily' and 'sexual' expression in accordance with the yet unwritten 'political manifesto of politically correct sex', experiment with their 'bodies and pleasures'.

The 'libertarian pluralist' positions within feminist and some sociological writings are far more accepting of diversity in pleasures but often operate with notions of a 'natural' and repressed 'sexuality'. Thus some exponents of this ideology seem to also employ an essentialist notion of 'sexual identity'. Pat (now Patrick) Califia (1988/1994/2001; Califia and Sweeney 1996) the American feminist who constantly engaged in attempts to explain and defend consensual 'SM' practices will be referred to throughout much of this work. Califia had to defend her [now his] feminist' position continuously towards 'moral feminism' as a practitioner of consensual 'SM'. He also implies the existence of a 'natural' longing for submission and domination. Both sides of these polarized positions rely on repressive understandings of power, while at the same time rejecting notions of autonomous 'sexual drives' and pointing to the social constructedness of 'desire'. The claim for 'truth' thus does not only arise out of the traditional sciences but is also to be found in much of feminist theory and practice. Jana Sawicki stated the similarities between radical and libertarian feminisms in reference to Ferguson's work as follows: "..., both involve universalist theories of sexuality, that is, they both reify 'male' and 'female' sexuality and thus fail to appreciate that sexuality is a historically and culturally specific construct... [this] assumes that there is some essential connection between gender and sexual practice" (Sawicki 1991: 30/31). 'Moral feminist's' elaborations, especially concerning the practice of consensual 'Sadomasochism' thus smack of the generalizations founded on social constructions of dominant ideology. Apart from also focusing far too much on 'sexuality' as the 'secret' of women's oppression, the relevance of the variety in experience is ignored. Thus: "..., feminists must explore the meaning of the diversity of sexual practices to those who practice them, to resurrect the 'subjugated knowledge' of sexuality elided within dominant culture" (Sawicki 1991: 31). Merck (1993) also accounts for the existence of a 'third camp' within feminism which attempts to offer a constructive critique of concepts of power and freedom that promotes a relational view of personal identity that is open to change (e.g. Butler 1990; Rubin 1984/94; Sawicki 1988). The 'queer' theory approach on consensual 'SM' by Halperin (1995) would, although not labelled 'feminist' also match this conceptualization and thus, these authors will be a point of reference throughout. This stream of thought acknowledges that socialization is never total determination and thus underlines the need for a 'politics of personal transformation'. Butler thus stated that: "There are no direct expressive or causal lines between sex, gender, gender presentation, sexual practice, fantasy and sexuality. None of those terms captures or determines the rest" (Butler in Jackson and Scott 1996: 165). Although these elements can sometimes correlate, they do not present fatalities. McClintock underlined in a similar fashion that consensual 'SM' 'body practices' only appear to 'servant' orthodox power (in Church Gibson 1993: 208). These 'politics of difference' (Sawicki 1991) which are informed by the works of Michel Foucault, see the possibility to effect political change in the personal and intimate sphere instead of a nihilistic rejection and repression of pleasures as advocated by the 'radicals'. 'Differences' are thus seen as resources of resistance and as occasions for dialogues that have the potential for re-creation and re-negotiation. In this respect, the distinction made by Foucault between 'practices' and 'identities' or 'subjectivities' is crucial, as pointed out by Carol Smart (in Holland and Adkins 1996). In many ways the practice and philosophy of consensual 'SM' is much closer to what Foucault would have termed a 'practice of resistance' (see Chapters 5 and 7) than mere 'liberation' that, as illustrated within much of feminist accounts, leads to different forms of domination. This point is further illustrated in Chapter 3 with examples of the empirical world.

2.4 The commodification of
the 'sexual' – the private as public

The previous section discussed how varying categories attempt to organize and regulate 'bodies' through 'sexuality' and 'perversions' and indicated that consensual 'Sadomasochism' is a site of political power struggles. The following section explores contemporary representations of 'sexuality' within the spheres of public representations which can, while not determine, crucially influence individual and collective perceptions and attitudes. As the obsession with commodities in capitalist-consumer culture had to be fostered, representations of 'sexuality' were given a major role in market-strategies.

One of the most important consequences of the commodification of 'bodies' and their 'sexuality' has been the breaking down of the strict division of public and private. A big proportion of the internet focuses on 'sexuality' and thus becomes potentially a new source for the further deployment of 'sexuality'. According to Aitkenhead (2003) about 200 million people are online worldwide whereby studies suggest that pornography constitutes between 20 and 30 per cent of all traffic on the internet. More than a third of the UK's 10 million regular internet users log onto porn-sites. Attwood (2005) explored the notion of the 'pornofication' of the cultural landscape referring to the mainstreaming of representations of 'sexual' activity and a proliferation of hard-core pornography propelled by the mass media. Boundaries between private and public discourse about 'sexuality' [at least accepted forms labelled as such] appear to be fading (Attwood 2002) and, together with the increasing availability of appropriate technologies, facilitate 'amateur porn productions' which do break down the former boundaries between producer and consumer of 'porn' (Ciclitira 2004).

Plummer (1996) explored the growth and change of the 'intimate' within the borderless space of modern media and argues that whereas the nineteenth century mass printed 'sexual stories' in tabloids etc. and socio-politically separate(d) audiences would read these, "... the new electronic media have blurred previously distinct spheres, such as those between men and women, young and old, gay and straight, black and white-making once segregated worlds more pervasively accessible" (Plummer in Weeks and Holland 1996: 35). While this is certainly commendable, it is further important to bear in mind that: "The familiarity of the Web can be deceptive: its increasing familiarity may constitute new hegemony. (...) ICTs and the WWW increasingly offer an apparent 'home' for members of sexual communities, but are also sites for the extension and diffusion of disembodied sexual capitalism, sexual consumer cultures and sexual pleasures (Bernstein, 2001)" (Hearn 2008: 40).

While the access to information through the internet is a constructive development it is clearly not without consequences:

"All 'privacy' is now potentially public. ... While many ICTs are experienced and represented as giving individuals access to 'more information', they also provide means for corporate entities to access far more information 'about us'" (Hearn 2008: 43). As part of what Hearn (2008) terms 'surveillant assemblages': "These are producing, and likely to further produce, new forms of the body and commodifications of the self, whereby flesh and sexualities are at least partly reduced to 'data doubles'" (Hearn 2008: 44). It is important to refer to Aas' work (2006) in this context of 'bodies' reduced to 'data' and/or 'codes', as like the 'docile body' of disciplinary power so greatly explored and commented on by Foucault (1975) these are historical constructs 'generated' at an intersection of 'truth' and power. Aas suggests that: "The coded body does not need to be disciplined, because its natural patterns are *in themselves* a sources of order" (Aas 2006: 153).

2.4.1   Commodified 'Sadomasochism'

"...'passive' and 'masochistic' sexual fantasies and practices, although seen as definitively 'feminine', are at least as frequently the experiences and practices of men. By a ratio of four to one, Nancy Friday informs us, men's fantasies are masochistic" (Segal 1994: 257). Apart from countering 'moral feminist' concerns about the alleged re-inscription of societal power positions through the 'bodily practices' of consensual 'SM', at least in the case of men joining in, these 'male' fantasies and experiences of men were reflected in part by the many related services offered by prostitutes in London's busy city centre. During the months I stayed in London I found the number of cards in phone boxes that offered professional 'SM'-services amazingly high. 'Normal sex' was comparatively rarely on offer on cards in public phoneboxes. Saner (2008) identified a 'mainstreaming' of 'sadomasochist' representations in the media as well as of BDSM behaviour forms within the UK and thus confirmed and extended the relevance of my own findings (Beckmann 2001a). However, usually such representations are usually decontextualized and do not focus on the importance of consent, negotiation and existential communication.

> Certainly the adage 'sex sells' is as old as media industries themselves, but the way that sex has become more pliable to the demands of a global economy is new. The need to repurpose contents allies mainstream with pornographic industries in the production of ephemeral sexual texts that both industries can shape to fit a desired time slot, page width and sponsorship without long-term commitment or repercussions. Sexual differences have become a standardized fare for marketing. (Esch and Mayer 2007 in Paasonen et al. 2007: 107)

With regards to the abundance of internet information and the facilitation of 'sexual' knowledges, Hearn (2008) is also cautious: "What may initially be self-help social-sexual communities of interest can become exclusionary, pay-to-use capitalist enterprises" (Hearn 2008: 41). Apart from increasing acceptance of LGBT 'sexualities' in varying spaces, Hearn (2008) expects a further blurring of 'sexual' categories.

"Sexuality is not necessarily co-existent with the intimate; nor does intimacy always connote the sexual. Yet modern forms of intimacy tend inevitably to throw up significant questions about sexual belonging, ethics and choice" (Weeks and Holland 1996: l). I found these to be central points that moved the practitioners of consensual 'SM' I interviewed (see Chapter 3) and, further, to be essential parts of discourses dealing with the 'postmodernization of intimacies' (e.g. Giddens 1990/1991 and Plummer 1995) and the conceptualization of 'Intimate Citizenship' as a means of sensitization (Van den Hoonard 1997; Plummer 1995/2003). Plummer stated once that if "...'intimate citizenship' seems an oxymoron, it also suggests a potential bridge between the personal and the political" (Plummer 2003: 15). This is precisely why an exploration of consensual 'SM' ethics is highly important in contemporary times in which everyone's 'life-world' is externally framed with 'sex' as commodity and simulation whereby at the same time a 'Sex uncovered-poll: "Homosexuality"' found that: "Same sex marriage has been legal in the UK since 2005, but 45 per cent of Britons still feel that gay couples should not be allowed to get married. (...) almost one in four Britons (24 per cent) believe that homosexual sex should be made illegal." (Sex uncovered poll: Homosexuality http://www.guardian.co.uk/lifeandstyle/2008/oct/26/relationships) and in which according to the findings of the Sex Education Forum (Bell 2007) commodified 'sexualised bodies' and stereotypically 'gendered' porn have seemingly replaced other forms of education in terms of 'sexualities' and relationships in contemporary Britain.

The experimental games of consensual 'SM', in contrast to the reductionist imagery of commodifying 'sexualities' and 'kink', allow for the discovery of new intensities and the diverse dimensions and potentials of 'lived bodies'. They also require the development of contextual ethics and, thereby do have the potential to bring about a 'political spirituality' on a practical level which would involve "...questioning through which people might start to depart from the historical limits of their identifications, ..." (Rajchman 1991: 108). The notion of a 'political spirituality' has obviously important implications for claims of a privileged position of same-sex attraction in order to facilitate 'transcendence of ego' as claimed by for example, Johnson (2000). The goal of some of these existential experiments in consensual 'SM', as well as in humanistic therapies, is the self-actualization of the human being and *not*, as in traditional psychologies, the personal adjustment to normative systems (e.g. social ordering and separating of human beings according to ascribed statuses of 'sex', 'gender', 'age', 'class', 'ableism', etc.).

2.5 'Pain'

As discussed at the beginning of this chapter the concept of 'lived body' is central to understanding the reductionism that is inherent to conventional, modern conceptions of 'body', 'sexuality', 'perversion', 'sadomasochism' and consumer culture's relationships to 'sexuality', thus I want to underline once again the advantage of the concept of 'lived body'. The 'lived body' concept suggests that bodily perception is incomplete as it is spatially spread and temporal, and thus requires constant reiteration. "If our existence is always indeterminate to varying degrees insofar as it is the unending process whereby hitherto meaningless, takes over meaning and, moreover, is ambiguous because the primary sensory meanings that are reached through our coexistence with others and things always have several meanings, then there can be no inflexible bodily structures that could once and for all determine our sexuality" (Bigwood in Welton 1998: 108).

In the concluding sections of this chapter it will become clear that the same fluidity holds true for perceptions of 'pain'. In contrast to most theories about 'Sadomasochism', and therefore in opposition to the social construction of 'Sadomasochism', the primacy of 'pleasure in pain' is, for the majority of my interviewees and for other practitioners of consensual 'SM' I met while conducting 'fieldwork' within the Scene, not a sufficiently valid explanation. Pat: "..., I don't just want it for the pleasure of the pain anyway. I like the connection with the other person" (Interview-file 1: 5).

Interpersonal communication and empathy are often far more relevant than the sensational means applied. However, a closer investigation of 'pain' is necessary in order to understand the strength and effect of the social construction of 'Sadomasochism' in its interdependence with a 'medical' and modern Western concept of 'pain', and in order to be able to appreciate the varieties in pain experience.

Szasz (1995) noted that from a psychoanalytical perspective pain is viewed as an isolated phenomenon that concerns the experiencing 'ego'. In this view pain is reduced to being an effect, a signal warning the 'ego' that something dangerous happened to the 'body'. Tart (1975) notes that: "While orthodox, Western psychology recognizes that pain can be a useful danger signal, warning us to attend to physical illness or to escape from a threatening situation, pain is otherwise looked upon as something to be avoided at all costs" (Tart 1975: 99). Within this understanding 'pain' is in itself interpreted as bad and as merely a physiological alarm sign. People consult doctors to eliminate their physical pains and legal drugs are given to 'cope' with mental pains. The idea that an individual actually appreciates or enjoys pain therefore seems both illogical and deeply disturbing for members of a society that is mostly orientated towards the hedonistic ideals of consumerism which embrace pleasure but only tolerate pain in 'legitimate' contexts (see Chapter 4).

2.5.1   Dimensions of pain experience

However, the dimensions of pain experience are wide ranging and should not be conceptualized as a single and unique quality which varies only in intensity. "Pain, ..., refers to a category of complex experiences, not to a specific sensation that varies only along a single intensity dimension. The word 'pain', in this formulation, is a linguistic label that categorizes an endless variety of qualities" (Melzack 1977: 41).

Melzack and Torgerson (1971) specify three main categories of 'qualities of pain'. The first category defines the *sensory qualities* of the experience of pain, which will vary in terms of "...temporal, spatial, pressure, thermal, and other properties" (Melzack 1977: 44). The second category defines the *affective qualities*, which will vary in terms of "...tension, fear, and autonomic properties that are part of the pain experience" (Melzack 1977: 44). Lastly, Melzack and Torgerson (1971) mention the category of the *evaluation* that is subjectively given to the overall intensity of the pain experience. As pain cannot be defined in terms of a single quality of experience with accordingly specified stimulus conditions, Melzack suggests a broader definition: "...pain may be defined in terms of a multidimensional space comprising several sensory and affective dimensions. The space comprises those subjective experiences which have both somatosensory and negative-affective components and that elicit behaviour aimed at stopping the conditions that produce them" (Melzack 1977: 46). While Melzack's gate-theory might appear dated, its enduring importance was underlined by Dickenson (2002).

Pain experiences have to be understood within the context of 'lived body' (Merleau-Ponty 1968) and thus in connection with a reflection of the total circumstances at a given time because only then a location of "...the position of the pain experience within the multidimensional space for the particular individual" (Melzack 1977: 47) is possible. In relation to the issue of pain within the context of consensual 'SM' this implies that any evaluation of degrees of pain experience must be context-orientated, which has profound implications for the scientific and legal level of the impact of the social construction of 'Sadomasochism'.

2.5.2 The psychophysical relationship in pain experiences

Melzack's data-analysis on the topic of psychological variables and their impact on the experience of pain suggests that the concept of a one-to-one relationship between the intensity of the noxious stimulation and the intensity of perceived pain has no basis. Their relationship is a relative one: "The same injury can have different effects on different people or even on the same person at different times" (Melzack 1977: 47).

The relationship between the stimulus and the perception varies as even early experiences with pain, the meaning given to pain and the culture on pain perception in which a given individual grows up are always different and might even change throughout her/his lifetime – even if the external circumstances and stimuli would be stable.

In relation to the criminalization of consensual 'SM', this implies that the concept of 'enjoying pain' and/or 'inflicting pain' in connection with these practices and their consequences does not have a valid foundation as pain as such is a relative variable that is highly individualistic and differently perceived.

Illustrating this point, one of the interviewees, here called Pat, explained to me how the techniques of 'play piercing' and 'beatings' result in different bodily sensations for her. Pat:

> When you do play piercing..., sometimes when I'm pierced I find it doesn't hurt at all, it doesn't feel anything, really. Just a, almost, almost nothing. Just a tiny sensation but usually at least some of them will give me a pain sensation and its a kind of strange sensation, ... I mean, when you get beaten or pierced or whatever, any kind of pain, you get endorphins in your body and the way they're released when you're pierced is a lot different I think because when you get a beating it's a very slow built-up and eventually you find that your body is full of endorphins and you're floating away. But with a piercing it kind of comes in rushes like when you're injected with something, almost. So, as you get the pain you get a kind of buzz and rush in your head, I think may be it has something to do with the fact that it's invasive, it pierces your skin, so your body is probably throwing a lot more endorphin out. At the same time, it does feel different and again I don't really relate to it unless it has some element of dominance in it. (Interview-file l: 7)

In a similar manner for Sue, pain is not the same if received by different means: "...my boyfriend is quite into pinching my nipples very, quite hard but if he doesn't do it gently to begin with he just ha, ha, clamps them very hard, I don't find that erotic at all. I find that's too hard but when it comes to ehm something like slapping or anything, you know, ... I think I'm quite reckless on the pain-level there" (Interview-file S.: 6).

2.5.3   The influence of affective processes on the perception of pain

The observations of the 'bodily practices' of consensual 'SM' and the information collected through interviews on pain experiences that relate to the 'scenes' that are enacted in these contexts, underline the importance of the affective dimensions of the pain experience. As most practitioners explicitly stated that their wounds appear to hurt less and heal better, when received during 'scenes' than outside this artificially set context, the affective bond of positive evaluation taken up to the wound, representing a positive experience, seem to support the bodily healing-processes. In this respect consensual 'SM'-related pain, and wound experiences appear to be in deep contrast to the pain experience of so-called 'post-traumatic pain syndromes', which can occur after negative experiences of pain (e.g. accidents, wounds resulting from domestic violence, pain caused by street violence, torture).

For many consensual 'SM'-practitioners sensations that conventionally would be termed 'pain' are evaluated as means to an end and if 'pain' continues to be felt days after 'the event', it is appreciated as a representation of bonding and/or as in remembrance of the experience of that specific 'scene'. A striking feature of many injuries and wounds obtained in the course of consensual 'SM' 'bodily practices', is that they do not hurt as much as when obtained within another context and further, that the healing process appears to be quicker. A potential explanation of this phenomenon is provided by the notion of 'DCBD' (Deliberately Caused Bodily Damage).

> *Bette:* I mean I was covered in bruises it was quite a, I mean it wasn't an enormously heavy but it was fairly heavy, it wasn't a light 'scene'. Also, if you get injuries in that way they don't hurt which I think is quite remarkable.
> *Andrea:* It's like a 'transcendental experience'?
> *Bette:* That's right, yeah. It has certainly a big spiritual element to it. With my partner I also have done occasionally, very, very occasionally quite heavy things. (Interview-file 4: 6)

In the work of Hussein and Fatoohi (1998) which deals with 'transcendental' abilities of the human body, the researchers concentrated on the DCBD abilities of followers of a Sufi School known as Tariqa Casnazaniyyah. The capabilities of these dervishes are contrasted with other practitioners of DCBD that occur in several other cultures. In their definition of the DCBD phenomena the authors explain the interesting characteristics of the various practices as follows:

> ... persons who practice quite dangerous feats in which they apply noxious stimuli to various parts of their bodies, yet with impunity. In these feats, damage is induced in parts of the human body, however, the body shows complete control over the detrimental consequences that would normally result. A typical feat of these Deliberately Caused Bodily Damage (DCBD) phenomena is inserting sharp objects, such as skewers, into various organs and tissues of the human body. ... Although DCBD phenomena are not necessarily piercing feats, the latter represent the majority and most remarkable instances of DCBD phenomena. (Hussein and Fatoohi 1998: 2)

A deeper insight into the spiritual dimensions of 'bodily practices' that involve intense sensations ('pain') will be given in Chapter 6.

2.5.4 Brain mechanisms responsible for the perception of pain

Traditionally it was assumed that pain sensation and response are subserved by a 'pain-centre' in the brain. But pain appears to be far more complex than this concept allowed. "Indeed, the concept is pure fiction, unless virtually the whole brain is considered to be the pain centre, because the thalamus, hypothalamus, brainstem reticular formation, limbic system, parietal cortex, and frontal cortex are all implicated in pain perception. Other brain areas are obviously involved in the emotional and motor features of pain" (Melzack 1977: 93).

In order to understand pain in all its dimensions, it is important not to underestimate the psychological dimensions of the pain experience, which are primarily the sensory- discriminative, motivational-affective, and cognitive-evaluative. One of the interviewees, here called George, illustrates the psychological dimensions of pain within the context of consensual 'SM' quite well: "... you know, she could, she will accept more pain if she's tied up than if not, like, you know, she has her mind set for that and then I build up slowly and pace it. Then she's able to 'take' harder blows, which before she wouldn't be able to do, ..." (Interview-file G.: 49).

Scarry (1985) views pain as deconstructing the self and the world, as self becomes reduced to the body and the world becomes reduced to the immediate surrounding. For Pat, one of my interviewees whom I introduce more fully within the next chapter, pain opens her up for sensuality: "I don't know why I like getting beaten I mean partly any intense sensation is pleasurable, so that's nice. But partly it hurts, it hurts awfully, it's like, if my body feels it then my body is there. I kind of, you know during sex I tend to, I can't, if I haven't really got a good connection with that person or something I tend to just wander off, my brain wonders off into some other place and I'm not really within my body."

> *Andrea*: So, it makes your body sort of aware of the sensations. It's like a gateway to sensual experiences for you?
>
> *Pat*: Yeah, I mean, I've noticed that for quite some time that, it's been apparent to me that with just ordinary sex it just doesn't work. I mean I can, I can do it, but it doesn't, I don't feel like I'm in my body and pain puts me into my body and having sexual intercourse or whatever sort of tends to put me out of my body in a way that I don't like, in a way that I'm dissociated from my body ... (Interview-file 1: 3)

The psychological side of pain experience thus seems to play a crucial role in consensual 'SM'-related pain experiences as well as pain experiences related to for example, sports and allows for interdependent changes on the level of the other two major psychological dimensions of the experience of pain. As "... cognitive activities such as cultural values, anxiety, attention and suggestion all have a profound effect on pain experience" (Melzack 1977: 102). As will be seen in Chapter 3, the Scene that developed around consensual 'SM' in London, evaluates the ability to 'take' experiences of pain that are connected to 'scenes' and/or semi permanent role-requirements, as positive achievements. They are perceived as symbols of strength and bonding (individually as well as socially) and therefore the cognitive-evaluative dimension of pain experience related to these 'bodily practices' will be a positive one.

The importance given to pain experiences on the Scene also enabled me to establish an empathetic bond with many practitioners of consensual 'SM'.

As my approach to this social research was guided by the feminist notion of 'engagement' (May 1993) as opposed to 'disengagement' (the traditional 'masculine paradigm' of research), the interviewees were able to enter into a dialogue with me in order to decrease the social distance between us. Within many of the initial questions the interviewees were focused on finding out about my own experiences with pain (both emotional and physical) and the way I dealt with these. As my experiences in this context were quite substantial, this appeared to be valued by a lot by the interviewees as after my responses they opened themselves up far more and developed a relationship of trust towards me. Through engaging in 'dialogic retrospection' (May 1993/2003) I was respected in terms of the 'frames of reference' of my informants and thus did not need to 'join in' in order to testify my abilities of understanding or 'taking' pain.

2.5.5 Transformations in the experience of pain – the impact of culture on the individual perception of pain

"...pain involves sensory, emotional and cognitive components. Although these interact, there is the suggestion that the emotional and cognitive components are learned. If these can be changed, then the experience of pain can be modified. This has been shown experimentally" (Kent and Dalgleish 1986: 263). The atmosphere of the clubs and the Scene of consensual 'SM' as such, might thus serve the function of a 'secondary socialization' and change the individuals learned psycho-physiological reactions towards sensations otherwise perceived as painful. The modification of pain experience also regularly occurs within consensual 'SM'-relationships as new sensations are introduced, selected and experienced again and again within the often varying contexts of the 'scenes'. The 'art of suffering' (Illich 1977), in other terms, ways of pain-management and the meaning ascribed to 'pain sensations' are changeable and interdependent with the socio-cultural context given (or chosen) by an individual. In the context of consensual 'SM', 'pain sensations' are understood in a positive manner, and, thus, in contrast to mainstream culture, the 'art of suffering' has a high social value. Similar to traditional cultures, the Scene that developed around consensual 'SM' provides a system of meaning for pain that is lacking in 'medical civilization' (Illich 1977), where:

People unlearn the acceptance of suffering as an inevitable part of their conscious coping with reality and learn to interpret every ache as an indicator of their need for padding or pampering. Traditional cultures confront pain, impairment, and death by interpreting them as challenges soliciting a response from the individual under stress; medical civilization turns them into demands made by individuals on the economy, into problems that can be managed or *produced* out of existence. Cultures are systems of meaning, cosmopolitan civilisation a system of techniques. Culture makes pain tolerable by integrating it into a meaningful setting; cosmopolitan civilisation detaches pain from any subjective or intersubjective context in order to annihilate it. (Illich 1977: 140/141)

Like traditional cultures, the 'bodily practices' of consensual 'SM' offer other understandings and other ways of dealing with issues and sensations of pain, which is positively valued, like impairment, which is sought after or accepted as a tool to highlight or bring about other sensations, or like suffering and death, which are understood as parts of life. Thus, within the Scene individuals have the possibility to unlearn the technical approach to pain and give sensations the idiosyncratic meaning that matches their very own perception. One of the general statements often heard within the Scene was thus: "It's all sensations, it depends how you use them."

The art of suffering, the management of sometimes extremely uncomfortable sensations is honoured and taught not only within the 'subculture' of consensual 'SM', but also in legitimized fields of pain-management, for example: extreme sports, the fitness-and beauty-sector and religious formations as well as in management-education, war-training (army) and natal-classes etc. "Behaviour modification therapies, wilderness training for the young, martial arts, and many sports embrace painful stimuli so that they can be mastered. Implicit in such activities is the belief that we can break our habitual responses to things that usually make us suffer" (Tart 1975: 87).

Summing up these reflections on the diversity of the psychological dimensions of pain experiences, it seems clear that the rapidly as well as interdependently conducting systems in the brain produce varying experiences of pain and, further, that psychological processes have a distinct and powerful impact on determining the quality and intensity of the individual pain experience. Apart from personal variables, the cultural background and the value given to pain appear to be important variables for the perception of pain. As the (sub)cultural value system of consensual 'SM' appears to be different from mainstream society, so are (in varying degrees) the social determinants that in part shape the individual perception of pain. As social determinants shape the individual anxiety, attention and interpretation of painful stimuli, my argument is that the attempt to estimate degrees of inflicted 'pain' without knowledge of the individual's situational and cultural context, as happened in the 'Spanner'-case and the following criminalization of certain 'bodily practices' of consensual 'SM' by the European

Court of Human Rights (see Chapter 3), represent a deeply flawed and inadequate way of dealing with these issues.

The 'bodily practices' of consensual 'SM' allow for self-experiments on the level of sensations of pain and provide specific knowledges for pain-management that are distributed often informally; for example, in conversations within clubs, the 'SM/Fetish' market and on private occasions such as 'SM'-picnics and parties.

Melzack's and Wall's 'gate theory' of pain (in Kent and Dalgleish 1986 and Dickenson 2002), which shows that emotional as well as evaluative reactions to painful stimuli (e.g. injuries) have a crucial impact on the individual's perception of pain, illustrates that attempts to create levels of legitimately administered pain, be it in connection with imprisonment and/or the criminalization of consensual 'SM', are bound to fail as they are unable to capture the full dimensions and individual and situational differences in pain perception.

The fact that there are individual approaches to pain is illustrated by the remarks of two of my interviewees. Tom and Bess experiment with painful sensations and they found out that they prefer different approaches to it.

> *Bess*: ...I mean at the moment I prefer a whip to a crop or a paddle because it wraps around you. I prefer long, slow sort of sensations rather than hard, sharp sensations. And he prefers a sharp, you know, something that makes him disappear. I'm the opposite way. I prefer a slow build-up in pain, really.
>
> *Tom*: Yeah, it has to be quite mild for pleasure. It's not intense [pain]. Also I find if you mix the pain with the pleasure, you can achieve a certain sort of like euphoric state? You know that basically is it all. You just take the pains. (Interview-file J.: 3)

In order to explain the difference between the two possible approaches and their effects, Tom described: "I mean it's like. It has to be that there's a major shock to the system. As Bess said if you build-up something, you slowly build up for it. It's cool. It's a nice way but it isn't at the shock. I find that the shock to the brain is less the endorphins get released a little bit more slowly. You just miss, it's not bang here, bang here there, out of it. Shock the body, shock the body with as much as the body can take. You want to release the endorphins because it's the endorphins I'm seeking not the pain" (Interview-file J.: 4).

In relation to the relationship between the 'masochist' and pain, Trigg (1970) compared Kenny's perspective on masochistic 'pain' with the philosophical approach of Wittgenstein to the duck-rabbit. "The fact that the masochist's sensation was produced by whipping gives us a reason for calling it 'pain'. The fact that he shows no 'pain-behaviour' gives us a reason for not calling it that" (Trigg 1970: 83).

In consensual 'SM', trust and the use of safewords (see Chapter 3) pre-vent the feeling of inevitability and the despair and hopelessness of other pain experiences (e.g. pain through disease and illness or through domestic violence or torture) from setting in. "Pain tension is more easily tolerable if, either in fantasy or reality, it can be escaped from, if it is avoidable, or if there is some escape hatch through which the tension can be released" (Leary in Solomon 1964: 244).

For some practitioners of consensual 'SM', the pain involved becomes a nearly therapeutic tool: Lara: "... a lot of things that we work out sexually do have to do with their [the practitioners] childhood and that those fantasies that are the most taboo and the most exciting, often have to do with things that have happened to us that we haven't resolved or ways that we have learned to deal with things that are abuse by eroticising it."

Andrea: Like overcoming the pain through erotic?
Lara: Yeah, the psychic pain, it might not even have been physical pain, but the psychic pain. You know, there's a lot of things that you can work out. (Interview-file L.: 15/16)

In this chapter I presented elaborations that deconstruct traditional, mechanistic, psychological and medical social constructions of 'body', 'sexuality' and 'pain' in favour of more open, fluid and flexible interpreta-tions of these complex elements of 'lived bodies'. These elaborations serve as a necessary introduction to the contextual and relational understandings of consensual 'SM' that follow in the next chapter. They further are the basis for the critique of the conventional and reductionist interpretations of 'bod-ily' concepts that guided the whole of the 'Spanner complex' which let to a scandalous miscarriage of justice. On a more theoretical level the elabora-tions of Chapter 2 also have the constructive potential to inform contem-porary debates on concepts of 'Intimate Citizenship' that are grounded in 'intimate choices'. (Plummer 1999 in Browning et al. 1999)

3
The 'Field': 'Lived Experiences' of Consensual 'SM' and 'Subjugated Knowledges'

In this chapter I explore the 'lived realities' of consensual 'SM' and its 'subjugated knowledges'. The first section presents an overview of the research methods I applied within the empirical part of the research on consensual 'SM'. The following sections introduce the reader to the subjects of my sample and also illustrate the different social reactions towards the label of 'Sadomasochism' and how they impact on individual lives. Topics around which data accumulated that was collected during interviews and 'participant observation' provide the 'grounded' structure of the next sections. These are: modes of self-understanding; motivations for the engagement in consensual 'SM'; consensual 'SM' on the Scene in London; the learning processes of consensual 'SM'; and, changes within the Scene around consensual 'SM' in London.

3.1   Qualitative research: An account of the methods

Chapters 1 and 2 of this book discussed the macro levels of the social construction of 'Sadomasochism' while this chapter focuses on the micro level and is based on my analysis of the data collected during the research I conducted in London. Given that my aim with this research lay in providing 'closeness' and 'authenticity' within my social scientific account, my approach lies in the tradition of ethnographic fieldwork.

During the time of my research in London, I conducted 'unstructured non-directive interviews' with 16 interviewees, who were contacted through 'snowball sampling' and 'relational outcroppings' (Lee 1993: 68). The choice of the access-methods of 'snowballing' and 'networking' appeared and turned out to be the most effective ones as I had to deal with a then extremely 'hidden' (as freshly semi-criminalized) and 'deviant' population (Lee 1993) with all its sociological problems. As the topic of this research project is a sensitive one, as it is, for example, dealing with the relatively private realm of 'sexuality' and also involves 'bodily practices' that are now indirectly and selectively criminalized, obtaining data was not an easy task to undertake.

3.1.1   Sampling a 'hidden population'

"...sampling becomes more difficult the more sensitive the topic under investigation, since potential informants will have more incentive to conceal their activities" (Lee 1993: 60). Due to the secrecy and the resulting problem of 'invisibility', access to the 'field' was crucially dependent on the information and trust I gained from the two 'gatekeepers' I found. May (1993) defines 'gatekeepers' as: "...those who control access to the information which the researcher seeks" (May 1993: 42). In this case, access to the population of interest was mostly conditioned by the possibilities of access of the 'gatekeepers' (one from the 'bi- and hetero'-consensual 'SM'-Scene; one from the lesbian 'butch-Scene') and the development of trust between myself as researcher and these two 'gatekeepers'.

As it turned out to be difficult to sample a relatively hidden population, Lee's suggestion of the employment of the combination of the strategies of 'networking' or 'snowballing' and 'relational outcropping' as a strategy for "...sampling 'special populations' which are rare and/or deviant in some way..." (Lee 1993: 61) seemed to provide an adequate approach. "Snowball sampling is ubiquitous in the study of deviant populations because it often represents the only way of gathering a sample" (Lee 1993: 66). The starting point of the 'network' sample was in this case my gatekeeper, here called Lara, as an informant for the gay/lesbian Scene around consensual 'SM' and an accidental contact I made with a member of the 'bi- and hetero' Scene while I was looking for accommodation in London. Lee defines the 'advantage' of the study of 'deviant' populations as follows:

> Where, as in the search for members of a rare population, the interest is in attributes rather than relations, one may gain some advantage in not having to predefine the sociometric criteria for inclusion in the sample. A pair of contacts in a chain need be linked by no more than knowledge of the existence of one another. Even so, in most cases-although this is rarely made clear-one is still sampling with reference to the social structure, though this time in an *implicit* manner. (Lee 1993: 66)

Biernacki and Waldorf (1981) have listed four suggestions to improve the sample variability and theoretical utility of 'network sampling' through enabling the researcher 'to pace and monitor the referral chains they generate'. After an initial phase in which enough contacts are made to start the research project, the researcher then "...should begin more to exercise more control over referral chains..." (in Lee 1993: 68). Concerning the sampling of members of the consensual 'SM' Scene this involved explicit efforts from my side to obtain information about the 'gay SM'-population as well as about the more easily obtainable data on 'bi-, hetero, and lesbian/butch'- consensual 'SM'-'body practices'. The third suggestion made by Biernacki and Waldorf, which Lee defines in accordance to Glaser and Strauss (1967) as being a process akin to theoretical sampling, involves: "... an attempt ... to identify specific kinds of respondents whose utility to the researcher lies in their ability to illuminate emerging theoretical formulations" (in Lee 1993: 68).

The interviews that I conducted as well as my fieldwork data generated through employing the social research method of 'participant as observer' within some of the consensual 'SM' clubs, made it apparent that the Scene around consensual 'SM' had undergone some interesting changes. As this process of change was mentioned very frequently, I identified the resulting 'generation gap' within the Scene in London as another important topic to research upon. This finding was the result of the employment of the sample method known as 'relational outcropping'. Lee describes this as: "... one method of sampling a rare or deviant population [which involves finding] some site in which its members congregate and to study them there" (Lee 1993: 69). My seeking out of 'relational outcroppings' within the Scene was partly limited by the code of secrecy that made some parties and clubs unobservable to the non-member in contrast to the abundance of fetish and 'SM' clubs that are currently in London. After some time within the 'field' and the collection of a reasonable amount of qualitative data, I followed the advice of the majority of my interviewees and started to extend my observations to include the semi-public events of the 'SM-Fetish-market' and on specific clubs and events recommended by them.

3.1.2 'Participant observation'

Initially I had planned to collect observational data by means of covert-participant observation because this method seemed to avoid the problem of 'reactivity' which is frequently focused upon in the literature on 'deviant populations' (Lee 1993). That literature suggests that the unawareness of being studied would make research participants feel less threatened by the research, while ensuring that participants continue their 'normal' behaviour even though it is labelled 'deviant' (Lee 1993: 143).

In the light of the ethical implications of engaging in covert social research methods, my commitment not to violate the freedom and privacy of the research subjects was very strong and even practical considerations prevented 'covert' observation. Schatzmann and Strauss (1973) pointed out that the use of a hidden identity requires the researcher to give up much of the mobility of social research as it prevents easy access to certain subgroups across jurisdictional or other lines.

The borderline between overt and covert methods is quite clearly drawn at the level of the role that the researcher adopts. If the researcher does not pretend to be someone who she or he is not, but explains his/her presence with honesty, the research is conducted in an overt manner. However, on the level of knowledge about the research project, the clear-cut distinction between overt and covert becomes blurred because social researchers generally do not know precisely what they will investigate at the beginning of the process of research. Even if these aims were already fixed, as in deductive orientated research projects, there would also be the problem of influencing people to behave in ways consistent with research related aims. Additionally there is the problem of meaning, because even if a researcher gives precise information about the content of the research project, the same information will have different meanings to different people. In this respect I tend to support Roth's opinion (Roth 1962 in Burgess 1990) that there is no clear cut distinction but rather a continuum between overt and covert research.

As part of the 'reflexivity of the research process' (May 1993) I decided to adopt the role of 'participant as observer' which implies, according to May, that a "...person adopts an overt role and makes her or his presence and intentions known to the group..., while during the process of observation the attempt to form a series of relationships with the subjects such that they serve as both respondents and informants..." (May 1993: 117) is being made. Whenever I went to any of the Scene-clubs the group or individuals that took me along were always informed of the purpose of my undertaking.

At the Scene-clubs themselves, I observed and asked questions only when the flow of events allowed me to do so. As the people at these clubs wanted to enjoy themselves, I had to respect their wish to 'play' without being a hindering disturbance. Especially since some of their 'modes of enjoyment' are criminalized and a number of clubs had been raided by the police, I did not want to increase the fears among the practitioners in the club of getting 'busted'. I did not dress in a typical 'Dom' or 'sub'-outfit but wore a rather 'untelling' black rubber-dress in order to adhere to the club's often rather strict dress-codes.

During the research process it was crucial to develop an understanding and 'feel' for the balance between the aim for authenticity and the finding of an appropriate distance that allows for proper research. Along with feminists and critical theorists, I do not believe in the notion of 'objective science' as the values of a researcher affect all aspects of a given research project and as the a priori requirement of the researcher's detachment in order to obtain 'objectivity' can anyway never be fully assured but merely reflects "...a limited idea of science through its separation of reason and emotion" (May 1993: 39).

My identity as a researcher was certainly and necessarily not a detached one and I frequently encountered the problem of 'multiple identities' that ethnographic fieldwork poses for researchers. Through my presence in the Scene for the collection of observational data and through the many interviews I conducted, I had become a trustworthy 'contact-person' for some people. On some occasions individuals, who were in need of help and support, contacted me in order to 'talk things over'. During my fieldwork I got to know many different people in the Scene that evolved around consensual 'SM-bodily-practices' who sometimes did not know each other. On a few occasions I therefore was able to introduce people to each other, which in one case helped to organize the set up of a consensual 'SM-workshop'. Through continuous contact with the Scene I also was able to inform people about upcoming events and venue-changes, when they were in need of this information. This view and approach to the research process might be best described by the term of 'dialogic retrospection', which is influenced by feminist-based research concepts and is defined as: "...an open and active exchange between the researcher and participant in a partnership of co-research" (Humm 1989 in May 1993: 39).

3.1.3 Unstructured, focused and in-depth interviews

In 'Quantity and Quality in Social Research' Bryman (1988) describes one of the crucial advantages of the unstructured but topic-focused form of interviewing in comparison to structured or semi-structured interview forms. Although it has an open-ended character:

"...rambling can be viewed as providing information because it reveals something about the interviewee's concerns. Unstructured interviewing in qualitative research, then, departs from survey interviewing not only in terms of format, but also in terms of its concern for the perspective of those being interviewed" (Bryman 1988: 47).

The major advantage of unstructured, focused interviewing is the fact that it allows the interviewees to express their views in terms of their own 'frames of reference', thus providing the possibility for the researcher to understand the meanings attributed to their 'life-worlds' (e.g. the 'bodily practices' of consensual 'SM' as well as the meanings the individual practitioners attribute to the label of 'Sadomasochism').

3.1.4 A quantitative method within a qualitatively orientated research design: The 'self-completion questionnaire'

Even though the general framework of my research design is qualitatively orientated and enabled me to engage in exploratory fieldwork (Shaffir and Stebbins 1991: 37f), a reflexive analysis of my pilot-work conducted in Edinburgh made apparent that securing of adequate information on the rather abstract topic of 'transcendence' would require different means. The unstructured, non-directive and reflexive interview-style (Rogers 1951) I employed gained me large amounts of fruitful data but the topic of 'transcendental experiences' that had been mentioned in different variations by some of my interviewees not always developed out of the flow of the interviews.

In order to collect data on this topic, I had to design a questionnaire as the term 'transcendence' itself is very complex and not used in everyday life. The use of this directive and deductive method of social research did not match my ethical considerations about social research but provided me with the opportunity to break down this difficult area. The questionnaire broke down this complex subject matter into understandable sub-questions which in turn facilitated the subsequent analysis and improved the validity and reliability of the data collected, as it enabled me to exclude errors or variations in the questions posed on a topic that is in itself difficult. For the purpose of this part of my research I therefore designed and introduced a 'self- completion questionnaire', which, on the basis of the trust gained through face-to-face interviews, I then asked my interviewees to take home. Instead of turning a part of my unstructured face-to-face interviews into a structured one (exclusively dealing with the topic in question), I found that the 'self-completion questionnaire' allowed the interviewees more time for the intensive reflections necessary to answer these questions. Through embedding the questionnaire within a framework of qualitative methods, I hoped to avoid the difficulty of its results being only valid at the very moment of its completion. I further encouraged the interviewees to make use of diaries for its completion and to engage in follow-up interviews. This process avoided the danger of a 'simplification of a complex social world' which takes 'no account of opinions across time' (May 1993: 86).

As the design of a questionnaire has an important impact on the quality of data gained, its construction has to be undertaken with a great deal of care. This is elaborated on further in Chapter 6 of this thesis.

Hoinville and Jowell (1987) state that the questionnaire design has to suit the aims of the research as well as the nature of its respondents as well as being clear, unambiguous, 'uniformly workable' and capable of engaging the respondents interest (ibid.: 27). I decided to make use of 'free-answer-questions' (open questions) because the merits of this type of question far outweigh any problems, especially when dealing with such a complex topic. "'Free-answer-questions' enable the researcher to elicit a wide variety of responses, they provide a background for interpreting answers to other questions and they also allow a possibility to introduce to the subject" (Payne 1973: 49).

Even though I was aware of the problems that open questions and their analysis pose, I gave priority to the greater freedom of expression it offers on the side of the respondent. Confronted with open questions, the individual is able to answer in a way that suits her/his interpretation of the questions and her/his personality. As open questions often pose problems for less articulate people, I hoped that my suggestion to use other means of answering the questionnaire and follow-up interviews would give sufficient support to them but none of the interviewees made use of this possibility. The vagueness and therefore the difficulty in describing experiences of a 'transcendental' nature and the fact that these experiences do have many varying features did not allow me to work with any kind of prefixed replies if I aimed at collecting meaningful data.

Answers to open questions further appeared to be valuable because they do provide vivid quotations which add to the credibility of the research on a so far under researched topic. The length of the questions depended to a large degree on the complexity of the topic. Complicated subject-matters that imply a variety of different facets like for example the various possible experiences of a 'transcendental nature' need to be put in several questions:

"Rather than rely on a single complex question, a series of simple questions should be asked, the number of such questions depending on the degree of simplicity required" (Moser and Kalton 1979: 321). Apart from trying to avoid ambiguous questions, leading questions and technical expressions, Moser and Kalton (1979) mention that the length of a questionnaire depends on the subject matter of the research and as the questionnaire is only dealing with one aspect of the research project, it only consists of ten questions and: "..., since questionnaire completion is a learning process with which the respondent will become increasingly at ease as he proceeds, the more difficult questions should come in the middle or towards the end" (Hoinville and Jowell 1987: 130).

In his book 'The Art of Asking Questions', Stanley L. Payne (1973) points out the most important issues that are to be thought of in the wording of questions. Payne recommends that we should not to take too much for granted in relation to the respondents' understanding of the researched upon topic. This is especially true for 'transcendental experiences' through 'bodily practices' of consensual 'SM'. Payne's solution to this problem lies in the development of a critical attitude towards our own questions, to question how much knowledge is taken for granted and he suggests to: "... substitute clarity for cleverness" (Payne 1973: 16). As the terminology had to be field-oriented, I decided not to use the word 'transcendence' within my questionnaire. "After we are sure that the issue is fully defined and that its limits are set to our satisfaction, then we can begin to translate it into simple words for public consumption" (Payne 1973: 27). Even the use of simple words could still have posed the problem of the 'phenomenon of unobservance', in that the answers just reveal what the respondent thinks the facts ought to be like. However, the unstructured interviews and observations in the Scene-clubs and at other consensual 'SM'-events enabled me to compare the results of the questionnaire with actual behaviour and understand or reflect the reasons for variations. In terms of the problem of response rates it was of advantage that the 'self-completion questionnaire' was embedded in several unstructured face-to-face interviews as well as in continuing field-contacts. Out of the 16 questionnaires that I distributed, 14 were completed and analysed. The two questionnaires that were not returned belonged to practitioners of consensual 'SM' who mainly 'played' in 'top-space' which, after the analysis of the data collected, turns out to be the less likely position to be in for the experience of 'transcendental states'. The 'self-completion questionnaire' on 'unusual experiences' during the practice of consensual 'SM' is contained within Chapter 6 of this book (6.2.8.).

3.2   The experiences of consensual 'SM'

The sample of this research consisted of individuals that I got to know over a ten month period in London, during which I conducted many qualitative interviews; handed out the self-designed questionnaires on the topic of consensual 'SM-bodily-practices' in relation to 'transcendental states'; and also engaged in 'participant observation' (without actual participation) within the London 'SM'-Scene.

The individual interviewees did not match the scientific stereotype mentioned by Gosselin and Wilson (in Howells 1984) of a correlation in the frequency of corporal punishment and interest in consensual 'SM'. The notion of varying degrees of 'commitment' (Becker 1960) to consensual 'SM' among my interviewees in contrast was useful. Becker described the characteristics of the explanatory variable of 'commitment' as behaviour that "...persists over some period of time....The diverse activities have in common the fact that they are seen by the actor as activities which, whatever their external diversity, serve him in pursuit of the same goal" and finally: "...the notion of consistent lines of activity seems to imply a rejection by the actor of feasible alternatives" (Becker 1960: 33). The individual informants that I encountered were 'committed' to the 'bodily practices' of consensual 'SM' to different degrees.

The 'bodily practices' of consensual 'SM' appeal to a variety of people with different degrees of 'commitment' and quite diverse backgrounds. Similar to Gosselin and Wilson's study this sample also does not show a direct correlation between frequency of corporal punishment and interest or engagement in consensual 'SM'-'bodily practices'. Although several of my informants did not experience corporal punishment, they still practice and enjoy consensual 'SM'. The sample confirmed Gosselin and Wilson's findings who described the socio-economic background of their sample as 'normal' (in Howells 1984).

3.2.1   The empirical field and the effects of the social censure of 'Sadomasochism'

While researching, I had to often deal with the phenomena of being in the role of what Becker (1963) termed the 'falsely accused'. Even though my 'deviance' only went as far as to be conducting a research on the topic of consensual 'SM', a lot of the people in my social environment as well as on the Scene (of consensual 'SM' and 'Fetishism') in London labelled me anyway. This experience allowed me an insight into the rigidity with which people apply labels and how a label changes the way people interact with an individual once labelled. Although my commitment to consensual 'SM' 'body practices' reduces itself to the level of professional research interests, my parents and my ex-partner believed that I was actively engaged with consensual 'SM' 'bodily practices' because I studied it. The psychotherapist whom I interviewed in London's 'Institute of Human Sexuality' was interested to find out about my 'SM-elements' as I was carrying out this specific research project. These are only a few of the many situations I encountered within the role of the 'falsely accused' which provided me with a 'lived experience' of the potential impacts of processes of labelling.

Through the interview with the psychotherapist who works at the London 'Institute of Human Sexuality', I gained an insight into the effects of official labelling. None of the clients he encountered in the context of his work were open about their 'bodily practices'; they remained 'closeted' and preferred to stay that way. The therapist informed me that in contrast to, for example, 'fetishism', which in his opinion is an exclusively male 'paraphilia', 'sadomasochists' could be found in both 'genders': "There are probably as many women as men in SM" (Interview-file Q.: l). He stated his belief that 'the broad area of SM', to his knowledge, is unusual; the clients with whom he works on their 'Sadomasochism' seem to obviously not enjoy their 'sexuality'. In his experience these are mostly men, who 'play' alone or 'unmatching couples' that do not cope with their different expectations regarding 'sexuality'. Another stark contrast to the people I interviewed, who were never officially labelled and who do not see the 'bodily practices' of consensual 'SM' as problematic in their lives, is the fact that these clients do not have any connection to others who share similar experiences or the Scene that evolved around consensual 'SM' and 'Fetishism' in London. It appeared as though his clients tried to avoid the stigmatization and the social reactions that go along with the label and therefore preferred to live isolated lives. As the social construction of the label 'Sadomasochism' implies a notion of psychopathology, they do not want to be identified with this 'social censure' (Sumner 1990) or be connected to any of the consensual 'SM'-support groups. "I would say that none of them seem to be in any kind of network. None of them have. ... They wouldn't want to identify" (Interview-file Q.: 4/5). The psychotherapist agreed that imposed and/ or internalized negative labels often prevent constructive work on problems and he added that negative labels would also lower self-esteem which in turn will worsen the compulsion to act out 'paraphilias'. In his opinion 'paraphilias', like 'Sadomasochism', are grounded in low self-esteem and thus negative labelling would be more than counterproductive in effect. My experiences with people in the 'field' was different. My interviewees did not show any self-esteem problems and thus, it might be that they are rather the result of lives spent in the 'closet' (i.e. as in the case of the psychotherapist's clients).

Research on the relationship between self-concepts and 'delinquency' has had disappointing results (Matsueda 1992). Matsueda thus suggested: "...the need for considering alternative conceptualizations of the self and its role in the process of social control" (Matsueda in Cullen and Burton 1994: 174). Matsueda's modification suggests a concept of self as 'being rooted in social interaction, comprising many dimensions and as providing a crucial link between self-control and social control' and considers the importance of labelling theories in the specification of 'the broader determinants of the self' in building up the argument that "...delinquency is in part determined by one's appraisals of self from the standpoint of others" (ibid.: 174). In view of the impression I gained of the 'self-esteem' of my interviewees I consider Matsueda's specification of 'self' an improvement as none of the people I encountered on the Scene seems to have particularities of 'global self-esteem'. Therefore Matsueda's framework that treats 'global self-esteem' as only one element of a multifaceted 'self' is indeed more fruitful as it appreciates that: "the critical locus of social control may be the process of role-taking and forming the self as an object with a specific set of meanings" (Matsueda in Cullen and Burton 1994: 175). This approach will be applied within the section of this chapter that deals with the modes of self-understanding on the side of my interviewees.

In the view of the psychotherapist there appears to be no specific 'SM-background' which also matches the results of my research: "They have a wide range of backgrounds, they may have cold parental environments, they may have public school type coldness or they may have not. They may have a very warm background and everything 'normal', normal as far as you can tell and according to their own accounts of it as well. And you think: 'Why is it like this?' And the answer is: 'Who knows.' I think there are hundreds of kinds of paraphilias" (Interview-file Q.: 4). Even though this therapist has an extraordinarily accepting approach towards consensual 'SM' in that he does not try to 'cure' it, like a majority of therapists might do, he still applies the term 'paraphilia' and he sees 'paraphilias' as implicitly problematic even though he gives his clients the choice to stick to them: "The crucial thing about it is that they ['paraphiliacs'] prefer those things to the loving partner. They are not just like embellishments, they are not like salt and pepper, they are the main course" (Interview-file Q.: 4).

After my experiences within the 'field', I believe that this is not generally true. Many interviewees either were in loving relationships or looked for them; some did not. In my opinion the fixation mentioned here might also be the result of the isolation in which clients of the Institute were living. They did not get a chance to meet others, who might have shown them that they are not 'weird', and they would not have had the chance to meet more 'matching' partners. Apart from these general findings, I found the psychotherapist's perception of 'masochists' very interesting: "Often when you meet people who are so-called 'masochists', even in a clearly sexual way, they are very difficult people, very, very controlling. So, it's almost as if they are the controlling ones, you know, the ones in charge" (Interview-file Q.: 3). Although I find it problematic to accept the suggestion that 'masochists' are supposed to be 'difficult people', the psychotherapist's comments about the masochist's power to control and to be in charge finds its empirical echo within the interviews and observations I conducted.

In 'Fetishism, Sadomasochism and Related Behaviors', the psychologists Gosselin and Wilson (in Howells 1984), point out that they:

> pay relatively little attention to the clinical literature, since the clinical subject represents only about 10 percent of those with these sexual variant patterns ... and is usually under legal or social pressure, feels excessive guilt, suffers marital discord and generally finds his sexual pattern a burden rather than merely a fact of life or a source of enjoyment. He is consequently unrepresentative of the variant population as a whole. (Gosselin and Wilson in Howells 1984: 89)

The official label thus profoundly impacts on a subject's behaviour. The information I gained at the 'London Institute of Human Sexuality' further verified Gosselin and Wilson's objections to the study of the 'clinical subject' or the 'secondary deviant' and therefore I decided to include only individuals within this research, who did not get officially labelled. The use of official statistics as a source of information to estimate the population who engage in consensual 'SM' as such, is, in my opinion, inefficient as it has proved to be for 'crime', not only because of the dark figure, but also because: "..., the size of the 'criminal' population is wholly determined by the exercise and experience of control, with particular members being periodically extruded into or included from the 'normal' population. ..." (Ditton 1979: 34).

3.2.2   Social reactions

The psychologists Gosselin and Wilson (1984) pointed out that 'these forms of sexual conduct', meaning consensual 'SM', are statistically unusual which, in my opinion, is probably mostly due to the social reactions that the 'social censure' (Sumner 1990) of 'Sadomasochism' provokes. In the field known as the 'sociology of deviance', Becker (1963) states my position that rejects a reading of 'deviance' as a characteristic of a person's actions but suggests that: "..., deviance is *not* a quality of the act the person commits, but rather a consequence of the application by others of rules and sanctions to an 'offender'. The deviant is one to whom that label has been successfully applied" (Becker 1963: 9). My analysis therefore begins with the social reactions the individuals I interviewed had and have to deal with or avoided by being 'closeted'.

Although the people I interviewed sometimes labelled themselves, the social reactions that followed either their 'sexual' practice or their 'coming out', clearly show the impact of the label 'Sadomasochism'.

On the level of the 'social body' the fear of 'Degradation ceremonies' keeps many practitioners of consensual 'SM' from being 'open' about their lives. Following Garfinkel (1972): "Any communicative work between persons whereby the public identity of an actor is transformed into something looked on as lower in the local scheme of social types, will be called a 'status degradation ceremony'" (Garfinkel 1972: 89). In relation to 'SM' 'Degradation ceremonies' are taking place on various levels (media, education, direct-talk) with different degrees of potential destruction. The aim of these ceremonies is always the 'ritual destruction' of the individual human being as social person. In its place, an 'Other' is constituted, now detected as the 'real person' in order to serve the moral indignation of the collectivity.

3.2.3   Family and friends

Even though Jane, who is in her thirties, identifies with the label 'pervert' in a positive way, her mother views her 'sexuality' as negatively different. "My mum knows that I'm a bit weird. She accepts it. I think she thinks it's her fault, you know. She thinks there is something wrong with me because I was abused as a child it must be. That's what a lot of people think" (Interview-file C.: 3). The traditional, modern 'scientific' stereotypes about 'Sadomasochism' show their destructive impact very clearly in this example. The mother perceives her daughter's 'sexuality' as 'wrong', as 'weird' and tries to trace down the causal connections which end up with an attribution of guilt on her own part. Another example is Diabolo: "I told most of my friends, only one doesn't know. Most of them just accepted it, they did not ask much. The others, well, they are not my friends, you can't call people like that friends anyway. My parents would not understand, they don't know. We only talk on a superficial level, they are conventional 'missionary-style'-people, too old to tell them" (Interview-file D.: 2). After the 'SM-PRIDE'-march which Diabolo joined, he remarked on the importance of keeping his discretion or 'face' towards his parents as they represent: "..., the last bastion of 'normality' upon me. But only because it would cause them pain if they knew I was into SM. I don't hope for one moment that they would understand it, or respect it, or acknowledge it as other than mental illness in their son and that can't be a good thing for them" (Interview-file D.: 4). The impact of the social censure of 'Sadomasochism' prevents, even blocks, the communication between Diabolo and his parents, as it did in Jane's case, through the stereotyping of consensual 'SM' as pathology and the resulting production of shame. George prefers to keep his 'bodily practices' of consensual 'SM' hidden from most people as he fears their possible reactions. He fears blackmail later on in his life and he is particularly concerned that his career as an academic would be in danger if people got to know his 'secret'. Therefore he does not join the Scene and he does not tell his friends about 'it', as "...they would dig at me...I haven't told anyone in my family such as I have a brother, I haven't told him, or any of my friends who I have from school that I still have as friends" (Interview-file G.: 20/24). Shiva does not tell anyone about her interest in consensual 'SM' as she had a painful experience, after she had told one of her long-term friends about it: "...then the other day she started making fun of me but saying that she wanted to come to a club." And she said: "But don't think that I'm coming because I'm into it. I'm just coming to have a laugh and if I didn't take it as a laugh, I consider you and Jake very demeaning. ...And I felt so totally betrayed. I've known her for years and years and years" (Interview-file 2: 6).

While it has become clear that the commodification of 'kink' in the recent decade facilitated the availability of clubs, access to other practitioners, representations and toys for practitioners of 'SM', the highly publicized case of Mr Mosley's commercial investment into the now mainstream world of commodified 'SM', revealed that negative stereotypes still have an impact on people's perceptions as part of his defence Mosley admitted his 'unfortunate interest' (Saner 2008: 5) in 'sadomasochism'. Apart from the problematic lack of the term 'consensual' in front of 'sadomasochism', and thus lacking a qualification of what is implied in the discussed activities, Mosley's own choice of words with regards to 'unfortunate' reflects an internalized (or at least represented as such) negative evaluation of 'SM'.

3.2.4 Subcultural groups

Even though subcultural groups frequently claim to be more liberal, they also set up internal rules and norms, often through identifying 'deviant' practices that are then excluded. The 'deployment of sexuality' thus also works within the minority groups themselves. Ryan, who came out as gay and lived a gay lifestyle, found it difficult to be open or 'come out' as a gay 'SMer' "Yeah, it is like 'coming out' especially on the gay Scene Yeah, I think when I went first on the Scene, experiences of pain or humiliation or 'rough sex', yeah? Like using dildos, 'fisting', piss, you know, those sort of sex, ... a lot of people, if you said: 'Oh, I'm into that.' They would block off, yeah. ...And now I'm not bothered. You know, I will tell people if they ask, I don't sort of float in it, you know what I mean. Yeah, but it was like a different experience of 'coming out'. ...I mean, I think, I mean I haven't 'come out' to everyone about 'SM'. You know I wouldn't tell straight friends necessarily..." (In R.: 3).

Pat, a now self-identified 'SM-dyke', had similar difficulties, even before experiencing the 'bodily practices' of consensual 'SM'. Pat: "A sort of power differential in sex was quite exciting for me. In my fantasies. I came out as a lesbian when I was fifteen, and I came out into the women's movement and it's all very equal, equal and, you know, and no one is allowed to fuck each other and no one is allowed to dominate each other."

Andrea: So it was strict rules there when you came out?

Pat: Yeah, for lesbians in the women's movement it was very much, you know, we're not going to emulate the power relations of heterosexuality, you know, heterosexuals is about male dominance and female submission, you know: 'We are not going to do that, we don't do that.' I was very confused because I knew I was attracted to women that's what I wanted to do primarily but the kind of sex was not very interesting. (Interview-file 1: 2)

In 'Out the other side' Sara Scott (1988) mentioned Melissa Benn's claim about the lesbian feminist debate on consensual 'SM' as essentially being about: "…a rejection by some lesbian feminists of a prescriptive public morality about sex" (Scott in McEwen and O'Sullivan 1988: 57) which is clearly illustrated by Pat's statements. A similar point is made by Ardill and O'Sullivan who accused the London Women's Liberation Movement of never actually discussing 'sexual practices' but instead focusing entirely on the 'politics of sexuality', thereby obviously leaving out the potential pleasures of the 'lived body'. Ardill and O'Sullivan perceive the main factor in the debates around lesbian feminist attitudes towards lesbian consensual 'SM' to be located in the organizing factor of 'identity' which is invested with a specific moral authority (Ardill and O'Sullivan in McEwen and O'Sullivan 1988: 124/125) leading thus to a hierarchical model of 'truth' that in effect made (makes) real communication and dialogue impossible.

It becomes very obvious then how power and knowledge are bound up together within the discourses on 'sexuality'. There is "…a multiplicity of discursive elements that can come into play in various strategies. It is this distribution that we must reconstruct, with the things said and those concealed, the enunciations required and those forbidden, that it comprises" (Foucault 1990: 100). The selectiveness of discourse is crucial here: as long as 'SM' is locatable within a context of commodification (e.g. medicalization, sensationalism, consumerism) there are various discourses about it; however, the potential of consensual 'SM' as a 'laboratory of life' or as an informal experiential space of exploration is not really covered. Consensual 'SM' as a space of education about the fragility of 'body', its interdependency with contexts and contested political status (e.g. aim to introduce assumed consent with regards to organ-donation, potential introduction of schemes to 'harvest' eggs from 'mentally ill' people, trafficking of 'bodies', etc. is neither an easily accessible knowledge.

3.2.5   Official social control

The atmosphere on the Scene of consensual 'SM' that I encountered was influenced by fears generated by the 'Spanner'-case [R.v.Brown; 1992–93] which was also a topic of major importance during many conversations and interviews. The following decision of the European Court of Human

Rights ([1997] Cr App Rep 44) (19.2.1997) furthered the criminalization of many variations of consensual 'SM'-'body practice' on a European scale. These examples of the selective legal regulation of 'unruly bodies' are therefore taken as illustrations of the official social reaction towards consensual 'SM'.

After the decision of the European Court of Human Rights to sanction the interventions of the British police and courts, many people on the Scene felt the need to be more cautious about going to the Scene-clubs. Bette described her personal experience of police-harassment at one 'SM-club': "I mean, I was at 'Whip' when at three minutes past two, sixty police-officers and lots of police-dogs and police-vans arrived. And the police-officers came into the club, I mean goodness knows what they thought they were going to find. I mean it's not exactly a violent place, neither one of them [the Scene-clubs]. I mean people were extremely polite to them, for all things considered but they were charged with 'disorderly house'. And the defense had to point out, one, that the police were lying about the extent of what they saw. ... So, the defense was first of all to say: 'Well, those were actually exaggerated by the police.' And secondly, to say: "Well, even if those sort of things were happening, you know if there was a bit of 'hanky-panky' going on, does that really outrage your sense of decency. Or should you be outraged by genocide in Bosnia in 1996. Is this really so outrageous?" So, we don't know on what basis the jury came to a decision but they did come to a majority verdict and said they were not guilty. I mean that doesn't mean there won't be further police-harassment in clubs" (Interview-file 4: 2).

Bentham, who in 1789 made the distinction between pain and pleasure the foundation of his plan for an ethical and legal code in the first sentence of his 'Principles of Morals and Legislation', would possibly be puzzled on the question of consensual 'SM'. As Morris writes: "Nothing remains separate once these two mighty opposites dissolve into an ambiguous mix, like the bodies in a Sadean melange where even gender grows indistinct. Like revolution, pain for Sade leads away from clarities" (Morris 1991: 237/238). The following will illustrate that this 'lack of clarity' in terms of conventional categories was a problem for the courts that were dealing with the Brown vs. Regina case. *The Times* commented on the Lords judgment in the Spanner case that the defendants: "... did all sorts of painful things to each other from which it is hard to imagine that pleasure could be derived" (*The Times* 12.3.93: 21) and Lord Templeman's comment in his ruling of the 'Spanner'-case was that: "... cruelty was uncivilized" (*Times Law Reports* 12.3.93: 42).

Phobic discourses function as a strategy of delegitimation of others and as an indirect legitimization of the socio-political status quo. The paradoxical combination of incoherence, propositional indeterminacy and social efficacy which is characteristic of phobic discourses only amplifies the effects of the social censure of 'Sadomasochism'.

In 1987 a police operation called 'Operation Spanner' acquired private videotapes which showed nearly 50 gay men involved in consensual 'SM'-'scenes'. Sixteen of these men were then arrested. In the years 1990/91 the trial against these 16 men took place. They were facing charges under Sections 20 and 47 of the Offences against the Person Act 1861. The initial trial judge ruled that consent was no defence to a charge of assault (Thompson 1994) and therefore the defendants, who at first had pleaded not guilty, had to change their pleas. On 19 December 1990 they were formally convicted. The ruling of the initial judge included the declaration: "...that it was the role of the court to draw the line between what was and was not acceptable in a civilized society, and that as sadomasochism was 'degrading and vicious' it was on the wrong side of the line" (Thompson 1994: 4). At the Court of Appeal the decision was later on upheld. Consensual 'SM' 'bodily practices' should never have been subject to an assault charge as they did involve consent which is definitely a 'civilized' form of interactive negotiation.

Section 20 of the Offences against the Person Act 1861 defines that an assault has taken place if a person: "...unlawfully and maliciously wound or inflict grievous bodily harm upon another person with or without a weapon or instrument". The problems of legal definition that occurred, as consensual 'SM' does not match the description of Section 20 and also would include legitimized activities like contact sports, teachers' disciplinary measurements etc., were avoided as "...all the judges used the fact that because the defendants had pleaded guilty to the charges after Judge Rant's [initial judge] ruling, they had admitted that they had wounded and caused actual bodily harm to each other!" (Thompson 1994: 5).

As the pain inflicted is actually perceived as pleasurable by the 'bottoming' practitioners themselves, even the concept of 'harm' would have been inappropriate in order to convict these three men which I will elaborate on at a later stage. Further, as it was a 'victimless crime' because no one complained of an offense being committed and because no one's privacy or decency was invaded by the consensual, private 'plays' of these men, the 'masochists' were [and had to be]constructed as the 'victims', even though "...the majority of the defendants were in the habit of switching roles" (Thompson 1994: 6).

Individual psychological and social harms were effected by the 'Spanner' case, thus through the official social reactions towards consensual 'SM' *and not through* the effects of the consensual 'play'. All of the defendants lost their jobs, several were thrown out of their flats and all of them were ousted as 'perverts'. Three of the men, were convicted and jailed for assault on consenting participants during the practice of consensual 'SM'. This judgment represents a miscarriage of justice with devastating effects. These victims of 'formations of domination' took their cases to the European Court of Human Rights in the hope to get the verdicts overruled on the ground that it breached Article 8 of the European Human Rights Convention. The

European Court of Human Rights [19.2.97] confirmed the legitimacy of the indirect criminalization of the 'bodily practices' of consensual 'SM' by the British courts. As these 'bodily practices' were undertaken in the private sphere and without causing lasting injuries, this decision violates the human right to privacy and makes the right over one's body questionable.

Article 8 of the European Human Rights Convention states that: "Everyone has the right to respect for his private and family life, his home and his correspondence." The Strasbourg judgment had thus to be based on the exception to the Article that covers 'the protection of health'. As consent forms a defence to assault in other instances of consensual encounters, like for example contact sports, operations for medical or aesthetic reasons, etc. from which physical harm and health problems can result, the judgment appears to be primarily a moral and political one.

Yet, rejecting the argument that behaviour involving private morality should not be open to state intervention, the Strasbourg court stated: "It is evident that the applicants' activities involved a significant degree of injury or wounding which could not be characterized as trifling or transient" (*The Independent* 20.2.97: 5). This confirms imposed limits to privacy in favour of 'the public need to safeguard health and safety' (*The Times* 20.2.97: 12).

The ruling of the European Court of Human Rights affirmed the entitlement of the United Kingdom: "... to seek to regulate through the operation of the criminal law activities which involve the infliction of physical harm, whether the activities occur in the course of sexual conduct or otherwise" (*The Independent* 20.2.97: 5).

As with other categories of 'perversion', legislation usually presumes non-consent and is therefore based on the presumption of violence, instead of consenting pleasure.

This observation obviously invites an investigation as to who is selectively labelled and criminalized and who is not. In 1995 a man stood trial for branding his wife's bottom with a hot knife blade and was found not guilty in the Court of Appeal. As the man had caused actual bodily harm to his consenting wife, he was initially found guilty of assault but the three appeal judges stated: "Sexual activity between husband and wife in the privacy of the matrimonial home is not, in our judgement, a matter of criminal investigation, let alone criminal prosecution" (*The Scotsman* March 96: 14). In the case of this 'heterosexual', married couple the judges showed ('patriarchal') empathy in their understanding of the behaviour of the defendant and the word 'victim' was not used. The fact of consent was given a big emphasis as the judge considered the woman's consent to be branded with the husband's initials on both sides of her bottom as 'showing her love' and accepted that she considered this as a 'desirable personal adornment' (ibid.). This system of 'proof' for consent and/or mutuality appears in this context to be based on patriarchal stereotypes of 'gender' and is also often found in cases of for example, rape or domestic violence wherein the victim is often presumed to have given, although hidden or unnoticed (e.g. revealing outfit as provoking), consent to the following acts of non-consensual violence.

In the context of the sensationalized revelations about Mr Mosley's commercial investment into commodified 'SM' in 2008, it is crucial to refer to the complexities involved in 'sexual' consent (see for example Cowling and Reynolds 2004), and one can notice an explicit lack of information about the crucial aspects of negotiating consent in the media coverage.

As part of his defence Mosley admitted his 'unfortunate interest' (Saner 2008: 5) in 'sadomasochism'. The problematic lack of the term 'consensual' in front of 'sadomasochism' lacks a qualification of what is really implied in the discussed activities whereby commercial contexts may make 'informed consent' on occasion rather problematic to negotiate in its full sense. Mosley's choice of words further seems to reflect the prevalence of negative stereotyping, however, clinical psychologist and sex therapist Stephenson Connolly stated within the same article: "If the rules are observed, it is a perfectly reasonable part of the very broad tapestry of normal human sexuality" (Saner 2008: 6). She further stated that most assumptions of her profession about consensual 'SM' practitioners were misguided after a study of 132 practitioners.

3.3   Modes of self-understanding in relation to and beyond the social constructions and 'scientific' categories of 'sexuality' and 'sadomasochism'

> Sexual behaviour is not, as is too often assumed, a superimposition of, on the one hand, desires which derive from natural instincts, and, on the other, of permissive or restrictive laws which tell us what we should or shouldn't do. Sexual behaviour is more than that. It is also the consciousness one has of what one is doing, what one makes of the experience, and the value one attaches to it.
>
> (Foucault in Lotringer 1996: 322)

The way in which people appreciate their sexual behaviour shapes the significance that is attached to it as "Sexuality's biological base is always experienced culturally, through a translation" (Ross, Ellen, Rapp and Rayna in Snitow et al. 1983: 51). The here explored 'Modes of self-understanding' serve as examples of how people, who practice consensual 'SM', diversely attach meanings to their practices and in several instances attach their identity to the constructed 'sadomasochistic sexuality'. Through these different individually expressed 'modes of self-understanding': "…the tension between history, scientific discourse and agency in shaping contemporary senses of self and social belonging" (Weeks and Holland 1996: 10) gets illustrated and the historical nature of 'sexual identities' thereby becomes apparent.

The establishment and the identification of 'perversions' is part of the 'deployment of sexuality' that works through "... knowledge-power an agent of transformation of human life" (Foucault 1990: 143). For Foucault therefore the claim of rights on the basis of the specificity of a category of 'sexuality' does not have the same politically liberating potential as the strategy of diverting from the discourses that are based on the 'apparatus of sexuality' would have. "the postmodern critique has exposed how modernity itself imposes constraints of a traditional kind-culturally imposed, not freely chosen-around the quasi-religious modern icon of science. Its cultural form is scientism, which sociologists of science argue is an *intrinsic element* of science as public knowledge. The culture of scientism has in effect imposed identity upon social actors by demanding their identification with particular social institutions and their ideologies, notably in constructions of risk, but also in definitions of sanity, proper sexual behaviour, and countless other 'rational' frames of modern social control" (Lash and Wynne in Beck 1994: 2/3).

The discourses of medicine, psychiatry, psychology and sexology (Chapter 2) conceive of the identity of an individual as located within her/his 'lived body' as a fixed, unified entity. The appeal to this same notion of identity, described as 'sexual orientation' and/or 'sexual inclination', was frequently used by the individuals I interviewed. In some cases the interviewees (re)-constructed their life-history on the basis of this notion of 'sexual identity'. This phenomenon is also very much present in Anthony Gidden's work on the 'Consequences of Modernity' (1990) which, in connection with 'Modernity and Self-Identity' (1991), explores modernity's distinctive form of reflexivity. Individually, this is often expressed by a reflexive shaping and re-shaping of personal biographical narratives.

3.3.1 Reconstructing 'sadomasochistic' life stories

Henry, one of my older interviewees, insisted to start the interview with a reconstruction: "If I first tell you, how I find myself in this sort of situation. Firstly, you know, when a youngster, a boy that's growing up, he has a nocturnal emission or a wet dream or whatever you want to call it. I can remember mine very clearly and what it was, my parents played quite a bit of 'Whist', you know the card-game 'Whist'. (...) And in my dream, as they were playing cards, this long carpet formed a tent, underneath them. And in my dream, I was under that tent, amongst a sea of legs. And suddenly, again in my dream, my head was gripped, you know, by my hair, by my aunt. And she forced my head there [her 'genitals'] and I was made to be there and just take it from there. And she was wearing nothing. Obviously, this is all a dream. And I suddenly found myself wet and sticky and its happened. And that to me, is the first sort of sign of submissiveness to ladies" (Interview-file H.: 1).

Henry thus quite clearly identifies his 'deviant' fantasies that do not revolve around the obligatory coitus, but still caused him to have 'sexual relief', to be the first 'signifiers' of his 'submissiveness' towards women. This reflects the powerful impact the 'psychiatrization of perversions' can have on individual conceptions and relations to 'self'.

In 'The History of Sexuality' (Vol. 1) Michel Foucault argued that the dominant culture's repression of marginal groups was responsible for creating the stereotypicality of elements that defined a deviant identity.

> *Andrea*:   Could you tell me about your experience with SM?
> *Diabolo*:   My experience with SM. How, how much do you want to know? I tell you the whole thing, a whole life-story as quick as I can. O.K. I was at a Spanner-meeting and they asked us, what our first experience of an 'SM-impulse' was. I said: 'When I was nine years old my favourite teacher, I stood outside her office and I thought I was going to be punished and got excited. I was a little bit frightened about it but more excited. In those times they still had caning so I thought I would get that but she just left me standing outside. Since then I did nothing, I was in the closet. (In D.: 1)

Apart from the fact that the notion of a 'SM'-impulse was an a priori in this situation, Diabolo tried to explain his interest and enjoyment of the 'bodily practices' of consensual 'SM' with recollections of 'deviant' fantasies. At a later interview Diabolo 'traced' his interests back to another situation. D.: "...I remember one aunt of mine used to watch wrestling on the television and that gave me an enormous erotic kind of impulse later on. I think that was a sort of very early, pre-puberscent sort of inclination towards a certain fascination" (In D.: 9).

Through a coincidence Diabolo felt forced to let go of his 'face' (Goffman 1967) of 'normality': "I just pretended that I was an ordinary heterosexual guy and I had no submissive inclinations or interest in SM. Until I had a girlfriend who was an acupuncturist and everything came out. Particularly when she got into electro-acupuncture to cure my arthritis. And it seemed to work as well, it did me a world of good but anyway there was no denying with her after that. And no denying to myself."

> *Andrea*:   So that was more or less the trigger that you thought: 'Well, now, now I do it.'?
> *D.*:   Yeah, then I knew that it was for real. That it wasn't just some sickness in my head. It transcended from fantasy into reality and then I'd taken a step and from then on it was just a matter of time, I think, until I found what I was looking for. (Interview-file D.: 3)

Through the perceived sensations of 'lived body' Diabolo felt able to reject the notion of 'pathology' and started to practice consensual 'SM'.

Asked about the meaning consensual 'SM' had for herself, Sue tried to remember the starting-point of her 'sexual inclinations' and thus applies the 'regulatory fictions' of power/knowledge (Foucault) onto herself: "I'm not really sure when my first inclinations towards S/M really started but I do know that I've always been sadomasochistic in a submissive rather than a dominant way ..., the first real sort of inclinations probably occurred about ehm two or three years ago" (In S. 2.: 1).

Berger and Luckmann (1966) argued that social identity is derived from a dialectical process between the individual and society. This dialectical phenomenon becomes apparent in some of the expressions of the inter- viewees. Pat, who defines herself as a lesbian 'bottom', stated: "..., well, even when I was a child I had a sort of strange attraction to things like, there was a program on TV called 'Branded', which was a TV-series about a man that was thrown out of the foreign legion and the beginning sequence was always him being, you know his buttons were ritually ripped of his jacket and then his sword got broken and he was sent off into the desert. I kind of identified with him, I felt like the outcast, the noble outcast. And I didn't quite understand that as a sexual feeling, I was only 8 years old or whatever. But ..."

Andrea: It was sort of identifying with someone being cast out?
Pat: Yes, and having this sort of and being, and being and, and, he was cast out but he was a shame and honorable at the same time, they, he was thrown out for something he didn't really do, you know that's the scenario for SM. I thought about that, since then I identified that as perhaps early, early, not roots but early signposts. (Interview-file 1: 1)

These examples show how deeply the traditional discourses of 'sexuality' are internalized by some interviewees. As they conceive their specific social- ization as *the* determination of their 'sexual identity', their view of 'self' remains more or less static. In this process separate and disparate events are 'melted' into a coherent life-history and the narrativization enables indi- viduals to construct a meaningful story of their lives.

Shiva: "My SM-practices are very light, but I started to discover that I had those interests when I was sixteen years old. I had a boyfriend then and we had a game of tennis and it annoyed me. And afterwards we went into the kitchen and he said: 'I am going to put you over my knee and spank you.' And he did and it gave me the most sexual 'high'" (Interview-file 2: 1). At a later point Shiva links 'those interests to experiences in her early child- hood: "When I was three I had a nurse-maid who used to spank me and I can remember it very distinctively, I wouldn't say it gave me a sexual high at three years old. I never forgot the experience and she used to come and try to humiliate me in public by parading me in the park in a nappy when I was three years old. And take me back to the house and put me over her knee, spank me and she told me that the fan that was going round and round would come down crashing on me and kill me if I was naughty" (Interview-file 2: 5).

Stereotypes about 'sexuality' and 'sadomasochism' are widespread in society and as families, schools and early friendships are generally not included in the private sphere of 'sexuality', most of my interviewees got labelled informally at a later point in their life through contacts within the Scene or they attached the label and/or modifications of it onto themselves after being influenced through discourses of 'sexuality' (e.g. books, magazines, contact ads).

3.3.2   The 'self-labellers'

> ... deviant behavior, or social roles based upon it, (.) become (.) a means of defense, attack or adaptation to the overt and covert problems created by the societal reaction to primary deviation.
>
> (Lemert 1967: 17).

Jane, who is in her thirties, believes that: "Probably I've always been a pervert" (Interview-file C.: 1).

In her view 'perversion' means to have a "... sexuality that isn't normal". She also connects it to a politically subversive attitude. For her thus to identify as a pervert is valuable: "I think it's a positive thing. I've always been politically subversive as well. So, it's an extension of that I suppose" (Interview-file C.: 1).

The use of the label 'pervert' in Jane's opinion: "makes people confront their own prejudices, especially when you use it as a term of endearment or with pride" (In C.: 3).

Jane explored variations of sexuality when she was aged 18–19: "I was exploring bondage and things like that without a label to it or things like that, you know, it was just great fun." As she cannot remember ever being labelled from the outside, she experienced her 'Coming out' different: "I wasn't doing it and hiding. It was like: 'Oh, now I've got a name for it" (Interview-file C.: 2).

One of my interviewees, Anthony, also uses the label 'pervert': "..., I call myself a black pervert and that's because I am outside the norm. So, basically I do believe that I have to justify myself. I have to be very clear about what I'm saying, about what I'm doing, if not then the system will then take you to task, saying: 'You're a pervert. Period'" (Interview-file A.: 4).

Lara identifies herself as a "... pussy-licking sadomite and a practicing pervert" (Interview-file L.: 10). She likes the self-construction of labels and is proud of hers. As consensual 'SM' within the 'new' Scene does not encourage fixed roles and identities but 'switching', as will be elaborated later in this chapter, re-inscriptions of identity are possible. After my fieldwork Lara once again created herself a new identity-label which reflects upon the fluidity of identities. This comes close to Foucault's rejection of the notion of 'sexual' identity and of an inner essence which would determine our 'sexuality'.

Pat, who was organizing the 'SM-dykes' in London identifies herself as an SM-dyke but mainly she emphasizes her role: "Well, I am primarily identified as a bottom" (Interview-file 1: 4).

These examples show how 'self-labelling' can become part of a discursive counter-practice, the resignification of terms that formerly served the human's scientific objectification within the psychiatrization of sexual expression can be transformed into a positive and powerful signifier of consensual 'SM'-identity. "... the word 'pervert' is switching from critical abuse to righteous, in-your-face affirmation" (Polhemus and Randall 1994: 5).

3.3.3 Freedom of the label

Some of the interviewees reject the label 'Sadomasochism'. These people do practice bodily practices which would be labelled consensual 'Sadomasochism' but, as they do not identify with this 'social censure', they do not limit their social contacts or their forms of 'sexual' expression to consensual 'SM'.

The process of 'deviancy amplification' (Wilkins 1964) that arises from 'secondary deviation', in which the label 'pervert' and/or 'Sadomasochist' gets incorporated within the self-image of the individual, did not take place. These examples are in distinct contrast to the 'self-labellers' modes of understanding as these interviewees do not perceive identity as static but they view personal identity as: "... constituted by the myriad of social relationships and practices in which the individual is engaged. Because these relationships are sometimes contradictory and often unstable, the identity that emerges is fragmented and dynamic" (Sawicki 1991: 41).

> *Bette*: I think part of the fact that I can enjoy lots of different things and lots of different types of people is because I wasn't brought up with those kind of (.). I mean the only problem with me is that because nothing is taboo it's very difficult for me to have sex with phantasies. You know because you are meant to have things of which you think they are terribly wrong. (Interview-file 4: 8)

Her view of herself is that of being different from other practitioners even though she enjoys the same 'plays': "I don't think I'm very typical as I say, for me, I'm perfectly happy not to have SM-relationships. I haven't spent my life doing it. It's just something I do sometimes" (ditto: 9).

Dean does not identify with the label either; he described himself as 'pansexual': "(.), I said I tried most things but it doesn't particularly appeal. I tend to go through phases, different things. Different things at different times. At the moment I'm not doing anything, at the moment so. Celibacy at the moment, so" (Interview-file a.: 1). The fluidity of human development and the changes that we are capable of, become apparent and expressed here. No specific label becomes attached and consensual 'SM' is understood as one way of enjoying intimate encounters rather than the basis of the identity.

George feels strongly about the lack of alternative terms, when he wants to avoid the use and implications of the label: "...I always want to say: I'm a sadist; but a sadist is a little queer because I don't want the kind of stuff...self serving excuses. I don't want to regard myself as a sadist...there is no better word at the moment" (Interview-file G.: 3).

Ryan, who practices what might be labelled as consensual 'SM' in various forms, with varying partners and who's also a contractual 'slave' of another interviewee, does not want to use the label 'Sadomasochism'. His distinction is a binary one: "..., you've heard the term 'vanilla-sex', yeah? I'm more interested in that sort of, not 'vanilla-sex', the other sort of sex. I don't want to label it, I don't want to call it 'deviance' or 'SM' even, but a different sort of sex. I've always been interested in that. Voyeurism, exhibitionism, yeah? Power games. I've not been interested so much in pain or torture" (Int R.: 1).

The lingering impact of the label 'Sadomasochism' as a signifier of 'pleasure in pain' and/or torture and its limitations becomes apparent here. Ryan wanted to avoid to be subjected to this limited view on his erotic explorations. He further wanted to avoid the application of the rigid role-split stereotyping that was a dominant feature of the traditional 'old SM scene' onto his practices and identity. Ryan: "..., I tell you why I do not use the label. I do use it, I do say to people 'SM' but because I'm versatile and I don't see myself as a 'slave' or a 'master' and for me it depends on the person, you know, as I've said. So that's why I just don't use the label" (Int. R.: 7).

Tom prefers to use the term 'body-art' as he finds it an all-embracing word for tattoos, piercings, fetishism and consensual 'SM': "That's what it is. It's all body-art" (Interview-file J.: 2).

3.4   Motivations for the engagement in consensual 'SM' 'bodily practices'

According to Blumer's interpretation, symbolic interactionism (1969) is based on three premises. Firstly that human beings act towards things on the basis of the meanings that these things have for them, secondly that these meanings are a product of social interaction in society and thirdly, that these meanings are modified through interpretative processes of each individual. The diversity of motivations for the engagement with the 'bodily practices' of consensual 'SM' reflect just this.

As 'Sadomasochism' is ascribed behaviour (Kuehl 1981), based on the comparison with the myth of 'natural sexuality', the attempt to draw back on physical or psychological deficiency-explanations would only be valid if this behaviour is not understandable to a sufficient degree (Weber). The empirical research on consensual 'SM' clearly revealed motivations that are understandable and sufficient. With regards to their 'cultural background', a modified version of Merton's anomy theory as developed by Hess (1993) seems enlightening to further understanding. Hess uses Merton's theory only to explain the motivation to 'deviate' but not 'deviant behaviour'. According to Merton (1968) social norms define legitimized and legal means to achieve certain cultural goals, whereby the discrepancy between the achievement of these goals and conforming means to realize these aims, results in the possibility to choose non-conforming means for the achievement of these cultural goals.

The most important aims mentioned by my interviewees thus are as follows

3.4.1 Consensual 'SM' as an alternative to 'normal genital sexuality'

For Ella the 'bodily practices' of consensual 'SM' were taken up as a possibility to enhance the sex life within her long-term marriage.

Ella: "... Well I've been married for about thirty-two years and really basically we started to getting into it as part of our sexual play. We started with tying each other up and doing little things and it developed from there. And then" (In E.: 1). This motivation could be understood as a choice to perform 'sex work' within the framework of marriage as elaborated by Duncombe and Marsden (in Weeks and Holland 1996) which appears to be a quite widespread social phenomenon in 'females' to comply to the cultural goal of 'sexual fulfilment' of 'their' men.

The effect Ella gets from consensual 'SM'-'play', she describes in great detail: "..., relaxed and sexy. I mean I have to say obviously it heightens up our sex life, there's no doubt about it. I mean because when you are doing something like that I mean it keeps you horny for days, basically, you know... you get into what you are doing, you get really sexually 'high' and it gets really sexually exciting. ... Yeah, I mean it's very much part of my life, it's part of both of our lives because it's important. Because sex is important to me. And I don't ever want to stop that. I mean it's an enjoyable activity if you like, if people say fishing is their hobby, O.K., sex is my hobby. But, yeah, you do, you feel really good. It's great" (In E.: 7).

For the next couple the choice of alternatives to genital 'sexuality' is the main motivation for their engagement with consensual 'SM' 'body practices'. Bess and Tom have a relatively new relationship, they also practice 'vanilla'-sex but enjoy novelty.

> Bess: There's nothing better than sweet, kind, loving ['vanilla sex']. There's nothing better than that but like everything, one diet gets boring. So the variety is really good. (In J.: 5)

For Ryan consensual 'SM'-'body practices' also serve as an alternative to penetrative 'sexuality' which he found to be mandatory within gay culture.

Ryan: "I suppose it started, my first sort of experiences 'SM'-wise, was seeing that film (...) and I was sort of, about 14, 15. ... And then watching it and actually being very turned on by the leather in it but also the power games. So I was sexually turned on. And then, another film that I saw was the ..."

> *Andrea*:   Ah, 'Querelle'?
> *Ryan*:   Again, I got it on video and I watched it and I was just ... And I suppose that sort of. ... And then I started experimenting with partners ... (Int R.: 1)

For Pat the 'bodily practices' of consensual 'SM' provide the possibility to have meaningful 'sexuality' within an environment of trust and safety: "... you can have all of that excitement in a place where you're feeling trust and where you're feeling safe, and where you're getting intense sensation and where you're communicating on a very intense level with the other person. And I think, I mean that's what people want from sex, isn't it? They want to communicate in an intense way with another person that they care about and that cares about them and that they trust. And that's what they want from sex, isn't it? I mean apart from casual sex but that's what people want from life. Meaningful sex-and that's what I get from S/M" (Interview-file 1: 8).

"The Scene is a place where 'perverse lingering' is being stripped of its negative connotations and celebrated as a constructive, positive alternative to the dead-end of 'instant gratification'" (Polhemus and Randall 1994: 185).

For Bette consensual 'SM' and 'ordinary sex' are similar in that both "... happen[s] to utilize sort of extreme physical sensations in order to bring pleasure, ..." (Interview-file 4: 1) but with very distinctive features. The meaning and existential importance of communication between the partners engaged appears to Bette a point of difference: "I think that SM-sex in a way is more conscious, more verbal and non-verbal communication between people throughout. I mean if somebody is being beaten, you ought to be looking at the person and trying to get it absolutely right. I mean that should be true in ordinary sex as well but I think it's more true of SM-sex than any other sex ... Men just go for their own pleasure. I think that part of the thing is the difference between intercourse and beating somebody, with intercourse, man having intercourse with a woman, there's a very direct sexual path, there's a very sexually fixed pleasure. And therefore he has a motive for just getting what he wants. But if what he does is not directly genital or sexual. I mean it may give immense satisfaction but the satisfaction it will give will be in the communication with the other person. The fact to get it right with the other person. The fact that it's turning the other person on. Unless this man is just violent. But assuming it's a proper SM-person. There isn't a direct path ..." (Interview-file 4: 5). Therefore Bette concludes that empathy is more crucial in consensual 'SM' than in 'ordinary sex' as consensual 'SM' depends directly on the communication between the partners as it otherwise would not work out. The dominant ideological and socially constructed 'sexuality' has been found to be unsatisfying as well as limiting, in Bette's opinion "...a lot of people miss out enormously on sex. Particularly men do, particularly heterosexual men do" (Interview-file 4: 7). After reading the 'Hite report on male sexuality' Bette was astonished:

"It's just so tragic in a way how limited, what they appear to enjoy is. And how little use, you know, they are just so genitally orientated. It's just so terribly, terribly sad. You just think, what they are missing out on. You haven't explored your mind or other parts of the body. Have you not been taught about being fucked yourself or what about your nipples. I mean all you do is with your penises. It's so sad. I mean putting your penis in isn't much communication. And I mean sex doesn't have to be like that. And being a man doesn't have to be like that" (Interview-file 4: 7).

This comment has clear parallels to Michel Foucault's criticism of the genital fixation of the concept of 'sexuality' and its effects of domination which for example often led (leads) to 'dominating body usages' on the side of human beings that had to prove (or maintain) their socially constructed patriarchal form of 'masculinity' and thus prevented 'communicative body usages'.

3.4.2 Consensual 'SM' 'bodily practices' as 'safer sex'

As several interviewees mentioned the possibility that interest in consensual 'SM' at that time in the late nineties could be related to AIDS, I asked for Bette's opinion and she replied: "Oh, absolutely. Because it's so, I mean we don't know of any case at all, where it's been caught in that way" (Interview-file 4: 11).

Bette engages in consensual 'SM' as well as 'ordinary sex' and notices that the feelings afterwards can be quite different, more obligating after 'ordinary sex' and she added: "...it's also a slight danger that you might catch something or get pregnant or something like that if you do something like that. There were two other equivalent people who I've done the opposite, I've done not SM but been to bed with. Sort of younger men, I mean that was fun but on the other hand. I mean it didn't change our relationship, I mean in some way it did change, but it was: 'What if I get pregnant? What if I get HIV?' I mean we did use condoms, it was O.K. But these were two other gay men. But it's not as carefree. The thing about SM, as long as it's properly regulated, you don't injure somebody, it's completely harmless. You cannot catch anything, you can't get pregnant, nothing can happen. So it's a very easy thing to do" (Interview-file 4: 11).

Jane confirmed that responsibility and 'safe sex' are important issues in the Scene, more so than in mainstream society: "..., it's a lot better, I mean, I much rather go to a party that is an S/M-party than a 'normal' party because, you know, that if somebody harasses you that's considered unacceptable and it's going to be dealt with. People are much more responsible usually about sex and there's a lot more emphasis on safe sex" (Interview-file C.: 7). Apart from individual self-responsibility which appears to be increased within the Scene, Jane mentioned that there is always the pressure of 'significant others': "Peer pressure to behave. So people who may be not necessarily sensible and respectful will be pressured into behaving like that" (Interview-file C.: 7).

The 'sexual' politics of AIDS employed modes of empowering knowledge in combination with the traditional modes of authorization and legitimization-power in order to administrate the public and private 'body' and its pleasures. In other words all the modalities of 'biopower' (Foucault) were applied in the fight for medical 'truth' and social regulation. "... repression is always a part of a much more complex strategy regarding sexuality. Things are not merely repressed. There is about sexuality a lot of defective regulations in which the negative effects of inhibition are counterbalanced by the positive effects of stimulation" (Foucault in Kritzman 1990: 9). The public responses to the AIDS crisis pointed to a need to conceptualize 'sexuality', after the manner of Foucault, as "an especially concentrated point of traversal [*point de passage*] for relations of power" (Halperin 1995: 27).

The UK's 'better late than never', 'safe-sex' campaigns established educational undertakings to prevent the further contamination of people with the HIV-virus and was very much focused on the use of alternative methods of sexual interaction in favour of penetrative sex to avoid any direct contacts with body-fluids, especially blood. Therefore diverse suggestions were presented to the scared public on how to have 'great sex without being at risk' and the involvement of fantasy and toys was promoted.

"It is the plague time. It is possible to eroticize latex. It's the only responsible thing to do. Exchanging fluids is suicide" (Swartz in Califia and Sweeney 1996: 177).

One effect of preventing 'unsafe sex' through educational sex discourses on a public level, I consider to be the rising interest in consensual 'SM' and 'Fetishism'. The intensification of both anxiety and of newly discovered pleasures was in my opinion the result of the societal reaction to AIDS. Within the 'new' Scene of consensual 'SM' safely performed (through use of rubber gloves and sterile equipment) 'play-piercings' and 'blood-sports' are innovative 'bodily practices' of consensual 'SM' that started to be practiced by gay and lesbian practitioners but quickly were taken up by the hetero/bi-Scene. These newly developed 'bodily practices' might be interpreted as a 'counterpractice' to the prescriptive avoidance of blood that was (is) particularly enforced within 'safe sex'-discourses.

3.4.3   The 'bodily practices' of consensual 'SM' as exploration of dimensions of 'lived body'

For Jane consensual 'SM' allows her to experience her 'lived body's' sensuality as well as emotions. "I enjoy everything that is sensually exciting and new ..., exploring feelings, emotional feelings" (Interview-file C.: 1).

Apart from being a strategy for drawing a borderline between reality and fantasy, consensual 'SM' serves Anthony as a space for exploration of 'bodily' possibilities and choice: "But we have to also separate fantasy from reality, I think that's what SM does for me as an individual. And also it is, I want to explore lots and lots of things, whether its SM, being tied up, watersports or whether its scatting-it provides this space. Where I can say this is for me or this is not for me, ..." (Interview-file 3: 2).

Instead of categories, individual explorations and 'lived experience' are important to Anthony and most other practitioners of consensual 'SM' I met.

For some practitioners consensual 'SM' provides a space which is free from the ordinary conventions of keeping a 'face' (Goffman 1967) and taboos and thus allows for a more 'authentic' (as founded on experience) relation to 'self' and others.

Mike: The major thing I get from it, is a tremendous sense of release and freedom. Because it's something that you can get into a very sort of primitive relationship with someone. It's very physical and it deals with very sort of dark elements. And it's a place, where you let it all go.

Andrea: You don't have to pretend anything?

Mike: No, you don't have to pretend. So, no one is gonna judge you. People are not gonna say: 'You are weird', when you're in a 'scene' with someone. (Interview-file S.: 3)

Some informants regarded consensual 'SM' as a possibility to transgress set limits of 'political correctness' through these 'bodily practices'.

Anthony: I did work around cross-dressing and drag. It was at a time I found cross-dressing and drag interesting for me. And then the work comes through that as well. SM came into my work and I found it interesting. I was also meeting other black men within various spaces who were into it. I'm actually curious by nature anyway. And I thought: 'What is this shit about?' Basically. And also about three years ago there was a lesbian and gay exhibition in the Brixton Art-gallery and on the invite it said that non-SM-related work would be accepted. And I felt concerned, here you have a platform for gay men and they say what is accepted and what is not. And I think that was another reason to say: 'Well, push those boundaries a bit further as well. I do believe SM and black people creates problematics for lots of black people. But those people miss an argument. First of all: there is consent, whereas slavery wasn't with consent. (Interview-file 3: 3)

3.4.4   The 'bodily practices' of consensual 'SM' as a possibility to transgress gay and lesbian stereotypes of 'sexuality'

> What I think is interesting now in relation to lesbian S/M is that they can get rid of certain stereotypes of femininity that have been used in the lesbian movement; a strategy that the movement has erected from the past. This strategy has been based on their oppression. But now, maybe, these tools, these weapons are obsolete. We can see that lesbian S/M tried to get rid of all those old stereotypes of femininity, of anti male attitude and so on.
>
> (Foucault in Lotringer 1996: 387)

Through the experiences I gained within the field of lesbian as well as gay consensual 'SM' I suggest that Foucault's comments are also valid for gay practitioners of these 'bodily practices' as Ryan's example shows.

During an interview with Ryan, who does not approve of labels because he finds them limiting, he brought up the topic of gay stereotyping and the 'liberating effect' of consensual 'SM':

> *Ryan*:   What I found, Andrea, on the Scene, when I first started, when we were young on the gay Scene is that, I've never been into penetrative sex, being penetrated, not because of being raped or anything like that, I've just never been inclined. And I find it painful, you know, when people try to, I've never found any pleasure in that. What I find, when I was on the Scene, when I was young, older men just wanted to do that to you. And this was just pre-AIDS, yeah? Late seventies, early eighties? So in a way 'S/M'-sex has actually helped me get round it. Because I remember, when I was very young, before I went to College in 82, you know, my first sexual experiences, when I was about fourteen to eighteen that I was getting a bit depressed, thinking: 'Oh, I'm not really gay because I don't get fucked.' You know, or: 'I don't want to fuck.' And I suppose 'SM'-sex was like a trigger of wakening me, to have a sexual possibility, which I found much more interesting.

The impact of stereotypes of 'sexual' behaviour even within the gay and lesbian Scene become obvious here.

> *Andrea*:   So it does not only overcome hetero-categories of sexuality but also gay categories of sexuality?
> *Ryan*:   Yeah, gay, gay, what's the word now? Gay stereotyping, you know, that we're all into anal sex. That's why a lot of heterosexual men are wary of gay men, 'cause they feel that all they want to do is just 'bugger' them. And that's not, that's not, you know, for me, it's

never been...I mean I have been, I have had anal sex but very few, very few occasions. (Interview-file R.: 6)

3.4.5 Consensual 'SM' as a possibility to experience the transformative potentials of 'lived body'

Bette enjoys many variations of sex, an important motivation for her to engage in consensual 'SM' is the relaxation she obtains from doing it, which she illustrated with an example: "I mean I find that kind of sex [consensual SM] very relaxing. I've got a serious eye-condition and I had some laser-treatment in the hospital. Physically it's not that painful but very upsetting. I was very uptight. It's quite a nasty thing to have done. This woman X. came around and..., she ended up beating me. And it was mainly unbelievably relaxing."

Andrea: It can release you from tension?

Bette: Yeah, absolutely. I just think physically if it's done well, you know it's very similar to being caressed. I mean I was covered in bruises, it was quite a, I mean it wasn't an enormously heavy but it was fairly heavy, it wasn't a light 'scene'. Also, if you get injuries in that way they don't hurt which I think is very interesting... It has certainly a big spiritual element to it. (Interview-file 4: 6)

Apart from experiencing sensations of release and freedom Henry, Pat, John as well as Mike enjoy to test and transgress their own limits and to transform the sensations that they expose themselves to.

"...you can just get on and do things that feel good and that are a lot of fun and that push your limits. To see, you know, what you can actually take. And for me it's a case of what I can take and whether I can convert that sensation into something enjoyable. So, there is a lot of, sort of personal combat and willpower involved, I suppose" (Interview-file S: 3).

The capacity of 'lived body' to overcome traumatic experiences of the past through consensual 'SM' is reflected also in this example: "When I was a baby, my dad or some other man shoved his penis in my tender mouth. My lover and I created a scene in which she became the perpetrator and I was 'little me'. She was harsh. I sucked her cock until I gagged; now I beg for her to spread me open and plunge into my throat. She gave me back my mouth. ... Our scenes are where we play and work with the old wounds. We know who we are by how we play, and my wife and I play hard" (Strong in Califia and Sweeney 1996: 196/197).

The motivations to engage in consensual 'SM' cited above illustrate that apart from being rooted in the contemporary cultural goal of the primacy of 'fulfilling sexual experiences' which is achieved by means of consensual 'SM', a lot of practitioners are interested in the exploration of the dimensions and potential limits of their 'lived bodies' by means of these 'bodily practices'. In that way they experience and potentially change their 'life-world' which is outlined in 'The Visible and the Invisible' by Merleau-Ponty: "The thickness of the body, far from rivaling that of the world, is on the contrary the sole means I have to go unto the heart of things, by making myself a world and by making them flesh" (Merleau-Ponty 1968: 135).

These narratives that allow a reading of consensual 'SM' as an experience of healing, clearly contradict not only scientific stereotypes of 'Sadomasochism' but further challenge the courts' conventional understanding of consensual 'SM' that appears to associate it (with the exception of the exertion of these 'bodily practices' within heterosexual relationships) intimately with the production of 'harm'. Even if physical marks or wounds are resulting the therapeutic effects can be potentially much more important to the practitioners.

3.5   Consensual 'SM' in practice

> It was a time of direct gestures, shameless discourse, and open transgression, when anatomies were shown and intermingled at will, ... it was a period when bodies 'made a display of themselves'.
>
> (Foucault 1990: 3)

This opening sequence of Foucault's 'History of Sexuality' (1990 Vol. 1), in which he illustrates a view of the relationship towards 'sexual' practices at the beginning of the seventeenth century, came immediately to my mind when I encountered the Scene of consensual 'SM' in London. In the so-called, 'Fetish Scene' and 'SM'- Scene, which do overlap, the exposure of bodies or body parts and their manipulation are also the most striking features of visual encounters. The display of interacting bodies that indulge in erotic experiments appeared like a flight from the everyday wholesale-product 'sex'.

As genital sexuality loses its socially reinforced importance and becomes a more or less rare by-product of the 'bodily practices' within this Scene, I was initially confronted with my own internalized and limited preconceptions about 'sadomasochistic sexuality'.

This also motivated me, as part of the reflexivity of research, to extensively deal with the deconstruction of the main social constructions that made the emergence and continue to maintain the social construction of 'Sadomasochism' possible (Chapter 2). It further convinced me to term consensual 'SM', 'bodily practices' instead of reducing its realities to a 'sexual' realm. This understanding of consensual 'SM' further allowed me to use Frank's (in Featherstone et al. 1991) concept of 'body usage' which he proposes to be less deterministic than the analytical approaches of Goffman. Frank's 'structuration theory of the body and society' is less nihilistic as it "... apprehend[s] the body as both medium and outcome of social 'body techniques' ['bodily practices'], and society as both medium and outcome of the sum of these techniques" (Frank in Featherstone 1991: 48).

In this view, both 'bodily practices' as well as social reproduction do not proceed linear but recursively which avoids the pitfalls of modern dichotomies that often hinder holistic understandings of 'lived bodies'.

The second striking feature within the Scene is the specific way in which 'lived bodies' empathetically interact as well as the tension that is imminent to these interactions and the 'pain' that is often involved.

The transformation of my own reactions to 'pain' in other people was one of the most challenging parts of my research: "This awareness of extreme loneliness is a peculiarity of the compassion we feel for bodily pain; it also sets this experience apart from any other experience, from compassion for the anguished, sorrowful, aggrieved, alien or crippled. In an extreme way, the sensation of bodily pain lacks the distance between cause and experience found in other forms of suffering" (Illich 1977: 148).

This represents the main difficulty I encountered on an intra-psychological level, before I had completely relativised my preconceptions about pain and rationalized its varying dimensions (Chapter 2), my observation of some of the corporal punishment-'scenes' were characterized first by an artificial blockade against compassion and then, after the internalization of the existence of various dimensions of 'pain', observation became easier.

In his work on eroticism, Bataille (in Richardson 1994) explains his perspective of the origin of the theory of taboo and transgression with reference to the work of Mauss (1979) which his student Roger Caillois (1950) set forth. In 'L'homme et le Sacre' ethnography is described as being concerned with peoples for whom time is divided into *profane time* and *sacred time*. *Profane time* here defines ordinary time in which work and the respect for the taboos is characteristic. *Sacred time* is defined as the time of celebrations "... that is in essence the time of transgressing the taboos. ... As far as eroticism goes, celebrations are often a time of sexual license" (Bataille in Richardson 1994: 257).

The London Scene as a whole, comprising a diversity of 'Fetish', 'SM'/'Fetish'-clubs as well as highly specialized 'underwear-clubs' etc. and exclusively consensual 'SM'-clubs thus could be understood as providing spaces for the celebration of 'sacred time'. During my research I further had the opportunity to visit private 'dungeons' as many practitioners of consensual 'SM' 'body practice' meet in privacy for 'SM'-parties, too.

3.5.1 Consensual 'SM'-'bodily practices' and the 'body' – the 'strategical use of the body'

In 'Social Research', Tim May (1993/2001) stated that it is neither possible nor desirable to try and note or remember all aspects of the setting, the people and the interactions during the 'participant observation'-process and the flow of data conducted by my research supports his statement. Therefore I centred my observations on the 'bodily practices' that took place during the club-events which I analysed within Frank's (in Featherstone et al. 1991) concept of 'body usage'.

Frank proposed four dimensions of 'embodied consciousness'. These are conceptualized as: control (relating to the predictability of the body's performances), desire (constitution of body itself in terms of desire, e.g. as lacking or producing), other-relatedness (body as monadic and closed or dyadic and open) and self-relatedness (association or dissociation of body consciousness with its corporeality) which generates 'styles of body usage' which ought to be understood as continua and not absolutes. These 'styles of body usage' thus denote ideal-typical styles of body-experience and body-deployment. The empirical world of consensual 'SM' 'body practices' in London gave the impression that in contrast to mainstream society which is dominated by 'mirroring body usages', generated by the endlessly reinforced desire to consume, the Scene fosters 'communicative body usages' generated by shared narratives, communal rituals and by the constant requirements for communication and recognition within this setting.

Apart from the most widely known and applied 'body practices' of consensual 'SM' which are bondage and flagellation, the ritualized interactions that were enacted and experienced during 'scenes', whether they were staged privately and/or semi-public, were: gagging, electroshocking, blindfolding, crucifying, suspending, piercing, clamping, suffocating, fisting (an innovative 'bodily practice' that developed in the gay Scene but is now very widespread and commodified), burning and, mostly in the bathrooms and/or toilets though, watersports (pissing on) and scatting.

These 'bodily practices' are always embedded within degrading 'scene'-scripts that are overtly based on rigid role patterns according to the socially constructed power positions they imitate. On a most of the time covert level, these 'scenes' are dependent and based on an intense and empathetic communication between the practitioners of this 'bodily practice'.

In deep contrast to this is the outward appearance as through the representations of unequal power through 'dresscodes' and through the clearly structured and hierarchical interaction patterns, the club-guests of diverse 'genders', do appear like extremities of power-differences. In contrast to 'bottom'/'top'-couples, the 'sub'/'dom'-couples interaction and 'play' depends to a much higher degree on elaborated role-play and power-difference representations. For example: while a female 'sub' (a 'transvestite') was kneeling at his/her mistresses' feet and holding her glass, the 'dom' was deeply involved in a conversation until she ordered her 'sub' to get up and return with more drinks.

In the Scene the supply of 'bottoms', 'subs' and 'slaves' seems to be endless, whereas 'tops', 'Doms' and 'Masters' are in short supply in the hetero/bi, as well as the lesbian/gay Scene. The gap is often closed by fee-charging professionals which usually provide most of their services to men. A fact that does not match feminist orthodoxy as Smart noted: "But that men do desire to be dominated, no matter how safely, does pose a conundrum for conventional ideas that male power leads to the simple and straightforward sexual domination of women" (Smart 1995: 115).

'Play' is different for 'bottoms' and 'tops', here the acting out of physical acts of 'punishment' and/or 'torture' are the main attraction for the participants. This kind of interaction can be illustrated by a 'scene' 'played' by Jane and one of her 'play'-partners, Mike, as these two have a relationship of 'top' and 'bottom'. Even though their 'dresscode' did not differ much from 'sub'/'dom'-outfits their interaction was not based on pretended power-difference from the start. When Mike felt interested to try out a new piece of equipment, he asked Jane if she would mind to 'top' him and only after Mike had assisted Jane in chaining him, their interaction patterns changed. Jane then started to slap Mike's bottom, gradually getting stronger in impact, and, after a while, she introduced a whip into the 'scene'. She then whipped Mike's back and bottom with a dog lead. Within Frank's (in Featherstone 1991) framework of 'body usage' continua, Jane applied a 'dominating' style of 'body usage' which on the one hand actively deconstructs an ideology of the 'female body' as passive, while on the other hand enforcing on the 'male body' an external control that it cannot exercise over himself.

Mike just hung upside down with his feet chained to a piece of solid wood that hung from the ceiling, while the intensifying impact of his 'top's' whiplash made him groan. As Jane and Mike knew each other very well and had negotiated that she will 'top' him, when they both feel like it, be it in 'S/M'-clubs or at private locations, they did not find it important to negotiate before each single 'scene'. Mike, who on these occasions has the function and role of the 'bottom', will 'take as much as he can' and potentially can stop the 'scene' by means of a 'safe-word' at any point in time. Mike's style of 'body usage' can be termed 'disciplined' as he applied a regime of self-regimentation which is aimed at the control of his 'bodily reactions'.

The most fundamental rule of consensual 'SM'-conduct is that everything is usually negotiated beforehand and consented upon which relates to a shared communicative style of 'body usage'. This might suggest that the setting up of an artificial relationship of power-inequality makes no sense but in order for the disciplined 'body usage' to be sustained, Frank stated that a sense of lack has to remain conscious and thus: "One device for sustaining the consciousness of lack is for the disciplined body to place itself in some hierarchy (military, monastic, other), in which it is perpetually, and itself justifiably, subordinated" (Frank in Featherstone et al. 1991: 55).

The 'scene' stopped, when both Jane as well as Mike had explored the 'potential' of this ceiling-equipment. Through their eye contact the 'scene' mutually finished and Jane helped Mike to 'come down'. This makes the difference of the 'bodily practices' of consensual 'SM' in contrast to, for example, drill within the military very clear. Whereas in the conventional settings of 'body usages' of domination and discipline, 'bodies' are usually monadic, the 'bodily practices' of consensual 'SM' rather function similar to communal rituals as they are fundamentally based on a dyadic form of other-relatedness.

'Coming down' means a physical as well as a mental 'come down'-process. Physically Mike's body, now burning and bruised, had to be let down slowly and his ankles had to be freed of his chains. Mike, who came to me after this 'scene', smiled intensely, while he told me that he would feel similar to being under the influence of a psychedelic trip through the amount of endomorphins released in his physical system.

Within the context of consensual 'SM' the conventional meanings of pain and pleasure as well as the traditional understandings of power relationships undergo thus important changes. No interaction or 'scene' is disturbed by any non-participant, unless the rules of consensual 'SM'-conduct are broken.

Another 'scene' involved the use of an Andrea's cross which was installed in such a way that it could be turned around. After negotiating with his 'slave' the details of the 'scene', the male 'top' tied his partner, who 'played' in 'bottom-space', to the cross and then turned the cross, with her still tied to it, upside down.

The 'top' then stimulated the 'bottom's' genitals for a while, before inserting a red candle into her vagina which he lit. While continuously holding eye contact with his 'slave', he then twisted and pulled her nipples, after which he stimulated her genital lips and whipped them. The 'top' then continued by turning the cross back to its original position which made the 'bottom's blood rush through her body. As she wasn't pierced (which is quite a common feature within the Scene) her master attached clamps to her genital lips and left his whip to hang there-off. The 'scene' ended when the 'bottom' signalled that she 'had enough'. Once again the medium of force that the 'dominating body usage' of the 'top' implies is always interdependent with the regimentation of the 'disciplined body usage' of the 'bottom'. As such both 'play'-partners continuously engage in 'communicative body usage' which crucially implies the recognition of the other.

According to Frank (in Featherstone et al. 1991), the essential quality of the ideal type of 'communicative body usage' is that it makes authentic interaction with the outside world possible and thus represents a process of invention. As with the 'scene' below most interactions between 'top' and 'bottom' aim at the introduction of new sensations which are consented upon. A lesbian 'mistress/slave'-couple made use of an installation that allowed people to be hung by their feet. The 'master', a woman dressed entirely in black latex outfit with high boots, negotiated with her 'slave' that she would be hung upside down and beaten, and then started slapping her 'slave's' exposed bottom. While she was then gently stroking her legs and bottom, she talked quietly to her, telling her plans and awaiting consent. The 'scene' developed into a whipping and genital-beating 'scene', after which the 'slave' then was carefully put down and pride showed on her and her 'mistress's' face.

Another 'scene', which involved three women, offers an illustration of the openness and communication within a 'scene' that involves more than two participants. A female 'master' and her 'slave' asked another woman if she wanted to 'play'. The 'scene' that developed between them consisted of the 'master' asking her 'slave' to lick the other woman's genitalia and then a closer genital act with a crop followed. The two 'slaves' were guided by the movements and orders of the female 'master' who made them perform an act that resembled intercourse while she moved the crop into the vagina of one of her 'slaves'.

After the 'scene', the female 'master' took her 'slave' over her shoulder and 'allowed' her to be licked by the other 'slave'-woman, after which she took a cheek of her slave in one of her hands and then slapped it with a proud smile. The 'slave' then kneeled down in front of her 'master', who then kissed the other 'slave' and arranged meeting-possibilities for further 'play' with this slave.

In some Scene-clubs there exists the possibility to obtain piercings as opposed to the engagement in 'play-piercings' during consensual 'SM'-'scenes'. One of the professional piercers who operate within these clubs also served one of my interviewees (Tom) as a 'Master'. As Tom wanted me to observe the ritual that had developed between him and 'Master V', they both started their 'scene' which was negotiated beforehand, in front of me.

First 'Master V' pulled out piercing needles that were about 30 cm long. Tom stood in front of me and looked into my eyes, knowing about my worries but wanting me to see and appreciate what he would go through and enjoy. When the needles got inserted [one through under his chin, two through his cheeks and another two through the skin of the scull on both sides up above his ears], I could see the pain in Tom's eyes and I got an idea of what he means, when he refers to the 'channelling' of pain. After the piercing throughout which 'Master V' kept eye contact with Tom, Tom proudly moved about the entire club to show the needles sticking out of his head, while 'Master V' informed me that Tom never likes to get the piercing-needles removed. Throughout this 'scene' the close and empathetical connection between 'Master' and 'slave' was impressive as well as the quasi-religious atmosphere that was present while the piercing took place. The 'communicative body usage' once again dominated the 'scene' of this 'Master' and his 'slave' which superficially appeared to be a relationship of dominance and submission.

The 'bodily practices' that developed between 'Master V' and 'slave' Tom represent an intense bonding-ritual, apart from providing Tom with the possibility to experience 'transcendental states' (Chapter 6).

The 'Fire'-club provided its guests with an interesting performance one night. This performance showed once again how the 'bodily practices' of consensual 'SM' can be means for intense 'bonding-rituals'.

During this 'scene' which was performed for the audience of 'serious play-ers', two gay men, two dykes and one femme pierced each other. These 'body practices' were undertaken very health consciously with the use of rubber gloves as well as sterile needles. The locations of these 'play-piercings' were on many places on their chest (two lines downwards each side) as well as on their stomachs. The insertion places were carefully felt and then selected and the five people did not appear to have much pain. After this all the needles were carefully attached to strings, which were used like connections from one 'lived body' to the next and a circle was built. Then music started and the 'players' moved around, first slowly, then faster. They also stretched their skins a lot by leaning backwards in this circle and by moving the strings, so that the tensions could be felt equally by all members of the circle. This 'scene' created a very ecstatic and 'bonding' atmosphere within the whole club. The symbolical meaning of the voluntary creation of 'bodily' holes could be interpreted as an opening up of 'lived bodies' to the world and to each other.

These few examples of the 'bodily practices' of consensual 'SM' already indicate that in contrast to the widespread and reinforced stereotypes about consensual 'Sadomasochism', these 'bodily practices' have more to do with the purposeful use of the 'body' by the conscious decisions and actions of human agents than with the uncontrolled enactment of sexual drives of a 'sadomasochistic libido'. This misconception was part of the basis on which the British courts' judgements were formed.

In contrast to most feminist accounts of consensual 'SM' that either condemn these 'bodily practices' (as shown in Chapter 2) as manifestations of patriarchal ideology, or which suggest that only the lesbian or gay variation of these 'bodily practices' represent practices that uniquely split 'gender' from 'sexuality', the experiences of the empirical world of London's Scene gave a different impression. In all the venues that I conducted my observations in, 'gender' did not determine the role-positions taken, thus the splitting of 'gender' from 'sexuality' is not a phenomenon exclusive to lesbians and/or gays. The turn away from genital fixation was also a feature encountered across the Scene and is not reducible to consensual 'SM'-play between women. Transgressive play with phallic signification and representations of other conventional power relationships is not an exclusively lesbian domain within consensual 'SM' which is also reflected in what is to follow.

3.5.2   A distinct feature of the Scene of
consensual 'SM': Societal categories count less

Golding once described a lesbian Scene-club as "...a peculiar place of exile;..." and as a "...distinct arena whose parameters can blur the edges,..." (in Kroker and Kroker 1993: 147/148). This special feature is created by the distinct code of conduct within the Scene of consensual 'SM' and through the limitlessness of these 'bodily practices' that are based on fantasy. The socially constructed differences between individuals do not count in this environment and individual pleasures and limits count for everything.

Diabolo: "..., I'm 48 years old and the SM-scene is more accepting of age-diversity as well as sexual diversity because they are not normal. And they don't have a normal age, there isn't a normal age to be an SMer for example. Whereas there is almost a normal age to be on a disco-dancefloor or in a backroom of some pub somewhere, you got to be twenty or something or at least pretend that you are. And I'm beyond all that. Yes, so there isn't age-ism, there isn't sexism, as there is amongst the so supposed 'normale'. And it's all part of people breaking free from stereotypical thinking about themselves and others" (Interview-file D: 3).

Apart from ageism, the cultural pressure of 'the body beautiful' (Chapter 2) is transgressed within most of the Scene-clubs, people of all ages, sizes and shapes are to be found there. Women and men do not hesitate to dress in skin-tight leather and rubber-outfits or to turn up in nude or half-nude states.

During my 'participant observations' in London's Scene another remarkable difference towards conventional 'club-culture' became obvious which is the presence and acceptance of 'disabled' people as active participants in 'play'. Comparing this feature of the Scene with the usual social reactions towards disabled 'bodies' is quite striking, as for example Kirsten Hearn's (1988) 'A Woman's Right to Cruise' illustrates for the lesbian movement and club-culture. As a lesbian disabled woman she accuses most of the lesbian movement of 'ableism' and notes about herself and other disabled lesbians:

> ..., our experience demonstrates that the reaction of severely able-bodied dykes when being cruised by one of us is likely to be embarrassment and terror. We are generally not taken seriously in these situations, since we are not supposed to have any sexual feelings whatsoever, let alone the ability to carry them out... Different women with different disabilities have different needs and abilities before, during and after sex. Some of us can only lie in certain positions or may have to use different parts of our bodies. (Hearn in Mc Ewen and O'Sullivan 1988: 50/51)

After this introduction to the London Scene that I encountered and that certainly will have been subjected to changes through the intense commodi-fication of 'sex' per ser in contemporary times, I do not want to attempt to give an impression of a 'perfect world' in the Scene. Like Polhemus and Randall, who researched within it, I too noticed: "As in any cross-section of society there are givers and takers, the used and their abusers, those who find themselves and the unfortunate few who get hopelessly lost" (Polhemus and Randall 1994: 202). However, and to sum up the so far presented, I would like to suggest that the 'bodily practices', their informal framework and reinforcement of rules on the Scene of consensual 'SM' as observed in London does provide a space for 'counterpractices'. It disconnects the fundamental philosophical pattern of the Western world which tied 'sexuality' to 'subjectivity' and 'truth' which in effect permanently shaped and limited human beings' relationships to themselves and each other. In the Scene and particularly in 'play' these patterns lose their limiting and often socially determining impact. These 'bodily practices' allow 'lived bodies' to experiment within the spaces of subject-and object position that they are usually assigned to by the apparatuses of domination.

3.5.3   Applied consensual 'SM'-scene-specific codes and meanings; and the learning process of these 'bodily practices'

> This subculture cuts across most, if not all, cultural and subcultural boundaries, ... Sexual sadomasochists are homosexual, heterosexual, or bisexual; they come from a variety of social, economic, racial, ethnic, geographic, and religious backgrounds; and they seek out others who share their predilections for their mutual satisfaction. Both to find other practitioners of sadomasochistic sex and to communicate their specific sexual desires to potential partners, ...
>
> (Murray and Murrell 1989: 4)

While I found this statement about the subculture of consensual 'SM' to be valid from my fieldwork-observations, it is illuminating to examine how these diverse practitioners gained access to the 'SM'-Scene and what they searched for within it.

As a lot of 'SM'-practitioners gained access to the Scene and/or individuals within it, through the internet, it appears to serve a big proportion of people as an access-tool.

When Mike described his entry into the Scene, it became apparent that access is nowadays not a big problem as long as an individual has access to a computer: "The simple answer is the internet because I've been reading and posting in the 'Bondage-newsgroup' and through that I saw the advert about the munches that were held here and went along to one. And that is how I met all the wonderful people, who have introduced me to the Scene over here. I also have been sort of given an 'in', to get in and I made a few more friends there, then I'm getting invited to a lot more things. So, I think since, let me think, since the end of July I've been to something every single weekend" (Interview-file S.: 5).

The obvious inclusive potential function of internet access is evident here; however, in an interview Patrick Califia offered a more differentiated perspective:

> The Internet makes it possible for just about anybody who's a member of any sort of minority to hook up with others who share that frame of reference. It's an amazing source of information and support for disabled people, political weirdoes of all stripes, spiritual splinter groups, and sexual minorities. If you have access to the technology (which is a political issue in and of itself), you can access an entire realm of fantasy. (...) It's

now possible to get printed information and live advice about safe S/M play that was completely unavailable just ten or fifteen years ago. Unfortunately, there's also some misinformation and some bad advice out there as well, and I worry that novices may have little or no way to screen what's accurate from what may be dangerous or insufficient information. People have a tendency to turn their common sense off when it comes to sexplay, and one of my primary concerns about S/M has always been to promote a lot of public education so we can all play hard without unwanted consequences. http://www.technodyke.com/features/patcalifa3.asp [accessed 15.10.08]

Another access-tool, which is not so high-tech, is the contactad section of specialized magazines as well as, in the case of Tom and Bess, an ordinary newspaper. Bess: "He advertised in the local paper and I was looking for a circle of friends. And he advertised body-art. He was a 'Body-art nut'. I thought: 'That sounds interesting.' So, I rang him up and that's how we got together" (Interview-file J.: 2).

Apart from direct contacts, no matter which mode of access is chosen, a coded language for the diverse activities as well as the intensity of 'play' is employed. According to Murray and Murrell (1989) most of the language-repertoire of consensual 'SM'-'body practice' (75 per cent) appears to have its origin in the twentieth century and has directly evolved for the specific needs of this 'subculture'. "..., members of the sadomasochistic community have developed a highly diversified language within the language of the main culture" (Murray and Murrell 1989: 4).

In order to obtain different meanings, language is crucially important, especially in the context of the 'SM'-Scene and the diversity of practices for which it stands, or for which it ideally provides the space.

The use of metaphorical patterns is a frequent phenomenon of this language: "... there are *fantasy* (golden shower [meaning urinating on someone or to be urinated on], ..., *toy* [the tools of the scenes, e.g. whips, dildos etc.], *violence and pain* (anal rape, cock and ball torture, ..., whipping), and *discipline* (corporal discipline, ..., dungeon, ...)" (Murray and Murrell 1989: 148). 'SM'-language thus appears to have evolved through the need to conceal activities which are deemed to be socially unacceptable. Within the Scene the intensity of consensual 'SM'-'body practice' is usually indicated by the use of the abbreviations of 'BD' and 'S/M'. Even though 'BD' generally is a specific form of consensual 'SM'-play, it gets used in a connotative manner on the 'Scene'. "BD and SM are most frequently perceived as different *intensities* of sadomasochistic activities, as though BD is automatically marked [+'light'] and SM is automatically marked [+heavy]" (Murray and Murrell 1989: 155).

Another specific quality of the language of consensual 'SM', according to Murray and Murrell, is the fact that it is mainly a written and not a spoken language. It follows the so-called Jakobson's 'code' of communication.

Moser and Kleinplatz more recently (in Langdridge and Barker 2007) commented on the difficulty of summing up a 'definite taxonomy of SM activities' as being "...hampered by the complexity of SM – or for that matter any other sexual interest" (Moser and Kleinplatz in Langdridge and Barker 2007: 53). Apart from the questionable desirability of such a 'taxonomy' and the fluctuations of the ever changing 'sexual' mores within societies they add that "SM is an understudied area of sexology" (Moser and Kleinplatz in Langdridge and Barker 2007: 53).

3.5.4   Learning the skills of
the 'bodily practices' of consensual 'SM'

As with any behaviour, consensual 'SM' 'body practice' has to be learned. The 'step' into the Scene therefore is, the start of a learning process.

Access to the Scene does not merely imply access to tools, outfits, setting and atmosphere, but also the access to people. These 'significant others' (Sutherland 1974) teach new individuals specific Scene-knowledges such as the appropriate rules of conduct of consensual 'SM', symbols and codes (language) with Scene-specific meanings and special traits for the diverse 'bodily practices'.

Weinberg's study, 'S and M: Studies in Sadomasochism' (1983), supports these findings whereby the authors pointed out that the ideological education of people on the Scene occupied a lot of time compared to the education of practical skills that are required for this 'bodily practice'.

Sutherland's theory of differential association (1974, ori. 1939) helps to appreciate the influence of the *Scene* as a subculture and the contacts an individual has with patterns of behaviour within it. The Scene provides a space to learn new behaviour patterns and to gain a different moral outlook onto activities that are not accepted by mainstream society.

Diabolo, who prefers to have contact with Scene-people described his understanding of the Scene in very similar words:

I think that when you go to the Scene it doesn't just happen, like when you go to a certain pub because it's on a convenient corner but you make a decision to go to the Scene because of an inner need. And that decision is a decision not only to accept but also in a sense to reject. Because as you said earlier, it's easier to have your own sexuality accepted, you're dealing with other people who also have their own sexuality accepted. So it's a sort of much wider, broader minded, tolerant, acceptable, more thoughtful, more sensitive social environment, generally. And the people are just nicer there and if they are not nice they don't last long. So there's a certain kind of social filter happening if the Scene is so small and related internationally, then if anybody is abusive on the Scene, they become notorious internationally, they become famous and pay a heavy social price for it. Perhaps that's the reason why we all behave so well. But there's just no comparison if you go to a SM/Fetish sort of club on a Friday or a Saturday night, although everyone is drinking, you never ever come across any form of misbehavior and yet any local pub, every pub, every club, every disco there's fights going on in the car-park. I don't trust 'normale' as the Germans say. And they don't trust me. (Interview-file D.: 2)

As becomes apparent through Diabolo's explanation, the Scene of consensual 'SM' has informal control-mechanisms which do not dogmatically exclude categories of people (as in mainstream society) but abusive actors, people, who use their potential power within consensual 'S/M'-'body practice' for other aims than the pleasure of the receiving part ('slave', 'bottom', 'sub').

The mere fact of the learning process of consensual 'SM'-skills as well as the mechanisms of informal control within the Scene, in order to prevent abusive and violent situations from occurring, once again shows the theories of 'sadomasochistic pathology' to be misleading. In Thompson's words: "As one had to learn a range of techniques in order to engage in a co-operative venture, one is made rather than born an active devotee; and these socially acquired skills become a means to distinguish between the socially harmless devotee and other people with violent criminal intent" (Thompson 1994: 146). In the context of the Scene the thus established rules of conduct serve as a mechanism of informal control, obliging the practitioners of consensual 'SM' to ethically constrain themselves as well as to expect certain forms of conduct from others.

The sense of trust, social bonding and the potential for participation for every 'lived body' that people encounter on the Scene stands in deep contrast to the often harsh, judgemental stereotypical and even abusive social reactions of mainstream culture.

Even though there are many books and safety-manuals available that potentially teach the interested individual how to practice and be safe with their 'bodily practices' of consensual 'SM', most people enjoy the 'family-character' within the Scene and learn their skills within it.

3.5.5 'Significant others'

Daniel Glaser (1978) developed Sutherland's approach further by focusing more on the 'significant others' within a subculture than on their behaviour patterns. The crucial point in Glaser's understanding lies in identification, 'differential association' also implies massmedia-figures as 'significant others'. His approach provides a basis for appreciating the influence of indirect sources of identification (e.g. Pat's identification with the 'hero' of the TV-series 'Branded' and Ryan's fascination with 'Querelle' and 'Cruising'.) The relationship between cultural representations and individual changes of attitude as well as behavioural changes have been a topic in Chapter 2 and will be further elaborated in Chapter 5.

Along with, and all through, the process of becoming members of the Scene, individuals learn to appreciate a set of values that is supported and reinforced on an informal basis, by the majority of Scene-participants (constant Scene-members as well as 'drifting members').

The concept of 'drift' (Matza 1964) seems to provide an adequate framework to explain the processes that are involved in becoming a practitioner of consensual 'SM'. The individuals I encountered within my research all (for diverse reasons) became detached from society's moral codes concerning 'sexuality' and/or the conventional uses of power.

The term developed by Matza, for the process that temporarily excuses or rationalizes the transgression of conventional values, once internalized by the individual itself and others, is 'neutralization'. Sykes and Matza (1957) distinguished five different 'techniques of neutralization':

1. denial of responsibility (responsibility is shifted to external factors, in the Scene reflective responsibility is strongly encouraged)
2. denial of injury (as wounds are regarded as valuable there is none)
3. denial of the victim (as there is negotiation and consent there is none)
4. condemnation of the condemners (which in the Scene applies as 'normal' or rather 'straight' society's own incidences of non-consensual power-play are invoked and justly condemned.)
5. appeal to higher loyalties (freedom and equal validity)

These techniques further the process of dissociation from the conventional moral and 'sexual' codes of society.

In contrast to Sykes and Matza (1957), who appear to assume that these 'neutralizations' have only a temporary effect, the empirical data collected within this research supports a rather different view. All individuals interviewed, independent of their duration within the Scene, held on to their critical attitude towards mainstream society and favoured the conduct rules of consensual 'SM'.

Agnew and Peters, who analysed predisposing and situational factors of the 'techniques of neutralization' (1986), point out that 'acceptance of neutralizations' is a predisposing factor in individuals to make use of different 'neutralizations'. Most of the interviewees had disillusioning experiences with the conventional (hypocratic) value-system of mainstream, capitalist-consumerist society as well as its neo-liberal 'order of things' and had therefore potentially less problems with the acceptance of neutralizations.

In Matza's concept of 'drift', the 'techniques of neutralization' are not as such sufficient to motivate an individual to 'drift' into 'deviance'. For this to happen, 'subterranean convergence' is crucial.

'Subterranean convergence' describes the process in which conventional morality and culture mixes with and thus gives support to the 'deviant morality'. In the context of consensual 'SM', these 'subterranean values' are to be found in the contexts of contemporary 'sexual representations and expectations', 'safe sex', 'body discourses' (see Chapter 2), the fascination and commodification of 'bodies', 'kink' and 'risk' (Chapter 5), and, last but not least, concerning the joining of the Scene, the formation of diverse 'tribes' that provide emotional community.

In 'Becoming Deviant' (1969), Matza noted that this process depends on the interaction of external uncontrollable factors and the 'free will' of the individual through affinity, affiliation and signification-processes which explains the diversity of individual involvement with consensual 'SM' in my sample.

To be able to participate in the culture of consensual 'SM', one has to learn its patterns of behaviour, codes of courtesy and get to know the different 'technologies' of 'playing'. In many cases the initiation of newcomers is taken into the hands of experienced long-term members of the community or long-term members of clubs, in some cases these are professional 'mistresses' and/or 'masters'.

After many years of 'playing' the 'straight' role with very limited sexual encounters Diabolo remembered:

> (.) I was in the closet but then I went to a club and I got to know my first mistress and she understood and initiated me. Since then I had several mistresses that I always had a trustful relationship with. (Interview-file D.: 1)

Diabolo said that he learned a lot of skills and possible scenarios but the crucial part he had to learn for himself: The balance between fantasy and reality.

> D.:   Yes. When it gets too much then it's just exasperating and anxiety inducing and then the pleasure goes. And it's, you got to experiment with yourself and live out those [fantasies] for quite a while, before you know really how you distil your fantasies into an actuality and that that process is full of mistakes and misunderstandings. And in my case none the worse for that. (Interview-file D.: 5)

Henry did not have the advantage of a club-scene because. 'In those days', he told me, there was not anything like it, therefore his mode of access was more or less entirely limited to the professional side. Henry: "(.) I looked and looked professionally for it, as a youngster, from the age of seventeen" (In H.: 2).

His search was not an easy task though:

> I've been, to use the professional term, 'rolled' three times. And that means, where I've been to visit a professional Lady and she's either

taken the money out of my pocket, while I wasn't looking or she's done something like this, one even sort of tied me to her bed and blindfolded me, and then came over and told me that she'd taken all the money out of my pocket: 'And I wasn't gonna do anything about it. There is nothing I could do.' And I said: 'Well, I hope you haven't, because I will have to.' And they think that you won't, because, you see, it's going to get into papers and your wife will know and all the rest of it ... (In –H.: 6)

After many discouraging experiences Henry was successful: "I found a very good professional, but it took me a lot of money that I couldn't afford, pocket money etcetera, before I found the right one..." (In H.: 2/3)

The access through professional 'mistresses', even though it turned out to be a good one for Henry, had humiliating aspects that stem from the general social reactions towards 'Sadomasochism' and 'perversion' which was reflected even in contemporary times when Mr Mosley's purchases on this level were publicized in 2008 (see Saner 2008).

Tom and Bess were learning the skills through friends, although Tom had quite a lot of self-experiment experiences with innovative 'body practices'. He recalled during an interview: "Experiment. Clamps, clothes pegs. I mean you can use pegs for clamping, pinching the flesh up... in all sorts of ways, you know. Put about like fifty clothespegs around your bollocks and have a wank, couldn't you? There's lots of things you can do that are not danger-ous" (In J.: 2).

After a period of auto-experimentation Tom felt that he wanted a relation-ship again, after the upsetting experience of divorce. He therefore advertised under 'body-art' and started his relationship with Bess. As both of them did not have experience in consensual 'SM'-'body practices', they were learning with the help of friends.

Bess: I don't know anything, just experiment. His friends are into it, so we go along. We are learning.
Tom: We are still learning.
Andrea: So it's a circle, private, intimate circle of friends?
Bess: Yes.
Andrea: Not Scene-people but people who meet in private, at houses?
Bess: The people might be in the Scene.? [looks at Tom]
Tom: Yeah, some are in the Scene.
Bess: They are fairly hard-core.
Tom: They've been in the Scene for a long time. Six or eight years.
Bess: Years and years. We are like their sort of proteges. Aren't we? At the moment.
Tom: Yeah. They're teaching me... I mean a piercer is no good without a pierce [someone who obtains a piercing]. Is it? (ditto)

Anthony started his explorations of consensual 'SM'-'body practice' and the learning process of its skills with the help of one ex-lover and friends. A.: "Well, actually I met, an ex-lover of mine was interested in some of that stuff anyway. And through him I began to like to get handcuffed, tied him up, bought some harnesses. And there were a few friends, we did meet privately and did some SM-'scenes' or whatever. They knew I wanted to explore this. They taught me how to tie someone up and, that's how I started exploring it, and then I met a few more people and I read also a lot around SM. Like practical."

Andrea: Like safety-books?
A.: Yeah. Safety-books or even from a critical perspective, there was a book by Gilles Deleuze, reading stuff on an intellectual level. It was interesting and I was also reading lots of fiction round SM. Like 'Venus in furs', 'The story of O.' These kind of books and then you got ideas what I might want to do in my own practices. So it was a mixture of three things that influenced the kind of sex that I want to have. (Interview-file 3: 4)

Shiva learned the skills she applied through her partner:

...we started making love in a way that was absolutely just what I always wanted. And the words, he introduced me to a whole lot of new words, like 'slave' because he is a 'dom' and I'm the 'sub' although I'd rather be a 'switch'. He is willing for me to try but he is not into being dominated, so there is no pleasure in it for me, like spanking him because he doesn't get anything out of it. We have bondage, slight bondage, in fact everything revolves round the talking, the way he talks to me which he does in a very quiet voice, very, very sensual, very sensuous. (Interview-file 2: 2)

As Pat and Bette used to have a long-term consensual 'SM'-relationship, Bette recalled: "...you don't know about me and Pat? You met Pat? We were obviously going to have something together, I mean she was very keen to explore her SM-side which she'd never done properly. I identify myself as a sort of 'top', so I had fun with her for quite a long time. About three years or so, we are still very close friends. But we have broken up from that, being in a relationship" (Interview-file 4: 6). As Bette already had a lot of skills in the 'bodily practices' of consensual 'SM' and defined herself as a 'top', she taught Pat the skills of 'bottoming' as well as 'topping'.

Within the Scene-clubs it is possible for everyone to obtain explanations of the use of various tools and each practitioner can try out which sensation he/she prefers. In the open and communicative atmosphere encountered on the Scene, people have the opportunity to obtain a 'feel' for diverse sensations if they submit to the internal rule of asking for consent.

'Piggy' stated that the search for the experience of diverse sensations is important to him: "...because I want to know what the sensation is like. When I was in the States recently, there was a guy in the 'Power exchange-club' and he was using two floggers, one in each hand. And I watched him work on someone and I was fascinated by this. And I thought: 'I wonder what it feels like to be on the receiving end.' So when he was relaxing, I went up to him and introduced myself and said: 'You know, I find that fascinating. I'd be really interested to know what it feels like. Would you mind?' And he said: 'No, no, no, help yourself! Bend over the flogging-stool and I'll show you.' So, that was entirely from within" (Interview-file S.: 5).

This example clearly shows the dynamics of this, on a symbolical level, hierarchical 'top'/'bottom'-relationship, where on the existential level, instead of domination, there exists a basis of mutual respect and negotiation. In this case the 'top' was actually overtly giving a service to an interested 'bottom'.

3.5.6   Dress codes and the passage into fantasy through 'fetishes'

Within the consensual 'SM' and 'Fetish'-subculture specific patterns of style developed, a dress code that influenced also the market-place of mainstream fashion. Leather, PVC, rubber and latex ('Skin Two') have at least a threefold function. They create a unified impression for others, (in order to) support the wearers self-image and thirdly besides an aesthetical function, they also can serve to advertise the wearers interests.

The 'SM'-dyke community used to employ the pocket/hankie codes that were developed by their gay counterparts but this feature of the Scene seems to have declined.

Pat: I say I'm not interested in dress code but I always wear a leather-vest and combat-trousers or a pair of jeans. Always wear my boots, so it's obvious that I'm kind of SM-person. My leather-vest has got all kinds of pins on it, different leather-clubs, so it's obvious that to anybody who's been around for a while that I'm into SM.

Andrea: But you don't represent to be a 'bottom' in a certain way?

Pat: And I do because I wear the keys and the chain on the right hand side, which is a code for being a 'bottom'. So, and a black hanky. You know the hanky-code. So, I wear all that on the right which means 'bottom'.

Andrea: So, that's already quite safe, so that people won't put you in the wrong position?

Pat: Yeah. So, I'm walking about, you know, advertising: 'This is a bottom.' And so when people, so people will know, and so if people are looking at me, in a way, you know, like they are attracted to me or they're interested in me, then I'm pretty confident that that person is not a bottom. Because why would they be interested in a 'bottom' if they are a 'bottom'. So, I'm already doing a bit of advertising, so I guess I don't have to worry about their clothes because I'm already advertising. (Interview-file 1: 16)

This may be representative of the impact of the general shift of meaning, representation and rules within the 'SM-scene', which will be discussed later in this chapter, on the individual, Pat does not find the dresscode important as the 'player' and his/her skills are more relevant to her.

Pat: I'm not fond of dress-codes because I'd rather just, you know, I don't want to go to a place where I have to be dressed up. I want to go to a place where I can be with other Sadomasochists and maybe play. To me it makes, it means nothing what someone is wearing. They could be wearing a jeans and a T-shirt or a flowery dress for all I care, you know.

Andrea: It depends on the person and how they play?

Pat: Yeah, it's the mental connection not about fetishizing clothing. Although, you know, I love leather you know, and if someone is wearing full leather then that's a turn-on. That's nice. But if it's a perfect stranger wearing full leather that's not of much interest. I'm not too keen on the dress-codes and I'm not really too keen on the club-scene. (Interview-file 1: 13)

For Bette dressing up is not particularly important or exciting, she stated: "..., I've always done it without. I only dress up when I have to, when I go to a club, interestingly enough. I think, I actually feel quite strongly about it from my own point of view. I think if you can't do something like dominate somebody without sort of dressing up in high-heel-boots and things, then in a way you're not that dominant anyhow. You ought to be able to do it in a dress. You notice I'm not in leather-gear now. I think there can be a sort of kinky turn-on but if you're really into that sort of mental thing then it shouldn't really be necessary" (Interview-file 4: 10).

'Dressing up' can in many cases function within the consensual 'SM'-scenario on a symbolic level as the 'dress code' as well as the tools for the actual acting out of a 'scene' and helping the practitioners to define and maintain their roles. The role of 'top', 'Master', etc. entails the control of the 'bottom' which on the symbolical level is underlined by for example, leather-gear and the wearing of whips and/or devices of restraint. The 'bottom', 'sub', etc. usually wears comparatively less and is often already restrained in one way or the other (e.g. chastity-belt or being led on a leash) in order to symbolically express devotion and submission which becomes further enhanced through the varying acts of humiliation that often introduce a 'scene'. For Clive Barker, the director of 'Hellraiser': "Dressing in furs, dressing in leather, dressing in tattoos, dressing in metal, is halfway to transforming the body" (Barker in Woodward 1993: 25).

The most common 'fetishes' within the Scene are certainly leather (clothes as well as 'toys', boots, uniforms, stilettos, corsets, restraint-instruments like ropes), latex and chains, sometimes also shit and piss and the 'play-tools' themselves. Townsend suggested to use the term 'situational fetishes' in order to include abstractions that go beyond objects and listed: "...: bondage (regardless of its materials), humiliation, punishment, and possibly the act of submission itself. All these abstractions, like their physical counterparts, form the central focus of your fantasies or mine... In fact, it is the actual use of most fetish items that form the core of the fantasy for us, not the object itself" (Townsend 1993: 87/88).

> *Andrea*: How important would you say is the dress? Is it to make a bor-
> derline between so-called reality and a 'scene'?
> *Ella*: I think dress, yes, I think it is. Because, I mean a lot of us like to live
> fantasies. I mean this is a fantasy-thing, really, in any respect. And I
> think most of us like to dress according to our fantasy-situation. ... It
> doesn't have to be leather, PVC or rubber in that sense of the word.
> *Andrea*: They have to fit your fantasies?
> *Ella*: They fit your fantasies. You know, you go looking for some-
> thing, ... The dress is a very important part of the fantasy-side of
> things, getting the clothes on gets you into that role and also it is
> very nice. I mean, you know, to put your PVC, your leathers or rub-
> ber on it puts you into a certain frame of mind, when you're setting
> out. I mean it is nice, to me it is important and also my partner is
> the same. (Interview-file E.: 6)

The detailed planning of consensual 'SM'-play in order to be able to come closer to a desired fantasy and also to create a 'mind-set' by bodily attires contradicts the constructed 'nature of sexual desire' which is deployed by the discourses of 'normalization' (Chapter 2). "It is a paradox that while sexual relations are pre-eminently the object of social control in human societies sexual desire is often taken to be something beyond social organization or rational control. The realm of the sexual is seen as *par excellence* the realm of the irrational, the anarchic-the realm of the senses" (Cowie in Segal and McIntosh 1992: 134).

Within the psychoanalytical tradition fantasy is understood as the 'staging of desire' (Cowie) as well as the conscious/unconscious foundation of subjectivity whereby the emphasis is put on the fact that fantasy allows for contradiction. In fantasy thus the individual can occupy any role or position according to his/her choice. This point is crucial in reference to 'moral' feminists critique of consensual 'SM' which focuses on its symbolically overt discourses and representations of 'gender' (power)-relationships instead of realizing the possibilities of identification that the fantasy at the core of the 'scenes' provides.

Military as well as medical 'scenes' have an attraction for many 'players' on the Scene. The relevance of military and medical roles and dress code derive their thrill from their assigned societal power positions.

Consensual 'SM'-play functions through fantasy-play and thereby often leads to catharsis of emotional energy. "Fantasy, and especially public forms of fantasy-films, stories, plays, television-in the main replace childish play for adults. ... Fantasies are actualized, but remain 'playacted' and this is the recurrent defense made by those engaging in consenting sadomasochism as well as by the besuited businessmen who pay women to dress them up as schoolgirls, servants, etc." (Cowie in Segal and McIntosh 1992: 149/150). For Anthony, masks have a particular attraction. He believes that because of our social roles that limit us to certain behaviours within defined situations, we constantly wear masks anyway. "I think people wearing physical masks or mental masks, you can hide behind any of them or not only for hiding, to protect as well. From whatever physical or mental. Masks are very interesting, and also for SM-sex, I like the idea of people dressing up for sex. That's what fascinates me in SM, people dressing up, like in theatre, performing roles. ... You can play out certain kinds of fantasies around for example, certain kinds of masks and hoods. Like bank robbers etc., you can have those kinds of 'scenes' as well" (Interview-file 3: 6).

The seeming 'authenticity' of the 'scene' thus helps to enact fantasies. "Pat Califia has argued that: The key word to understand S/M is *fantasy*. The roles, dialogue, fetish costumes, and sexual activity are part of a drama or ritual" (Cowie in Segal and McIntosh 1992: 149).

3.5.7 Parallels to the 'symbolic play' of children

The make-believe games of children within which they represent and practice their understanding of the surrounding social world are less focused on one topic (e.g. power relations in consensual 'SM') and they often do not involve much preparation as they are mostly spontaneous, but nevertheless they do show similarities to 'SM' 'play' on a structural level.

The book 'Symbolic Play' by Inge Bretherton (1984), in which the social and cognitive study of pretence in the symbolic plays of children is undertaken, focuses on temporal-causal-spatial frameworks (e.g. event schemata, scripts, stories) as opposed to the rather limited former approach that understood representation merely as the study of disembedded symbols or taxonomic structures.

Within this concept the notion of metacommunication (Bateson 1972) which describes the ability to mark off pretence from everyday reality through the children's agreement on: "This is play", is very important and is also relevant within the context of a 'scene'. In consensual 'SM' the notion of metacommunication plays an important part during the negotiations that the 'set-up' of a 'scene' requires, here the distribution of the roles, the plot (open for variations) and the code-word and/or safe-gesture for possible abrupt endings of a play are discussed. This metacommunication allows the players to structure the on-coming 'scene' and thereby to gain security within this creative setting. "..., the ability to represent 'what ifs', to engage in subjunctive thought..., is one of the most intriguing aspects of human cognition" (Bretherton 1984: 3).

Bretherton points to evidence that shows that representations of 'symbolic play' are organized in terms of event schemata or scripts which are 'skeletal frameworks of everyday events' and that they are thus not to be reducible to an organization of taxonomic structures and classification hierarchies.

In the context of consensual 'SM', the representation of power relationships that are in a broader sense isomorphic with reality, serve also as a basis for the figurative frameworks established for a 'scene'.

> ..., children use event schemata as raw material to create a fictive reality that does not merely simulate but transforms their affective-cognitive map of the social world. These transformations are analyzed in the emergence of a subjunctive capacity. ... By changing various parameters of an event schema, children can create a variety of more-or less-fantastic alternatives to everyday reality. ... not that symbolic play faithfully reflects children's ability to represent the social world but that it constitutes play with that ability. (Bretherton 1984: 7)

This is very much true for consensual 'SM' as well, as the 'scenes' do not reflect the practitioners (dis-) ability to represent different power relations which they encountered within the societal world, but they allow them to play with that ability for their own purposes. The distinction between mere representation and the play with representations is relevant not only concerning a possible 'transcendence' of socio-politically determining categories through the practice of consensual 'SM'-play, but also as a possible counterargument for a feminist anti-sadomasochism position such as this: "What I'm concerned about is one part of sadomasochism, the master and slave relationship. ... Some of the things that I have seen and heard about succumbing to the power of someone else are devastating for me as a Black woman, having grown up in Black culture and being subjected to someone else's power, and having to live with that all my life" (Sims in Linden et al. 1982: 100).

The role responsibilities and the relational and contextual responsibility that are necessary to ensure the safety and comfort of both parties involved in a 'scene' often require sensitivities that, at least in Western capitalist cultures, are not self-understood as they are more or less opposed to the reinforced egoism required for success in capitalist-consumer society.

> The empathy between Top and bottom has to be even deeper and more complete than in any other form of sexual relationship. If the S cannot

feel and understand what the M is feeling and experiencing, there is no way for him to perform adequately. (Townsend 1993: 23/24)

3.5.8 Specific skills of consensual play

> The process whereby coercion becomes consent is achieved by old-fashioned coquettishness rather than intimidation or violence.
> (Anthony 1995: 120)

Seduction and conspiracy are then the psychological tools applied by 'top' and 'bottom' in order to be able to 'play'. The ability to act is another crucial component for a successful 'play' session.

> As every good actor knows, the effectiveness of the performance increases with commitment. Method acting involves intense preparation and fanatical concentration, with the objective of doing as much as possible to conceal-from himself no less than anybody else-the actor's real personality, so that the role he is playing fills the vacuum: *he becomes* the character. (Anthony 1995: 160)

The dominance-display of 'tops' depends most of the time rather on the emotional powers and empathy of the 'top' than on physical displays of dominance. The application of emotional, moral and/or physical pressure and the administration of physical 'punishments' to facilitate the other's pleasure, require a reflexive and empathic individual.

Anthony explained the role responsibility of 'tops' to me: "..., if you are a 'top' you have to be aware of how your 'bottom' is feeling at every single stage. A 'top' has to take responsibility, like a 'bottom' has also to take responsibility. A 'top' has to be aware of how exactly his 'bottom' is feeling. Is he O.K., can he breath O.K. ... Is he mentally O.K. Sometimes a 'bottom' might say: 'Yes, I'm O.K. ' But they might not be O.K. as well. So it must be like a unit, you must have a sixth sense. You have to pick up on body language, breathing. And you might say: 'Well, actually, I don't think, you're O.K.'"

> Andrea: Because some 'bottoms' want to push and push their limits to so much an extent that it might be not alright for them, even though they think they are fine.?
> A.: Yes, yes. (Interview-file 3: 7)

The most important elements within the interplay of 'tops' and 'bottoms' therefore appear to be reflexivity and empathy. The trust needed for these edge-experiments on the side of the 'bottom', must be matched by the empathy gained through experience on side of the 'top' that allows him/her to take the other to the very idiosyncratic limits of pain and/or pleasure. The 'top' ideally must be able to 'tell' the exact condition of the 'bottom', the slight and fragile dividing line between the feeling of being hurt and feeling a painful pleasure. This also appears to be a thrill for most 'tops', the knowledge/experience of the whole individual that enables the 'top' to control the 'bottom' to his/her own benefit.

Within the Scene the words: "A good top has to be a bottom first" constitute the 'Golden Rule' of consensual 'SM' and are known to most practitioners. Townsend (1993) calls this the apprenticeship of a 'top' and although several 'tops' in my sample as well as in the gay 'SM'-community he describes, did not have this experience he cautions: "To be worth anything, you must know how it feels, and the only way you can properly experience this is to be on the bottom" (Townsend 1993: 79).

Apart from the 'creation of a proper self-image' of the 'top', Townsend mentions the points that Anthony illustrated as crucial for a 'top', as well as the knowledge of practical skills which does not only imply the proper skill for the use of the tools but also an understanding of the different materials used.

'Bottoms', 'subs' or 'slaves' do not only carry out tasks and/or get 'punished' but also develop a certain attitude towards the services they provide for their 'Tops', 'Doms' or 'Masters': "I pride myself (don't let anyone tell you real submissives aren't proud) on remembering how my dominants drink their coffee, fold their Jockey shorts, and like their necks rubbed. This is my art, my vocation" (Campell in Califia and Sweeney 1996: 185).

In order to feel more happy and balanced the 'submissive' has to fulfil his/ her needs for belonging and serving and therefore, according to Campell: "The collar that Daddy or Master or Mistress places around my neck reminds me that no matter how insane the world is, there is an island of acceptance and care for me, a place to come home to. When I play as a masochist, all I need to do is show up, communicate with my top, and keep breathing. ... But the joy I get from service is as intellectual and emotional as it is physical. Caring for another's person and possessions is a mark of intimacy, affection, and respect. I may be a fetishist, but I won't do just anyone's leathers" (Campell in Califia and Sweeney 1996: 186). The fulfilment of the need to serve and belong in this context as opposed to within 'conditions of domination' does not imply unselective and general submission, nor passivity but choice.

Townsend described in the 'Leatherman's Handbook II' (1993) how the dichotomy of 'Sadism' and 'Masochism' that in former times had matched the 'playing' of distinct and exclusive roles of 'S' or 'M' within the gay 'SM'-community now has given way to a majority of 'switch-hitters'. These observations find parallels in Gosselin and Wilson's findings (in Howells 1984) as well as within the results of my empirical research in London. As will be illustrated, the 'old Scene' in London was characterized by rigid roles while the 'new Scene' embraces 'switching'.

Only very few of the people I interviewed were not 'switching' to experience both sides of this consensual power game. Diabolo: "I do whatever my mistress tells me to. I do not like to switch. I did it sometimes, when one of my mistresses wanted me to but I do not like to 'top', it does not feel right. Only when I am asked to. In the Scene people often switch or do gay stuff, I don't. I prefer to serve my mistress. Sometimes I can do small 'scenes' in clubs, like for example in 'The Entrance' but mainly I serve one mistress" (Interview-file D.: 1).

Within the current 'hetero/bi'-Scene of consensual 'SM' there exists nearly an idealism of 'switching', many couples encourage each other to try out different tools as well as positions.

3.5.9 Safety in consensual 'SM'

The emphasis on safety, responsibility and communication is widespread within the Scene although particularly strong within the 'S/M'-dykes community. In 'The Lesbian S/M Safety Manual' (Califia 1988) the first important part of a 'scene' in the framework of a lesson for a 'sadist' is thus the negotiation before it. "Careful and complete negotiation can make the difference between a scene that is safe and hot, and one that you will shudder to remember. It is also an excellent way for the top to begin to take control. The bottom should be asked about her vanilla-sex history; any medical problems (asthma, back problems, poor circulation, diabetes, haemophilia, etc.) which may affect her flexibility, pain tolerance or limits; prior experience with S/M; a list of things she absolutely will not do, might do, and wants to do; fantasies; if she has used a safeword...in the past...; and her reason for wanting to play with the person who is asking her all these rude, personal questions" (Califia 1988: 45/46).

The same rules of negotiation-consent apply to both 'players' as it is a consensual 'body practice' therefore the 'top' obviously also can make use of a safeword. In comparison to 'vanilla-sex' ['hetero-, gay-' or bi-] encounters the focus on safety and personal agency is far more pronounced. In 'vanilla sex', health and safety concerns are reduced to pregnancy prevention and/or the prevention of disease transmission. The framework of negotiation within consensual 'SM' ensures a more holistic understanding of the partners 'lived bodies' involved and obliges the practitioners to communicate. Within the hetero-, gay- and bi-'SM' circles I often encountered less rigid patterns of negotiation in comparison to the 'SM'-dykes but the importance of safewords was never put into doubt.

> *Diabolo*: I am a weak whimp but I try to take as much as possible and as I know my mistress usually very well, she will know what I dislike and like. My code-system is like the traffic lights. Green: You can go. Yellow: Be aware. Red: Stop. But I don't like to say 'Red' and I didn't have to so far. (Interview-file D.: 1)

3.5.10   Changes within the Scene of consensual 'SM' in London

> The practice of S/M is the creation of pleasure, and there is an identity with [i.e., a personal identity attached to] creation. And that's why S/M is really a subculture. It's a process of invention.
>
> (Foucault in Halperin 1995: 86)

Michel Foucault saw consensual 'SM' as being a part of wider practices of subcultural community formation and the results of the empirical part of this research support his opinion. In view of the American Scene of consensual 'SM' Pat Califia noted: "We even have enough history and experience as a community to have a generation gap" (Califia and Sweeney 1996: xiii). Through the interviews and observations I conducted in London it became obvious that the London Scene had to deal with a similar phenomenon.

The 'old' Scene

Diabolo gave me a short description of the beginning of the Scene : "There was something called the 'Mackintosh-club' that was where 'perverts' just used to wear Mackintoshes and have afternoon-teas and have a very formal, restrained relationship, where nothing was done but everything was thought about. The 'Mackintosh-society' existed in the sort of fifties, perhaps even earlier, I don't know, it was a minute little sect of perverts, who used to meet in England, which was the earliest sort of club as far as I know, what one might call a 'Fetish-scene'. Then there was club 'Maitresse' but again it was a fetish-Scene, more than precisely an SM-club. So that one got a mixture of transvestites, transsexuals, SMers, gays, lesbians, heterosexuals, rubber-people, silk and satin-people, leather-people and other things and many, many other things in some remote way, all cramped into this club called 'Maitresse'. This created the explosion into 'Der Putsch' and 'Torture Garden' and 'Submission' and 'Club Whiplash' and everything since" (Interview-file D.: 6/7). Apart from the new variety of clubs, the atmosphere and the internal rules within the clubs have changed. This appears like a reflection of mainstream-society's transformations too as the defining limits of 'sexuality' have shifted and become more fluid.

The 'old' Scene was, according to my informants, characterized by small numbers of people that frequented the rather unspecific events and clubs on offer. It was further a Scene that provided a sense of continuity for its members. Ella: "…When we used to go to the 'Putsch', I mean the 'Putsch' was basically, I mean after 'Maitresse', the only club at the time."

> *Andrea*:   And everybody went there?
> *Ella*:   Everybody went there, but the thing was that because the same people went all the time you actually built up friends, right? You met people, when new people came they were instantly recognized as new and so therefore you would go and introduce yourself, chat

or whatever. The same that happened to us. I would have never got into the things or not knowing things if it hadn't been for this lady L. that I met, who was so generous, who started talking to us, who introduced us to her friends. And that is how it was, people were very welcoming, you know. (Interview-file E.: 16)

A very descriptive as well as personal explanation of the 'old Scene' was provided by one of the oldest members of the Scene. Henry: "..., the club-scene here has developed, there was a very good club, some years and years ago, club 'Maitresse'. (...), my current Lady, the one with whom I've been for ten years, she was probably the leading light there. All of the people gathered around her table, nobody dare go to her table, when she walked in that table was empty, ready for her. And men would clutter around, she had a few Lady-friends, who were there. And then, they were in fetish dress, everyone and you wouldn't have got in there without a reasonable fetish dress. And there would be a little bit of dancing and a little bit of play at tables, may be, you know: 'Right, put the nipple-clamps on!', or something like this. And with handcuffs on: 'Please, may I have a drink?', 'You wait. You wait!'. This sort of thing. But at midnight, somewhere around midnight, the mood of the music would change and it would be sort of like: 'Kiss those boots of shiny, shiny leather' or 'Camina Burana', something like that, that changed the mood. And then she would stand up, dragged, whoever she was with, onto the floor and all the other 'Mistresses' would follow. And then on the floor, in various corners, they would do various things to their various 'slaves'" (Interview-file H.: 22).

Other features of the 'old' Scene around consensual 'SM' involved rather rigid role-distributions. As the 'old Scene' was very small, the lack of vari-ations within the role-play and role-choice had sometimes negative conse-quences. With regard to the theory of 'differential association' (Sutherland), the Scene in former times only provided a limited choice of patterns of con-sensual 'SM'-behaviour and the distribution of the roles of 'dom' and 'sub' were orientated much more than nowadays along a (reversed) gender-axis.

> *Ella:* ...I got into the dominant thing in a way not through choice but I think in some ways because at the time that was how the scene was seen. I mean I didn't know, you must remember I was quite naive. (Interview-file E.: 1)

The limitations of role models for consensual 'SM'-practitioners made Ella adapt to the role of a 'Dom' as it was expected of her as a woman. To keep her 'face' (Goffman 1967) she went along with the expectations of the subculture and learned the skills: "I think the first time anything happened was at one of these 'Skin Two'-things, when somebody came up and asked to lick my shoes. And I can remember thinking: 'Oh my god, what am I supposed to do?' I had no idea what was going on here, you know, and it was quite a strange experience but at the same time it was quite exciting. It was something that had never happened before, you know. And it is very difficult because it was a very gradual process, you can't actually put your foot on it, really. I mean in those days things were different really, there were a lot more submissives, who would come up to you for something. I mean I was blocked and I was totally naive, I was inexperienced, I didn't know what I was supposed to do. But I learned an awful lot from people like her [a dominant professional Mistress], who had lots of experience that I didn't have and I watched other people do things. And I did it. And."

>*Andre*:   So you grew into the role?
>*Ella*:   I grew into the role, really and maintained it for quite some time. Until I suppose really fairly recently, when I began to rethink things because I learned through rethinking things that I actually wasn't getting a real buzz out of what I was doing. (Interview-file E.: 2)

Now through reflections and diverse role behaviour patterns within the current Scene, especially the notion of 'switching', Ella discovered how to obtain more pleasure:

>I like doing things and I like a variety of the things that I do and I realize that being stuck as a dominant in fact denied me certain sexual and sensual pleasure that I actually needed. I wasn't getting it from just dominance alone, it wasn't doing anything for me sexually. It fulfilled other things, it was enjoyable to do, I enjoyed sometimes a sense of power but on its own it was not enough. So I have actually found that I like the combination of the two. (Interview-file E.: 3)

Ella's husband, who defines himself as a 'dominant' initially had the same problems as men in the old Scene were 'submissives'. As a result he did not 'play' and got excluded. Ella: "I mean initially, obviously, it tended to be that my partner was left out somewhat and it was because, when we started with the club-Scene, women were the dominants and the males were submissive and male dominance was rare" (Interview-file E.: 3).

Like Ella, who socialized as a consensual 'SM'er mainly within the hetero-, and bisexual 'SM'-Scene, Lara, who was always in close touch with the lesbian Scene, also was confronted with potentially limiting role-expectations within the Scene: "..., you know, I'm too strong a personality to come of as a 'bottom'. You know, I've started off as a 'bottom' because I believed that's what you were supposed to do, that's the best way to do it and I think I'm right. But then I, you know, decided that I'd learned enough and I didn't really enjoy that position, ..." (In L.: 15).

Dean, who works in one of the retail businesses that revolves around consensual 'SM' for many years, stated as well: "Initially, the people I first met were very stuck in roles, they were very role-playing. I suppose when I first sort of discovered the Scene most of the people I met were gay men. They tended to be very much into their little roles and rituals. You know: 'He's the dominant one, he's the submissive one.' Not just in sex, in their sort of lives in general, in their sort of partnerships in general" (Interview-file a.: 2).

The 'new' Scene

Although Ella suffered through the rigidity of the role-divisions within the old Scene, she misses the security and orientation these structures provided. As many other interviewees, Ella does not approve of the use a lot of men make of the Scene and 'scenes' within it. Ella: "you could walk into the 'Putsch' and every single male you knew was going to be a submissive, if I walk into a club now I don't know what these single males are because most of them are not" (Interview-file E.: 4/5).

Henry commented on male behaviour in the 'new' Scene-clubs: "...But what I do object to in clubs occasionally is, if for instance we are at a club, ..., if I come up to you and you're in the club there and I say to you: 'Excuse me Madame, but I'm very much into water sports. Will you use me?' Alright, now, you mustn't feel offended because you're in a club, where these things happen. ...On the other hand, if you say: 'That's not for me. I don't do these sort of things.' Then, I mustn't feel offended of being refused and that's the way it goes. And that's exactly as the clubs should be taken. ...Now, that's fine but what I do object to is a man, just walking into the 'Ladies' and standing there, playing with himself and saying: 'Please use me. Please use me.' If you just go in there for the normal function and you got someone like that there, now, that's not on."

Andrea: It's non-consensual.
Henry: Yes, that's right. Absolutely! Nonconsensual, ...That's the only thing in the whole clubs that I object to and I'm very strong on that. (Interview-file H.: 12)

For the interviewees who have been involved with the Scene for many years, the 'new' Scene can be described in terms of three major lacks concerning involvement, conduct and integrity.

Ella: "Yeah, I mean, I think people are just looking for buzzes in life and they drop into us and drop into something else. The real dedicated people that are into it are still around because we know them but I mean there are very few of them left from the original people that we knew. The trouble is new people coming in are not doing the same. So you're not getting any hard-core from the new people that are staying. They, they, I don't know, where they go, they just drift of" (Interview-file E.: 16). And during an earlier interview Ella mentioned: "The 'Entrance' is the best of them because it's the most action-packed. (...)You know, I mean I sometimes think that us SMers are total good people that are brought into it to be the cabaret. You know, we bring the punters in. You know, they've got the equipment and we start playing with it, it gives something new to people to go in and see. Whether they perhaps go to a night-club and have a drink and watch a top-less dancer, you know. It's that kind of attitude that I'm very much against, where before it tended to be very much more involvement. People, every-body did things, now it's a few people do things and a proportion go there to watch or I don't know what, chat or whatever..." (In E.: 16).

As the clubs on the Scene have exploded in number and diversity, the commercialization of 'kinky perviness' has become a distinct feature in many of the clubs. "I think the problem lies in the fact being that people are making money out of it. I mean I have to say that like 'Whiplash' which R. does, now R. isn't into the Scene at all. He is doing it to make money and the same with 'Torture Garden' and most of 'Submission', what they want is people. They don't really care what they are doing when you get there, they don't really care what they are wearing. I mean they know that to them the success of a club is three thousand people turned up. And that is to them a successful night. And they call themselves fetishists, they call themselves SMers, they are rubbish. They are not, because it doesn't mean anything. (...) But what you get in 'Whiplash', you get the 'Club-Dom', she turns up, she scoops up seven or eight of the only submissive males around and has them the entire evening, takes over the dance-floor, so nobody can dance, walks around the place with them and everybody stands around and watches her and boring, boring, boring. What's happening now is, we get fashion-shows at these clubs, I mean we get these shows and I think."

Andrea: So, it's really commercialized?
Ella: Yes, and that's what I don't like because we don't need all that. We should be doing the things, we shouldn't have people doing things for us. (Interview-file E.: 6)

A lot of gay consensual 'SM' was practiced on London's Hampstead Heath. Since a number of years the changes noticed by interviewees of Scene-clubs also seem to have come about the 'Heath-Scene':

Ryan: ..., I think it has changed. I think, they got rid of a lot of the trees and bushes and stuff, so it's a lot more open. You still get a lot of people down there but it's not as, for me, it's not as 'deviant' as it used to be.
Andrea: Has it become more known, so more people just come to look?
Ryan: Yeah, look, exactly. Yeah, rather than have sex.
Andrea: Like all over the scene.

Ryan: Yeah..., there are more people that go to, there are more people that know about it. But it hasn't spoiled it for me totally and I still get a thrill, when I go up there. (Int. R.: 2)

The last distinct feature of the 'new' Scene concerns the diversity of 'bodily practices'. This is partly due to technological innovations, for example, the frequent use and exploration of 'violet wands' (electric devices) and specifically equipped face-masks (for feeding and 'suffocation') which I observed during my fieldwork.

Once a month the 'SM/Fetish'-market in central London offered the possibility to browse through stalls with 'play'-equipment. The changes that occurred within the Scene also became apparent in new variations of traditional 'play-tools' on offer. Whereas the old market mostly displayed black outfits and tools, the new market may be catching up with the boom of 'sex-scene-clubs' and provides the customers now with a choice of coloured whips and coloured outfits. As the Scene experienced a shift from rigid role-patterns and stereotypical role-distribution towards more openness and fluidity, the retailers adjusted. Not all new 'bodily practices' are connected to innovative equipment though, as, Lara explained that: "...the practices, the sexual practices people are engaged in now are very different....It wasn't very common to have cuttings for example or play-piercings..." (Interview-file L.: 3). 'Bodily practices' that involve blood but are performed according to safety-rules (e.g. by means of rubber gloves and sterile 'cutting' and/or 'piercing'-equipment) are quite widespread within the 'new' Scene in London which might be a counter-practice to the 'blood'-fear inducing 'safe sex' education to prevent the spread of HIV (see Chapter 2).

Changes also occurred in the way 'scenes' are approached. Whereas role-play was in former times always involved in these 'bodily practices', the 'new' Scene is more direct in its approach on consensual 'SM'.

Dean: I think as it's got more open. How can I put it? May be it's younger people are more into just doing it. It's not the role-play. Let's just get on with it and do it. I think that seems to be a feature of it. (Interview-file a.: 2)

The limininal spaces that the Scene in London offers, are since recent years an attraction-point for various kinds of people who, as illustrated above, often do not engage in the 'bodily practices' of consensual SM'. The reasons for this shift and the parallel rise of the term 'kinky', point to the transformations of meaning that triggered this socio-cultural phenomenon. As the term 'kinky' arose as an alternative to the consumerist wholesale of sex, it soon also became commodified and fostered the establishment of a new market of 'trendy kinkyness'. A lot of clubs, magazines and retail businesses developed around this new trend and thus attracted many people.

In order to account for the increase in 'drifting members' of the Scene, as well as for much of the changes noticed on the Scene I consider broader social and psychological determinants to be of crucial importance. In recent times the notion of 'individualism' gave way to the 'postmodern' notion of the 'de-centred subject': "The de-centred subject has a greater capacity to engage in a controlled de-control of the emotions and explore figural tendencies, immediate sensations and affective experiences formerly regarded as threatening, as something which needs to be kept at bay or strictly controlled" (Featherstone 1993: 101).

Even though the feature of confusing and disorientating mixtures of signs and an 'aestheticization of everyday life' (Featherstone 1993) is not historically new, its occurrence though, formerly reduced to carnivals (e.g. fairs of the Middle Ages), has changed massively, as today it appears a constant, all-embracing feature of life.

Maffesoli's 'The Time of the Tribes' (1996) suggested the emergence of heterogenous 'tribes' within the context of Western societies. These 'postmodern tribes' are fluid and allow the temporary members to suit their needs by 'switching' in between. In the context of the empirical research on consensual 'SM', it is thus possible to regard the fluctuation of 'drifting members' of the 'Fetish'/'SM'-Scene in contrast to the stability provided by the 'old Scene', as part of a general shift towards the 'tribes'.

After these insights into the 'life-worlds' of consensual 'SM' that revealed the 'power/knowledge' expert discourses of modernity to be inadequate to describe the 'lived experiences' of consensual 'SM', the next chapter will focus on other, fundamental constructions of modernity and reveal their inherent contradictions.

4
'Sadomasochism' – a Social Construction and Its Use

Chapter 3 introduced and discussed the meaning of consensual 'SM' 'bodily practices' for my interviewees and analysed the 'subjugated knowledges' contained within these 'bodily practices' and thus within the 'life-worlds' of consensual 'SM'. This chapter demonstrates that representations of the label 'Sadomasochism' are not fixed but flexible, thus allowing for attachments with diverse signifiers. "However, temporary meanings may emerge, both contingent and partial. Sadomasochism inhabits meaning by means of incomplete and historically specific attachments with other signifiers, for example violence, martyrdom, suffering, which in turn form attachments with each other, and with other signifiers. This conceptualization of sadomasochism accords with what Derrida calls the 'dissemination' of the text" (Valier 1994: 1).

In this part of the book some of the recurring elements of the social construction of 'Sadomasochism' that are deployed by means of representations in the media, are examined and their impact on some of the subjects of the research project are pointed out. Public representations of 'Sadomasochism' are contradicted by the 'lived experiences' and 'subjugated knowledges' of practitioners of consensual 'SM' as presented in Chapter 3, especially since both spheres are dealing with different relationships of power. As public representations of consensual 'SM' often operate as signifiers of conventional and thus unconsensual power relationships, the origins of these signifiers have to be located and contrasted with the 'life-worlds' of consensual 'SM' practitioners. This chapter further suggests that the social construction and category of 'Sadomasochism' in many ways serves to secure the reproduction of unequal power relationships within society. Unequal power relationships are inherently violent, yet such violence is generally assumed to be characteristic of and ascribed to consensual 'SM'. Thus, the following sections discuss prevalent understandings and operations of power within society and examine the unconsensual 'conditions of domination' implicit in socio-political and cultural structures as opposed to the negotiated limits and the fluidity of power within consensual 'SM' 'bodily practices'. The

latter sections of this chapter illustrate instances of modern institutionalized and thus legitimized pain-distribution and their effects in the socio-
political realm as well as on the human beings involved, while contrasting
these with the distribution and meaning of 'pain' within the context of
consensual 'SM'.

4.1   Public representations of 'Sadomasochism' versus realities of consensual 'SM'-'bodily practice'

As has already been illustrated in Chapter 2 the contemporary exploitation
of 'sexuality' as commodity has led to an apparent public tolerance towards
these 'bodily practices'. Yet this tolerance turns out to be superficial, as old
signifiers and stereotypes of 'SM' are still evoked within public discourse
and considered to be 'truths' while an authentic, contextual understanding is not provided. Most information on the practice of consensual 'SM'
still serves to mystify this form of human interaction and thus prevents
authentic understanding (see also Barker in Langdridge and Barker 2007
and Beckmann 2001).

   One of the most commonly used representations and signifiers of 'SM',
'flagellation', is the focus of Anthony's 'Thy Rod and Staff' (1995). Anthony
points out that in contemporary Western cultures the term serves as a
representation "... the impulses for which it stands are generally held to be
embarrassing, incomprehensible, ludicrous, distasteful, bizarre, lunatic,
criminal or irredeemably wicked" (Anthony 1995: 15). Thus, even one single technique under the wide-ranging possibilities of 'S/M' already serves as
a negative signifier.

   The 'sexually perverse' connotations of the term 'flagellation' have,
according to Anthony, a priori prevented a fruitful discussion on a lay level
which, in my opinion, holds true for consensual 'Sadomasochism' in general as well. As the traditional western relationship between sex and shame
became expressed in the construction of 'sexual perversion': "..., the degree
of reticence is therefore directly related to the 'normality' of the sexual
activity in question" (Anthony 1995: 16).

   The general direction of the social construction as well as of stereotypes
of 'Sadomasochism' are represented in the 'Daily Mail's' headline during
the Spanner-appeal: "Torture gang take Britain to Court" (19.10.96: 16) to
announce that the three convicted consensual 'SM'ers would take their case
in front of the European Court of Human Rights. The association of consensual 'SM' with the act of torture makes the complete misunderstanding
of these 'bodily practices' apparent, even though the report continues in
stating that: "All consented" (ibid.). The use of the term 'torture', which
distinctively excludes any notion of negotiated consent is still considered
to be appropriate in describing consensual 'SM' practices. Thus, representations and signifiers of violence are still associated with and attached to

these consensual 'bodily practices'. Another term within this discursive context is highly value-laden though less obvious. In choosing the word 'gang' the immediate association produced in the readership will be that of a 'criminal' group or association with some degree of organization. This and similar portrayals of consensual 'SM' in the press contribute in a crucial way to the reinforcement of prejudices and fear among members of main stream society.

Another illustration of the operation of the social censure and an additional part of the 'discourses of sexuality' can be found in *The Times* (20.2.1997: 12). In an article on the Strasbourg judgement on the 'Spanner'-case *The Times* reports that the videos the police acquired would show: "... them engaging with 44 other men in violent sexual acts involving whips, sandpaper and fish-hooks." Later on in this article the word 'abuse' gets used several times to indicate the nature of these consenting acts: "The sex acts involved genital abuse with hot wax, sandpaper, fish-hooks and needles, and ritualistic beatings with spiked belts, stinging nettles and a cat-o'-nine-tails. Those receiving the abuse used a codeword if they wanted the 'punishment' to stop" (*The Times*, 20.2.97: 12). While the code word is mentioned in this representation, the use of the term 'abuse' operates in ascribing violence onto consensual 'SM' practice. Further, although the association of consensual 'SM' with abuse is in itself very misleading, it additionally provokes associations of consensual 'SM' with the widely covered topic of child abuse. It is particularly striking and contributes to the continuing mystification of 'realities of consensual "SM"' that, although the existence and actual use of the 'codeword', which is one of the most crucial and distinct structural elements of consensual 'SM'-'body practice', appears to be worth mentioning, its meaning and function within this context is not elaborated on.

The Times commented on the Lords' judgement in the 'Spanner case' that the defendants "... did all sorts of painful things to each other from which it is hard to imagine that pleasure could be derived" (*The Times* 12.3.93: 21). As elaborated at length in Chapter 2 conventional modernist concepts of 'pain' and 'pleasure' do not capture the 'lived experience' of a potential continuum, a fluidity, of pleasurable and painful sensations nor 'their' culturally variable specifications and expressions or the diversity of sensations documented within accounts of the Scene (see Chapters 3 and 6). The unreflected use of these 'normalizing' terms as categories of 'truth' within these comments reveal the lasting legacy and next to complete collective internalization of Bentham's 'pleasure/pain'-principle which is not only one of the fundamental elements of utilitarian thought and the basis of Hobbes' notion of the 'social contract' but also one of the central premises for the social construction and public representations of 'Sadomasochism'.

The commodification of 'SM' (Beckmann 2001) implies that decontextualized elements of consensual 'SM' have become part of the 'subterranean values' of many consumerist societies, however: "Mainstream media depictions and everyday perceptions of 'SM' are largely negative, perpetuating psychiatric and legal perspectives of [consensual] SM practices as pathological and on a 'slippery slope' towards criminal behaviour (...)" (Barker in Langdridge and Barker 2007: 261).

4.1.1   The impact of the social censure of 'Sadomasochism' on individual perceptions

The function of a social censure (Sumner 1990: 26) is not explanation, but denunciation, and signification, with the aim of regulation something gets marked as in need of intervention. Social censures are "...negative categories of moral ideology..." (Sumner 1990: 21). As 'Sadomasochism' is thus a negative category of moral ideology, the Brown vs. Regina case was biased from the onset as such categories and the connected stereotypes formed the basis of the legal decision making process which found a summarizing expression in Lord Templeman's comment in his ruling of the 'Spanner'-case that this "...cruelty was uncivilised" (*Times Law Reports* 12.3.93: 42). Examples of the impact of the social construction of 'Sadomasochism' on individuals can be found within the narratives of practitioners of these 'bodily practices'. Without a directive question from my side, several interviewees told me about the ideas they had about consensual 'SM' before they engaged in this 'bodily practice'. The stereotypical ideas constructed around 'Sadomasochism' resulted in fear on the part of these individuals.

Diabolo lived in the closet until consensual 'SM' became demystified through experience: "The fear that SM is violence and that it's oppressive and all these simple suppositions. Which haunted me for twenty-five years and kept me away" (Interview-file D.: 3).

Although Diabolo now terms the representations of consensual 'SM' within the public sphere 'simple suppositions', it becomes very clear how much these potentially influence the individual's attitude and behaviour, in this case over a period of more than two decades.

Even though he could be considered a member of a younger generation, Anthony shared the same feelings about consensual 'SM': "I think to me, I think over the last four or five years I've flirted with S/M. I've always been scared to get into SM, I thought it's about pain, abuse and violence. I guess over the last year I've embraced it properly" (Interview-file 3: 1).

After the initial internalization of negative meanings that are attached to consensual 'SM', the actual experience of these 'bodily practices' allowed these practitioners to deconstruct existing stereotypes and discover similar 'subterranean values' (Matza and Sykes 1961) within mainstream culture.

"(.), there's no such thing like s/m-sex because SM is so personal. Whereas in this culture it's portrayed like: SM is about leather, it's about rubber...I think what is interesting is that most people practice SM-sex without realizing it's SM-sex" (Interview-file 3: 2).

As in recent times there occurred a 'mainstreaming' of 'sadomasochist' representations in the media as well as of BDSM behaviour forms (Saner 2008) one might assume and hope that these negative feelings of shame should vanish. The 'sexualization' and 'pornofication' of society led to a shift in public attitude which is represented by the fact that not the 'bodily practices' themselves but assumptions about the scenario and characters played were the focus of the media's attention in the media spectacle surrounding Mr. Mosley (e.g. Cheston: 'Dominatrix told to video Mosley giving "Sieg heil"' in *Evening Standard* 09.07.08) it appears important to revisit the legal legacy of the Spanner case and engage in 'politics'. "To show law in its nonrelation to life and life in its nonrelation to law means to open a space between them for human action, which once claimed for itself the name of 'politics'" (Agamben 2005: 88).

4.1.2   Understandings and relationships of power in society

In order to maintain the operations of stereotypes of 'Sadomasochism' as well as the disciplinary functions of the sexological and psychiatric category of the 'sadomasochist', a certain structuring and understanding of power must be assumed and, in large degrees, present in the public sphere.

> In the classical era power was transparent, epitomised by the command-power of the king, while in modern society power has become diffused and its location becomes almost mysterious. This shift is epitomised in the visibility of political power and the often veiled reality of economic power. (Hunt and Wickham 1994: 45)

Although this shift of power occurred a majority of people still envision and understand power as being located in certain individuals that symbolically represent power (e.g. politicians, 'royalties', doctors etc.) and/or they refer to law as the exercise of power which has a long tradition in the Western world: "In Western societies since the Middle Ages, the exercise of power has always been formulated in terms of the law" (Foucault 1990: 87). Therefore the language, representations and the principle that law has to be the very form of power, has deeply shaped our understanding of power and its exercise.

As several crucial elements of feudalism still dominate a majority of human beings lives within Western (post-) industrial societies, it does not seem surprising that power is not understood in its diffusion and complexity. To illustrate this point Anthony provides an example for the continuing presence of feudalist elements that can be found operating within the educational sector:

> School is a classic hierarchy: 'it compels attendance and obedience, and attempts to compel loyalty; it exerts discipline by means of reward and

punishment; it frequently allows-or, more often, compels-those within its walls to wear special clothing proclaiming their status; and it arranges its ranks and the transmission of power in the classic feudal pyramid (principal, deputies, senior staff, staff, senior pupils, junior pupils). All this is held somehow to be effective training for the democratic way of life, but in fact impresses the opposite social principle-hierarchy-on the youthful mind. (Anthony 1995: 132)

The triumph of the economic imperative that lead to an improved school system also (re-) produced the traditional relationships of the classical era. Within the Western world human beings 'bodies' are thus socio-culturally positioned and inscribed with hierarchical, unequal power relationships that are often represented and experienced as static.

In contrast to these ultimately deterministic understandings of power, Foucault conceptualized power never as a substance, as the property of persons or of institutions but a fluid relation that was immanent to social relations. "I am not positing a substance of resistance versus a substance of power. I am just saying: as soon as there is a power relation, there is a possibility of resistance" (Foucault in Kritzman 1990: 123). It is this immanence that makes it very difficult to identify and confront power in conventional society. Complex interacting and most of the time invisible relations of power that are unevenly concentrated through selective distribution and institutional stabilization are often not recognized as potentially changeable as their socio-cultural relativity and thus their utter constructedness is not reflected and acted upon. The resulting and, to a big degree, unreflected upon, collectively maintained, 'concentrations of power' establish 'conditions of domination' that impact on the relationships people have to themselves and others. These 'concentrations of power', together with their diverse socio-political and cultural mystifications and resulting informal and formal expressions are often perceived as given and are therefore in danger of remaining static. The resulting state of inequality in society affects the quality of social relations between people as in "...more equal societies, people are much more likely to trust each other, measures of social capital and social cohesion show that community life is stronger, and homicide rates and levels of violence are consistently lower" (Wilkinson 2005: 33). Within contemporary UK society violence is very much evident (state violence as well as conventional forms of violence through gun crimes and rapes etc.) and this does not mean that people living in this country are essentially more violence-prone but: "When there is large-scale or widespread violence in a society, either cultural characteristics, societal conditions or, most likely, a combination of the two are exerting influence" (Staub 2003: 289). In what is to follow a selection of socio-political and cultural 'conditions of domination' are discussed in relationship to Chancer's (1994) notion of a 'sadomasochistic dynamic' inherent to the social world.

4.1.3   Exploring 'conditions of domination' within society

Rigid power positions and understandings of power imply and effect an inflexibility of dynamics within the relationships that develop between individuals as well as institutions which most of the time are not contextualized and reflected upon. In her book 'Sadomasochism In Everyday Life', Lynn C. Chancer (1994) thus pointed out that there is a 'sadomasochistic dynamic' endemic in the relations between 'self' and 'other' within society. The social world is thus pre-structured in terms of unequal power relationships. This dynamic consists of symbiotic relationships and mutual dependencies that appear in forms such as sexism, racism, homophobia etc. Consensual 'SM' 'bodily practices' mock and mimic this societal dynamic which represents in phenomenological terminology 'objective society' as 'sedimented intersubjectivity' (Merleau-Ponty 1968).

Though always only provisional, the event structures that became sedimented, present 'lived bodies' with quite a limiting framework for inter-relational experiences: "We are living in a society sadomasochistic in that it bombards us with experiences of domination and subordination far more regularly than it exposes us to sensations and inklings of freedom and reciprocity" (Chancer 1994: 2).

What follows is an exploration of various legitimized 'conditions of domination' that are operating within conventional, so-called 'normal' and 'civilized society' that are characterized by inequality and thus by inherent violence. Even with regard to the negotiation of intimacy, societal concepts and institutions provide us with blueprints for the production and reinforcement of inequality.

This section will explore the underlying models of power of the notion of 'romantic love' in comparison to concepts of consensual 'SM'.

Even though the notion of 'romantic love' and 'SM' appear as opposites, there are striking parallels. In 'Love as Passion' Luhmann (1986) explored the codification of intimacy and analysed love's mystifications that were treated as refinements within the codification of 'romantic love'. "The various paradoxes (conquering self-subjugation, desired suffering, vision in blindness, a preference for illness, for imprisonment, and sweet martyrdom) converge in what the code proposes is central to love, namely: *immoderateness, excessiveness.* Regardless of the great importance attached to moderate behaviour, in the case of love this counts as a decisive error. Excessiveness itself becomes the measure of all behaviour" (Luhmann 1986: 67). In contrast to this societal concept, practitioners of consensual 'SM' are suspicious of the consequences of submitting to the ideal of 'romantic love'. Jane remembers her experiences with 'romantic love' before she engaged in consensual 'SM': "When I look back and I see people, you know, being in love with being in love and they go from one trauma to another trauma to the next emotional crisis with people they are in love with. I just don't think that's fun either. And I've been able to have lots of fun-relationships with no heaviness" (Interview-file C.: 5).

One of the most crucial ideological tools that 'educates' human beings for their 'gendered' experiences of sex within the socio-political framework of patriarchal heterosexuality is the notion of 'romantic love'. The difference between this notion within the sedimented socio-political setting of 'conditions of domination' as opposed to negotiated and collectively consented 'scenes' with individually set limits (based on communication and contextual reflection), as is the case in consensual 'SM', is striking. Within the setting of consensual 'SM' there is the profound and definite obligation to power equality based on negotiations and consent which facilitate the growth of feelings and experiences of intersubjectivity between 'lived bodies'. This is not the case in mainstream predominantly heteronormative representations of 'sexuality': "With male (hetero) sexuality continuing to be constructed as *visual* (e.g. Moghaddam and Braun 2004), with desire based on the aesthetic, such accounts reinforce a traditional model of male sexuality, and female sexuality alongside it" (Braun 2005: 413). This patriarchal blueprint for mainstream porn continues to make vast amounts of money and has become part of the mainstream: "...the porn industry outweights the other leading elements of popular cultural entertainment such as music, film and sports: a situation which has caused Linda Williams (2004), a leading authority on porn studies, to argue that the long-standing cultural status of pornography as obscene (*off*-scene) has finally passed into history, with the genre now very much *on*-scene" (Hardy 2008: 60).

This trend might have, apart from eventual boredom, potentially quite wide ranging consequences as according to social learning theorists the consumption of porn and porn-like advertisements, music videos etc. could be interpreted as constituting ways of learning behaviour (Malamuth 1985 cited in Russell 1998). In contrast to this potentially problematic broader socialization and enculturation, the dynamics of consensual 'SM' are based on consent reached through explicit communication and not on socially constructed obligations and expectations. In this context it is further important to recall the 'subjugated knowledge' about the 'real' power relationship between consensual 'SM' partners as discussed in Chapter 3. Here the 'top' (who is superficially 'in power') always is limited by the will of the 'bottom' (the superficially 'powerless' one). In contrast to conventional societal power arrangements, in consensual 'SM', the limits of the 'Other' are ultimately *always* the limits of the one in power. Thus, the one lacking power, the 'bottom' is never helpless as the interdependence of the participants in this power exchange game is clear to everyone. This stands in deep contrast to what Chancer (1994) had termed the inherent 'sadomasochistic dynamic' of Western patriarchal capitalist societies that continue to enforce a non-consensual 'sadomasochistic' dynamic in relationships. Radner (2008) suggests that 'sexuality' is compulsory in the present times because of 'its' intertwining with consumerism which reinvests into patriarchal and capitalist relationships: "For a woman to be desirable (and thus to identify herself as 'woman') she must be adept at manipulating and presenting herself according to the strict codes of consumer culture. As recent television shows such as *The L Word* (Shown on Showtime since 2001) demonstrate, the lesbian subject is not exempt" (Radner 2008: 98).

The works of Rich (1980) and Foucault (1990) and Binnie (2008) emphasized the importance of critically exploring the interconnections between 'sexuality (ies)' and wider socio-political and economic processes, however, only a few authors (Badgett 2001; Gluckman and Reed 1997; Hennessy 2000) explored these interrelationships.

While the author of this work identifies certainly as a 'pro-sex' feminist critical social scientist, it is important in this context to point to the fact that within the UK: "The Department for Culture, Media and Sport does not differentiate between lap-dancing venues and other forms of entertainment, despite evidential links between the proliferation of adult venues and the sex industry (Bindel 2004). The DCMS's stance appears to welcome the sexualization of women as an acceptable form of commerce" (Eden in Lilith Report 2007: 10). This heteronormative 'normalization' and socio-legal reinforcement of the 'sexual' commodification of women generates existentially alienating relationships as the report found evidence that the current licensing policy helps to foster the illusion that all women are sexually available.

This needs to be understood contextually as in the UK a rape is reported every 34 minutes (while some will never be reported or recorded as such) and as, according to the aforementioned report 26 per cent of people believe that an 'inappropriately' dressed woman is 'asking for it' (Lilith Report 2007). The report explored the impact of lap-dancing in Camden Town, north London and found that after the opening of four large lap-dancing clubs in the area, incidents of rape in Camden rose by 50 per cent, while sexual assault rose by 57 per cent compared to three years prior to the arrival of these establishments. The 'normalized' commercialization of 'sexual bodies' does appear to generate harms in terms of non-consensual 'sexual' encounters and does not facilitate 'sexual' openness, communication and/or empathy.

While representations and simulations of 'sexiness' are currently seen as desirable and working in the 'sex' industry is constructed as 'normal' and even empowering (e.g. Levy 2005), the links to human trafficking and the clear disempowerment and exploitation through economical pressures have to be acknowledged and problematized as frequently: "The club management take on more women than are needed in a night so it really becomes dog eat dog" (Bell 2008: 18). This problematic capitalist exploitation obviously leads to non-consensual delivery of 'sexual' services.

The total commodification of 'sex' within capitalist-consumer societies does not only have 'sexual' abuse as a potential consequence but further may have dramatic economical and emotional implications as: "Statistics show that addiction to the porn and sex industries is the third biggest cause of debt in the UK, while sex and relationship therapists are seeing an increase in the number of men suffering from sex addiction" (Bell 2008: 18).

In this context it is crucial to refer to Chancer (1994) as to her one of the main origins of an unconsensual 'sadomasochistic' social structure is the institutionalization of patriarchy (with its destructive and unequal relationship concepts of romantic love and marriage). This extends itself into male domination within institutions of coercive power (e.g. military, technology, sciences) that still persists although there have been transformations of this 'gender' segregation on a superficial level. "In the case of patriarchy, a tendency toward sadistic exercising of power and masochistic experiencing of powerlessness has been bifurcated along the lines of gender, with each side symbiotically requiring services only the other can provide" (Chancer 1994: 33). However, this socially constructed symbiosis does not have a big potential for generating a 'happy ending' in eternal bliss. When Bell asked Elena a former lap-dancer if she thought that lap-dancing is damaging to men too, she replied: "Stag do's, in particular, made me think there must be a lot of crossed wires about it", she says. "I think men are fed just as much bullshit about their sexual identity as women are...I don't think that it makes anybody happier" (Bell 2008: 18).

It would be easy to be tempted to believe that the economic imperative of 'sexual license' only applies within the heteronormative sphere, however, while it is important to celebrate socio-legal successes with regards to same-sex 'sexualities' within the UK, Stychin's (2003) work highlights the reproduction of neoliberal agendas with regards to the revision to UK immigration policy in the context of same-sex relationships: "...by making distinctions between economically valued sexual citizens and those who are excluded by their inability to pay" (Binnie 2008: 102).

It appears thus that despite much needed socio-legal changes with regards to public acknowledgements of people's relationships, heteronormative, unequal patriarchal representations of 'sexuality' and accompanying expectations of 'role' behaviour still prevail within a framework of a dominant capitalist-materialist hierarchical 'order of things'.

"So is that the way things will be from now on? Crude economic logic would suggest that as long as there is a correlation between sex and revenue, the volume of explicit material will increase. Moreover, to maximize the financial return from sex, it is necessary to shock, and that means perpetually pushing back the boundaries" (Behr 2008: 7). The market is huge even if one only considers the internet level: "The number of X-rated sites on the net has been put at anything up to 7 million, and £70 million a year, it has been suggested, would be a conservative guess at the annual revenue generated by internet porn. Beyond a certain point, these figures begin to feel meaningless; £70m, £100m – it scarcely seems to matter. And as any statistic is likely to be outdated before it has been published, the effect of these numbers is not so much to inform as simply to awe. If they are half way close to the truth, our relationship with porn begins to seep into the banal. Pornography is treated more like fast food than sex; a casual everyday snack" (Aitkenhead 2003: 1).

Unless labelled as an addiction the 'normalized' consumption of com-modified 'sex' is not ever explored though: "... the emotional consequences of casual porn use, or the effects of its cultural ubiquity, are completely ignored. Whether porn might be harmful to a non-addict is never even examined. In this straightforward formula, if you can hold down a job, pay the bills and avoid grossing your wife out, where's the problem?" (Aitkenhead 2003: 1).

Aitkenhead refers to Donnerstein's research involving so-called 'normal' men who stated: "Even porn which wasn't violent made the men twice as likely to say they felt aggressive towards women. This is not to say that porn turns men into rapists; it doesn't need to, for it trespasses on the mind more subtly. The evidence proves that porn invites its audience to view women differently – as inferiors, as objects, only good for sex. This is the problem with ['heterosexual' mainstream] pornography; it alters the way men look at women. There is no 'at risk' profile because it affects everyone – and it even alters the way women look at themselves. Few women have truthfully never wondered, when they are in bed, whether a part of them might be impersonating the women they see in porn, who are impersonating women enjoying sex" (Aitkenhead 2003: 1).

Levy (2005) in the US context found much evidence of vaginoplasty oper-ations etc. to have become 'fashionable' within the last ten years as well as a mainstreaming of Brazilian wax 'beauty care' regimes which appear to con-firm that to many women porn-consumption per se does not have to imply 'liberation' of some inherent 'sexuality' or an increased 'female' confidence in 'sex' but rather perpetuated already internalized feelings of 'female' phys-ical inadequacy and 'female' competition. Naomi Wolf (2003) illustrates this increased pressure on 'females': "Well, I am 40, and mine is the last female generation to experience that sense of sexual confidence and secur-ity in what we had to offer. Our younger sisters had to compete with video porn in the eighties and nineties, when intercourse was not hot enough. Now you have to offer—or flirtatiously suggest—the lesbian scene, the ejac-ulate-in-the-face scene. Being naked is not enough; you have to be buff, be tan with no tan lines, have the surgically hoisted breasts and the Brazilian bikini wax—just like porn stars. (In my gym, the 40-year-old women have adult pubic hair; the twentysomethings have all been trimmed and styled.) Pornography is addictive; the baseline gets ratcheted up. By the new millennium, a vagina—which, by the way, used to have a pretty high 'exchange value', as Marxist economists would say—wasn't enough; it barely registered on the thrill scale. All mainstream porn—and certainly the Internet—made routine use of all available female orifices" (Wolf in *NY Magazine* October 20: 2003: 1).

Apart from reflecting the aforementioned shift in 'sexual' mores, the web's 'Triple-A Engine' – access, affordability, and anonymity – is suggested to drive the online pornography industry (Cooper 1998). As it is 'males' who still predominantly consume internet porn, the 'male' audience is according to Wolf likely to be less 'turned on' to have real-life 'sex' because of overexposure to porn: "The onslaught of porn is responsible for deadening male libido in relation to real women, and leading men to see fewer and fewer women as 'porn-worthy'. Far from having to fend off porn-crazed young men, young women are worrying that as mere flesh and blood, they can scarcely get, let alone hold, their attention" (ibid). Wolf therefore suggests abstaining from porn but not due to moral concerns but as "greater supply of the stimulant equals diminished capacity" (ibid).

4.1.4   The social-psychological effects of 'conditions of domination'

The ideological presuppositions and social power structures that serve to stabilize conditions should not only be challenged and changed but also serve as a tool for the understanding of the potential consequences of an erotisation of power.

The social-psychological approach of Chancer (1994), suggests that unconsensual 'sadomasochistic' forms of social organization do parallel an unconsensual 'sadomasochistic' social psychology within society.

This holds true not only for patriarchy but also for the institution of capitalism which divides human beings into powerful/powerless agents "...., the relationship between worker and capitalist is also inclined in a highly symbiotic direction, creating a literally life-and-death situation:..." (ibid.: 34). The effects that the habitual experience of subordination have on the consciousness of a human being were already implicit in Marxist theory. Objective relationships of dependency become by means of (degrees of) individual internalization, subjective ones. In order to describe the struggle for the legitimacy of the individual 'self' within an unconsensual dependency situation that makes this legitimacy entirely conditional upon the approval of the other, Chancer (1994) coined the term 'conditional psychology'.

The notion of 'conditional psychology' is the exact opposite of the equal participation and consensuality in so-called 'sadomasochistic' practices. Chancer's notion of 'conditional psychology' has to my mind even more relevance within the context of consumer cultures as this 'anti-social' environment increases the degree to which human beings are symbiotically tied up to the 'gaze' and judgement of others, while at the same time the 'internal supervisor' also increases 'its' hold within the individual. In a world of next to complete commodification, where each individual appears to operate on a continuum from being commodified to commodifying, a 'sadistic position' within this non-consensual societal setting, has more appeal in relation to the rules of the market-place. The display of distance and unavailability appear to create a higher demand in others which clearly reflects the value of 'self' in the unconsensual conditions of domination in capitalist-consumer societies.

Capitalism, patriarchy and racism as forms of social organization therefore clearly stabilize and increase unconsensual hierarchical power relationships and symbiotic over-dependency to flourish within social relationships. This has wide-ranging consequences as the degree of inequality in society dramatically affects the quality of social relations between people.

4.1.5   The unconsensual 'Sadomasochism' of societal 'conditions of domination'

"Sexuality both generates wider social relations and is refracted through the prism of society. As such sexual feelings and activities express all the contradictions of power relations-of gender, class, and race" (Ross and Rapp in Snitow et al. 1983: 53). The 'social censure' (Sumner 1990) of 'Sadomasochism' is serving the purpose of veiling the all pervading societal unconsensual 'sadomasochistic dynamic' (Chancer 1994) of Western capitalist societies. This serves the needs of the ideologies of patriarchy and ethnocentrism as well as the overarching aims of capitalist-consumer cultures. Chancer (1994) lists four interrelated criteria for this unconsensual sadomasochistic dynamic, which is 'a very particular but common social relationship based on power and powerlessness, dominance and submission', that she detects as giving Western cultures a direction of orientation.

Chancer's first criterion is the existence of 'an excessive attachment exist [ing] for both parties' that is a symbiotic dependence, which might be physical but which is crucially psychic in character. With regards to the data collected within the London Scene (see Chapter 3) there does not seem to be an 'excessive attachment' of symbiotic dependence that characterizes the consensual 'players'. The accounts of the 'field' revealed that most of them do experience other forms of 'sexual' and/or 'bodily' practices and appear able to 'switch' both – their 'play'-partners as well as their assumed positions of power.

Chancer's second criterion is that an interaction following a sadomasochistic dynamic "... has a repetitive and ritualistic character in that the sadist is consistently drawn toward a position of control while the masochist is just as constantly in the persona of the more controlled" (Chancer 1994: 3). This repetitive structure does not allow for either of the interacting parties to "assume or unassume their respective roles by an arbitrary or simple exertion of will" (ibid.). As my research-data has shown this second criteria does not cover the consensual and negotiated interactions of 'SM' that my interviewees are/were practising, as their interrelationships are/were based on shared and negotiated pleasures and limits that might be interrupted and/or stopped by either party at any point in time.

Thirdly Chancer points out that this societal unconsensual sadomasochistic dynamic is regularized but that "...it is also a dialectical form of interaction, constantly changing and moving, in flux as the actions of the sadist bring about reactions on the part of the masochist and vice versa" (Chancer 1994: 4). The conventional representations of a static victim and victimizer-relationships that are implicit to the social construction of 'Sadomasochism', does not live up to the actual fluidity of social reality. The potential for transformations of power are never captured by representations of 'SM'.

Chancer's last criterion, which she finds is the most central of all the four and thus as determining the existence of an unconsensual sadomasochistic dynamic is "...whether individuals (or groups) positioned masochistically face severe consequences should they question, talk about, or challenge the power of those individuals (or groups) who are structurally more powerful" (Chancer 1994: 5).

Anthony, one of my informants illustrated the crucial difference between sadomasochistic power relationships within society and consensual 'SM', when he talked about his relationship with his 'slave'. As Anthony 'plays' the 'top' he arranges the 'set-up' of the 'scene' before his 'slave' arrives. His 'slave' knows that Anthony would never choose any 'scene' or sensation that he dislikes: "He knows I wouldn't but everything is discussed before we do anything anyway. There are certain things that he told me he doesn't like and I don't do that kind of stuff. Even though he's my slave by contract I respect him as a person-it sounds like a contradiction. I can say: 'Yes, he is my slave, yes, he is my bottom, but I still respect him as a person'" (Interview-file 3: 8). This perspective that decreases the power inherent to societal categories and roles is more humane, more 'enlightened' and 'civilized' than it's socially conditioned counterpart in a societal reality in which the status of power means everything and powerlessness implies the end of dignity. It is obvious that the societal reality of the operation of unfettered market forces causes widespread social harm but is not pathologized and/or criminalized: "...the neo-liberal economic paradigm is fundamentally harmful – it wrecks lives and creates harm on a wide scale – and these features are not some aberration, but integral and necessary aspects of this form of economic and political organisation" (Tombs and Hillyard 2004: 32).

Increasing areas of social life have been subjected to the discipline of market forces (Smart 2003) and as a consequence, the side- and long-term effects of socio-economic and politically reinforced inequality begin to reveal themselves: "Alongside economic insecurity a new set of social problems has emerged – widespread mental illness, systematic loneliness, growing numbers of psychologically damaged children, eating disorders, obesity, alcoholism and drug addiction" (Shah and Rutherford 2006: 28).

To Lara the conditions of inequality of power immanent in society represent non-consensual 'Sadomasochism' that stand in deep contrast to consensual 'SM': "What S/M people always say and with what I agree with is that abuse goes on whether you call it like that, non-consensual S/M goes on in society. But the difference is when you're negotiating a contract and you're saying: 'This is what I want to do with you'" (Interview-file L.: 13/14). In consensual 'SM', in contrast to the unconsensual 'sadomasochism' inherent to society, the occurrence of power abuse is far less likely, as even before any interaction takes place reflective negotiations are entered into that serve to ensure an equally pleasurable exchange. Consensual 'SM' therefore allows for a far more reflective and communicated dealing with power in relationships that does foster decision making based on informed consent.

In relation to the analysis of power relations Michel Foucault had pointed out during an interview in 1984 that: "...; one sometimes encounters what may be called situations or states of domination in which the power relations, instead of being mobile, allowing the various participants to adopt strategies modifying them, remain blocked, frozen" (in Lotringer 1996: 434). This concept of 'state of domination' which Foucault described here comes very close to Chancer's notion of 'condition' characterizing the societal non-consensual sadomasochistic dynamic that is part of 'normality' and not diagnosed as pathological. The analytical distinction that Chancer employed throughout her book between 'limits' and 'conditions' is crucial to keep in mind when contrasting societal 'sadomasochism' to the consensual 'bodily practices' of 'SM'. 'Limits' are not exercised for the sake of power alone but: "...rather, the goal may be to facilitate eventual transcendence of the hierarchical relationship as the less powerful party to it (...) progressively approaches a level of parity with the more powerful one" (Chancer 1994: 5). In contrast to 'limits', 'conditions' "...signify the punishing and enraged repercussions that will almost always ensue should the person(s) situated masochistically try to break from a symbiotic bond" (Chancer 1994: 6). In the very moment when 'conditions' come to exist, non-consensual sadomasochism will develop on the micro level within relationships and/or the macro level of a given society. As already explored in Chapter 3 the 'conditions' set by conventional society mentioned by Chancer, are, in the context of consensual 'SM' practice, replaced by negotiated and consensually agreed upon 'limits'. Thus consensual 'SM' 'body practice' does not even qualify to be a stabilizing factor for societal power relationships.

4.1.6   Concluding thoughts

The conditions of domination immanent to capitalist, patriarchal, ageist and abelist societies which foster unconsensual 'sadomasochistic dynamics' within social relationships have also confronted and affected several of my interviewees. This does not, however, imply an arrival at a deterministic stance due to a belief in a next to complete internalization of societal inequalities and practices of power. Within the concept of 'lived body' inscriptions of power as well as other 'signs' offered to individual perceptions "...are not separable from their living significance,..." (Bigwood in Welton 1998: 107) and thus are subject to change. In this context it is important to remember the account of one of my informants, Anthony, who experienced the impact of the societal power conditions of the social construction of 'race' as a black man, consensual power games are to be seen very different from the life under unconsensual 'conditions of domination'. "I do believe SM and black people creates problematics for lots of black people. But those people miss an argument. First of all: There is a consent, whereas slavery wasn't with consent" (Interview-file 3: 3).

Anthony expressed that he feels that the practice of consensual 'SM' has changed him in relation to concerns of power. "It does give you a different sense or a different perspective into the power and how power does get played out. Whereby several years ago I might overlook certain things, now I'm into saying: 'No.' I think S/M-sex has given me the chance to do that" (Interview-file 3: 5). It becomes obvious that 'playing' with power relations can be 'empowering' as it allows the players to understand the potential of both the dominant as well as the submissive power positions better. This awareness in turn will make apparent how reversible and interdependent these positions are. This new perspective of 'empowerment' is especially beneficial with respect to people who have been allocated submissive positions within non-consensual societal relationships of power (e.g. 'females', etc.) as it enables individuals and/or groups that are discursively socio-politically categorized as inferior to discover their potential for change.

These insights into the dynamics of power that can be acquired on an experimental level in the 'bodily practices' of consensual 'SM' come close to Michel Foucault's understanding of 'power as a dynamic situation'. This reading of power allows for a positive and constructive reading of power as opposed to the nihilism Foucault was often accused of. Power for Foucault: "...produces possibilities of action, of choice and, ultimately, it produces the conditions for the exercise of freedom (just as freedom constitutes a condition for the exercise of power). Power is therefore not opposed to freedom. And freedom, correspondingly, is not freedom *from* power – it is not a privileged zone outside power, unconstrained by power – but a potentiality internal to power, even an effect of power" (Halperin 1995: 17). That dynamic understanding of power is still rarely to be found in 'common sense' perceptions of power amongst members of so-called 'normal' society was illustrated by an interviewee who is professionally engaged with the Scene.

Dean got involved with the 'Spanner-campaign' as a lot of the 'all time' customers of the bondage-equipment retail business he works for started the campaign. In the course of his involvement for the campaign he had talked to many barristers and he remarked: "And it's like hitting your head against a brick-wall, the authorities, the state, whoever they are, those people, them, whoever they are, they can't get this simple fact that it's not an abusive partnership, it's the exact opposite, into their heads. You know the 'bottom' is always in control, the 'top' is not in control, the 'bottom' is in control. ... May be it's because they are such authority-freaks, they've got to be in charge. They can't understand anything other than that, to them if somebody is a 'top', then they must be in charge because that's the way they are. They can't understand anything other than that: 'total control'. But you can talk to these people until you're blue in the face, they don't, they will not understand ..." (Interview-file a: 12).

4.2   Modern institutionalized forms of pain-distribution, legitimized suffering and the production of 'truth'

One of the major signifiers of the social construction of 'Sadomasochism' is violence understood as the infliction of 'pain' onto another 'body'. The following elaborations aim to explore the meanings of suffering attached to the signifier violence. The legitimized distribution of 'pain' and thus the state authorized exertion of violence is revealed to be implicit in many societal relationships and institutions that thus constitute 'conditions of domination' (Foucault in Kritzman 1990) set up by the requirements of modern nation states as well as modernity in a more general sense. After contrasting the purposes and effects of (un) consensual but legitimized 'pain' distribution to the selectively criminalized forms of explorations of 'pain' within the context of consensual 'SM', the utilitarian calculus of pleasure and pain that underlies modern thought and practice even in contemporary so-called 'postmodern' times is problematized.

4.2.1   Pain as punishment and tool of 'normalization'

Anthony (1995) suggested that there exist a variety of interpretations of corporal punishment: "From early Victorian times through to our own day, physical chastisement has been perceived variously and often simultaneously ... as (1) a legitimate and desirable form of punishment for children, criminals, soldiers, sailors and other animals; (2) an act of religious or mystical devotion; (3) a sexual perversion; (4) a type of physio-therapy; (5) a form of insanity; (6) a commercial activity; with mutual exclusivity by no means taken for granted" (Anthony 1995: 6).

As already explored in Chapter 2, the definition of 'suffering', where it begins and where it ends and, most crucially, under which circumstances human suffering is legitimized, has socio-political and cultural determinants, apart from individual specifities. Part of the normative cultural framework of mainstream Western capitalist-consumer society determines if suffering is constructed and thus perceived as legitimized. Within a modern utilitarian Western socio-political context suffering is considered to be meaningful and legitimate under war-, sport-, health-, 'beauty', 'age' defying, fitness-maximizing, population-regulating etc. circumstances. Suffering can thus be understood to be part of the operations of 'biopower', of the regulation of society and the subjugation of the 'bodies' of its members.

Larger imperatives legitimize suffering in social situations as for example the suffering of the newly born baby is implicit to the medical practice of the 'natal spank' but would never be considered as the infliction of bodily harm or even assault. Another example to refer to in this context is "...the birth of an intersex child [that] is typically treated by the medical establishment as a 'psychosocial emergency', requiring decisions to be made as soon as possible about how the child should be surgically assigned..." (Grabham 2007: 30). The 'normalization' of 'atypical' genitals and associated suffering is legitimated via medicalizing and pathologizing discursive practices that illustrate starkly the 'bodily effects of culture' that are so well explored by Fausto-Sterling (2005) in terms of inscriptions of 'sexual' differences onto 'bodies'.

Traditional modes of childrearing and school-sanctions also often implied the use of pain and, in effect, suffering on the side of the punished and/or disciplined individual in order to cause changes of behaviour and character.

Within the context of my empirical work the issue of societal power relationships and practices that create double-bind situations came up and the possible impact of these was explored by one of my interviewees called Pat: "Well, I think there's a lot to be said. ... And why, may be, is it that so many of us, in this generation, are into S/M? May be it's because a lot of us had parents that were pretending to bring us up in a good way but they were still doing the same kind of abuse on us like parents before. You know, parents a hundred years ago would routinely beat their children and it was thought of as a good thing that they were doing but now people are being hypocritical and beat their children in secret. ...lying about it. And so there is all this double-standard going on: 'Oh, no. It's wrong to beat your children.' And yet they beat their children" (Interview-file 1: 33). In other words, the goal of 'normalization' legitimizes individual and social suffering although it continues to generate alienation in human beings social and intimate relationships.

Even though Anthony remarks that officially sanctioned corporal punishment is very much less a feature within the context of Western societies, he points out that: "...corporal punishment lingers embarrassingly on, usually on individual or family bases, in most countries of the Western club-excepting those, like Sweden, where it has become altogether illegal to smack a child" (Anthony 1995: 29). The 'parental right to smack' children remains confirmed by the British government of 'New Labour' thus re-inscribing the institutionalized hierarchical power relationships between parents and their children. Within the UK the numbers of deliberate harms done to youngsters (NHS figures show there are now 22,000 hospital cases a year according to *The Observer* (20.04.2008)) show the impact of such problematic discourses and legislation in favour of non-consensual 'SM' between socio-politically ascribed powerful 'adults' and powerless 'children'.

"A large part of social suffering stems from the poverty of people's relationship to the educational system, which not only shapes social identities but also the image they have of their destiny (which undoubtedly helps to explain what is called the passivity of the dominated...)" (Bourdieu 1998: 43).

Since the late 1970s, education's role has been increasingly defined in terms of its relevance to the needs of commerce and industry – with a correspondingly reduced emphasis on its role for generating a more just, caring and democratic set of social relations than the unjust status quo (Beckmann and Cooper 2004/2005).

However, as education is obviously used as a governmental tool of 'normalization' it is unsurprising that a report submitted to the Commons Education Select Committee in June 2007 by the General Teaching Council called for all national exams for under-16-year-olds to be banned because of the suffering they constituted:

...the stress caused by over-testing is poisoning attitudes towards education.... [E]xams are failing to improve standards, leaving pupils demotivated and stressed and encouraging bored teenagers to drop out of school.... [T]eachers are being forced to 'drill' pupils to pass tests instead of giving a broad education.... Psychologists have reported going into schools at unprecedented rates to tackle exam stress, with children as young as six suffering from anxiety. (Asthana 2007: 1)

4.2.2 Turning utilitarian belief systems around through 'lived experience': How non-consensually distributed 'pain' can become 'pleasure'

Apart from the already mentioned forms of apparently legitimized induced suffering, pain also plays an important role in the training of the 'bodies' of soldiers for war. In Theweleit's (1978) psychoanalytic exploration of fascism the interrelatedness of 'body' and 'self', thus the 'lived body', becomes the focus as the production of a fascistic masculinity is based on cadet-training in which deprivations, beatings and strenuous exercises (pain as discipline) create 'men of steel'. "... the body swallows attack after attack until it becomes addicted" (Theweleit 1978: 147). In his account flogging within the hierarchical conditions of the cadet-training changes "... the desire for bodily warmth into a perception of the heat of bodily pain; the desire for contact into a perception of the whiplash" (ibid.). He then points out to the connection between bodily pain and the development of a 'new' self: "All forms of beating are, as we have seen, intimately familiar to the soldier male. Painful encroachments by external agencies on his bodily periphery-onslaughts on his musculature-are integral to the process whereby the not-yet-fully-born acquires something approaching the psychic agency of the ego, a 'stable' body-ego. It is tempting, then, to assume the beatings he himself administers to be in some way connected to the production of his own ego" (Theweleit 1978: 289).

Apart from re-inscribing the unconsensual power relationships, there are potentially other, unintended and 'bio-politically' undesired consequences resulting from unconsensual 'body usages' of domination (Frank).

> How differently would one deal with youth, if one could more clearly see the remote effects of the usual mode of treatment, which is employed always without discrimination, frequently without discretion! ... Who would believe that this childish punishment, afflicted upon me when only eight years old by a woman of thirty, disposed of my tastes, my desires, my passions, and my own self for the remainder of my life, and that in a manner exactly contrary to that which should have been the natural result? ... To lie at the feet of an imperious mistress, to obey her commands, to ask her forgiveness-this was for me a sweet enjoyment ... (Rousseau 1782: 10–13)

This part of Rousseau's 'Confessions' is one of the earliest connections made between the societal unconsensual use of 'corporal punishment' and 'sexuality' which was then perceived and censured as being essentially 'unnatural'. As early as 1886 Krafft-Ebing stated against corporal punishment that the beating of boys on the buttocks can at times generate the first arousals of the 'sex urge'.

Scott (1938) wrote a book on the topic of corporal punishment of children that was aimed and even restricted to a selected readership of members of the medical and legal professions, scientists, anthropologists, psychologists, sociologists, criminologists and social workers. With his work Scott tried to make a case against the use of corporal punishment with the main argument that it would lead to an 'unhealthy sexual excitation' in the so treated child. He stated that: "In children and adolescents there is a risk of *any form* of castigation on the buttocks or anal region stirring up sexual activity" (Scott 1938: 210). Although Scott did of course implicitly conform to the norms of a 'natural sexuality', thus labelling other experiences as 'perverse', he also clearly pointed to the frequency and thus 'normality' of these phenomena: "Every sexologist knows that the number of cases of individuals who have experienced sexual feelings while being whipped is a considerable one, and in nearly every instance where the anomaly has persisted in adult life the victim is able to trace the beginning of his perverse interest in flagellation to a flogging received at school or elsewhere" (Scott 1938: xx).

In many interviews that I conducted within the Scene, although not in all of them, the experience of 'pain as discipline' was mentioned. Several interviewees had been subjected to painful sensations that aimed at 'disciplining' them, be it at home or at school. George, who was never hit at home, remembers this practice of disciplinary action from his schooldays: "... at school I found the idea of being beaten rather terrifying because at the time, where I lived in Scotland, not now, but ... they did use the belt on children in primary school. ... Yes. A little six year old making faces or something" (Interview-file G.: 7/8). Although the use of corporal punishment within legitimized contexts is positively sanctioned and socio-politically re-enforced, its potential 'sexualizing' effects on the 'lived bodies' of individuals are 'rewarded' with social censures like 'perversity'.

In contrast to this paradox immanent to society, within the Scene of consensual 'SM', the corporal punishment of children is not an accepted form of behaviour. Anthony quotes the editor of 'Skin Two' ('SM'/Fetish magazine) Tim Woodward, as his views on this issue represent the standard attitude within the Scene: "Corporal punishment is tremendous fun for adults, but out of the question for children. Everybody should spank their partner and cuddle up afterwards. But hitting children? No thank you" (Woodward in Anthony 1995: 44). Flagellation and other forms of corporal punishment are only nominally punishments within the 'scene'. Within the context of consensual 'SM' they serve to allow for catharsis and/or they serve as an aphrodisiac.

"Within the nation-state, the state, through its institutions, monopolizes both legislation and violence" (Stratton 1996: 10). The notion of 'legitimate force' points to the inherent yet usually hidden violence of the institution of law and reveals a fundamental paradox: "... while law purports to substitute itself for violence – in the form of a civilised, and civilizing, alternative – it retains, and depends on, an immanent violence of its own" (Weait in Langdridge and Barker 2007: 63). There is thus effectively a stately monopoly on unconsensual pain-distribution which is currently illustrated by for example, the widespread use of so-called 'anti-social' behaviour orders that: "... are primarily being used against the mentally ill, the elderly, the very young, drug and alcohol addicts, sex workers and beggars ... vulnerable people with complex problems. The order does nothing for such problems. ... It is a national scandal that as a result of Asbos 10 young people a week are being jailed, and that beggars and prostitutes are being imprisoned even though begging and prostitution are non-imprisonable offences" (Foot 2005: 20).

This stately monopoly on unconsensual pain-distribution is, amongst other examples, currently further illustrated in terms of techniques of neutralization or "juridical othering" (Jamieson and McEvoy 2005), global military interventions (Chomsky 2005), the use of indefinite detention in facilities such as Guantanamo Bay and Abu Ghraib (Hersh 2005) and the employment of torture (Hitchens 2008) as seemingly 'acceptable' methods in the execution of war in the quest to 'bring' 'civilization' to 'othered' countries as well as to 'enemies within'. To Agamben (2005) it is the very concepts of 'law' and 'state' themselves that are at stake in the present context of a 'state of exception':

"Indeed, the state of exception has today reached its maximum worldwide deployment. The normative aspect of law can thus be obliterated and contradicted with impunity by a governmental violence that – while ignoring international law externally and producing a permanent state of exception internally – nevertheless still claims to be applying the law" (Agamben 2005: 87).

4.2.3   The hidden pains of stately administered punishment

Referring to Derrida's philosophical works, Turner (2008) summed up that: "...in so far as the law is a command of the state and in so far as the state has a monopoly of force in a given territory, then the legitimacy of the law requires that the origins of law have to be disguised. Law pretends to have no history and no context; it is a form of pure authority. If law has its historical origins in state violence, how can law be an ordering of violence without itself being an instance of arbitrary violence?" (Turner 2008: 2)

The modern period brought about changes in the representations of power, especially concerning its relationship to juridical practices. Displays of power were replaced by the 'panoptic schema' (Foucault 1975) that revolved around the 'gaze'. This omnipresent surveillance of the 'gaze' covered the whole social body while remaining invisible. Modern 'enlightened' societies were characterized by a disappearance of the 'spectacle of punishment' (Foucault 1975) and developed much more refined and less visible forms of stately pain-distribution as forms of punishment. One of the central forms of stately delivered pain is the imprisonment of human beings. In 'Crime control as industry', Nils Christie (1993) focused on the punishment of imprisonment as it is, apart from Capital punishment, the strongest power at the disposal of the state in order to control its population. The different degrees of punishment distributed by the legal system of any country are measured in terms of what Christie calls the 'levels of intended pain'. He remarks: "except for Capital Punishment and physical torture...nothing is so total, in constraints, in degradation, and in its display of power, as is the prison" (Christie 1993: 23).

The 'level of intended pain' used against an offender is interrelated to the view that the executive organs, trained and disciplined themselves according to the state's ideology, have of the identity of the one who is about to be punished. "..., with the offender seen as the non-person, a thing, there are no limits to possible atrocities" Cohen (1992: 12). The notion of 'levels of intended pain' – distribution appear to originate from a strong and sedimented belief in a simplistic and reductionist calculus of 'pleasure/pain' that underlies modern utilitarian thought. This belief generates the reductionist, ill-informed, universalizing idea that individual suffering is comparable. The supplementary social construction of a species of 'perverts' that find 'pleasure in pain' that served as an 'explanation' of 'masochism', is not only flawed and artificial (in terms of not representing or capturing the 'life-world') but often leads further to the consequential misconception (and at times mistreatment) of so-called 'masochists' in terms of an application of 'any pain is nice for them' prejudices. On a symbolical level it therefore appears that the 'bodily practices' of consensual 'SM' that mimic and overtly spectaculize traditional forms of stately distributed 'pain as punishment' and/or torture, thereby indirectly undermine the state's privileged monopoly on the power to punish.

4.2.4 The ultimate use of the other's pain: Torture

The most calculated form of human's infliction of pain onto other human beings is torture. The term and the practice of torture is often associated with and has become a signifier of the social construction of 'SM'. At the same time, it is also used within the Scene as part of the coded language of consensual 'SM'. In order to illuminate and contrast the meaning of 'torture' in 'SM' with the notion of torture as conventionally understood, the following discussion explores key dimensions of the discourses and practices of torture on both macro as well as micro levels of given societies.

In his work 'Discipline and Punish: The birth of the Prison', Michel Foucault suggested a view of penal torture as a 'calculated art of pain' aiming to produce: "...the most exquisite agonies" (Foucault 1975: 35). The practices of torture are used in various countries for the purposes of punishment, social control as well as for the production of 'truth' (in terms of being a means to 'extract' information out of the 'body' of a human being), they are thus directly aimed at the destruction and/or prevention of resistance against state power.

The central point of torture then is the intention and the acting out of techniques that decrease the stability of the physio-psychological well-being and in effect, the 'self' of the victim.

Another feature to be considered is the circumstances in which torture is applied. Most research on the nature of pain, ..., is directed towards acute or chronic pain caused by accident or disease, and such research recognizes the body's own capacity for producing pain inhibitors and focuses upon creating the optimal conditions for recovery from pain.

In the torture process, however, the conditions under which torture is applied are specifically designed to enhance the experience of pain, to block the operation of natural pain inhibitors, to prevent optimal conditions for recovery from pain, and to increase the pain in as many ways as possible. (Peters 1985: 171)

The crucial difference to consensual 'SM' becomes obvious as, apart from the non-consensual context, even in apparent 'torture-scenes' the care for the 'bottom's' 'lived body' is always the focus of the 'top's' activities.

Stover and Nightingale also underline the interconnectedness of physical and mental pain in the torture-experience. "In terms of the character of stress experienced, the physical assault of burning the body with lighted cigarettes and the psychological assault implicit in sensory deprivation techniques fall at points on a single physical-psychological continuum" (Stover and Nightingale 1985: 6). Physical torture is inevitably often automatically combined with mental torture but both forms occur separate as well.

Torture is intended to somehow generate 'truth' (e.g. a confession or information of the victim and/or a transformation of a 'deviant' belief), whether to 'extract' or 'produce' the victim's 'truth' or in the case of deterrence, torture is always: "... the deliberate infliction of pain by one person on another in an attempt to break down the will of the victim" (Stover and Nightingale 1985: 4). As such the instrumental application of violence is an important concern for criminology (Hamm 2004; Katz 1987; Melossi 1994; Schinkel 2004) and in the context of state violence, or at least the threat of it, is used as a tool of socio-political control that is officially presented as a form of 'crime' or 'terrorism' prevention, 'legitimate' punishment and/or conflict resolution.

In the context of torture, the essential features of the instrumental application of violence as noted by Stover and Nightingale are (a) the involvement of (at least) two persons – the perpetrator and the victim; (b) the effective physical control over the victim by the perpetrator; (c) the intent and purpose of the infliction of pain lies in the breaking of the will and humanity of the victim; and (d) "..., torture usually entails purposeful, systematic activity. The torturer's intent is, variously, to obtain information, a confession, or a recantation from the victim or a third party, to punish the victim or others" (Stover and Nightingale 1985: 5).

Apart from the macro level of the functions and operations of torture that stand in deep contrast to the consensual 'bodily practices' of consensual 'SM', the micro level of torture represented by the attitudes of practitioners of torture reveal the profound differences between both practices. "Essential to torture is the sense that the interrogator controls everything, even life itself" (Robertson and Amnesty International, 1984: 19). The power of the torturer is therefore absolute.

On the other hand, in consensual 'SM', the power of the 'top' that 'plays' for example a 'torture-scene' with his/her 'bottom' is limited by the conditions consensually negotiated beforehand and, in the last instance, by the use of a 'safe-word' and/or 'safe-gesture' by the 'bottom'. The differences between consensual 'SM torture' and torture as conventionally understood become even clearer when looking at torturers' experiences of a process of 'second socialization'. For example, military and/or police training programs for the instruction of security personnel in torture or, using the more civilized sounding term of 'interrogation techniques', is not the privilege of societies labelled as 'uncivilised' or 'barbaric' but a frequent feature of police and military-education in contemporary Western societies (e.g. at the International Police Academy (IPA) in Washington, DC etc.). In these contexts the classical justification of the use of violence through expediency is drilled into human beings. The justification to torture individuals, to inflict pain on them and produce suffering in their bodies is taken as a 'necessary evil', a 'good reason', in order to protect and secure the social and political 'body'.

"Concentrated in the torturer's electrode or syringe is the power and responsibility of the state" (Robertson and Amnesty International 1984: 4). In the process of becoming a torturer there appears to be initially a continuous use of 'techniques of neutralization' (Sykes and Matza 1957) that allow the practitioners of torture to disassociate from a sense of responsibility for their actions which, once again, reveals the profound difference to consensual 'SM' practice, where reflection and responsibility are considered to be fundamentally important and collectively reinforced (see Chapter 3). In consensual 'SM'-play the 'bottom' is *never* helpless and can abruptly stop the whole 'scene'. The justification of consensual 'SM' 'torture-scenes' lies in the pleasure derived from its practice for both of the parties. Even though ideological justifications for the use of torture appear to be crucial at the initial stages of the 'second socialization' of a professional torturer, a routine of torture soon sets in that often serves practicing torturers as a legitimization to act out vengeance against detainees. Again, in contrast to this, within the context of consensual 'SM', the power of the 'top' is limited by the will of the 'bottom', at any one point in time action will immediately stop if the 'safe-word' is said or, if verbal communication is impossible (e.g. through the use of a gag or body-bag), an agreed upon signal is given. Within consensual 'SM' as opposed to torture, the limits of the 'Other' are the limits of the one in power.

The official secrecy of torture stands in big contrast to the open display of consensual 'SM's 'torture-play'. While governments avoid the presence of witnesses and apply more and more complicated psychological, electronic and pharmacological techniques which result in intensely painful sensations and suffering but do not leave obvious signs of physical traumas, practitioners of consensual 'SM' do not hide but wear and present their marks of physical traumas with pride. While the sensations, experience and pleasure generated in consensual 'SM' tend to strengthen the bonds or respect between the 'players', conventional, non-consensual violence can be understood further as undermining the integrity of the individual, community, or government that puts it to use as fear is substituted for respect (Bourke 2005; Clarke 2006; Furedi 2002). The use of violence to enforce a position is likely to result in counter-violence and undermine the possibility of dialogue, conflict-resolution and/or empathy.

4.2.5   The aim of torture: The extraction of 'truth'

Torture was part of the ancient Greek and Roman legal sanctions against slaves and therefore shaped our understanding of the connection between human suffering and the production of 'truth'. "That truth is unitary, that truth may finally be extracted by torture, is part of our legacy from the Greeks and, therefore, part of our idea of truth... the logic of our philosophical tradition, of some of our inherited beliefs about truth, leads almost inevitably to conceiving of the body of the other as the site from which truth can be produced, and to using violence if necessary to extract that truth" (duBois 1991: 5/6). In the course of duBois elaborations on the Greek and Roman origins of the word 'torture', she found that in both cultures the original meaning and use of *'basanos'* or *'lapis Lydius'* was subject to change as the socio-political contexts altered. "The Sophoclean language, and its ambiguity, reveal the gradual transition of the meaning of the word *basanos* from 'test' to 'torture'. The literal meaning, 'touchstone', gives way to a figurative meaning, 'test', then over time changes to 'torture', as the analogy is extended to the testing of human bodies in juridical procedures for the Athenian courts" (duBois 1991: 21). *'Basanos'* became a feature not only of legal processes but also of the relations between ancient states.

In this classical Greek culture slavery was legal and the torture and punishment of slaves was only part of the 'normalized' and ubiquitous (duBois 2003) institution of slavery. The test of 'truth', the process of torture was applied on slaves under the general assumption that: "...the slave, because of his or her servile status, will not spontaneously produce a pure statement, cannot be trusted to do so....The truth is generated by torture from the speech of the slave; the sounds of the slave on the rack must by definition contain truth, which the torture produces" (duBois 1991: 36). In the case of the use of torture as a legal instrument in courts it was thus never applied on Athenian citizens but only on their slaves. Free men and women were compelled by oaths to talk the 'truth' in court as a lie under oath might have implied the loss of the rights of a citizen. The privilege of giving a free testimony was never on the side of the slave as he/she was believed to lie anyway and as slaves were not considered to be free agents. This socially constructed distinction between slaves and 'free agents' formed one of the oppositions ancient culture was essentially based upon. As the threat to be enslaved themselves constantly accompanied the 'free agents' of the ancient

Greek world (duBois 1991) sustaining this constructed opposition appeared important to them. Within the Greek legal system the calculated infliction of human agony on the bodies of slaves came to represent a guarantee for 'truth'-production.

"..., the slave can testify when his body is tortured because he recognizes reason without possessing it" (duBois 1991: 66). In the case of a Master denying his slave to be tortured for evidence purposes negative assumptions about the Master's credibility will be made by the polis. Even though the result of torture could be true or false, evidence produced under torture of slaves was attributed a higher value than evidence derived of the free speech of the Master.

The very ambiguity of evidence derived from torture, ..., replicates the ambiguity of social status on which it depends. ... The two issues are linked in the body of the tortured, who on the rack, on the wheel, under the whip assumes a relationship to truth. Truth is constituted as residing in the body of the slave; because he can apprehend reason, without possessing reason, under coercion he is assumed to speak the truth. ... The slave, incapable of reasoning, can only produce truth under coercion. ... As Gernet says, 'Proof is institutional. Proof, and therefore truth, are constituted by the Greeks as best found in the evidence derived from torture. Truth, *aletheia*, comes from elsewhere, from another place, from the place of the other'. (duBois 1991: 68)

The practice of torture thus appears to have been a tool for the separation of human beings and helped to reinforce the Greek notion of 'truth' as an accessible secret.

This metaphysical and Platonian notion of 'truth' is an exclusive and absolute 'truth' which is only accessible to socially and politically privileged human beings which enjoyed high positions within Athen's oligarchy.

Notions of unitary 'truth' are, as seen throughout this work, still part of our legacy from the Greeks and thus entail the possibility to extract 'truth' from 'bodies' of the 'Other'. Thus: "...one is inevitably and inextricably implicated in the positing of the other. The ancient democracy depended on torture; the ancient democrats used torture to know themselves" (duBois 1991: 142).

This chapter gave examples of the monopoly of [thinly and badly veiled] violence of the state, represented in one of its most non-consensual and abhorrent forms, by torture of 'othered' people[s]. The differences between torture as conventionally understood and 'torture' in consensual 'SM' substantiate my argument that any attempt to condemn this practice as uncivilized (as has happened within the Brown vs. Regina trial) has to be regarded as uninformed and that it crucially misses the dubious origins of our understanding of civilization and democracy. In the next chapter I will argue that the social construction of consensual 'SM' is interdependent with other more fundamental constructions of modernity that reveal to be inherently contradictory. The latter parts of Chapter 5 then offer suggestions for the potential broader social meanings and functions of consensual 'SM'.

5
Challenging Claims of a Non-violent Modernity

The previous chapter, in analysing signifiers of the social constructions of 'Sadomasochism', demonstrated how these are intimately connected with power relationships and illustrated how public representations of 'SM' bodily practices contradict the 'subjugated knowledges' and 'lived experiences' of practitioners of consensual 'SM'. These contradictions were evident in the examples presented and, in particular, in my discussion of the distinction between the practice of 'torture' within consensual 'SM' as opposed to how torture is conventionally understood and represented. In this chapter the broader social meanings of both the social censure of 'Sadomasochism' on an ideological-symbolic level as well as the socio-cultural meanings of the social phenomenon of consensual 'SM' 'body practices' are analysed. The chapter begins by discussing the concept of 'civilization', represented in its highest form by the 'Enlightenment' and its supplementary construction of 'wilderness', which serve as a point of departure for an explorative reflection on the socio-ideological operations of these constructed dualisms and their relation to the 'bodily practices' of consensual 'Sadomasochism'. Inherent contradictions within these dualisms and within conventional interpretations of consensual 'SM' that are based on the modern 'order of things' (Foucault 1971) are noted and then compared to the 'lived experiences' of consensual 'SM' practitioners.

One of the consequences of the formation of modern power-knowledge-subject relations that is of central relevance to this piece of work is the selective legitimacy of 'risk taking' and potential resulting production of 'harm' within 'risk societies' (Beck 1994). As the notion of 'risk' appears to be one factor that attracts some people to engage in these 'bodily practices', the latter sections of this chapter compare the operations of the discourses and practices surrounding this notion and contrast legitimate forms of 'risk-taking' activities with 'risk-taking' activities that are selectively rendered illegal. In this context the permissiveness of 'risk taking' and related potential production of harm will be problematized.

5.1   The dichotomy of 'Enlightenment' and 'wilderness' or surveilling the boundaries of social constructions

> The materialist view of the individual was responsible for that central characteristic of the new technology of sex, which Foucault defined as the demand that the social body as a whole and 'virtually all of its individuals' place themselves under surveillance. Surveillance was necessary because the new desiring individual, imagined as fundamentally egotistical, threatened constantly to undermine the requirements of the social. Sade captured this same need for surveillance in his endless obsession with establishing rules.
>
> (Hunt in Stanton 1992: 91)

This obsession with control and compulsion for rules, de Sade shared not only with his 'enlightened' era but this heritage still continues to be a dominant feature of contemporary times.

It appears to be legally and morally acceptable to ignore the factuality of 'civilized' consent that was established between a group of people as Lord Templeman's comment in his ruling over the so-called 'Spanner'-case explicitly labelled the behaviour of the 'playing' men "...uncivilized" (*Times Law Reports* 12.3.93: 42). The modern binarism of 'civilization'/'wilderness' make this comment a value judgment that effectively dismisses the 'lived experience' of consensual 'SM'. The experiences and the understanding of consensual 'SM' practitioners presented in Chapter 3 gave a different impression of their interactions. The planning of 'scenes', the crucial importance of negotiations to establish consent and the amount of time invested in these private 'bodily practices', conventionally represented as 'perverse', do not really suggest a lack of 'civilization' but rather a sophisticated application of one of its assumed core-preconditions [the control of the 'sex drive']. "...SM exhibits a high degree of theatricality; which belies the simplistic assertion that no one is able to control their desires. On the contrary, active SM is the perfect means by which one learns to do just that" (Thompson 1994: 160).

One of the interviewees, Anthony, describes his perception and experiences of the 'bodily practices' of consensual 'SM' in connection to time which I found to be representative for most people I encountered on London's Scene:

> Basically, I think good SM-sex is very controlled, very controlled. At every stage, extremely controlled. I think that the system likes to paint the idea that it's deviant sex and it's wild. Most people hear misconceptions around SM-sex and that's what they are used to hear. You have to talk to an insider to know how it is exactly. If I'm having a 'scene' with my Asian 'slave' for example, I might plan for two hours what exactly is going to

happen. From the minute he rings that doorbell, exactly what will happen. If it's for water sports for instance, I have to set up the bathroom in a particular way, move things out, bring things in, change the lights, clean things up. It's a lot of hard work. (Interview-file 3: 8)

Instead of a 'wild', uncontrolled exchange, consensual 'SM' requires a lot of preparation a priori. It is important to acknowledge that in comparison to most routinized 'heterosexual' coitus-encounters, the 'bodily practices' of consensual 'SM' require a much more profound investment of time. This quantitative and, effectively, qualitative difference runs counter to the meta-narrative of modern progress.

Within his 'Five Lectures', Marcuse explained the relevance of the evaluation of time as a central characteristic of the modern view of progress:

Time is understood as a straight line or endlessly rising curve, as a becoming that devalues all mere existence. The present is experienced with regard to the more or less uncertain future...In this linearly experienced time, fulfilled time, the duration of gratification, the permanence of individual happiness, and time as peace can be represented only as superhuman or subhuman: as eternal bliss, which is possible and conceivable only after existence here on earth has ceased, or as the idea that the wish for the perpetuation of the happy moment is itself the inhuman or anti-human force that surrenders man to the devil. (Marcuse 1970: 32)

5.1.1 'Self'-mastery in consensual 'SM' in contrast to 'commodified life'

Another example that illustrates the degrees of (self-) control exercised by practitioners of consensual 'SM' and further the 'care for the self' ('lived body') that has to be undertaken for these 'bodily practices', is being provided by Henry. After years of being whipped, Henry had to set himself limits to the exercise of his most enjoyed 'bodily practices' as he feels these to be necessary to protect his body. Henry compares it to the limits of playing hockey at an old age, which he had to stop a year ago. Henry:

But if you get an injury at hockey, when you are older, the bruises and the scars last that much longer as you get older. They just last longer. And that's what's happening with me now. The scar-tissue, you're getting scar-tissue on top of scar-tissue and it's breaking down now. And that's what I've got to be careful of, I've got to be sensible. Because whatever you do, common sense must prevail. And that's important....But I do really feel, I still want to do as much, perhaps a bigger gap in between. Instead of doing it every day or every other day or something like this or three times a week. Now it might be once a fortnight, but pretty heavy....But now, everybody, who's been caned an immense amount has one spot on their bottom. The old gluteus maximus that opens up very quickly. I can tell you now, if my Lady caned me twelve strokes hard with the cane, if she hits that spot, it's gonna open up, within twelve. And it's worrying. (Interview-file H.: 19)

Consensual 'SM' implies the 'care for the self' as only through processes of continuous reflection one's own changing limits can be accessed. This often means that precautions are taken within the context of these 'bodily practices' according to individual evaluation and deriving sets of limits. In contrast to mainstream society, in which even the most unlikely 'risks' are assessed by experts and insured by profit oriented corporations, the risks that are being taken are self-assessed and self-legitimated. Diabolo for example nearly gave up one of his 'bodily practices' as he felt it became to much for his body: "...I used to enjoy hanging a lot but I did it too often. {Holding and showing his throat.} I cannot do that too often nowadays" (Interview-file D.: 2).

The notions of 'wilderness' and 'animality' in connection to consensual 'SM' therefore should rather be seen as strategical devices of power. In 'Discourses of sexuality', Mae G. Henderson mentions Hayden White's explanation of this kind of device, which in his words is a "...'culturally self-authenticating device' intended to 'confirm the value of [the] dialectical antithesis between 'civilization'...and 'humanity'" (Henderson in Stanton 1992: 324). These 'culturally self-authenticating devices' are elements of the conceptualization of 'Otherness' that can be used as an image of a form of subhumanity. These devices thus serve, through a process of negative self-identification on the side of the receiving individual, as a confirmation of a sense of superiority on the sender's side. In labelling the 'bodily practices' of consensual 'SM' selectively uncivilized, the allegedly 'civilized' behaviour of mainstream society receives an indirect confirmation which points to the origin of this 'social censure': "...S/M, as Foucault puts it, 'is not a name given to a practice as old as Eros; it is a massive cultural fact which appeared precisely at the end of the eighteenth century, and which constitutes one of the greatest conversions of Western imagination: unreason transformed into delirium of the heart'" (McClintock in Gibson and Gibson 1993: 207). The consequences of the thereby constructed concepts of 'Otherness' reduce history and human lives to a struggle between 'culture' and 'nature', thereby preventing any genuine understandings and leading to meaningless interpretations and discourses around constructed purities.

5.1.2   The violence of 'civilized' rationality

Before the Court of Appeal in 1992, Lord Lane thus dictated: "The satisfying of the sado-masochistic libido does not come within the category of good reason" (Kershaw 1992: 10). Apart from the problematic use of the pathologizing concept of 'sadomasochistic libido' (see Chapter 2) this statement evokes associations with other negative signifiers surrounding 'SM'. Cruelty and violence are signifiers of the social construction of 'Sadomasochism' and are often suggested to be in direct opposition to rationality but:

> ...what is most dangerous in violence is its rationality. Of course violence itself is terrible. But the deepest root of violence and its permanence come out of the form of the rationality we use. The idea has been that if we live in the world of reason, we can get rid of violence. This is quite wrong. Between violence and rationality there is no incompatibility. My problem is not to put reason on trial, but to know what is this rationality so compatible with violence. (Foucault in Lotringer 1991: 299)

In 'The Order of Things' (1971) Foucault remarked that modern thought was unable to propose a morality. Even the noble origins of Western civilization, Ancient Greek culture, that led many 'Westerners' to see themselves as: "...privileged, as nobly obliged to guide the whole benighted world toward Western culture's version of democracy and enlightenment" (duBois 1991: 4) was saturated and founded on violence to 'Others'. The hegemonic narrative of the noble origins of Western civilization continues to be forced onto others as it has become the sole discourse about Western history.

Its origin in classical antiquity, as already mentioned in Chapter 4, was inherently bound up with the notion of a unique 'truth' which is also part of the Greek legacy (Plato) and which was thought to be extractable from the 'body' by torture. For Page duBois this does not imply that torture was invented by the Greeks nor that torture is only part of the philosophy of the West, but these origins allow for the deconstruction of a myth of 'civilization' as violence free. Her aim is thus: "...to refuse to adopt the moral stance of those who pretend that torture is the work of 'others', that it belongs to the third world, that we can condemn it from afar. ...The very idea of truth we receive from the Greeks, ..., is inextricably linked with the practice of torture, which has almost always been the ultimate attempt to discover a secret 'always out of reach'" (duBois 1991: 7). In the 'enlightened' world reason became the signifier of 'truth', attempting to establish thereby the 'truth' of rationality for all human beings which had (has) the violent effect of the exclusion of difference. The philosophy of the 'truth' of reason thus generated 'conditions of domination'.

In contemporary Britain there appears to be evidence for an enforced loss of the spheres of the 'social' and the 'political' that can be interpreted as posing a 'risk' to 'democracy'. The 'harms of British education' have been addressed in more depths in the context of other articles (Beckmann and Cooper 2004, 2005) but it is important to note that the 'educated subject' is rationally fabricated according to the perceived 'needs' of a so-called 'free market' while the pedagogical methods and the process of education are now degraded to a mere 'side effect'. Pedagogy and the process of education, however, are crucial in terms of the enframing of the educational process and in terms of educating pupils and students also in socio-political ways. This reductionism within the education system obviously constitutes another example for the compatiblity of rationality and violence as this sets unconsensual 'conditions of domination' and leads to socio-cultural impoverishment.

When young people decided to actively engage with their 'citizenship' in 2003 by walking out of schools in protest at the war in Iraq "...the dominant view of the educational establishment was that the strikes represented an 'unruly' excuse to truant" (Cunningham and Lavalette 2004: 259). While even so-called 'truanting' is now semi-criminalized, the crucial point is obviously that: "In a country where children and young people are thought to display high levels of political apathy, the justifications that pupils gave for their actions were remarkably considered, reasoned and articulate..." (Cunnigham and Lavalette 2004: 260).

In a true democracy opposition voices need to be heard and visible and not simply discounted, however, the dualism inherent to the dominant discoursive formation of 'security' sets political freedom as 'its' opposite.

This discourse is boosted by other contextual factors: "The role of the media is probably the most problematic in this respect. Elchardus (2002) speaks of a 'drama democracy' in which fact and fiction have become undistinguishable. 'Reality TV' has to some extent become more real than our own everyday reality and 'soap stars' have become our community" (van Swaaningen 2005: 298).

Such pseudo-community engagement is definitely safer for people in the UK as: "No act has been passed over the past 20 years with the aim of preventing antisocial behaviour, disorderly conduct, trespass, harassment and terrorism that has not also been deployed to criminalise a peaceful public engagement in politics" (Monbiot 2005: 27).

5.1.3 The 'progressive' production and selective surveillance of 'risks' and 'harm'

The development of technological reason within the framework of 'progress' signified a kind of reason that was/is indifferent to questions of justice or freedom. In 'One dimensional man', Marcuse rejected the traditional notion of the 'neutrality' of technology as:

> Technology as such cannot be isolated from the use to which it is put; the technological society is a system of domination which operates already in the concept and construction of techniques. The way in which a society organizes the life of its members involves an initial *choice* between historical alternatives which are determined by the inherited level of the material and intellectual culture. The choice itself results from the play of the dominant interests. It *anticipates* specific modes of transforming and utilizing man and nature and rejects other modes. (Marcuse 1964: xvi)

The fatality of rejecting other modes of development becomes especially apparent in the dimensions of 'risk production' which accompanied (and continue to accompany) the fulfilment of the 'masterplan' of technological, scientific and economical progress.

Pfohl, in describing and deconstructing the 'constitutive violence of white patriarchal CAPITAL' notes: "When something becomes a *structural possibility* it is constituted as positively necessary, factually objective and morally valued or economic" (Pfohl in Kroker 1993: 186). In 'Venus in Microsoft' (1993) Stephen Pfohl characterized artificial intelligence and virtual reality as the 'masterful dream of purified enlightenment'. This modern dream impacts intensely on human life as: "We live and die rationally and productively. We know that destruction is the price of progress as death is the price of life, that renunciation and toil are the prerequisites for gratification and joy, that business must go on, and that the Alternatives are Utopian. This ideology belongs to the established societal apparatus; it is a requisite for its continuous functioning and part of its rationality" (Marcuse 1964: 145).

In relation to the contemporary 'order of things' it is helpful to refer to the article "Practices of calculation-Economic representations and risk management" in which Kalthoff (2005) refers back to Heidegger's elaborations on the social role of technology. In terms of risk management in the context of financial markets he concludes that: "...the manufacture of economic representation through practices and tools of representation shapes economic practices. The reference to Heidegger's philosophy of modern technology (enframing) reminds us that such a reality is constituted by ordering systems which frame (human and non-human) activities and which only know an end in itself" (Kalthoff 2005: 90). This obviously signifies that the myth of the necessity of the reign of the unfettered market as omnipotent and as all determining is merely yet another tool of public manipulation within capitalist societies in which the "...cultural ethos of the pursuit of individual happiness, free-market capitalism and the rule of law – [is constructed as] the fate of the world: 'the universalization of Western liberal democracy as the final form of human government'" (Morrison 2006: 2).

Beck remarked that there occurred a decisive shift: "..., while in classical industrial society the 'logic' of wealth production dominates the 'logic' of risk production, in the risk society this relationship is reversed" (Beck 1994: 12).

While it is evident that the greed of wealth production overrides ethical thought and decision-making processes as well as legislation and/or inforcement in the billion dollar beauty and fashion market within capitalist societies, it is crucial to emphasize the interrelationship of legitimized cosmetic 'body' interventions and increasing inequalities in the UK as well as the problematic permissiveness with regards to this legitimized (as commodified) risk-taking activities and the consensual 'bodily practices' of 'SM'.

Referring to Bourdieu's work, Quart (2003) observed that the trend in youthful plastic surgery obviously also fosters divisions alongside material inequalities: "The girls who have plastic surgery use their improved bodies as proof of their supremacy to those who simply survive as they live out their days in fat, small-breasted, ordinary bodies that are destined more for laboring than for shopping" (Quart 2003: 152).

This trend thus clearly operates as a practice of acquiring 'cultural capital'. "Kids are forced to embrace the instrumental logic of consumerism at an earlier-than-ever age" (Quart 2003: XXV). Gordon (2008) for example refers to a London based 'luxurious child-only salon' in which parents book manicures, pedicures, styling and makeovers for their children, the co-owner stated that: "...British parents [are, *sic*] still 'conservative' compared to Americans. So far his youngest customer for a manicure or pedicure has been six, whereas salons in Los Angeles and New York regularly treat children as young as two" (Gordon 2008: 14).

Robinson stated that: "...adult men are seduced by the allure of childhood innocence and it is maintained that in all children lurks the flirt, the Lolita, waiting to overpower the unsuspecting adult" (Robinson 2005 in Mason and Fattore 2005: 69).

The clothing company Abercrombie and Fitch for example appeared to sense big profit as it started to sell thongs in 2002 depicting cherries and words such as 'wink, wink' and 'eye candy' to preteen girls (Quart 2003). Other corporations that profit from such non-consensual forms of 'symbolic violence' were for example ASDA (black lace underwear for 9 year old children) and last but not least Playboy via the widely marketed Duvet covers, pillow cases, watches and mobile cases embossed with Hugh Heffner's Playboy bunny symbol. This symbol clearly symbolizes commodified 'sex' in the form of 'hetero-porn' and it is surprising that in a 'paedophilia'-condemning era this symbol was featuring in the displays for 'back to school' merchandise at WH Smith and obviously sold.

Representations such as these alongside highly sexualized advertisements, magazines for young people as well as 'sexed up' music videos that are frequently consumed by prepubescent persons are likely to have an impact on their consumers as: "the co-constitutive, co-productive ways in which consumers, working with market-generated materials, forge a coherent, if diversified and often fragmented sense of self" (Arnould and Thompson 2005: 13). Thus, predominantly reductionist 'identities' are consumed, regulated and produced within our surrounding culture and these are able to generate meanings via symbolic systems of representation (Woodward 1997).

> Today's adolescent girls are surrounded by more exposed flesh than girls of previous generations, especially from the quasi-pornography of the laddie magazines *Maxim, FHM,* and *Gear.* Those magazines, no longer relegated to the pornographic brown wrappers of yore, display teen starlet cover girls, complete with their prerequisite, unnaturally firm bosoms, (...) [while] Music videos have had a similar effect. (Quart 2003: 162)

Thus it is more than obvious that: "Teen girls who get the breast enhancements wish to be erotic objects of consumption, following the not-so-hidden currents in the general culture that both eroticizes teenage girls and punishes those who act on their libidinal impulses" (Quart 2003: 157). This is but one of the socio-political and cultural contradictions within capitalist-consumerist societies that on the one hand foster the alienation of people from the diversity and [in cases of older botox and surgery consumers] the frailness of 'embodiment' and, on the other hand criminalizes those who have come to desire the products of such unfettered marketing ['paedophiles']. It is further important to note that while the UK government takes a stance against teenage-pregnancies, in a context in which teenagers learn about 'sex' via media porn consumption, one of the media's foci is on so-called 'celebrity'-pregnancies seemingly without reflecting on the potential impact this may have on young people's concepts of 'self' in the synoptic space of contemporary media-society.

While so-called 'teenagers' frequently have feelings of inadequacy, of deficiency, of not belonging, the burgeoning market of cosmetic surgery tries (often successfully) to exploit these emotions and concerns. Quart discovered "... a surgery site that claims 'successful plastic surgery may result in reversal of the social withdrawal that so often accompanies teens who feel "different"'" (Quart 2003: 154). The risks involved in growing up with such unfettered commodification and superficial imagery is also impacting on boys as their consumerism-generated sense of inadequacy is now also being fought by 'body projects' as 'emotional palliative' (Quart 2003). Apart from surgical interventions, the use of steroids is a mode of self-construction with a list of potential risks: "The possible side effects of steroids include stunted bone growth, liver damage, and shrunken testicles" (Quart 2003: 168).

Transformations of 'bodies' that involve woundings are only legal when they 'submit' to the ideologies of consumer culture that serve the purposes of 'normalization' and not when they were consensually agreed upon by the parties involved.

Thus, the 'universal reign of the normative' (Foucault 1975) works not only through the 'categories of normality' as applied by the 'judges of normality' but also through the justifying concepts of 'prevention', 'care' and 'risk'.

The demarcation of a borderline between legitimate 'bodily practices' and illegitimacy in consumer culture cannot even logically be comprehensible by reference to health and safety concerns. The consumer culture specific explosion of eating disorder syndromes and now the phenomenon of 'poly-surgical addiction' illustrate the systemic results of the promotion of normalizing 'body-images': "Medical science has now designated a new category of 'polysurgical addicts' (or, in more causal references, 'scalpel slaves') who return for operation after operation, in perpetual quest of the elusive yet ruthlessly normalizing goal, the perfect body" (Bordo in Welton 1998: 46).

The taking of risks for health and safety under the auspices and hands of experts of 'normalization' are selectively allowed and thus confirms that: "...the body is a battleground whose self determination has to be fought for" (Bordo in Welton 1998: 53).

In a context in which Roughgarden (2004) like others suggests that the 'body' is re-constituted (e.g. the 'natural' givenness of 'gender', genetic engineering, xenographs, cloning etc.) and in which the socio-legal control over 'bodies' appears to be extended (e.g. smoking-ban, the suggested non-consensual use of cells of 'mentally ill', the rise of synthetic biology, etc.) individual and self-determined ownership of one's body (like in consensual 'SM' practice) seems to be utopia in a culture in which the body can be commodified and legitimately transformed to the bitter end as long as it serves the purposes of 'normalization' (see Chapter 2). This development of a rational approach on 'risk' will be at the costs of those 'lived bodies' who do not submit to the legitimate paths and goal of 'normalization'. It further impacts on the selective permissiveness of 'risk'-activities and potential 'harm'-production.

The taking of risks seems to function as a means of social distinction in terms of cultural capital in contemporary culture. Moreover, if 'risk'-taking has become a form of 'cultural capital' and is by now commodified in many ways, the criminalization of the 'bodily practices' of consensual 'SM' on the grounds of potential risks concerning health and safety, appear like political judgements in pursuit of the 'normalization' of 'lived bodies'.

> Shilling argues that in a culture that is dominated by risk, uncertainty and doubt, the body has come to form a secure site over which individuals are able to exert at least some control: 'Investing in the body provides people with a means of self expression... If one feels unable to exert control over an increasingly complex society, at least one can have some effect on the size, shape and appearance of one's body' (1993: 7). (Bunton and Burrows in Bunton et al. 1995: 212)

As shown people use their control over their 'bodies' in order to hand it over to the 'agencies of normalization' which help them, while taking a risk to the 'body's' health, to submit to the 'sexed up' 'beauty imperative' of consumer culture and thereby potentially gain some sense of safety and security. The same effects are often achieved by people who choose to engage in self-created and consensually negotiated 'body practices'. An assessment of the potential 'harm' that can result from engagement with both legitimate as well as illegitimate 'risk' taking activities is a complex undertaking. Traditionally 'harm' is a concept that is defined individualistically and further institutionalized within the power/knowledge realms of medicine and law (Feinberg 1987). An analysis and evaluation of the 'harm' produced in diverse contexts would therefore merely result in an overly individualistic and utilitarian account. Additionally, many consensual 'SM' practices involve 'harm' that is (a) not perceived as such; (b) that enhances the meaningfulness and drama of the enacted ritual (similar to initiation rites, see Favazza 1996: 231/232); and (c) in no relation to the positive, life-enhancing meaning that the 'bodily practices' have for individual practitioners. Although courts appear to find this unproblematic to do, an evaluation of the 'harms' potentially produced in consensual 'SM' practice as opposed to within procedures of 'normalization' is more than likely to produce socioculturally biased results.

Consensual 'SM' 'body practices' imply the 'strategical use of body' (Chapter 3) and also the taking of self-set and negotiated risks involving the 'lived body' which are part of the thrill and the challenge that some people enjoy through these 'plays'. Pat explained: "Even if the 'scene' involves something that is frightening you really a lot, which is wonderful because you know at the same time that you're actually safe" (Interview-file 1: 8). The 'bodily practices' of consensual 'SM' seem to be able to provide a sense of security and safety within the context of a 'controlled risk' taken within the framework of trust and the rules of conduct of consensual 'SM'.

5.2   The potential broader social meanings of the rising interest in the 'bodily practices' of consensual 'SM'

The 'bodily practices' of consensual 'SM' can be read as being 'transgressive' in relation to diverse organizing categories that are enforced by various discourses of 'normalization' (Chapters 2, 4 and 5).

This and the subsequent sections of this chapter provide several interpretations of the broader social meanings that these 'bodily practices' and the engagement with them in contemporary 'late modern' consumer cultures might have. Apart from the motivations of my interviewees (Chapter 3) which are likely to be indicative of the motivations of others who are interested and/or engaging in the 'bodily practices' of consensual 'SM' and the Scene, there are other potential much broader social meanings which require to be examined. In what follows, my argument is that the Scene provides a space for the (re-) signification of 'lived bodies' through 'bodily practices' that are accompanied by 'dislocated' signs and symbols. The diversity of representations (discourses and narratives) thus created can further be utilized as tools for ongoing explorations and experiences of 'lived bodies', their changing limits and thus can be interpreted as [re]-discovering or learning 'skin knowledges' (Howes 2005). Diprose (2002) argued that the ambiguity of bodily existence cannot be interpreted, as sometimes the Lacanian accounts of the mirror stage, as the alienation of the subject in the other, but in contrast as the productive opening of new possibilities of existence. Her model of 'intercorporeal generosity' can be related to the 'bodily practices' of consensual 'SM' as her model implies a concept of 'freedom' with limitations based on the capacity (Merleau-Ponty's notion of 'tolerance') to give and receive corporeality from the other. This understanding is reflected in much of the intersubjective experiences that were experienced by the practitioners in Chapter 3.

The various possibilities of transgression and/or transcendence within the context of these 'bodily practices' in terms of societal hierarchies (e.g. 'class', 'gender', 'race', 'age') also relate alternative patterns of discourse. Such alternative discourses are of crucial importance in contemporary times as Tyler (2004) found that the increasing incorporation of management discourses and techniques into 'sexuality' and 'sexual' relations via contemporary mainstream cultural resources (e.g. lifestyle magazines) to be eroding and arresting the intersubjective elements of the 'erotic' and suggested: "Erotic sex, as Rose put it, is clearly about much more than just pleasure; it is a way in which individuals can express themselves and find an intersubjective release from the fragmenting and alienating effects of organized society (Marcuse, 1955)" (Tyler 2004: 100).

5.2.1 The re-signification of the 'body' through the 'bodily practices' of consensual 'SM'

With reference to Bourdieu's work of 1979, Bunton and Burrows wrote: "...one will make choices in everyday consumption rituals that reflect the habitus of [his/her] group. The habitus of any particular group which is determined socio-culturally thus becomes incorporated into body shape and is passed on...by way of processes of acculturation..., 'lifestyles are seen as groupings of commodity consumption involving shared symbolic codes of stylized behaviour, adornment and taste" (Bunton and Burrows in Bunton et al. 1995: 213).

The symbolic meanings given to 'normalizing' commodities and practices are thus important to decipher as they appear to be in contrast with the meanings given to the 'bodily practices' of consensual 'SM'. Ella, pointed to the advantage of the 'new' Scene as having less set rules and regulations in terms of roles and 'bodily practices' and she alluded to a different set of meanings within the Scene: "It's just interesting, finding out about yourself, really. I think that's the whole thing about the Scene that one must be actually more open minded..." (Interview-file E.: 12). Meanings ascribed by socio-cultural structures therefore lose their usually all pervasive power within this context. The 'bodily practices' of consensual 'SM' involve 'play' within negotiated structures that depend on empathetic communication and 'open bodies' and thus are not oriented towards commodity consumption and 'closed bodies'.

In contrast to mainstream society's reinforced attempts to hide blood, sweat, urine etc. from sight and even self-perception, the attitude of consensual 'SM' practitioners to these bodily fluids and thus to the 'open body' is less paranoid and on occasions a reason for pride in accomplishment. Henry for example, who first had to develop enough trust towards me, 'rewarded' me by showing me a photo collection of some of his 'beating-scenes' and proudly pointed to the blood that covered his back.

Another contrast between mainstream consumer ideology and 'bodies' in the context of consensual 'SM' that was already addressed before is the fact that the lifting of 'bodily boundaries' is only legitimised for so-called 'good reasons' (see Chapter 2). The self-setting of bodily limits, the 'work' on new ones as well as the experience of being in-and out-side of one's 'body' in the context of consensual 'SM' could therefore also be understood as active attempts of a re-signification of 'body'. Consensual 'SM'-practice requires 'open bodies' (e.g. 'bottoms' as well as 'switches', but in the sense of 'lived body', 'tops' will have to be included too) and therefore disrupts the notion of a 'closed', self-possessed and therefore 'safe' body. Especially the orifices of the body which usually have to be protected (e.g. eating with the mouth closed) are extensively used in diverse 'scenes', while other 'bodily practices' even create new orifices (e.g. 'play'-piercing). As the image of the intact, the 'functional body' is not only a 'closed body' but also a sterile and hygienic one, the use of bodily fluids in consensual 'SM' which is tabooed in Western societies disrupts the regular understanding of 'body use'. It should be clear that the contrast between these 'bodily practices' and the sterile, norma-tive use of 'body' in Western consumer societies could not be deeper, as for example advertisements suggesting that ordinary toilet-paper is not clean enough, while soapy-moisturized ones are. Deodorants are not considered to be good enough if they don't 'protect' the wearer and his/her environ-ment for at least 20 hours from the smell of sweat and last but not least, the obsession with panty liners that are not only 'safe' but also invisible, matches the ideology of the normative 'body' and its usage.

Consensual 'SM' is often associated with uncontrolled, wild exchanges and, excesses of body-fluids of varying kinds, thus mainstream society tends to reject this possibility of 'communicative body usage' as this would threaten the concept of the 'closed self-possessed body', a 'body' that is closed but consuming. The limits of transformation of 'body' reflect the limits of the consumer-realm as is illustrated in Bordo's chapter on the 'Material Girl' (1995) in her book 'Unbearable Weight...' portrayed 'plas-ticity' as the postmodern paradigm for the consumer capitalist but essen-tially modern imagination of 'human freedom from bodily determination'. She notes:

> Popular culture does not apply any brakes [to the disdain for material lim-its of 'body' in pursuit of 'normalization'] to these fantasies of rearrange-ment and self-transformation. Rather, we are constantly told that we can 'choose' our own bodies. (Bordo in Welton 1998: 46)

Nevertheless, this choice is only a conditional one as the judgment of the European Court of Human Rights on consensual 'SM' 'body practices' has demonstrated. Transformations of 'bodies' that involve woundings that are not 'transient' and 'triffling' are only legal when they 'submit' to the ideologies of consumer culture that serve the purposes of normalization.

The 'universal reign of the normative' is operating in this context via justifying concepts of 'prevention' and 'care'. The criminalization of consensual 'SM' based on selectively applied 'health and safety'-precautions thus turns out to be another instance of the inscription of the schizo-concept of 'disciplined-consumption' on 'bodies' in order to regulate the social body towards capitalist-consumerism.

5.2.2   The re-enchantment of the 'body' through experiential exploration and communication

'Bodies' acquire meanings through their signification within historically specific discourses and the era of contemporary consumer culture offers only limited and reductionistic patterns of meaning in reference to 'bodies'.

The 'consuming self' of contemporary society is a representational being, permanently engaged in the construction of 'body image'. The sense of 'self' in consumer societies is thus in danger of being reduced to the 'body-image': "...it is the body-image that plays the determining role in the evaluation of the self in the public arena" (Turner in Falk 1994: xiii).

As shown in Chapter 3 within the consensual 'SM'-Scene in London this relationship is reversed as the individual abilities of 'tops' and 'bottoms' are evaluated and compared, thus 'body-images' are relevant only as a means to enhance experiences of 'lived bodies'. The dominance-display of most 'tops' is not reducible to 'body-images', it depends far more on emotional, cognitive and technological skills and the development of empathy. The same holds true for the 'bottoms', as their most crucial attribute is the optional willingness to be open to experiences and experimentations with sensations as well as their responsiveness. These attributes of 'tops' and 'bottoms' can be associated with notions of attunement and/or a form of thinking "through the affective field of the other" (Diprose 2002: 143).

These 'bodily practices' thus provide a way beyond the tendency of human beings to become "culturally enmired subjects" (Butler 1990) by means of alterations of the 'body'. The domain of the 'ugly' as well as the domain of age are revalorized within the Scene which poses a challenge to the prevalent 'technological beauty imperative' (Morgan in Welton 1998) and the ableist as well as ageist dimensions of consumerist ideology.

The collective subordination of 'lived bodies' to current ideals of 'beauty'-ideals involve prescriptive strategies of 'body'-control and in the realms of elective cosmetic surgery this control is even mediated by technology and the 'authorized' experts. In consensual 'SM' 'bodily interventions' and 'transformations' are a joint creative, imaginative and idiosyncratically meaningful undertaking of consenting individuals. The Scene in London offers its members as well as 'drifting members' possibilities of exploration in terms of alternatives to conventional 'body usage' and 'bodily practices'. As such especially the 'new Scene' can be read as representing possible moments of community in a celebration of the 'lived body' as opposed to the 'normalizing' concern with 'body-images'. The 'paradigm of plasticity' (Bordo 1993) fosters 'body practices' like 'body-sculpting' (e.g. body building, dieting) and elective cosmetic surgery procedures, thus promoting the achievement of normalizing and homogenizing 'body images'.

The Scene in contrast to this reductionism, promotes experimentation and exploration: "...somebody may start off in the Scene as a dominant or submissive in everybody elses eyes but we're all finding where we are in things. It's only ever by doing things that you can find out what works for you" (Interview-file E.: 12). The 'new' Scene of consensual 'SM' offers the practitioners disordered/deregulated spaces for the display, interaction and experiencing of 'lived bodies'. The creative use of 'lived bodies' is encouraged and thus stands in deep contrast to the reductionistic and alienating contemporary notion of the 'body plastic' (Bordo 1993).

The psychiatrist Favazza who worked on the wide area of the social phenomenon of self-mutilation and body modification, also mentioned the possibility of individual 'bodies' consenting to mutilation/modification by other bodies in a non-pathologizing way. Concerning the motivation for these 'body practices' Favazza noted: "...it provides temporary relief from a host of painful symptoms such as anxiety, depersonalization, and desperation. ... it also touches upon the very profound human experiences of salvation, healing, and orderliness" (Favazza 1996: xix). It appears though that specific contextualized and consensual 'harms' generate so many benefits that it becomes problematic to talk of 'harm'. Favazza also considered the social phenomenon of body piercing, a form of body modification that has found many devotees as well as fashion-'victims' within the last decades. Fakir Musafar whom Favazza describes as 'the guru philosopher of the 'modern primitives' movement', that encompasses diverse 'body-practitioners' as well as consensual 'SM'-practitioners, outlined the deeper motivation for 'body play': "...we had all rejected the Western cultural biases about ownership and use of the body" (Musafar in Favazza 1996: 326). The 'Modern Primitive movement' promotes experimentation with the experiences of 'body', for example as a means of expression or a 'reclaiming' of the 'body' (often after abuse experiences)and as a means of self-exploration. These are aims that are shared by many practitioners of consensual 'SM' and thus might explain some of the interest in these 'bodily practices'. Fakir Musafar termed this the "...search and experiment with the previously forbidden 'body side' of life" (Musafar in Favazza 1996: 327).

The primacy of sensations and experience as opposed to mere 'body-image' find expression in the 'spectacles of bodily practices' of consensual 'SM' which bring the tactile and existential dimensions of social existence to the foreground and indirectly invite for participation. This sensual attitude prevalent in the Scene-clubs, among Scene-members as well as 'drifting members', could be termed 'dionysiac' (Maffesoli 1996) and thus be interpreted as a break with the representational distance created through the cult of 'body image'. Although the 'bodily practices' of consensual 'SM' involve the *use of representations,* these function as a strategical tool to facilitate pleasure and help to enable people to enter into more experiental and intense communication and as illustrated (see Chapters 3 and 6), they can on occasion create the possibilities for collective experiences. "The spectacle, in various forms, assumes the function of communion" (Maffesoli 1996: 77).

Shared sentiments as well as effective ties have a bonding function which is essential to any social existence. According to Bell, Durkheim understood religion as the consciousness of society: "And since social life in all its aspects is made possible only by a system of symbols, that consciousness becomes fixed upon some object which becomes sacred" (Bell 1975: 394). Within the Scene of consensual 'SM' the 'body' as experienced through a diversity of sensations, through for example, displaced traditional 'body practices' as well as the active exploration of innovative ones, is thus 're-enchanted' and achieves a 'sacred' character. Religion is the symbolization of the social bond which becomes expressed through communion and a 'common transcendental voice':

> Durkheim argued that religion does not derive from a belief in the supernatural or in gods but from the division of the world – things, times, persons – into the sacred and profane. If religion is declining, it is because the realm of the sacred has been shrinking, because the shared sentiments and affective ties between men [sic] have become diffuse and weak. The primordial elements that provide men with common identification and affective reciprocity-family, synagogue and church, community-have become attenuated, and men have lost the capacity to maintain sustained relations with each other in both time and place. To say then that 'God is dead' is, in effect, to say that the social bonds have snapped and society is dead. (Bell 1975: 395)

Nietzsche's advent of nihilism then can be seen as being 'prevented' when new bonds arise and temporary membership in diverse 'tribes' such as the Scene and, more specifically the 'SM'-scene, allow the individual to regain the feeling of participation and 'social bonding'. The potential spiritual aspects of the 'bodily practices' of consensual 'SM' will be further elaborated on in Chapter 6.

5.2.3 Consensual 'SM' as a 'remapping of bodies': The 'desexualization' of pleasure

Consensual 'SM' can be interpreted as disconnecting the fundamental philosophical pattern of the Western world which tied 'sexuality', 'subjectivity' and 'truth' together and in turn shaped human beings relationship to themselves.

In 'History of Sexuality' (1990) Foucault suggested that *the only way* to go beyond an identification of ourselves with our 'sex drive' or 'genital desire' would be a return to 'bodies and pleasures'. Foucault's notion of 'desexualization of pleasure' which he saw represented by consensual 'SM' play, implies not a complete rejection of all acts that might be conceived as 'sexual' or genital but the detaching of 'sexual' pleasure from its institutionalized genital dependence and thus its specifically constructed localization in the individual 'body'. At this point it is helpful to refer to Bette's 'subjugated knowledges' that in parts were already explored in 3.4.1.

According to Bette this is a crucial difference between 'vanilla sex' and consensual 'SM': "I think that part of the thing is the difference between intercourse and beating somebody, with intercourse, man having intercourse with a woman, there's a very direct sexual path, there's a very sexually fixed pleasure. And therefore he has a motive for just getting what he wants. But if what he does is not directly genital or sexual. I mean it may give immense satisfaction but the satisfaction it will give will be in the communication with the other person. The fact to get it right with the other person" (Interview-file 4.: 5). The intense relationship that develops among the 'players' within the 'scenes' is thus the guiding motivation for many practitioners of these 'bodily practices' and might be another factor that could explain the rising interest in consensual 'SM'.

After reading the 'Hite report on male sexuality', Bette was astonished: "It's just so tragic in a way how limited, what they appear to enjoy is. And how little use, you know, they are just so genitally orientated. It's just so terribly, terribly sad. You just think, what they are missing out on. You haven't explored your mind or other parts of the body. Have you not been taught about being fucked yourself or what about your nipples. I mean all you do is with your penises. It's so sad. I mean putting your penis in isn't much communication. And I mean sex doesn't have to be like that. And being a man doesn't have to be like that" (Interview-file 4: 7). This comment shows clear parallels to Michel Foucault's criticism of the genital fixation of the concept of 'sexuality' which reduces pleasure to the genitals. In consensual 'SM' pleasure is coded quite differently, for the context of pornography it was suggested that: "In contrast to both heterosexual and homosexual pornographies, sexual identities and sexual pleasures are presented in this type of pornography as more a function of performance than of biology. It is this performance of perverse desires which do not follow the expected routes of sexual identity (hetero or homo) or gender (male or female) that keeps both viewer and protagonists guessing about desires and pleasures that take surprising twists and turns" (Snitow et al. 1983: 250/251).

As consensual 'SM' often involves the use of the genital zones for other purposes than the reaching of orgasm and as it also eroticizes regions of the 'body' formerly not considered to be worth stimulating, these 'bodily practices' symbolize also a 'remapping' of the individual 'body' and a redistribution of the sensations of the 'body'. Changing social constructions of the 'body' are of an existential nature as they: "influence (.) not only how the body is treated but also how life is lived" (Synnott 1993: 37).

Consensual 'SM' might therefore be considered as potentially freeing the individual retrospectively from the internalized social constructions of 'sexuality' that were part of the individual's past. In Ricoeur's terms the (re)configuration of the past enables the individual to refigure the future (Ricoeur 1988). Through the creation of counter-narratives and 'bodily practices' that reconstitute individuality, consensual 'SM'-practice might be an important device in the individual reconfiguration of the past and innovative figuration of future.

5.2.4   Transcending dualisms – consensual 'SM' as a possibility to overcome the constructed binarisms of modernity and as potential transformation of the relationship to 'Other'

In 'Social Selves' (1991) Ian Burkitt undertook an interdisciplinary overview of notions of 'self'. Their shared problematic appeared to be the persistent inherent and/or inherent dualism of society and individual. The notion of humans as psychological 'monades', as 'self-contained' and isolated psychological beings leads to a completely inadequate understanding of the human 'self'. This basic but fundamental misunderstanding of 'self' Burkitt detects for example in Freud's psychoanalytical theory of personality which reinforced a notion of "...the human body as a mechanism that accumulated and discharged energy through a process that is usually labelled as his 'hydraulic theory of biological functioning', ..." (Burkitt 1991: 19).

In Freud's influential view the human being then had to adapt to its environment by means of the development of a 'reality principle' to survive in its given environment. The 'reality principle' then forces the human being to be more aware of their surrounding environments and develop the 'ego'/'I' which partly works against the 'id'/'it' of the 'pleasure principle'. Cultural values, rules and moral commands of a given society then through internalization force the development of the 'super-ego' or 'over-I' within the human personality. As Freud pictured the inner drives of the 'it' as powerful and often as threatening the culture functioning as a superstructure incorporated in the 'ego' or 'I' served to repress many of them.

In contrast Burkitt points out that society and social relationships with other human beings are fundamentally important for the development and construction of individual identities and that therefore the 'self' cannot be innate or given in human beings. In order to understand the 'social self', according to Burkitt, a dialectical approach is needed:

> By this I do not mean a circular mode of theorizing, wherein society affects the individual in some respects while the individual affects society in others. A dialectical relationship is one in which a new dimension is created by the reciprocal relations and effects of objects or humans. In this respect, the self is the new dimension which is created in the active relationship between human bodies in their material environment. ... The state of selfconscious 'individuality', where each individual takes on their own identity, is not innate or prior to society but only comes into existence *through* social relations. (Burkitt 1991: 189/190)

The 'self' is thus relational by 'nature', which comes close to Foucault's notion of the 'self' as a strategical possibility (Halperin 1995). The interdependence of 'self' and environment, thus the 'lived body' in its potentiality of change and fluidity can be directly experienced within Scene-clubs and provide the practitioners with the possibility of 'transcendence' of the social constructions of separation. "...; we are speaking of a time, a space, a home-land, a-thing, a quasi-location quite a bit stranger than fiction and infinitely more reliable than truth..., we pass into a place beyond a natural limit, pulled as it were, 'over there', over into the elsewhere of sexual mutation, curiosity, and paradoxical decay. Indeed, the 'we' and the 'them', the 'I' and the 'you', bleed into one another, stain at the center, flicker in the distance without for a moment missing the rhythm or the spaces in between this thing we have for so long called the Self" (Golding in Kroker 1993: 147/148). This description of a former lesbian 'SM'-club in London, captures the potential philosophical depth of the consensual 'SM'-Scene and its rituals.

Within traditional Western sciences the assumption of a split between the body and the mind is a central assumption. According to this orthodox perspective consciousness and volition are located within the central nervous system and 'order' the 'servant', 'slave' body to act as demanded. However, 'body'/'mind' have an interdependent relationship which for example also becomes apparent when psycho-somatic illnesses are being treated as well as in the notion of 'body-memory'. The physical body is obviously more than "... a passive servo-mechanism, but an active partner in the development of our consciousness" (Tart 1975: 82). In a critique of traditional psychoanalysis James W. Jones (1991) stated:

> ... all of modern culture, has been dominated by a split between the public and the private worlds. ... Opposing this dichotomy of public and private, objective and subjective, Winnicott clearly sees that a 'third part of the life of a human being, a part that we cannot ignore, is an intermediate

area of *experiencing*, to which inner reality and external life both contribute. It is an area that is not challenged because no claim is made on
its behalf except that it shall exist as a resting-place for the individual
engaged in the perpetual human task of keeping inner and outer reality
separate yet interrelated.' (Jones 1991: 57)

The intermediate area between inner and outer reality "... is a product of the
experience of the individual person ... in the environment" (ibid.).

The concept of 'lived body' caters for all the dimensions of experienced
'embodiment' and is also less deterministic as it allows for change, a potential for change that is experienced by most practitioners of consensual 'SM'.
During an interview Pat illustrated this "..., you know, it is learning to accept
heavy pain. It's something, you know, you won't be able to do it just over-
night. You can't go straight from, just from nothing to being beaten black
and blue with no preparation, mental preparation at all because it's nothing
that your body really wants to accept. My mind wants it but your body has
to be trained. Well I think so, I felt so" (Interview-file 1: 5).

The 'lived bodies' that practice consensual 'SM' are often overcoming the
traditional dualism of body/mind through the experiences that are provided
through individual practices and through the 'open bodies/minds'- atmosphere within most of the clubs of the Scene.

In referring to Norbert Elias' work Featherstone explains: "The grotesque
body and the carnival represent the otherness which is excluded from the
process of middle-class identity and culture" (Featherstone 1993: 79). The
relationship between societies and their carnivals is mainly one of symbolic
inversion and transgression as the distinction of high and low, classical and
grotesque etc. are mutually constructed and deformed. Seen from this perspective some 'scenes'/'plays' of consensual 'SM' could be characterized as
having 'carnivalesque' features. "The carnivals, festivals and fairs in early
modern Europe celebrated transgressions of the classical and official culture with symbolic inversions and promotions of grotesque bodily pleasures. They provided sites of 'ordered disorder' in which otherness and desire
could be explored ..." (Featherstone 1993: 119).

"Because sex sells, a dramatic liberalisation of [representations and simulations of] carnality was [became] inevitable" (Behr 2008: 7/8). In terms
of the 'pornofication' and/or 'sexualization' of everyday life it is helpful to
consider the potential broader effects on the population as: "... the promise
of simplification: brought to its logical limit, simplification means a lot of
sameness and a bare minimum of variety" (Bauman 2001: 148). The commodity 'sex' now available 24/7 might become bereft of excitement and/or
meaning.

'The Time of the Tribes' (Maffesoli 1996) proposes that contemporary
Western societies are experiencing the decline of individualism within

Mass societies. The consequences of the break-up of mass culture are in Michel Maffesoli's view effecting the emergence of heterogeneous 'tribes'. These 'tribes' are distinctively postmodern as they enforce a strong group solidarity with mechanisms of integration and inclusion but do not rely on continuous memberships. The 'powers of discipline' within these 'tribes' Maffesoli describes as 'weak' as they merely can lead to the shunning of members or their exclusion. A crucial element of the 'tribes' is according to Maffesoli the actualization of group membership by means of rituals, type of dress and a group-specific style of adornment which all serve the espousing of shared values. Maffesoli thus explored a new 'aesthetic paradigm' which generates masses of people to join and gather in temporary emotional communities. These 'postmodern tribes' are fluid and allow the temporary members to suit their needs by 'switching' in between. In the context of the empirical research on consensual 'SM' it is possible to regard the fluctuation of 'drifting members' of the 'Fetish'/'SM'-Scene in contrast to the stability provided by the 'old Scene' as part of a general shift towards the 'tribes'. As the notion of 'Kinky sex' as a trendy alternative to the wholesale of 'sex' and also as a variant of 'safe sex' (that is well exploited to the needs of the market) has established itself as a 'normalizing' strategy which leaves the realm of the 'perversions' intact, the Scene-clubs now attract wider parts of the population. As elaborated in Chapter 3 the liminal spaces that the Scene in London has to offer are, in recent years, an attraction point for various kinds of people. This shift and the parallel rise of the term 'kinky' point to transformations of meaning that triggered this socio-cultural development.

The rigid geographical mapping of spaces of 'perversion' and 'normal' 'pleasure-domes' become blurred and thus allow for the dissolution of binary concepts. On the level of the 'body' Halperin suggested an additional dimension of the practice of consensual 'S/M' in a similar direction: "...S/M represents an encounter between the modern subject of sexuality and the otherness of his or her body. Insofar as that encounter produces changes in the relations among subjectivity, sexuality, pleasure, and the body, S/M qualifies as a potentially self-transformative practice..." (Halperin 1995: 88/89).

Golding who described the atmosphere within the 'Clit-club', remarked that even via entry self-transformation is promoted: "Gone are the old identities born of either/or distinctions, with their addenda self-referential prophecies of a decidedly discrete Other. For it's a strange kind of spill over, this neither/nor transgression, one which escapes the usual Law of binary divisions like masculine/feminine, black/white, gay/straight, community/individual, public/private, life/death, truth/fiction, and so forth. Simultaneously, it refuses any melted ambiguity between Self and the Other" (Golding in Kroker 1993: 148). The potentially more open 'lived bodies' of consensual

'SM' and alternatives to traditional 'body usages' and 'body practices' make it possible to explore the wide areas of the whole human being. The following Chapter 6 on consensual 'SM' as spiritual exercise expands on this topic and points to another quite complex potential broader social meaning of the rising interest in consensual 'SM' 'bodily practices'.

6
Consensual 'SM' as a Spiritual Practice and the Experience of 'Transcendence'

In Chapter 5 I argued that the contradictions inherent to modern dualisms are mirrored by the conventional, misleading interpretations of consensual 'SM'. These were demonstrated to be completely detached from the 'life-world' of consensual 'SM' that relates to other, broader socio-cultural phenomena and meanings. This chapter focuses on one specific, additional potential deeper meaning that consensual 'SM' 'bodily practices' might have for some practitioners.

> ... sadomasochistic, cross-dressing and other sexual rituals have much in common with dramatic, religious and magical rites, for example in the use of pseudo-aggression, menace, special clothing, compulsion, restraint, chastisement and ordeal to acquire powers, expand self-awareness or alter identity boundaries. (Gosselin and Wilson in Howells 1984: 107)

As much of what I observed within the Scene appeared to have a more profound meaning to the practitioners than was readily describable (see Chapter 3) and as several authors pointed to a spiritual dimension of consensual 'SM', I considered it important to investigate this experiential level of these 'bodily practices'. This chapter therefore explores the notion of consensual 'SM' as spiritual exercise from various angles as the rising interest in these 'bodily practices' might also be connected to this potential function of consensual 'SM'.

During both, the whole of the 'Operation Spanner', as well as throughout the two following court proceedings, this potential of the 'bodily practices' of consensual 'SM' for practitioners was never mentioned. An acknowledgement of this critically meaningful aspect would quite obviously have increased their chances of legal standing. From this perspective a comparative view of other spiritual traditions that have relevance in the understanding of consensual 'SM' as a potentially spiritual practice, appears to be crucial. Within this first section of Chapter 6, parallels and differences that arise out of this comparative perspective will be discussed and an appreciation of the spiritual dimension of consensual 'SM', its deducted existential legitimacy and its potential meanings within contemporary culture will be explored. The last part of this section ends with a discussion of different frameworks that are offered to understand the notion of 'transcendence'.

After this historio-cultural comparative introduction to the understanding of consensual 'SM' as spiritual practice, the sections under Chapter 6 refer to some of the theoretical sources that underline and explain this perspective on the 'bodily practices' of consensual 'SM'. Following the discussion of theoretical sources, empirical data collected around this notion and its experiential implications will be explored. The analysis of the empirical material suggests that consensual 'SM' indeed functions for some practitioners as a spiritual exercise and thus the notion of 'transcendental experiences' through these 'bodily practices' finds its validation in the 'life-worlds' of consensual 'SM'.

6.1 Concepts of 'transcendence' in relation to the 'bodily practices' of consensual 'SM'

In order to explore potential parallels between religious and mystical ritualistic practices and consensual 'SM'-rituals, this section provides an account of a diversity of historical as well as still practised ritual practices and their related concepts of 'transcendence'. Apart from pointing out existing parallels, this section aims to provide an introduction to the socio-cultural and motivational backgrounds indicative of the potential broader social meanings of the rising interest in and engagement with consensual 'SM'.

These motivational backgrounds further point to the need to alter existing legal practice concerning cases of consensual 'SM' as they, as will be elaborated below, reveal that an existential human need of expression and personal insight is catered for through 'transcendental states' obtained through the exercise of these 'bodily practices'.

One crucially important line of distinction between the concepts of transcendence discussed in this section is their implicit or explicit relationship to the 'lived body' and, in effect, to 'sexuality'. Foucault's distinction between cultural conceptions of 'sexuality' and their relationship to the 'lived body' is particularly relevant in this context as these originated first in religious, mystical and magical contexts. In 'The History of Sexuality' (1990 Vol. 1), Foucault suggested that historically two great distinct procedures for the production of the 'truth of sex' existed within the diverse cultures of this world. He distinguished between societies that practice an 'ars erotica' and the mainly Western societies that developed a 'scientia sexualis'.

> In the erotic art, truth is drawn from pleasure itself, understood as a practice and accumulated as experience; pleasure is not considered in

relation to an absolute law of the permitted and the forbidden, nor by reference to a criterion of utility, but first and foremost in relation to itself; it is experienced as pleasure, evaluated in terms of its intensity, its specific quality, its duration, its reverberations in the body and the soul. (Foucault 1990: 57)

The resulting knowledge, based on experience, has to be deflected back into 'sexual' practice to 'shape' the experience from within and in order to aim for the amplification of its effects. The transmission of these knowledges of *ars erotica* happened traditionally through the relationship to a master who held them as secrets. This secrecy was believed to be necessary in order to keep its effectiveness and virtue which would be lost if the knowledge was divulged.

Foucault took account of many cultures in which an ars erotica was employed but he especially focused on ancient Greece and forms of Christianity (e.g. the notions of martyrdom/self-sacrifice) that, for him, had a lot in common with an ars erotica.

In order to reach a deeper understanding of cultural traditions which endow an ars erotica and its implications on the micro (e.g. relationship to 'self' and others) and macro levels of society, this section of Chapter 6 looks more closely at some traditions which appear to have similarities with elements of the concept and ritual of consensual 'SM' as spiritual exercise. The institution of transformation through ritual ordeal and/or sexual ecstasy has an ancient tradition in many cultures and some have striking parallels in the 'bodily practices' of consensual 'SM'.

6.1.1 'Transcendence' in the context of institutionalized religion and parallels to consensual 'SM'

The social relevance and function of religion can already be deducted from the origin of the term. The word religion's etymological definition, which is rooted in the Latin term 'religare', means to bind fast and implies notions of binding, compulsiveness and obligation. It also includes moral and customary aspects of religion: "Religion demands behaviours, loyalties, commitment" (La Barre 1972: 9). According to Durkheim (1965 ori. 1915), the totemic celebration of a group's own sacred in-group-ness is the most elementary form of religious life. Within the Scene that developed around consensual 'SM', the sense of secrecy and diverse membership procedures as well as the commitment to a specific code of conduct and a specific philosophy of life, could therefore be seen as elements of the 'religious life' of the Scene.

On the level of the individual, religion fulfils human needs for, for example, identification and recognition, again similar to the functions that consensual 'SM' potentially provides. For example, the psychoanalyst Jessica Benjamin views 'desire for recognition' as the most fundamental parallel between consensual 'SM' and religion: "..., sexual eroticism appears as the heir to religious eroticism; that is, in sexuality we have a new religion or a substitute for one. The original erotic component, the desire for recognition, seems to emerge in sadomasochism, as it once did in the lives and confessions of saints" (Benjamin in Snitow et al. 1983: 281).

Within the Christian belief-system, the renunciation of one's will and the following of the will of God is a highly valued behaviour and the only path for a true believer.

Medieval devotionalism, for example, which was encouraged by the Franciscan movement, involved the 'giving up of one's will' and was accompanied by 'bodily practices' that led to a feeling of identity with Christ experienced by the worshiper.

Parallels to consensual 'SM' can be detected in this concept of transcendence in a modified form. In consensual 'SM' the will of the 'bottom' is at times given up and/or 'tested' within the frame work of a trusting, consensual relationship to the 'top'. For example, in the ritualistic giving up of one's control (as opposed to one's will e.g. in the 'bottom'-role) to the control of the 'top', in the employment of methods of deprivation like bondage for spiritual retreat and in the so often mentioned feeling of unity and identity felt by the 'bottom' with the 'top'. During 'scenes' the connection between 'top' and 'bottom' becomes highly intensified as many interviewees alike Mike and Ella mentioned: "I become quite disconnected from everything except my top" (Que. M.: 1).

When she was in the position of the 'bottom' or 'sub', Ella described: "Whilst involved in a 'scene' I am actually living it. All outside world disappears. For that period I am only aware of myself and my Master. This is because my need at that time is to be totally controlled, hence I have no will, no thoughts of my own. I hand over myself completely and when I'm really into it nothing is able to distract me. I don't see him as my partner but as a totally different person" (Que. E.: 1).

Although Michel Foucault seemed fascinated by the Christian ideas of martyrdom and self-sacrifice and remarked: "No truth about the self is without the sacrifice of the self" (Miller 1994: 324), he rejected the techniques applied within the Christian context.

The Christian techniques for the subjection of 'self' are unconditional obedience, interminable examination and exhaustive confession, in which the aim is the renunciation of self through perpetual interpretation, therefore:"...the continual mortification entailed by a permanent hermeneutic and renunciation of the self makes of that symbolic death an everyday event" (Bernauer 1992: 165). This 'symbolic death' in the Christian context was especially focused on the 'sinful body' as the site of sensuality, yet, the 'bodily practices' that developed in this connection were themselves producing pleasures. Scott, for example, wrote about Carmelite nun Sister Maria Magdalene of Pazzi: "...who found pleasure in being publicly whipped on her buttocks". On one occasion she cried: "Enough! Fan no longer the flame that consumes me: this is not the death I long for; it comes with all too much pleasure and delight" (Scott 1938: 118).

Flagellant-processions toured throughout Europe from the eleventh century onwards, travelling on pilgrimages. Here discipline of the physical body was meant to liberate the spirit from sensuality. As it became apparent that these 'scourgings' increased sensuality, the Pope opposed them and members of these sects were tortured by the Inquisition.

The phenomenon of martyrdom also implied sensuous pleasures. In 'A Preface to transgression' (Bouchard 1963), Foucault explained his understanding of Christian mysticism. For Foucault Christian mysticism is the precursor of transgression as in it sexuality, rapture, and ecstasy existed at the heart of the divine. This understanding of Christian mysticism comes close to von Sacher-Masoch's explorations on martyrdom in comparison to 'masochism', whereby in his portrayal the 'masochist' is not victimized. In a conversation between Severin and 'Venus', Severin explains: "the martyrs were supersensual beings who found positive pleasure in pain and who sought horrible tortures, even death, as others seek enjoyment" (von Sacher-Masoch in Deleuze 1989: 172). In this view of martyrdom, von Sacher-Masoch and Foucault find themselves supported by Nietzsche who's Zarathustra proclaimed that: "Man is the cruellest animal towards himself; and with all who call themselves 'sinners' and 'bearers of the Cross' and 'penitents' do not overlook the sensual pleasure that is in this complaint and accusation!" (Nietzsche 1966 in Deleuze 1989: 235).

This Christian notion of 'transcendence' is therefore (erotic) pleasure through suffering. The ideal of 'religious suffering' has a long tradition in Christianity, be it Catholic or Protestant. In Knott's (1993) opinion, the stories of the early Christian martyrs all reflect the idea of a 'trial of truth' in which the physical evidence of suffering becomes the central component in the victory of 'truth'. "The greater the physical abuse the victims of persecution endure, the more impressive their spiritual victory and the more telling the contrast between the abused body of the martyr and the glorified body of the saint" (Knott 1993: 10). Martyrdom was seen as a confirmation of the power of God and therefore as comforting for the community of faithful believers. Further it also demonstrated the victory of faith over the physical torment that the authority, be it imperial or ecclesiastical, was ready to inflict. "What should have been marks of shame, physical humiliations reserved for the lowest order of criminals, became badges of the highest spiritual dignity in the eyes of Christians" (Knott 1993: 37).

The ideal of 'mastery' in the suffering of pain and the highly positive value attached to the marks of suffering appear to be similar in Christianity and consensual 'SM'. Many practitioners of consensual 'SM' that 'played' in 'bottom'-space regarded their wounds as tokens of devotion, as memories, as attesting their volition and as symbols of bonding.

Within the Christian belief-system, the body is portrayed as separate from the mind and as mainly being an enemy. This dualistic polarization of body and soul has dramatic consequences as the joy of the body has to be sacrificed for the salvation of the soul. Christianity thus does not embrace any ars erotica as only in negation of the bodily pleasures salvation of the soul can be found.

6.1.2   The distinction of 'Dionysian' and 'Apollonian' cultural practices and consensual 'SM'

In his reflections on the 'body social', Synnott discusses Benedict's comparison of the Apollonian culture and the Dionysian culture, originating in Nietzsche's distinction of Greek tragedies. The Dionysian culture "...of most of the Indian nations of North America and Mexico as a whole: 'They valued all violent experience, all means by which human beings may break through the usual sensory routine, and to all such experiences they attributed the highest value'" (Synnott 1968: 58). A fundamental Dionysian practice common to all but the Pueblos, Benedict argues, is that they "...seek the vision by fasting, by torture, by drugs and alcohol" (Benedict 1968: 62). By transcending the senses, one sees the truth, becomes powerful, and finds the unique 'self'. Classic examples are the Sun Dance of the Western Plains and the Peyote Cult.... "Thus the Apollonian-Dionysian personalities and cultures are not, of course, exclusive to the Indian nations of the Americas. The Dionysian seeks 'to escape from the boundaries imposed upon him by his five senses, to break through into another order of experience...to achieve success' (Benedict 1968: 56)" (Synnott 1993: 145).

Starkloff stated about the native American religious rites of the 'Sun Dance' as well as the 'Peyote Cult' that even though they are based on ancient rites, their development in the late eighteenth and nineteenth century, fulfilled the purpose of bonding – of bringing the now separated native American tribes back together. He remarked that in these contexts the sensual, corporal experiences can be at once a personal and a communal spiritual experience of high intensity. "..., a state of higher consciousness came, as with Zen training and yoga, through severe self-discipline and self-emptying" (Starkloff 1974: 108).

In Starkloff's opinion native American ascetism has been often misunderstood as 'masochism'. The constant awareness of suffering, the return of the tribal division of labour for occasions like the Sun Dance and their relation to religious suffering should, in Starkloff's opinion, be seen as functional in the quest for survival. In comparison with the Scene especially the bonding-ritual of the lesbian and gay practitioners of consensual 'SM' (see Chapter 3) springs to mind here, in which they pierced their chests at various points and danced, connected to each other by pain, while slowly pulling their pierced skins further and further apart.

On a symbolic level this ritual could be read as an intense bonding practice that unites factually disenfranchised members of both, the minority groups with their often prescriptive 'political correctness' (e.g. feminist/ lesbian) and/or stereotypical expectations (e.g. mandatory anal sex in parts of gay culture) about 'sex', as well as dominant culture's socio-political outside pressures of 'normalization'.

"If the suffering of ascetic self-denial is a religious experience, one can perhaps better understand the incredible capacity of the historical Indian tribes to endure the near genocide undergone for some three hundred years" (Starkloff 1974: 118).

As in Christian tradition, the marks of suffering serve as marks of identification for the individual and the community of believers within the native American belief-system. For the traditional native American, personal, individual morality is social morality, they are no separate categories. As with Christianity, within the traditional native American belief-system, religious asceticism has a profound effect on the individual's personal growth as well as indirectly on the life of the tribe. The more suffering (representing offerings to the Creator), the greater the favour asked from the Creator.

Starkloff states that the tradition of asceticism within the native American cultures should be seen positively as it has provided their people with acquired 'self'-knowledge. In my opinion this holds true for consensual 'SM' as well because the aim is to explore the limits of 'self' as defined by the 'lived body'.

Within his answers to the questionnaire Henry explains this notion in the second section of this chapter in which he describes the relationship between his willpower and its effect on the body as an art of self-exploration.

As the notion of the 'Dionysian' serves comparative purposes within psychological and sociological accounts, it appears to be worthwhile to gain a more fundamental understanding of the origins and traditions of the cult of Dionysus.

The cult of Dionysus celebrates the 'twice-born' god, born first prematurely to a mortal lover of Zeus. In reaction to Hera's jealous anger, Zeus rescues his child by sewing the premature foetus into his thigh from where it is born for the second time (Eliade 1978). Dionysus assumed many diverse manifestations, when being celebrated and worshipped in ancient Greece. His followers consisted of groups that were multi-formal. Dionysus "...is certainly the only Greek god who, revealing himself under different aspects, dazzles and attracts both peasants and the intellectual elite, politicians and contemplatives, orgiastics and ascetics" (Eliade 1978: 372).

The figure of Dionysus was androgyne and represented a figure that would lead people to go mad, therefore the exercise of control over Dionysian celebrants became a political topic. Ptolemy IV, for example, ordered that all members of the cult of Dionysus had to register in Alexandria.

Eliade tried to explain opposition towards the cult of Dionysus:

Dionysus was bound to incite resistance and persecution, for the religious experience that he inspired threatened an entire lifestyle and a universe of values. ... But the opposition was also the expression of a more intimate drama, and one that is abundantly documented in the history of religions: resistance to every absolute religious experience, because such experience can be realized only by denying everything else (by whatever term this may be designated: equilibrium, personality, consciousness, reason, etc.). (Eliade 1978: 359)

This 'threat' appears to exist also for society in relation to the 'bodily practices' of consensual 'SM' as, for example, 'technologies of government' are appropriated by its practitioners in order to derive pleasure from them. As elaborated in Chapter 2 the 'bodily practices' of consensual 'SM' also imply the transgression of the existing modern scientific 'order of things' apart from the transgression of the non-consensual 'SM' inherent to Western patriarchal capitalist-consumer societies (Chancer 1994).

Eliade stated that: "Dionysus is a god who shows himself suddenly and then disappears mysteriously" (Eliade 1978: 359). In 'Dionysus-In Excess Of Metaphysics', Sallis describes Dionysus as a withdrawn figure and in excess of metaphysics: "How is it that the figure of Dionysus withholds itself from direct disclosure in an image? It is because, in both senses of the word, there is nothing to be disclosed – no being, no ground, not even Being... but only the abyss of indetermination, nothing" (Sallis 1988 in Krell and Wood 1988: 6).

The crucial parallel to Foucault's concept of transcendence here, lies in the notion of indetermination which is central to Foucault's philosophy and which is emphasized further in connection to the cult of Dionysus.

Eliade, who places Dionysus among the gods of vegetation, relates him also to the totality of life: "...as is shown by his relations with water and germination, blood or sperm, and by the excess of vitality manifested in his animal epiphanies (bull, lion, goat). His unexpected manifestations and disappearances in a way reflect the appearances and occultation of life-that is, the alternation of life and death and, in the last analysis, their unity" (Eliade 1978: 360). On a symbolical level this holds true for consensual 'SM' as well as 'scenes' that make use of, for example, representations of death and/or use blood, also symbolically celebrate a notion of 'life in death'.

Sallis presents the Dionysian as a revelation of the abyss:

...the dissolution of ground and of determination... it is the exceeding of any limit by which the self would be defined and constituted as an interior space of self possession. This exceeding, this being in excess of subjectivity, is at the same time the dissolution of subjectivity, the utter disruption of determinate selfhood, being torn to pieces. The Dionysian state is an abysmal loss of self... of ecstasy, a state of being utterly outside oneself... Dionysian ecstasy, being-outside-oneself, would be a matter not simply of relating an inside to an outside but rather of shifting the 'inside' into the 'outside', displacing it, disrupting the very logic of the opposition inside/outside. The Dionysian, this ecstasy bursting forth from nature itself, would be a deconstruction indeed of subjectivity. (Sallis 1988 in Krell and Wood 1988: 3/11)

Again parallels can be drawn to the Scene in London, particularly in terms of the practice of 'switching' which implies the swapping of subject/object positions that are usually assigned to people without their consent and further in terms of the specifically open atmosphere in Scene-clubs as described by the philosopher Golding (1993). She described the atmosphere at a consensual 'SM'-club in London as a space of 'the-impossible-but-actual-limit-to-the-outside/otherside-of-otherness', a location of an exiled identity: "This is a peculiar identity: one that must always bear an excess, the excessiveness of the game itself, the perverse and excessive game of self, of mastery and submission, all up for negotiation and reformulation" (Golding in Kroker and Kroker 1993: 26/27).

6.1.3 Contrasting the Christian and the Dionysian concepts of 'transcendence'

Nietzsche's contrasting of Dionysus and Christ as the affirmation of life against the depreciation of life is discussed by Gilles Deleuze (1989). Both were martyred, Dionysus by being ripped into pieces and Christ on the cross, and both returned to life. In Deleuze's view and in his interpretation of Nietzsche, the meaning of these two martyrdoms are different:

"In Dionysos and in Christ the martyr is the same, the passion is the same. It is the same phenomenon but in two opposed senses. On the one hand, the life that justifies suffering, that affirms suffering; on the other hand the suffering that accuses life, that testifies against it, that makes life something that must be justified. For Christianity the fact of suffering in life means primarily that life is not just, that it is even essentially unjust, that it pays for an essential injustice by suffering, it is blameworthy because it suffers" (Deleuze 1989: 15).

Deleuze does not understand this opposition of Dionysos and Christ as a dialectical one, but as "opposition to the dialectic itself: differential affirmation against dialectical negation, against all nihilism ..." (ibid.: 17). Further, in Deleuze's view, Nietzsche's characterization of Christ may now be applicable on morality and science: "We must then acknowledge that morality has replaced religion as a dogma and that science is increasingly replacing morality. ... Morality is the continuation of religion but by other means; knowledge is the continuation of religion but by other means" (ibid.: 17).

The lack of areas of spirituality that were formerly satisfied by religious rituals left a void in Western consumer societies. The filling of this void might be one of the broader social meanings that the increased motivation to engage in the 'bodily practices' of consensual 'SM' in contemporary consumer culture signals.

If the essentially limiting institutions of morality and science have 'replaced' and/or de-based traditional religion, then it does not astound any more that mystical and magical elements regained more importance in contemporary Western societies.

6.1.4   The meanings and functions of mysticism in relation to consensual 'SM'

Evelyn Underhill's understanding of mysticism, as cited by Ellwood (1980) enlightens the relationship between transcendental experiences and consensual 'SM'.

> ..., she spoke of mysticism as a quest for truth and reality that goes beyond merely sensory or intellectual spheres, taking on the aspect of a personal passion that must know directly ultimate reality without mediation of mind or sense. She quoted Coventry Patmore to the effect that mysticism is 'the science of ultimates... the science of self-evident Reality, which cannot be "reasoned about", because it is the object of pure reason or perception'. (Ellwood 1980: 14)

The 'bodily practices' of consensual 'SM' could be interpreted as one form of mysticism in which the 'lived body', and in particular its sensuous capacities, are used as a medium. In their research under the heading 'Modern Primitives' Vale and Juno interviewed pierced, tattooed, otherwise 'bodily' modified individuals (e.g. the founder of the Modern Primitive Movement, Musafar Fakir) and practitioners of consensual 'SM', to gain an understanding of the diverse meanings the body can have as an artistic medium. They point out that pain still did not lose its shock value and that: "The most extreme practitioners of SM probe the psychic territory of pain in search of an 'ultimate', mystical proof that in their relationship (between the 'S' and the 'M'), the meaning of 'trust' has been explored to its final limits, stopping just short of the infliction/experiencing of death itself" (Vale and Juno 1989: 5).

The search for authenticity in experience, bonding and trust was also mentioned by some of my interviewees. The people I encountered on the Scene showed a great dislike for 'conditions of domination' (Foucault in e.g. Kritzman 1990; Lotringer 1996) inherent to society and they tried actively to improve and develop ways of relating to each other.

In recourse to Ornstein and Bacon, Frits Staal (1975) noted about the problematic of studying mystical experiences within the traditional sciences: "...nothing can be known with certainty without experience. Experience, according to him [Bacon], is twofold, and includes inner experience, which covers mathematical as well as mystical intuitions. Argument or 'logic' is separate from these. What Ornstein suggests in addition is that argument or logic is not applicable to experience" (Staal 1975: 117).

Staal pointed to an additional problem as: "Mystical experiences are often seen to follow events which cannot be described as prerequisites or methods. Such events are often dramatic and tragic, and they help to shape the mystic's life" (Staal 1975: 135).

With regard to the subjects of this research, one could see this initial, 'by chance' trigger of 'the wish to convert' into another dimension of life, as being for example, the various experiences of serious power abuse recollected by some interviewees, however, several interviewees did not experience 'disillusioning', 'deconstructing' and 'disruptive' events like that. Typically the interviewees without any experience of 'heavy life-events' rather longed for more excitement and 'disruption'.

The methods adopted by mystics have secular justifications according to Staal but always entail a combination of mental and physical elements. Within the later sections of this chapter this is also confirmed and reflected by many of the responses of practitioners of consensual 'SM' to the self-completion questionnaire on 'transcendental experiences'. It appears thus, that every method applied to the 'lived body' will have effects on the whole of the person and therefore transgresses any rigid body/mind split constructions that ignore the complexity of 'lived bodies'.

As another a priori, another prerequisite for mystical experiences, Staal mentions the "...withdrawal of the senses. This is likely to be associated with asceticism and otherworldliness" (Staal 1975: 136). Within their censuring social environment, this withdrawal was in some of my interviewees' lives, a necessity of 'social survival' as their sensual existence often had to be hidden and reduced to rare moments. The artificial and ritual 'withdrawal of the senses' within the 'bodily practices' of consensual 'SM', is practiced by 'bottoms', 'subs' and 'slaves' in varying ways and to different degrees depending on their aims and on the quality of the 'top', 'Dom' or 'Master', who allows the possibility of the experience of the 'withdrawal of the senses' (e.g. forms of sensory deprivation).

Apart from fasting, meditation and breathing exercises have a long tradition in being used by mystics of varying belief systems such as Christianity, Yoga, Buddhism and Taoism (Staal 1975). All these practices allow the individual to first increase the mental awareness and then to decrease the control of the movement of mental fluctuations. Apart from the obvious parallel between these breathing exercises and the consensual 'SM'-practice of temporary suffocation, most of these 'bodily practices' change the breathing-pattern and/or, ability of the 'bottoming' party.

The diverse practices listed above are closely related to the concept of 'detachment' which within the context of Western religions and understandings implies morality. "The mystical significance of detachment does not lie in the realm of ethics. It is an aspect of most of the techniques for training the mind. ... Detachment is to some extent a prerequisite for the other methods, but it is in turn increased by their practice" (Staal 1975: 138/139).

In terms of consensual 'SM' this detachment might be assured a priori through the artificial, theatrical setting that, perhaps due to its ritualistic appearance, allows individuals to detach from the 'outside world' and to completely enter into the world of a 'scene'.

"But any device that diverts the mind's attention from its habitual content is helpful" (Staal 1975: 139).

Within the context of consensual 'SM' the creation of potentially dangerous situations, the induction of fear, the excitement of taboos, 'pain' and 'pleasure', the whole range of 'bodily practices' of consensual 'SM' appears to tend to distract the mind from its habits and preoccupations of thought. The moral stricture that mysticism is subjected to within the Western world and in Islam hinders a proper understanding and appreciation in terms of this broader and open conceptualization that matches consensual 'SM' practices.

Ellwood attempted to present an analytical tool for mystical experiences that is not based and limited by ideological expressions and therefore appears to be a helpful source. In his account many diverse approaches suggest that mystical experience is divisible into three stages, of which the first one is the 'trigger' and/or 'background influence'. The term 'trigger' "...may be some what unfortunate in that it seems to imply an overly mechanical, reductionistic explanation for mystical experience. The writings of the mystics themselves, ..., are full of expressions of the wonder, subtlety, and unexpectedness of their encounters with the transcendent" (Ellwood 1980: 68).

The rituals of a 'scene' and the bodily sensations connected to them, might be termed the 'trigger' of potential mystical experiences within the context of consensual 'SM'. All interviewees who have reported to have 'transcendental experiences', also stated that these experiences were at first totally unexpected and often so subtle that a lot of reflection was needed to recollect them.

The second analytical stage of mystical experience, as suggested by Ellwood, is

> the first moment in the mystical experience proper and its most intense point: a sudden, seemingly spontaneous flash of absolute power or ecstasy. It does not last long in its intense phase, but it imparts enough intensity to leave the experiencer shaken yet enraptured for minutes or even hours afterward. It might make an impression that will last a lifetime, especially when associated inseparably with a meaningful interpretation. (Ellwood 1980: 69)

This impression of 'lifelong validity of experience' is very much parallel to Pat's interpretation of her 'transcendental journey' later in this chapter.

The qualitative content of the mystical experience is nearly indefinable as it is so diverse: "The matter of visual, audial, or conceptual content in the ecstatic moment is, however, problematical. Others report only a marvellous emptiness of thought, a void of bliss" (Ellwood 1980: 69).

The third stage of mystical experience is "... the afterglow, when the intensity recedes and associated ideas and images appear ...; it is rather an associative state, when the experiencer begins the work of relating the experience to other experiences or ideas, particularly those that give meaning to the experience and his or her life" (Ellwood 1980: 69/70).

The integration of the mystical experience into one's individual worldview by means of interpretation might have diverse results as the results of the questionnaire showed. The answers clearly reflect the diversity of potential interpretations as well as the differing consequences that these 'unusual experiences' gained during the 'bodily practices' of consensual 'SM' had for my interviewees.

"In Tantrism or Taoism, ..., sexual practices are judged only in terms of their efficacy in relation to mystical experience. If they assist, they are welcome; if they interfere, they are not; and if neither, they are neutral" (Staal 1975: 140).

In contrast to other religious and/or mystical contexts (e.g. Islam, Christianity etc.) which reject and/or condemn the 'body' and 'sexuality' on the basis moral exclusion, 'sexuality' is utilized especially in the tantric traditions of Indian civilization. "In Tantrism, sexual practices which would be rejected if they were held to be conducive to an increase in mental tension are on the contrary utilized in order to bring about greater detachment from the rules of morality" (Staal 1975: 140).

The diverse means of achieving detachment in this context, are believed to help the individual mind to divert its attention from its habitual content, whereas within the West the 'detachment' of mystical experiences from morality is strongly sanctioned. The counter-example of tantric detachment must be understood within the context of Indian societies. "By introducing sexual practices, Tantrism undermines in the first place the value system of the caste hierarchy, and thus frees the mind from numerous fluctuations ... the view that mysticism is connected with passivity and/or irresponsibility is pure prejudice" (Staal 1975: 141).

This view of mysticism also matches Vale and Juno's suggestions as to the reason of the 'revival of the primitive':

All the 'modern primitive' practices being revived-so called 'permanent' tattooing, piercing, and scarification-underscore the realization that death itself, ..., must be stared straight in the face, ... Death remains the standard whereby the authenticity and depth of all activities may be judged. ... Our most inestimable resource, the unfettered imagination, continues to be grounded in the only truly precious possession we can ever have and know, and which is ours to do with what we will: the human body. (Vale and Juno 1989: 5)

Mysticism in terms of the understanding of 'Modern Primitives', is an active philosophically inspired search for new values and meanings for the individual as well as for society in general and not a passive act of regression. This view reflects another possible interpretation of the potential broader social meanings the rising interest and engagement in the 'bodily practices' of consensual 'SM' might have in contemporary consumer cultures.

A mystical tradition which is centred around the figure of a 'master' was mentioned by Pat (Que. P.: 4–6), when she termed one of her most intense experiences of consensual 'SM' of a transcendental quality a 'shamanic journey'.

Eliade (in Couliano 1991) defined shamanism as a 'technique of ecstasy' as opposed to a proper religion. Shamanism consists of a system of ecstatic and therapeutic methods that enable human beings to make contact with the universe of the spirits which exists parallel to the 'here and now' world in shamanistic belief-systems. Apart from mere contact, it is attempted to gain the support of the spirits in order to improve the management of individual or group affairs.

In archaic time the shaman was a religious specialist with spiritual powers. In the case of a successful initiation, the shaman would be able to go into trances, detect reasons for illnesses, fly into the world of the gods and the dead and could communicate with spirits about the existential needs of the community. The initiation of the shaman had to be painful as this would allow for new insights, Ellwood quotes an Inuit shaman: "... 'All true wisdom is only to be found far from men, out in the great solitude, and it can only be acquired by suffering. Privations and sufferings are the only things that can open a man's mind to that which is hidden from others'" (Ellwood 1980: 45).

In 'I am the leatherfaerie shaman', Norman (1991) points to the parallels between shamanism and consensual 'SM' apart from the application of similar methods. Like shamanism the 'bodily practices' of consensual 'SM' can be an "... ongoing process of initiation and a continuous search for new experience and knowledge of 'self' ..." (in Thompson 1991: 280).

As a crucial precondition for a pleasurable 'scene', the 'top', often a former 'bottom', also ideally has learned to 'control personal spirits' in order to empathize with the 'spirits' of her/his 'bottoms' through the journey of a 'scene', which sometimes, and apparently not that rarely, allows for 'transcendental experiences'. During a 'scene', the 'top', similar to a shaman, makes use of objects that symbolize societal power, for example, instruments of corporal punishment of humans or instruments representing the power of the science of medicine over the individual 'body'. These tools function in terms of providing a setting of 'spiritual atmosphere' that is meant to enable the 'bottom' to reach 'ecstasy' and possibly 'transcendental states'.

6.1.5 'Transcendence' of societal values:
The relationship between the Scene and society

> it is important to emphasize the tradition within popular culture of transgression, protest, the carnivalesque and liminal excesses. ...The popular tradition of carnivals, fairs and festivals provided symbolic inversions and transgressions of the official 'civilised' culture and favoured excitement, uncontrolled emotions and the direct and vulgar grotesque bodily pleasures of fattening food, intoxicating drink and sexual promiscuity. ...These were liminal spaces, in which the everyday world was turned upside down and in which the tabooed and fantastic were possible, in which impossible dreams could be expressed. The liminal, according to Victor Turner..., points to the emphasis within these essentially delimited transitional or threshold phases upon anti-structure and communitas, the generation of a sense of unmediated community, emotional fusion and ecstatic oneness.
>
> (Featherstone 1993: 22)

The Scene that developed around the 'bodily practices' of consensual 'SM', serves also as such a 'liminal space'; everything can, as long as it is negotiated about and done in consent, be acted out. Even though there is the basic rule of 'consent', the atmosphere within the 'genuine' clubs is very much that of an anti-structure and communitas that bonds the members together. Anti-structure also involves the rejection of 'status quo' meanings.

Meaning, for the individual as well as for groups, is derived by means of language, symbols etc. from a given society, in other words through the 'social construction of reality' (Berger and Luckmann 1966), the dialectical chain of human projection invests human lives in society with meaning. The processes of externalization, objectification and internalization continuously reinforce the reality construction of a given society.

In his reflections on the relationship between culture and the individual, Aldous Huxley suggested that: "A culture cannot be discriminatingly accepted, much less be modified, except by persons who have seen through it – by persons who have cut holes in the confining stockade of verbalized symbols and so are able to look at the world and, by reflection, at themselves in a new and relatively unprejudiced way" (Huxley in Solomon 1964: 31).

As people need to be prepared for the process of 'hole cutting' the option of the integration of culture comparisons within society's formal education appears to be valuable but insufficient as the whole of the person, the 'lived body', must be captured in order to change. In Aldous Huxley's opinion the experience of LSD induced altered states of consciousness allows for this particular kind of 'training' as the highly intense and unusual experiences enable the individual to be more 'open' to change.

Within the context of scientific research on the effects of LSD and other psychedelic substances on the human consciousness, the central metaphor employed by Timothy Leary in order to explain the 'psychedelic effect' was: "You have to go out of your mind to use your head" (Leary in Solomon 1964: 16).

The goal of going beyond our normal conceptual framework which is indicated in this metaphor was shared by most of the great religions and mysticisms, a few of which have been mentioned within this section of Chapter 6 as well as by practitioners of consensual 'SM'.

For Leary (1964), the yearning and potential of human beings for transcendence (which are related to culturally determined fears, Chapter 4) is a fundamental characteristic of human beings. The liberational aspects and possibilities of 'transcendental experiences' listed by him, can be summarized as a potential cognitive 'transcendence' that allows for new insights as well as a social 'transcendence' that allows for openness to new experiences as social inhibitions are lost. Further Leary mentions a psychological 'transcendence' allowing for discovering the individual 'self' beyond the usual limits of seeing your 'self' as well as cultural 'transcendence' which allows for the envisioning of new institutional solutions. The last liberational possibility Leary suggests is an ontological 'transcendence' that allows the internal freedom of choice of movement between different levels of consciousness.

The de-centring of the 'self' by means of 'transcendental experiences', appear to allow for the most fundamental changes in consciousness and often also result in behavioural changes. As all behaviour is learned and culturally determined, it is changeable. In order to explain behavioural changes, Leary (1964) employed the notion of a 'game' to define 'a learned cultural sequence.

"Psychology, religion, politics are games, too, learned, cultural sequences with clearly definable roles, rules, rituals, goals, jargons, values" (Leary in Solomon 1964: 99). The problem with these complex 'games' listed above in comparison with for example, sports and consensual 'SM', is that they are less explicitly games.

> Worst of all is the not knowing that it is a game. Baseball is a clean and successful game because it is seen as a game. You can shift positions. (...) You can quit, start a new game. Culturally, stability is maintained by keeping the members of any cultural group from seeing that the roles, rules, goals, rituals, language, and values are game structures. ... Cultural institutions encourage the delusion that the games of life are inevitable givens involving natural laws of behavior. These fixed delusions tend to rigidify behavior patterns. (Leary in Solomon 1964: 100)

The game of consensual 'SM' symbolically points to the game-character of 'normal life', which in Foucauldian terms, is often determined by socio-political relationships of power that turn rigid and thus effect 'conditions of domination'. Consensual 'SM' is always clearly a game with all the advantages of a game, one can start and stop when one likes (sometimes laid down by contract) and the flexibility of the game is ensured by the possibility of 'switching' and by the fantasy and empathy developing within the game situation ('scene').

In Leary's opinion the "... most effective approach to the 'practical' games of life is that of applied mysticism. Identify the game structure of the event. Make sure that you do not apply the rules and concepts of other games in this situation. ... The process of getting beyond the game structure, beyond the subject-object commitments, the dualities-this process is called the mystic experience" (Leary in Solomon 1964: 103/104). This points to the problematic relationship of 'moral' and/or 'radical feminism' towards consensual 'SM'. The arguments against consensual 'SM' as well as the selective 'celebration' of lesbian 'SM', suggest that the representations and concepts of societal power relationships with their explicit and implicit rules are stabilized and reinforced within the setting of the 'scenes' of these 'bodily practices'.

These arguments from 'moral' and 'radical' feminists alike do not try to go beyond the game structures of society and thus promote a positivistic view of human beings based on (sometimes selective) socio-political determinism.

Leary lists diverse methods that expand consciousness beyond game limits such as traumatic limit-experiences, electric shock, extreme fatigue, sensory deprivation, etc. that all 'cut through the game'. "Certain forms of sensory stimulation alter consciousness beyond games. The sexual orgasm is certainly the most frequent and natural, although so brief and so built into interpersonal courtship games that it has lost much of its mystical meaning in the West" (Leary in Solomon 1964: 106).

In consumer society in which orgasms get consumed, counted and chemically achieved, the notion of a mystical experience through orgasm, might only survive in a few human beings.

The consequence of 'transcendental experiences' is, according to Leary, the 'unplugged mind'. "Not the 'id'; no dark, evil impulses. These alleged negative 'forces' are, of course, part of the game, being simply anti rules. What is left is something that Western culture knows little about: the open brain, the uncensored cortex-alert and open to a broad sweep" (Leary in Solomon 1964: 106). The atmosphere within the Scene encourages the exploration of new understandings and the progressive decline in meaning of traditional ones. On the individual level the experience of 'discret altered states of consciousness' (Tart 1975), of 'transcendence' or of 'peak-experiences' (Maslow 1970) that several interviewees reported and which probably is experienced by many others, appears to have a direct impact on the social atmosphere within the Scene as well as on individuals.

Mystical experience has such an inner ring of authenticity that it also authenticates whatever areas of life, indeed whatever life-styles, with which it is symbolically associated. When an individual's life is sufficiently different as to have only questionable social legitimation, this individual naturally craves a corresponding inner authentication. Mystical experience can answer to this need. (Ellwood 1980: 142)

Michel Foucault believed in the value of experience and, further, that in order to move beyond our identifications with 'sex-desire' (due to the prevalence of the 'scientia sexualis' within the Western world), a return to 'bodies and pleasures' would be needed which could promote an 'economy of pleasure' not based on 'sexual' norms nor on the liberation of a constructed 'sexdesire'. Thus, Foucault's notion of a return to bodies and pleasures entails rather: "...a creation of anarchy within the body, where its hierarchies, its localizations and designations, its organicity, if you will, is in the process of disintegrating..." (Foucault in Miller 1994: 274).

Parallels to Foucault's explorations can be found in parts of Thompson's 'Leatherfolk'. Herein, Norman, who practices 'leatherfarie shamanism' explains his view of the purpose of shamanism and consensual 'SM': "Such practices are not done with intent to cause harm, but to break cultural conditioning and put one in altered states of consciousness in order to repattern the mind. We often learn best through suffering. An intense experience will have lasting effects, cause permanent change, and open the self to new experiences" (Norman in Thompson 1991: 279).

The effects of 'mystical' and/or 'transcendental' experiences through the 'bodily practices' of consensual 'SM' may be seen in the development of an 'empowered' attitude and/or behaviour changes of individuals. Jane for example once stated: "I'm not going to turn around and blame the abuse. Obviously I condemn the abuse and I think it's wrong and awful and terrible. I'm responsible for my own emotions and my feelings" (Interview-file J.: 4).

In my opinion Jane's remark 'transcends' the stereotypical concepts of child-abuse victims. The effect of this formal and informal stereotyping often amount to a 'secondary victimization' in terms of ascribing a passive 'victim-role' onto the concerned human beings. In contrast to this 'societal reality' Jane's account of dealing with child-abuse experiences is far more positive and active, especially the notion of responsibility for oneself and care for one's emotions breaks with the rather deterministic approaches of aetiological concepts.

Another interviewee appears to express Foucault's aim of 'abolishing the internal supervisor' and/or the 'panopticon of everyday life'. Anthony believes in choices that transcend the socially set boundaries not by principle but as a strategy to achieve more freedom. "We've already lived in a repressive culture anyway, this is why I keep pushing my boundaries to see what works for me, you know what I'm saying?...I think people have to make their own choices without that power within: you can't do this, you can't do that" (Interview-file 3: 3).

The 'bodily practices' of consensual 'SM' appear to provide some practitioners with the possibility of experiencing 'spirituality'. This feature of consensual 'SM'-practice is also an element of many diverse religions and mystical belief systems that also involve the body as a whole. Consensual 'SM' can therefore satisfy the longing for religious and spiritual experiences for some practitioners and further provide them with the possibility of self-actualization (e.g. through experience of 'boundary situations', etc.). In 'Psychology of Religion' (1997), Wulff referred to the relationship between 'bodily states' and religious or spiritual experience and pointed out: "..., it is impossible to find any religious experience or behaviour that is not grounded in the fact of embodiment" (Wulff 1997: 49/50).

As not only my interviewees in London but also several other sources that are related to the empirical world (e.g. Foucault, Thompson, Califia, Bastian) point to the phenomena of 'transcendental states' through the practice of consensual 'SM', it is reasonable to assume this to be a relatively frequent feature of the 'bodily practices'.

Conceptual frameworks for similar holistic 'self'-explorations with the employment of helpful tools do exist, for example in belief systems that imply rewards for suffering (Christianity) or that provide methods that allow the individual to engage in an existential quest (e.g. Shamanism, Tantrism) throughout all times and cultures. The phenomena of 'transcendental experiences' through the 'bodily practices' of consensual 'SM', should thus be regarded as an important aspect of the commitment (Becker 1960) that practitioners of consensual 'SM' can develop towards their 'plays'. This degree of (religious, spiritual or quasi-religious) commitment of individual 'players' should be taken into account, when the issue of the degrees of 'bodily harm' in the context of consensual 'SM'-play are discussed.

6.2   The 'bodily practices' of consensual 'SM' as spiritual exercise

"An inverse relationship has generally been assumed between delinquency and *religiosity*. Although earlier studies found a small negative relation between delinquency and religious attendance, inconsistent findings have been reported.... It was suggested that the influence of religion on delinquency is most likely to be mediated via the type of family and friends it dictates" (Blackburn 1995: 200). Ronald Blackburn's 'The Psychology of Criminal Conduct' presents contemporary theories of psychology, sociology and social psychology on the topics of 'deviance' and offending behaviour that also covers the area of 'sexual deviations', including 'SM'. The relationship between spirituality and '(sexual) deviance' is, however, a neglected area in social research so far.

Horn et al. do refer to studies that explored the relationship between sexuality and spirituality (e.g. Wade 2000, MacKnee 2002 and Murray-Swank et al. 2005); in which "... individuals experienced connections with God and with their partner [which] resulted in a breakdown of 'dualism in all forms' that reconciled body and spirit, male and female, human and nature" (Horn et al. 2005: 83). However, these studies were all exclusively concerned with heterosexual relationships and 'vanilla sex' and thus quite selectively within the heteronormative sphere.

Califia's book 'Sensuous magic' defines a 'SM orgasm' as: "The reaching of an emotional, psychological, or spiritual state of catharsis, ecstasy, or transcendence during an S/M scene without having a genital orgasm" (Califia 1994: 151), I consider the exploration and empirical research on consensual 'SM' and spirituality to be of relevance.

Michel Foucault, himself a practitioner of consensual 'SM', mentioned his aims and hopes for 'transcendence' through these 'bodily practices' several times (Miller 1994). According to Foucault's own experiences 'transcendental states through "SM"-practice' are:"... potentially self-destructive yet mysteriously revealing states of dissociation..." (in Miller 1994: 30) that allow a completely different view of the world and open up possibilities for the 'invention' of a new self.

Other related sources that refer to the 'transcendental' dimension of consensual 'SM' are to be found in the works of Pat Califia as well as Mark Thompson, who both enjoy the practices of consensual 'SM' and have described the possibility of achieving similar states. In his book 'Chainmale 3SM' Bastian stated: "... this whole Leather thing has very little to do with Leather as defined within erotic parameters, and lots to do with life in more general terms... when something so profoundly effects so much of everyday life, it becomes very much a part of existence. It is soul and it is spiritual" (Bastian 2002: 112).

Mark Thompson's explorations on this topic are a bit more extended and he explained that the notion of 'SM' as a basis for greater spiritual awareness was only very slowly acknowledged by the practitioners themselves due to the difficulty of description: "It is little wonder that we sometimes refer to them as religious experiences, because that's what they can feel like. Those who experience the rites of passage that I went searching for over twenty years ago *and are transformed by them* have come to form a kind of fraternity – a brotherhood or sisterhood of those who have traveled within to confront the Inner Self" (Thompson 1991: 172).

Under the heading 'New Age leather', Thompson explains the notion of consensual 'SM' as a possible meditation path in more practical detail:

When leather and S/M scenes were done in a certain way, we achieved a different level of awareness – we felt transformed into someone whom it felt better to be. ... Some of us referred to it as the 'S/M high', because when it happened, it felt similar to but better than the best drug experiences we had shared earlier with LSD (acid) and other such drugs during the sixties. Because the element of ecstatic transformation was common to these experiences, they felt spiritual to many of us. (Thompson 1991: 172)

As all the sources are themselves directly linked to the social world through the personal experiences of their authors, the topic of 'transcendence' through consensual 'SM' has empirical relevance, especially as there appears to be no empirical data and/or theories which directly focus on this aspect of consensual 'SM'. The theoretical relevance of this topic was implicitly already stated by Foucault himself, when he commented on the relationship between 'limit experience' (e.g. 'transcendental experiences through "S/M"') and the 'history of truth'. Foucault admitted that when starting from some personally transformative 'limit experience', "it is necessary to open the way for a transformation, a metamorphosis, that is not simply individual but has a character accessible to others" (Miller 1994: 32).

Within the specific context of my research project my aim was to find out if Michel Foucault's frequent but rather vague suggestions about the use of consensual 'SM' for the possible 'transcendence' of culturally learned and internalized categories of for example, sex and sexuality and a new 'mapping' of the 'lived body' are:

(a) shared motivations and/or experiences of other practitioners of consensual 'SM'
(b) a priori or gained motivations

Apart from the exploration of the motivations, I also intended to find out more about the quality and the impact of these experiences for the practising people.

6.2.1 The questionnaire on 'transcendental experiences' through the 'bodily practices' of consensual 'SM'

Guided by Foucault's project to find out about the way 'truth' is formed in relationships between knowledge and power within social practices (Foucault 1980), I intended to explore his notion of *the only way* to go beyond this 'truth' ('transcendence'). I thus had to make use of multiple methods which give different perspectives on this complicated subject. Overcoming our identification of ourselves with 'truth' that shapes our relationship to ourselves as well as others, as for example, in the case of 'sexuality' (identification of human beings with their 'sex-desire' or 'genital desire'), through a return to 'bodies' and 'pleasures' (by means of e.g. consensual 'SM' and potentially 'transcendental experiences' reached through these practices), was one central concern of Michel Foucault's life and work (see Miller 1994). These ideas that were informed by 'lived experience' appeared to be worthwhile to explore further, even with the medium of a self-completion questionnaire.

As explained in the methodological section of this piece of work I had to design a questionnaire for the purpose of data collection on this topic. In common with McLaughlin, I believe that: "...questionnaires can tap meanings if adequately designed and piloted and that the divide which is often thought to exist between quantitative and qualitative research, actually 'impoverishes' the aim of understanding and explaining human relations (McLaughlin 1991)" (May 1993: 88).

Which methods of interpretation are being used by people to attribute meaning to their social environment and to themselves is one of the central concerns of this work. Within this part of my work I therefore don't elaborate on the methodological aspects of the design of the 'self-completion questionnaire' I employed but on the issues that revolve around its difficult contents.

Apart from methodological and structural requirements the other determining factor for the design of a questionnaire is, according to May (1993), the amount of resources that are available beforehand.

In the case of 'transcendental' experiences through the practices of consensual 'SM' there was an absence of former research-material or directly focused theoretical works. Therefore I had to organize my literature review in an interdisciplinary fashion, alongside psychological and parapsychological books that deal with so-called 'transcendental experiences' in other contexts (mainly by Grof 1985 and Tart 1975) and literature that explored 'transcendental experiences' in religious contexts (e.g. Maxwell and Tschudin 1990 and Jones 1991) which will be introduced below.

Even in 2006 Martin still remarked that there does not exist much empirical research on transcendent 'sexual' experiences, referring to Wade's work (2000) as one of the notable few. Westhaver (2005) pointed to a lack of incorporation of the 'ineffable body' as being characteristic for much of academic work but especially evident within the realm of 'sexual' health research and promotion. Consequently: "...we exclude an aspect of the subject-ineffable bodily experience, the self shattered in the face of pleasure-that is constitutive of what we are" (Westhaver 2005: 357).

6.2.2   The possibility of 'transcendence' within the setting of a 'boundary situation'

In 'The History of Sexuality' (Vol. 1), Michel Foucault suggested that *the only way* to go beyond an identification of ourselves with our 'sex drive' or 'genital desire' would be a return to 'bodies and pleasures' and he often used the term 'transcendence' in this connection.

As human beings we are rather reluctant to change in general. To open up the complex structures of the 'self' for possible change our 'lived bodies' need intense raptures. Human beings reliance upon systems of significant symbols for orientation, communication and safety result in an eager control of the 'self'. If Foucault's notion of a 'deployment of sexuality' is valid, then the social construction of 'sexuality' was the basis for an apparatus of subjection of human beings. Our 'lived bodies' and 'selves' are 'sexed' and 'sexualized' and thus deeply subjected to 'truth'.

To *go beyond* the moral imprisonment built within us, through the internalization of 'truth' (as constructed predominantly by legitimized discourses and experts but also by the media), Michel Foucault believed that we have to abolish the 'internal supervisor'. Progress of the individual 'self' and the abolition of the 'internal supervisor', according to Foucault, is possible through 'limit-experiences'. In connection to the notion of 'limit-experience' Foucault understood consensual 'SM' as a 'social experiment' which explores radical 'politics' of the 'self'. Similar concept's to Foucault's can also be found in the philosophy of Jaspers as well as Merleau-Ponty's notion of 'lived body' and in the psychologies of Maslow and Tart. These concepts are all guided by the belief in individual change through intense experiences. The artificial creation of a 'boundary situation' (Jaspers 1951) or 'peak-experience' (Maslow 1970) through the context of consensual 'SM' (e.g. 'scenes' involve the deliberate exposure of an individual to experiences of mental and/or physical 'pain') can thus be regarded as allowing for possible changes of 'self'.

6.2.3   The definition of 'boundary situation'

Based on the philosophy of Karl Jaspers, 'boundary situations' (e.g. struggle, suffering, guilt, death) are common to all human beings and: "...open up existence to the reality of transcendence" (Schrag 1971: 164). These 'boundary situations' are special insofar as, although nearly everything within our empirical existence can be organized and planned, using common categories that structure our life and culture, inside a 'boundary situation' the human being has to confront an extreme situation unprepared, thus in a 'lawless state'. Known and well-approved behaviour and/or thought mechanisms do not provide the necessary resources to deal with these situations-new solutions must be found.

"...wonder, doubt, the experience of ultimate situations, are indeed sources of philosophy, but the ultimate source is the will to authentic communication, which embraces all the rest" (Jaspers 1951: 26). Remembering the value most practitioners attached to the intense communication before, during and after 'scenes' (see Chapter 3), it appears as though the wish to engage in 'authentic communication' is already a given precondition for most practitioners of consensual 'SM' as these 'bodily practices' require intense, authentic communication from the outset. Despite their differences, Jaspers (1951) shared Foucault's critique of the absolute and exclusive claims of scientific theories, the value of communication and the aim of a change in 'being'.

Truth for Jaspers as for Foucault has to be founded on experience and is always uncertain, fragmented and experimental. This untraditional, quite 'postmodern' approach then has important consequences for philosophy:

> Consequently philosophy demands: seek constant communication, risk it without reserve, renounce the defiant self-assertion which forces itself upon you in ever new disguises, live in the hope that in your very renunciation you will in some incalculable way be given back to yourself. ... To philosophize is then at once to learn how to live and to know how to die. Because of the uncertainty of temporal existence life is always an experiment... let us go our way, without knowing the whole, ... (Jaspers 1951: 124/125)

6.2.4   The concept of 'peak experience'

> an ecstatic experience similar to the religious mystical unitive experience, but triggered by situations such as love, dancing, childbirth, sex, aesthetic insight, etc.
>
> (in Maxwell and Tschudin 1990: 198)

Based on a fundamental criticism of traditional psychoanalysis and behaviourism, Abraham Maslow suggested that psychology ought to be a combination of observation and introspection rather than to focus on one or the other in order to gain an understanding of the whole personality. In 1962 Maslow conducted a study of individuals who had had spontaneous 'mystical states' or 'peak-experiences'. He opposed the interpretation of such phenomena as pathological and instead considered them to be supernormal (but not 'supernatural') and associated them with self-realization tendencies within the human being. Maslow's studies on 'self-actualization' found that the experience of dramatic 'peak-experiences' which are also described as a 'cognition of being', 'mystic' experience or 'oceanic', form a central part of the 'self-actualizing' individuals lives he studied and provoked constructive personality changes.

Under the premise that societies have become too technologized and people too detached from emotions, resulting in alienation and de-humanization, this holistic view of human beings considers experiental and physical means as helpful to promote personality change aiming for "...individual growth or self-actualization, rather than adjustment" (Grof 1985: 179).

The experimental procedures of consensual 'SM' are also aiming at the 'whole' of the human being, its 'lived body' and work with non-verbal and physical means in addition to verbal ones. The goal of some of these existential experiments in consensual 'SM' as well as in humanistic therapies is the self-actualization of the human being and *not* as in traditional psychologies the personal adjustment to normative systems (e.g. social ordering and separating of human beings according to ascribed statuses of 'gender', 'age', 'class', 'ableism', etc.).

A common feature of 'boundary situations', 'peak-experiences' and the consensual 'SM'-'laboratory of life' (Foucault) is that, exposed to situations like this, the individual is, in confrontation with this 'existential situation', unable to apply its 'normal' habitual thought processes and behaviour patterns (including the 'internal supervisor'). The 'void' created by the experience of 'boundary situations' and the existential experience of an absolute borderline, throws the individual back onto itself as it is experiencing a loss of all security within this 'limit-experience of the self'.

"... one [has] to be ready to *convert* one's self and one's whole way of seeing the world, ..." (Foucault in Miller 1994: 325). Given these individual preconditions, Foucault believed that transcendence of the culturally coded 'self' could be achieved in the 'boundary situation'-setting of consensual 'SM-scenes'. Alike Jaspers and Maslow, Foucault believed that human beings can only look for 'truth' in experience and in order to transcend fixed identifications of themselves based on 'sex-desire', Foucault considered an authentic return to 'bodies' and 'pleasures' for example, within the 'laboratory of life' of consensual 'SM' to be a promising possibility. "With the help of the right 'instruments'... and 'symbols' ..., one might be able, ... 'to invent oneself' – to make a new 'self' appear ..." (Foucault in Miller 1994: 269).

In Foucault's opinion these 'bodily practices' offer a way to discover 'new forms of life', because one's thinking (about the 'self' and its orientation through organizing, limiting and hierarchical categories) would get ruptured and shattered through the suffering-pleasure obtained in this special 'limit-experience'.

6.2.5 'Transcendental experiences' and 'discrete altered states of consciousness' (d-ASC)

While Wade's research (2000) also employed categories developed by Grof (1985) as indicators of 'transcendental experiences', my own research drew on Grof (1985), Tart (1975) and further included Maxwell and Tschudin's (1990) categories. The book 'Seeing The Invisible' (1990) explores modern religious and other transcendent experiences. Herein the editors Meg Maxwell and Verena Tschudin introduce four 'Common elements of religious and other transcendent experiences' which the psychologist William James had found to be the psychological criteria of mystic experience. "James describes four elements as characteristic of mystical states: there is an ineffability about them (they cannot be adequately described); a noetic quality is present (a sense of 'knowing' of a different order); there is transiency (the experience is short-lived); and there is passivity (the experience is received and happens despite what the person is doing at the time)" (Maxwell and Tschudin 1990: 17). These elements already point towards the difficulties implicit in a research on 'transcendental states': the problems of wording. There are no adequate words or symbols readily available to describe internal experiences like this as they are often too sublime in character to be properly expressed.

I therefore had to begin to establish an understanding of 'transcendence' and its various meanings in an exploratory manner because of the often rather vague definitions of this term. This vagueness is due to the lack of interest within the conventional scientific/academic arena which results in a lack of discourse, reflected by a lack of adequate language (terminology). Therefore the topic of 'transcendental states' proved to be a difficult one which is represented by its basic criteria "...ineffability (it cannot really be described), ..." (Ellwood 1980: 15). It was thus going to be 'hard to put into words' for the respondents to the questionnaire.

6.2.6   d-ASCs and their relevance to human beings

> ..., desire for religious experiences, increased by the breakdown of the traditional value system of our culture, is responsible for people seeking out ASCs by various means.
>
> (Tart 1975: 13)

As early as 1975 the transpersonal psychologist Charles T. Tart, who studied and researched various 'States of consciousness', pointed to the lack of scientific research on, what he termed *'discrete altered state of consciousness'* or 'd-ASC':

> These types of experience are not limited to ASCs induced by drugs, of course, but can occur in meditative states and other kinds of ASCs. Yet, these kinds of experiences of ecstasy, other 'dimensions', mystical union, rapture, beauty, space-and-time transcendence, and transpersonal knowledge are simply not dealt with adequately in conventional scientific approaches. They are either not dealt with at all or are swept into the wastebasket category of 'subjective' and 'pathological' experiences. These kinds of experiences will not disappear if we crack down more on psychedelic drugs [or in contemporary times on ecstasy and crack cocaine etc.; remark of the author] (an obviously impossible task-obvious to everyone but the government), for immense numbers of people are now practicing various nondrug techniques, such as meditation and yoga, for producing ASCs. (Tart 1975a: 12)

The explorative research on 'transcendental states during the practice of consensual 'SM' therefore took place on sensitive grounds as there was a lack of words to adequately express experiences formerly unnoticed, unnamed and perhaps therefore unreflected upon. Very much in contrast to the area of 'sexual' behaviours in which sexology, psychiatry, psychology and various media provide discourses and endless specifying categories, the area of *'discrete altered states of consciousness'* offers a lot of scientific silence and neglect to be discovered.

6.2.7   The theoretical possibility of the experience of 'transcendental states' within the context of consensual 'SM'

In his book 'Foucault and Derrida-The other side of reason', Roy Boyne concludes his understanding of Foucault's last books which come close to my own understanding of them: "... [they], do begin to present a counter-vision to the experience of modern culture. Like some contemporary Descartes, Foucault offers the possibility especially in *The Use of Pleasure*, that there are political resources within the self that have remained untapped and forgotten for millennia" (Boyne 1990: 126). The 're-regulation of the self' involves the experience of a loss of the former 'self'. This in my opinion explains Foucault's aim for 'transcendental experiences' (altered states of consciousness; here called d-ASC) in the 'bodily practices' of consensual 'SM'.

The invention of 'new forms of life' in which one's habitual way of thinking and relating to oneself (through organizing, limiting and hierarchical categories) is ruptured and shattered through the intense suffering-pleasure obtained during consensual 'SM', can thus be linked to states of dissociation resulting from d-ASCs. During an interview in 1981 Foucault (in Miller 1994: 30) explained the appeal of extreme forms of passion in terms of a linkage between 'suffering-pleasure' to an ability to 'see the world completely differently' through potentially self-destructive yet also revealing states of intense dissociation.

In order to understand the connections between 'suffering-pleasure' and a possible change of consciousness, literature that especially deals with different states of consciousness proved to be helpful. The psychologist Charles T. Tart (1975) describes two basic operations that are essential for reaching an "altered state of consciousness". The first operation is the *application of disrupting forces* to the basic 'normal' state of consciousness, which Tart calls the 'baseline' state of consciousness.

A disruption of the 'baseline' state of consciousness can be achieved through "... psychological and/or physiological actions that disrupt the stabilization processes..." (Tart 1975: 7) of the 'self'. As these processes require interference or a withdrawal of 'attention/awareness energy' to be disrupted, the rupture needs to be intense, according to Tart.

The second operation that Tart finds essential is the *application of patterning forces* which has to follow a successful 'rupture' of the integrity of the 'self', which brings structures as well as subsystems of it to their limits of functioning and beyond. During this 'chaotic period' within the 'self', psychological and/or physical actions are able to pattern new structures and subsystems for a new self. The 'bodily practices' of consensual 'SM' could thus be seen as another way to alter consciousness, like religious trance and/or the intake of consciousness altering substances. As consensual 'SM' directly focuses on power relations, which are within this context used by people for their own means, the practice of consensual 'SM' might have much more complex effects, even in the long run, for people who practice it. As social power relations are almost always hidden, unnegotiated as well as rigidly positioned and ascribed, the playful and therefore 'creative' way of dealing with them within consensual 'SM'-settings can be interpreted in terms of 'creative appropriation' and 'resignification' (Halperin 1995). The 'switching' of power positions within the context of consensual 'SM' and the focus on pleasure as opposed to the adaptation to and silent 'suffering' under given 'conditions of domination' (Foucault) of societal power inequalities have an additionally relativating character. Practitioners of consensual 'SM' are possibly more aware of their imminent abilities to resist the dogmatic belief in given social constructions that often imply power differences based on the hierarchical and binary structures after experiences like this.

"These large shifts in ego sense in d-ASCs may later modify the ordinary d-SoC functioning of the Sense of Identity sub-system" (Tart 1975: 134) to describe the possible consequences of the experience of an altered state of consciousness. A new 'scripting of the self' seems thus to be an option in consensual 'SM', the result might be what Tart termed an 'Ego-Transcendent Identity' that breaks with its habitual responses:

> ..., it is said to reduce one's sense of separation from others while at the same time conferring a greater personhood. One is simultaneously less and more than his or her former self, newly connected with the world at large but also more powerful, independent, and self-sufficient. Such experience typically confers a confluence of freedom and security that does not depend upon this or that set of a confluence of freedom and security that does not depend upon this or that set of behaviours. (Tart 1975: 87)

The shared view within the literature on 'transcendental experiences' is that the common indicator for such experiences is a highly subjective one: the feelings of the individual.

> Science, as an organized social effort has been incredibly successful in dealing with the set of experiences we attribute to physical reality, and it has historically become associated with the philosophy of physicalism, the belief that physical reality exists independently of our perception of it, and is the ultimate reality. ... Unfortunately (for those accepting physicalistic philosophy), the vast majority of important phenomena of d-ASCs and spiritual phenomena have no known physical manifestations: they are purely internal experiences. ... Science has not had any important degree of success in reducing any of these phenomena to a physical basis,

so the result has been that they are ignored by not being studied. But, insofar as science deals with *knowledge*, it can distinguish itself from the philosophy of physicalism and deal with experiential knowledge. (Tart 1975: 21)

According to Grof, the common determinator of 'transpersonal experiences' is the individual's obviously subjective feeling and impression that her/his consciousness has expanded beyond the 'normal' limitations of the 'ego' boundaries and that during these experiences the dimensions of time and space, which usually give human beings a basic orientation, have been 'transcended'. In order to be able to account for experiential knowledge on transcendental states through the practice of consensual 'SM', I therefore had to gain access to the subjective experiences of my interviewees which involved the development of a trustful atmosphere between the individual interviewee and me, so that they would feel encouraged to reply honestly to these extremely personal and complex questions.

While trying to recollect experiences I had myself which had a 'transcendental character', I realized that remembering occasions like that require a more detailed knowledge about common elements of 'transcendental experiences' as they provide an orientation. Otherwise the problematic abstract quality of this term with rather vague specifications would make it impossible to collect meaningful data on this topic. Therefore I decided to construct the questions alongside Charles T. Tart's 'Experiential criteria for detecting an altered state of consciousness' (1975) and Maxwell and Tschudin's 'Common elements of religious and other transcendent experiences' (1990). I further took Grof's contributions on this topic into account as these sources provided me with accounts of elements that are common to individual 'transcendental experiences'.

The development of a framework of questions that make sense, that are understandable (without imposing the idea of 'transcendental states' through consensual 'SM'), and that would still relate reasonably authenticly to experiences of people who have experienced 'transcendental states' in other contexts, was my aim for the questionnaire design. In order to gain sensible responses on abstract topics, the abstract concept has to be broken down into a series of questions (Hoinville and Jowell 1987) and unfamiliar words and phrases should not appear within the questionnaire. This will prevent that inappropriate assumptions about the respondents knowledge and/or vocabulary will make a response to the questionnaire impossible.

6.2.8 Empirical data on experiences of 'transcendental states' through the practice of consensual 'SM'

Within this section, as was in Chapter 3, it is my ambition to provide as much space as possible for the diversity of 'subjugated knowledges' (Sawicki

1991) of practitioners of consensual 'SM' that are otherwise often silenced and/or distorted. However, as some answers to the individual questions are very interesting in their complexity but too long to be featured at length, they had to be cut down without losing their meaningfulness.

1   *Did you ever have experiences during the practice of S/M that you find hard to put into words? For example: Did you experience changes in the way you usually see, smell, hear, feel ...?*
To this question most of the interviewees were able to give positive answers, therefore 'proving' the criterion of the 'ineffiability' of these experiences.

For Jane this seemed to be a general feature of her practices of consensual 'SM' as she wrote: "[I] Always have experiences which are difficult to articulate. I suppose they are comparable with drug induced altered states." And Jane added that she: "... tend[s] to feel vulnerable after S/M experiences. Almost like a drug 'comedown'" (Que.J.: 1).

Pat's answer was very focused on changes that occur in her perception of physical pain, she stated: "... the way I feel is different because after a little while pain doesn't feel like pain. So, the body, the skin feels different" (Que. P.: 2). Pat explained these changes through the impact of released endorphins that gradually change her perception of pain, while she's getting hit. In recollection of other 'undescribable experiences' during consensual 'SM'-play, Pat further remarked that she mostly had her eyes shut but if she did not, she could perceive the room in which she played as being further away, and: "sometimes it's like a distance, it's that, well, almost watching myself. Or sometimes just that the room seems like misty or far away" (Que. P.: 2). In addition Pat felt that the way she moves changes sometimes while she 'plays': "I mean sometimes, also, I have to move slower or I feel like I'm moving slower. Sometimes it might feel like the air actually has a consistency. That I'm moving through the air, so it takes a long time to get from one place to another" (Que. P.: 2). Shiva answered the question about experiences that she finds hard to put into words with the short formulation of: "An arousal rush" (Que. S.: 1).

Anthony's answer to the first question began with an interesting distinction as he usually plays the 'top'. He stated that his 'undescribable experiences' *only* relate to the time he 'bottomed'. He wrote: "I believe unusual experiences can only come from the position of the bottom/slave because as bottom/slave you are more in tune with your emotions and are willing to let your body go with the flow" (Que.3: 1). The position which allows most for 'letting go', for passivity and the giving up of control seems to be the most promising one for 'transcendental states'. The 'bottom' does not have to decide anything (apart from the possibility of using the safe word or gesture) and thus is able to let go of the 'internal supervisor' while the 'top' monitors. This finding became further substantiated by other responses to the questionnaire.

As Dean viewed his consensual 'SM'-plays as merely another possibility of having 'sex' he wrote: "...the feelings they produce are similar to any pleasurable sexual experience. Sensations are sharpened and experiences seem more intense, more memorable" (Que.a: 1).

For Diabolo the same holds true, yet he emphasized intensity and further remarked upon changes concerning the perception of time: "Time sometimes seems suspended, that is, I don't notice the passing of time during some S/M experiences, after which I'm surprised at the lateness. Feelings change as per any other sexual experience, but for me more so. I also have feelings of being 'mentally' naked and weightless" (Que. D.: 1). The notions of 'timelessness' and 'mental nakedness' clearly indicate that the usual concepts and categories that structure not only time and space, but further, our thoughts and actions, lose their profound impact during 'play'.

Henry, who is purely 'playing' the 'bottom' and has practised consensual 'SM' for over 40 years, repeated that only the sense of feeling and the sense of hearing would be altered, when he 'plays'. In order to explain the alterations in the way he feels during heavy 'play', he chose to compare it to the way his feelings change during the practice of running a marathon: "...you start out fairly hard and that's quite hard, you're struggling then, and you're all right until you get past a certain point, ...and then, having done that, the next patch, you've gone up a steep pain-curve.... If I have a caning from the person, whom this place is, or anyone else, the first twenty or thirty, I think: 'I can't take this. This is ridiculous. I mean, I ought to be taking it. I've taken more than this. I'll have to give up. I'll have to give up.' And I, that's when I battle myself. Because that pain is intense. It's worse than anything at that stage and you think: 'I can't do it. There's something wrong with me. I can't "take" it tonight.' And you have to fight yourself and say: 'Hang on in there! Hang on in there!' And then the body's reaction to that caning, what it does is, ...then I've got to the threshold. Now, they can go on. Now they can go on. They are not going to hurt me now..." (Que.H.: 20/21). Henry described that a sense of numbness overcomes his body at that stage of a marathon as well as at that stage of a heavy 'scene' that allows him to continue his 'bodily quests'. Henry: "Yes. The body's reaction let's you 'take it' then. The body has said: 'Something is wrong in this area.' And it puts blood to that area and protects that area. And you get this quite thick pad. If anyone, who 'takes it' hard, you can see it. Physically see it. Then you, you're feeling, you can feel it but it's not [discomforting]" (Que. H.: 21). Henry: "..., the feel is different and then, when I'm on that high plateau, especially the last bit, ...not only the feel but the sensitivity of that, on that last bit. I'm too old now but in the very young days, I would have an orgasm, as they, as you, were coming to the last lot, when they're really going to town, as I say" (Que. H.: 23).

As I conducted the interview in which Tom describes his 'unusual experience' through the 'bodily practices' of consensual 'SM' together with his girlfriend Bess, I will quote her description of the event in which Tom got a cigarette stubbed out on the palm of his hand consensual with, and by, his girlfriend.

> *Bess*:   ... I tried to knock most of the end of the cigarette before I did it because to have it done to me, I'll be horrified to have a cigarette burning into the palm of my hand. Anyway I did it but not hard enough. So it was in his hands, burning, and we looked at each other and then the breakdown appeared. And it was like a delayed reaction? And then I put the ashtray in front of him and he emptied the cigarette into the ashtray and then he moved and went back. And his eyes rolled back and he went back into the bed. And he was back out. He was totally mmh in another world? And his legs were shacking and his back was arching and his head was back. That lasted, it's hard to say but maybe 30 seconds, may be a minute but no longer, I don't think. And then his eyes came back and he sat up. ... It looked as if it was a really good trip.
>
> *Tom*:   I lost it, mind!
>
> *Bess*:   And also, when it happened, when he sort of went back in like a trance, it was like, the atmosphere was like really tense, almost like being in church. You know, when you get that sort of stillness? I can't really explain but it was, he was in a sort of trance, he was gone and I was watching him. It was quite amazing. (Interview-file J.: 5/6)

This description of consensual 'SM' of Tom and Bess even explicitly refers to a spiritual atmosphere that developed through the intense 'bodily practices' of consensual 'SM'.

The following response of Mike does not only illustrate the closeness between a 'top' and a 'bottom' but can further be related to the notion of 'transiency' which is, according to Maxwell and Tschudin (1990), an important and common element of 'transcendental' experiences and there-fore was explicitly asked for in question 3. Mike: "I become quite discon-nected from everything except my top. For example, at a party recently, I was 'scening' with someone and there was some disturbance going on nearby but it seemed very distant. It also seemed simultaneously speeded up and slowed down. ... I know that doesn't make sense, but it didn't seem real at all ... just something happening 'over there' " (Que.M.: 1).

Ella remarked that her 'unusual experiences' only happen while she is 'bottoming', which she now does more often as she used to 'top' exclusively through the role-expectations within the 'old Scene'. While she 'tops' some-one she notes: "I never feel anything but myself..." (Que. E.: 1). In contrast to this Ella described her 'bottom' experiences: "Whilst involved in a 'scene' I am actually living it. All outside world disappears. For that period I am only aware of myself and my Master. This is because my need at that time is to be totally controlled, hence I have no will, no thoughts of my own. I hand over myself completely and when I'm really into it nothing is able to distract me. I don't see him as my partner but as a totally different person" (Que.E.: 1). Once again the merits of being in 'bottom'-space, in terms of letting go of control ('no will') and the internal supervisor ('no thoughts'), are underlined.

Sue remarked a change in the way she sees: "Physically, occasionally during the practice, when the pain dealt out has built up to a (for myself) high and constant level, it seems that my sense of seeing or eyesight has become sharpened. I am very myopic, so it is not a true feeling of focus as my eyesight does not physically improve during that time, but there is the sense that an object which I am perhaps concentrating on looking at during a scene can become 'sharper' in my mind" (Que. 5: 1).

George who usually plays in 'top'-space answered that he does not notice any significant changes while being engaged in consensual 'SM', but he mentioned: "However, I do think my ability to imagine reality as something different becomes stronger during s-m, without there being any particular kind of role-play" (Que. G.: 1).

2 *During the practice of S/M, did you experience changes in the way you normally perceive your body? Did you feel different in it or did your body react or move differently?*
The second question of the questionnaire that deals with changes of the perception of one's body during consensual 'SM' was answered in a very direct way by Jane. She wrote: "Sometimes I feel like my mind and my genitals are one with nothing in between" (Que.J.: 1).

Pat's experiences of a different body-perception include her different perception of the body-response to pain, a slower way of body-movement and a perception of being distant which does not only include her body but also her partner's: "Or there's a veil in-between me and everything else, while I'm in some kind of a force-field with me and the person that I'm with. And since I'm in this force-field, everything else seems far away" (Que.P.: 2).

Shiva's comment to this question was her observation that she moves her body differently, while being spanked which she does not ever do in other situations. "I always arch my back" (Que.S.: 1).

The psychologist Tart mentions about 'altered states of consciousness': "In d-ASCs, people often report either greatly increased or decreased control over their emotions. In addition to changes in the degree of control over emotions, the intensity of emotions themselves may also change in d-ASCs" (Tart 1975: 124). In recollection of a very intense 'scene' Shiva illustrates these changes in an interview: "... the peak was so high that I was so absolutely sobbing with sheer shock" (Interview-file 2.: 4). During an interview Ella also described that: "..., I have seen myself and I have seen other people, through a very intense scene and when it's actually finished, I've actually burst into tears. Without realizing you suddenly just go..." (Interview-file E.: 21).

Anthony recalled: "The only experience I can relate to is being spanked and the intensity of the pleasure took me somewhere else. My body reacted differently because I was letting go. I have this theory that in regards to our sexual..., a few people have the key that unlocks this door and they can tap into something. That's the feeling I'm trying to explain. Or to put it another way: If you think about all the sexual partners you've had, only a handful or even less do it for you" (Que.3: 1). The relevance of a 'sexual' element in 'transcendental states' through consensual 'SM' appears to be related to individual motivation and past experiences which seems to also account for different evolutions of the consensual 'SM' learning-experience. This is further illustrated by Dean's answer: "The only changes I can think of are that experiences that would normally be unpleasant are transformed into pleasant ones by the addition of the sexual element" (Que.3: 1).

Diabolo's response to this question was very focused on the role-reversal that takes place during 'scenes' as he only 'bottoms': "..., 'normally' I tend to be influential in a group, positive, even assertive but through S/M I reverse roles to be passive, subordinate, creating a change in physical sensation. Sometimes, a day or two later, I enjoy the after-effects of marks etc., which give me a long 'tingle', recalling and prolonging the event" (Que.D.: 1). Diabolo's description illustrates how 'play' allows for explorations and practices of 'self' in terms of enabling the practitioners to experiment with subject-and object positions, usually ascribed and fixed by socio-cultural constructions, like 'gender', 'class', 'age', etc.

Henry already had indicated that the 'bodily practices' do have changing effects on 'lived bodies' throughout life and he further offered another individual example for alterations in the perception of the 'body'. Henry: "...And I know a young lady, who's very much attached to this lady here, who 'takes' a brilliant, brilliant caning but if you do anything else to her in the matter of pain, if you whipped her back or anything else – not interested. Because she transfers her feeling from her gluteus maximus to her vagina and has an orgasm by doing it" (Que. H.: 25/26).

Tom noticed changes in how he perceives thoughts and his consciousness in general: "...I put myself through pain because the inside has to come out. You know, I can release the inside by coming out with the pain" (Que.T.: 1). When Tom uses his willpower for pain-transformation processes he terms it, like several other practitioners, 'channelling'. 'Channelling' seems to be based on willpower and concentration and often involves an individually different body-position as this description of Tom during an interview shows. Tom: "I couldn't put my head into the right position to be able to shoot it up. Some people shoot it down their legs, some people shoot it up.

Like in their head. ... Once you channel it through your body, the sensation, you understand the sensation you are getting and you can push the sensation. It's very difficult to explain, unless you've been there. You can push it through your body, sort of, it forms as it leaves your body. It's like piercing, it's like being pierced again but pleasantly. Which is good, it's a release. It's like having a good dump, a good shit. And it goes out and comes through a bit but it gets more intense and more intense and it's a build-up. And then you, you lose it. Yeah? And you don't feel anything after that. You know?" (Interview-file J.: 6).

The phenomenon of 'depersonalization' which occurred frequently in the answers to the questionnaire, is traditionally used by psychiatrists to describe pathologies as a reduction in one's sense of personal identity is considered to be dangerous, at least worrying. However: "At the higher levels of spiritual experience, personal identity temporarily disappears altogether as the person becomes aware of and identified with higher spiritual forces or entities. Failure to lose one's sense of personal identity is frequently regarded as failure to achieve success in the spiritual discipline" (Tart 1975: 85/86).

Mike's and Ella's responses clearly address the phenomenon of 'depersonalization'. Mike: "..., although sometimes the disconnectedness causes me to feel like I'm watching myself perform ... especially if I'm being humiliated and made to perform 'tricks' infront of others – then part of me sits back and watches in amusement" (Que. M.: 1).

Ella stated that she does feel different about her body: "...in as much as I become incredibly submissive and in this way my body does not belong to me but to my Master to do with as he pleases. My body reacts unconsciously to what he is doing and it is utterly pleasurable. I find myself doing and behaving in a way that is somehow out of my control. I do not respond in any conscious way but in some kind of instinctual way. Very hard to explain in words" (Que. E.: 1).

For Sue her perception of her body changed as well: "... I feel rather more at ease in it, ... out with the physical reaction to a build-up of pain (which is rhythmic flinching in advance of impact), my body reacts and moves as in a restive state" (Que.5: 1).

George only perceived changes of his body when he occupied the 'bottom'-space, which he does not do very often. George: "While passive, yes. It feels more feminine, or perhaps more childish" (Que. G.: 1). As 'femininity' often still is stereotypically associated with 'passivity', the choice of wording reflects the impact of these stereotypes of 'gender' and how they shape our relation to 'self'.

Ryan noticed changes in the way he perceived his body: "I think I do feel stronger. ... Sometimes the reason why I engage in S/M-sex is that my perception of my body changes, ..." (Que.R.: 2). He mostly perceived these changes while he was 'topping' someone but: "Even when you're 'bottoming' sometimes, and you're being 'topped' by an absolutely, what I would term 'gorgeous physical man'" (Que. R.: 2). Ryan's changes in body-perception seem to originate in the value he puts onto the looks of his partner.

3   *While engaged in S/M-practices, did you feel different in your relation to time? Did 'clocktime' become irrelevant, did it disappear or become meaningless and did another notion of time become important?*
To the question about the relationship towards time during engagement in these 'bodily practices' Jane mentioned that: "Very often time flies quickly during S/M play" (Que.J.: 1) and Pat stated that: "Time [clocktime] has disappeared... several hours have gone by, suddenly" (Que.P.: 2).

A different time-measurement gained importance when Pat practiced consensual 'SM': "... You know, the ticking of the clock itself is gone. You know, they ['tops' timing of actions] are the clock" (Que.P.: 2). The last words of Pat's reply were very emphasized as she wanted to point out that another structure of time becomes of foremost importance. A 'body-clock' takes over which is interdependent with the 'top''s timing that is guided itself contextually by the top's empathy for the other's 'lived body'. This perception could be seen as matching Howes' (2005) notion of 'skin knowledge' very well.

In Shiva's recollection of 'playing' and her relationship to time, she mentioned that another notion of time determines the 'scene' as her concentration is centred onto playing: "I'm focussed on my upcoming 'Miss Domina'-play" (Que. S.: 1).

For Anthony the 'clock-time' lost its importance completely: "Time becomes irrelevant because even though I used contracts in my 'scenes' for let's say two hours, because the body then goes through so many emotions and feelings." To Anthony the set-up of the play-room (usually in black) adds to the lacking importance of 'clocktime' (Que.3.: 1). As Anthony compared the experiences to day-dreaming he mentioned also that one just 'loses track' of time, while being in this state.

In Dean's view people tend to lose track of time, while they enjoy themselves anyway and therefore he does not perceive this as a particularity of consensual 'SM'. (Que.a: 1)

Diabolo sometimes experienced time as 'suspended' and did not notice the passing of time, therefore he wrote: "I particularly like long sessions to allow greatest time lapse" (Que.D.: 1).

Henry told me that 'clocktime' became irrelevant, but another sense of time, which is completely determined by the situation, became relevant.

Henry: "Oh, yes, but there are other ways of time. ... I have been put into either a 'privation-cell' [deprivation-cell] or into bondage with a blindfold. There's a thing called a 'body-bag', you know the 'body-bag'? ... Now, you do lose the sense for time there and you think you've been there for hours and hours, and you've been in there for fifty minutes or an hour and a quarter... because you don't know whether it's light or dark, you got no clue.

And so you lose sense of time like that immensely ..." (Que. H.: 27/28). Henry further described the time-management taking place within him during deprivation-'scenes': "... the important thing that I found was never to panic in these situations. In the 'body-bag' for instance, ..., I had no idea what the time was. ... And that is very worrying, but what you have to do is talk to yourself in various ways. Firstly, when you are so enclosed, the easiest thing is to panic and you, I have to physically say to myself inwardly: 'Don't panic. She wouldn't have left you in a place, where you are going to die. Don't panic. You'll be worse if you panic. Stay quiet! Stay calm! Breath normally. Don't hyperventilate, breath normally.' You need to do this, to talk to yourself in that way" (Que. H.: 29).

In Tom's opinion time became irrelevant as he found that once one is engaged in these 'bodily practices' and especially if one has 'transcendental' experiences, one is: "... Too busy within yourself, to sort lots of shit out" (Que.T.: 2). For Mike the concept of time also generally disappeared during consensual 'SM': "Sometimes a fifteen minute scene feels like it lasted hours, other times an hour-long scene feels like it lasted only a few minutes. When I'm in bottom space I'm so focused on the moment-to-moment sensations that I ignore anything in the background that indicates a passage of time" (Que.M.: 1).

Like many practitioners, who either 'bottom' or 'switch', Ella also finds that 'clocktime' became irrelevant during 'scenes': "All I can say about this is that clocktime stops. In other words I have no idea of what the time is or how much time has passed until the scene is over" (Que. E.: 1). Sue also stated that 'clocktime': "... sometimes did become irrelevant when the scene was a lengthy one, ..." (Que.S.: 2). While George experienced as well that time "... goes more quickly..." (Que.G.: 1). Unless work-pressure enhanced the importance of 'clocktime' during his frequent visits to the consensual 'SM' area of the 'Heath', Ryan commented: "No, clocktime doesn't mean anything to me..., the only time you wait for is when the sun goes up, very late at night" (Que. R.: 2).

4   *Did you notice changes in the perception of your memories during S/M-practice? Did they for example seem like 'an outside-flow of events'?*
In connection to this question Jane recollected: "I often have difficulty remembering the order in which things occurred" (Que.J.: 1). For Pat changes in perception do occur, yet she underlined that this only accounts for 'good scenes' in which her body-perception had already changed: "... then, you know, my body is not mine anymore. You know, it's just happening, you know. So, it's a matter of trusting that person to be able to let that happen. And it's a rare thing" (Que. P.: 3). Given these a priori conditions, she is entirely focused on the 'top' and then: "... sometimes my mind would wander, you know. And I would be getting pictures of places, where I've been at other times" (Que. P.: 3). During 'play' Pat had recollections of memories

that just seem to 'float' in, again confirming a state in which the 'internal supervisor' is not in control.

As Shiva put emphasis on the importance of the voice of her partner that 'guided' her through her experiences, she did not recollect any changes in her perception of memories but: "I'm only concentrating on the fore-play speech of my 'top'" (Que. S.: 1). Anthony as well as Dean did not find important changes in memory-perception during 'scenes', while Diabolo appears to 'foster' this sensation: "Yes, in fantasy sex, I'm also 'outside looking in', so I like mirrors during a session to allow an 'outsider's' view" (Que. D.: 1).

Henry also noticed changes in the perception of his memories: "Yes, you're outside of your self...because although I'm enjoying it, it's a hell of a trauma to 'take'....Just set your mind, if I'm going to have a really heavy beating, I will ask people to leave me alone for about three minutes and I'll either stand and cover my face up like this [Henry demonstrates.] or I'll sit in a corner and just think: 'You gonna go through this and you're gonna 'take' it. And you're not going to let your 'Dominant' down, your partner down. She wants to give it and you're going to 'take' it.' You know and I work on myself like this and by doing so, ehm, because I'm concentrating then, on what I've determined I'm gonna concentrate on to overcome the trauma, I have actually failed to count....'What happened to forty-eight?' 'Oh, I'm sorry 'Mistress.' or 'I'm sorry, Madame.' And then, they hold this thing above you, which says: 'If you fail, if you get the counting wrong, we start from one again.' So, that, you know, concentrates the mind quite well, actually" (Que. H.: 28). Henry himself provided an explanation for these changes: "...I do take my mind away from what they are doing because I want to concentrate on my own thing to be able to withstand the trauma. To go through that mental barrier, that pain-barrier, I concentrate on that" (Que.H.: 29).

Tom's immediate reaction to this question was that he had 'flashframes'. He tried to explain: "..., let's just say my concept of pain isn't the same, ..., as you understand pain. But the word 'pain' to me is like a memory and a feeling of the memory, ..." (Que.T.: 2). Especially in connection to the various dimensions of 'pain' in relation to 'lived bodies' (see also Chapter 2) Tom's elaboration is crucial, as it once again shows that 'scientific' generalizations usually applied to the 'lived body' are far too limiting.

Mike's as well as George's responses account for changes of memory perception. Mike: "I certainly find it very difficult to recall the scene in chronological order-something I'm generally very good at. Memories of scenes tend to be made up of a fairly random swirl of sensations and events from the scene. If I try to describe the scene several times to different people, I think I describe it in a different order each time!" (Que. M.: 1). And George stated: "Memory and anticipation definitely seem less worrisome. Anxiety about the future, built upon memory of the past, is definitely less pronounced" (Que. G.: 1). The focus of perception during 'play' is thus on the 'here and now' which allows for intense and potentially transformative experiences of the 'lived body'.

5 *Did you ever have illusions and/or hallucinations during a 'scene'-Experiences that you might have had before in the form of for example, fever dreams, substance-related states...?*
The experience of hallucinations and illusions during the practice of consensual 'SM' seem to be rare, most interviewees responded that they did not experience either of these. Shiva, however, describes her experiences as: "It's a bit like speed" (Que. S.: 1) in her answer to the comparative part of the question. Pat can recollect having visions of a particular place and atmosphere when she was engaged in a very good 'scene': "...a vision of maybe when I was in South America and was just, had my near-death experience. And I was very glad to be alive and I have a picture of the scene there, the view that I was having from the mountains or whatever. And that has happened to me a few times. The same 'scene', the same vision I've had of the place" (Que. P.: 3). When I asked Pat about the 'trigger' of special experiences like this in consensual 'SM' she explained: "Well, it seems to be that when I've been getting sensations for a long time and really my body has kind of become less important and I'm focussed on what the other person is doing. And I've just given my control up to that person. You know, usually from an intense beating or something... at the same time... the sensations in my body just don't feel like pain anymore. And time is gone away. And then I seem to have a link to that other time. The other time sort of comes back and I see the picture of what. You know, my eyes are probably closed but I'm getting a vision of the blue sky and the thin air and everything feels like I was there again" (Que. P.: 3).

Anthony uses a comparison to explain the state he feels to be in while having these experiences: "It's like day dreaming, you move away from the physical body into a mental state and you loose track of how long you've been away" (Que. 3.: 1).

Diabolo admitted that most of his 'unusual experiences' have been 'assisted' by cannabis and/or magic mushrooms but he has recollections from past 'scenes', when: "...I had a strong fixation on certain scenarios, which when enacted, have had a certain visionary quality, like an outside film" (Que.D.: 1). Dean's negative response underlines the importance of being in a specific frame of mind: "However, I rarely experienced any hallucinations whilst experimenting with psychoactive substances, even in comparatively large amounts, so this is perhaps due to my mind set rather than the nature of the scene" (Que. A: 2).

Tom did not have any illusions beside his 'flashframes' already mentioned and Mike, Henry and Ryan were unable to recollect any either. And although Ella was unsure about the answer to this question, she wrote: "I have never hallucinated but as many of our 'scenes' are fantasy based, I do actually have the illusion and belief that the events being enacted are really happening" (Que. E.: 1).

6   *Excluding substance-induced states: Did you feel that these experiences happened to you without your actual influence?*
Pat's answer expresses the importance of the trusting relationship between the 'bottom' and the 'top' as a precondition of these experiences. Pat: "Well, yeah, they were happening because of what was happening to me physically, they were happening. I couldn't make them happen by myself. You know, they require the other person to be there, to, to do that. I couldn't do it by myself. I couldn't give up my control to myself. It has to be another person, taking that and taking responsibility in a way for me to feel safe and let go and this to happen" (Que. P.: 4).

Shiva mentioned a particular intense 'scene' that had a deep impact on her in an interview: "..., the peak was so high that I was so absolutely sobbing with sheer shock through being in another world. I felt I've been transported to another world" (Interview-file 2.: 4). Shiva suggests an explanation for these experiences: "I think that the rush comes through my own mind" (Que. S.: 1). While Shiva emphasizes herself as a source for these experiences and Henry's explanations focused on how he has to mentally prepare himself to be able to reach these experiences (see answer to question 4), in Anthony's opinion it is complicated to distinguish where the actual influence came from: "It's difficult to be clear whether this experience happened without my actual influence but all I can say is from this one experience, the body felt almost borderless but then everything was operating on a mental level – I would even say spiritual level..." (Que.3.: 2).

Sue, George and Ryan do not believe that these experiences happened to them without their own influence either. While Ella's response suggests that: "...some kind of conscious wanting to believe must be there initially. Then the illusion takes over" (Que. E.: 1). This suggestion appears valid as in Dean's opinion his mind-set does not allow him to be not in control and therefore: "...I rarely feel out of control in any situation. Indeed I tend to avoid such situations, perhaps to my disadvantage at times" (Que.a: 2).

Some practitioners do use substances that alter their state of mind and thus their responses are less revealing. Tom: "No, 'cause I was on drugs. In one form or another even if it's just a cigarette. I'm a drug-user but I'm not an addict and I'm pretty together" (Que. T.: 2). And Diabolo who regularly uses a diversity of substances, answers: "No, not yet. I'm sorry to say" (Que. D.: 1).

7   *Do you relate these experiences, given you had some of them, to physical or rather to mental parts of a 'scene'? In other words: Do you have an explanation for what caused you to have these experiences?*
Jane wrote: "Probably a combination of physical and psychological sensation. But I believe that they are chemically induced by endorphins or

hormones" (Que. J.: 1). Pat attributes these experiences to a combination of mental and physical parts of a 'scene' that made these experiences possible. For the mental part she states: "If I'm put into a certain 'headspace', the other person is controlling me, then it makes it easier for it to happen." But she does not underestimate the physical components: "there has to be a physical part as well, to put my body aside" (Que. P.: 4). As Pat defines herself as a 'bottom' and rarely 'switches', the beatings she receives from the 'top', within a framework of mutual understanding, serve as physical triggers while the intensely trusting relationship with the 'top' prepares her mentally: "…I relate it to the chemical stuff going on. I relate it to having been, you know, physically, have physical experience and the chemical changes that go by. I mean, it's a drug inside your body that your body is releasing. So, I guess it's that but it also has to do with, well, it doesn't just happen, if I'm just getting hit, just by itself. I have to have some kind of, there is this bond that goes on and the person has to. The person is there, you know, they are there. I'm trusting that person, I'm giving parts of my control up to them and hopefully all of my control. But it's very difficult for me, to actually take my feet of the ground…, there has to be a mutual thing. It has to come both ways" (Que. P.: 4).

Shiva strongly believes that the impact of her mind allows for these changes to happen (Que. S.: 1), while in Dean's view the lack of frequency of consensual 'SM' within his life-context is responsible for changes in perception: "I would attribute any changes in perception, however slight, to the fact that I was engaged in some 'out of the ordinary' practice, rather than the actual physical sensation caused by the practice" (Que. a: 2).

Henry also considers his own willpower to be responsible for the experiences he had. His response further illustrates once again the importance given to the second socialization within the 'Scene': "…The answer really is that I do focus on something on a 'scene' for myself, so that I can translate the pain to a pleasure. If you can't do that, the pain is just going to get more intense. I do, as already stated, concentrate on a 'scene'…When people come up to me in a club or where ever I am and they've seen me 'take' a beating and they say: 'I could never "take" that. I could never "take" what you can'. And I keep saying to them: 'It is not a competition. The only person you've got to beat is yourself.' And, you know: 'Compete with yourself.' And so I took a hundred strokes quite hard, if I can 'take' a hundred and twenty this week I'll be happier. Or if I can 'take' them this much harder this week I'll be happier. But not to say, because we've all got our limits, our own threshold of pain and all you've got to do is advance your own threshold, not go up to anyone else's. That's not what it's all about" (Que. H.: 30). Henry's answer clearly reflects the crucial importance of 'self'-exploration with regards to 'limits of pain' as opposed to understanding it in terms of a competition with others as is the case in much of contact sports, to achieve these 'altered states'.

Tom perceives the physical reactions of his body (endorphins) as just a bonus on top of his 'transcendental experiences'. He suggested a single existential 'trigger' for these experiences: "I woke up one day and I got into realities" (Que.T.: 2).

For Mike, the mental part of a 'scene' is the crucial element: "It's definitely a mind thing. Partly self-induced as I consciously open up my mind to drop into bottom space where there is no pain and where it doesn't matter what I'm made to do...that's how I rationalize the way I get enjoyment out of submission and being beaten. Partly induced by the effects of being in bottom space: once I'm there, the time sense goes and the sensations change" (Que. M.: 1). Mike puts emphasis onto the fact that he, as a 'control-freak', prefers the state in which all his external control has gone and he found that these experiences were satisfying as: "...afterwards I know I've overcome many of my own barriers to push myself that far – I have achieved a victory of internal control over self by forcing the 'self' to submit entirely to someone else's external control" (Que. M.: 2).

In Ella's opinion a combination of physical and mental elements 'caused' these experiences but within her answer she focuses more on the mental dimension: "There is the 'scene'-setting involved, such as the set up of the room and the clothing both are wearing. Also, very important, is the ability of the dominant to be totally convincing and as involved in the 'scene' as myself. Any slight feeling of non-involvement or uncomfortableness can be easily detectable and would prevent me being able to surrender myself completely, mentally and physically, and lose myself in the 'scene'" (Que. E.: 1). This again underlines the crucial interdependence of 'top(s)' and 'bottom(s)' in consensual 'SM' as opposed to the stereotype of a hierarchical non-consensual relationship.

George's answer reflects the difficulty to define and/or detect altered states of consciousness: "I don't know if I experienced much in the way of altered states of consciousness. However, I would be more inclined to regard them if they ever came my way as illusions, time and space as real, rather than the other way around" (Que. G.: 1), while in Diabolo's opinion the 'trigger' is merely 'sexual': "The liberation of sexual release needs a poet to describe" (Que. D.: 1).

8   Did you expect to experience these kinds of sensations of S/M-practice?
Jane expected these sensations as she relates them to other mind altering experiences and contexts: "Yes – because of my experience with drugs" (Que.J.: 1).

Pat did not expect to have experiences like that through consensual 'SM' but, after having had some of them she now does expect them to happen again. (Que.P.: 6)

Shiva did not expect these experiences a priori, but relates them to unreflected experiences within her past: "I did experience them by accident, when I was sixteen. From then on I knew I needed this for this rush" (Que.S.: 2). As most of the interviewees, Anthony did not expect these experiences through consensual 'SM' and he elaborates: "...because the impression is that its strictly physical but I now believe 'pain' can transform into something else" (Que.3: 2). Here it becomes very obvious how these 'bodily practices' engage the whole 'lived body' which implies an overcoming of the conventional dualism of 'body' and 'mind'.

Like Anthony and Tom, Dean did not expect any of these sensations, he only: "...expected S/M to be exciting and 'different' (which it can be)" (Que. a: 2). And Diabolo remarks: "No, for all my earlier life, I was frightened of my S/M inclination and repressed them, so life began at forty in discovering the real potentials of S/M" (Que. D.: 1).

Henry explains that previous experience of these sensations lets him sometimes expect them, for example, when a heavy beating is planned. He once again refers to the importance of the necessary preconditions: "...I want to be sure that it's O.K. and safe to give up control completely, otherwise I do not get the same out of it" (Que H.: a).

For Mike it was not an initial expectation either but it is has now become a 'gained expectation': "...I had no idea how I would respond to heavier play until I tried it. I suppose that I judge a scene now on whether I experience the disconnection, time distortion and euphoria that I associate with a good scene" (Que. M.: 1).

For Ella these experiences were new too, especially since she only started to 'bottom' recently: "For many years I played at being dominant. A role really set on me rather than one of choosing" (Que.E.: 2).

Sue had read about the physical experience of 'sharpening eyesight' beforehand and therefore knew: "...that this is quite a usual reaction to the infliction of pain and so it did not seem strange" (Que. S.: 2). George's answer reflects the 'gained expectation' of many of the other practitioners: "Well, those that I have, I would expect to feel. And are part of the fun of the S and M" (Que. G.: 1).

9 *Do you especially seek for experiences like this in S/M? Do you have other ways or means to reach similar ones?*
Pat remembers that she formerly was motivated to take drugs in order to gain 'self'-knowledge but that these did not fulfill her needs as much as those experiences she has from consensual 'SM'. Pat: "Well, yes. Now, I mean that I had these experiences I want to have them again. And, no, I don't have other ways or means to reach ones. I don't know the only thing that was similar was taking hallucinogenic drugs but that was a different altered state and not the same. And I don't do that anymore. I'm not taking any drugs now. So there are other things, other ways, take me other places and they are not the places, where I want to go. It's the kind of S/M-ones that I want" (Que. P.: 6).

Shiva does look for 'peak-experiences' through consensual 'SM' and she states that she does not have other means to achieve them. (Que. S.: 2), while Anthony who identifies and 'plays' predominantly within 'top space', responded: "I do not especially seek for these experiences like this in S/M, my concern is that the bottom seeks out these experiences" (Que.3: 2). For Diabolo who 'plays' in 'bottom space' the bond he has to his 'Mistress' is also highly important: "...it takes a relationship to achieve the empathy..." (Que. D.: 1).

According to Dean his lack of these experiences is due to too little practice: "S/M practices aren't a major part of my life. I have a too casual approach to them for any significant experience to take place. Drug use, particularly when I was younger, was my chosen route to 'alternative states', although this is, of course, a very limited way of achieving this" (Que. a: 2).

Henry relates these experiences within his answer to the way in which he uses his willpower (or 'stubbornness' as he calls it) also in dealing with difficult situations in which a power-difference is socially determined (e.g. in dealing with the police) (Que. H., a). In contrast Ella seeks for these experiences only as part of the indulgence in these 'bodily practices': "There is no other activity that can produce them" (Que. E.: 2). And Mike who initially did not seek for 'transcendental' experiences in consensual 'SM', also states: "Now that I know they can occur I desire them as part of a scene" (Que. M.: 1).

To Ryan these experiences are only achievable through 'play': "No, I don't have other ways actually, ..." (Que. R.: 3). While Sue also does not have other means to reach these states, she explains: "I tend to view consensual 'SM' as a separate experience in itself and whatever comes from that is the result of these practices, it's exclusive to it" (Que.5: 2). Sue further mentions that she aims to achieve a level of pain whereby she becomes faint, which she did not realize so far. However, in George's view music can be another means to reach similar experiences: "I would suggest that music produces a similar feeling in me. Of femininity, cheerfulness, freedom. Possibly even at a stronger level – but without the overpowering sensations associated with sex" (Que. G.: 1).

10   *Through the practice of S/M in connection to these 'undescribable experiences' – Did you feel lastingly different about yourself? Did you relate in a new way to your life or to life in general?*

In Pat's opinion transformations occurred: "Well, yes. Especially that one time that I was telling you about because I really felt like I'd been reborn and that I found information from my childhood or from a long time ago. That really helped me. That led me to be able to take a new path in my life" (Que. P.: 6). For Pat therefore the experience of 'transcendental states' through consensual 'SM' represent a positive changing point in her life and also an intense way to learn about her 'self': "...it's self-knowledge, it's looking for self-knowledge" (Que. P.: 6). The preconditions of consensual 'SM' in terms of a practice of 'care of the self' (Foucault 1990) are underlined in their importance here also as an a priori to the experience of 'transcendental states'. This implies the requirement of a constant reflexive mode that inform a contextual and relational personal ethics on the level of the practitioners. Pat elaborates on the different degrees of transformative experiences: "... I always feel, after a really good 'scene' I always feel very calm and different about myself. I might feel really frustrated beforehand and really need to scream or something. And afterwards I'm feeling relaxed and so on" (Que. P.: 7).

Pat described a particular experience that she found 'healing' and 'life-changing' which she defined as crucial to her life. As the 'scene' described in my opinion gives an impressive example of the potential realities of 'lived bodies' in consensual 'SM', I quote it lengthily: "I'd been, I was with this person, who, we'd been having a 'scene' for may be about four hours and she had started the 'scene' of by, basically making me, taking away some of my control. You know, she hit me round the face and put her hands around my throat and made sure that I knew that she was the boss. And I was feeling quite young. I started to feel quite young, you know, may be twelve years old or something. And then she put me into restraints and she beat me for about two hours. So, I was, you know, I had a lot of pain, a lot of sensations like that and ... all I cared about was just doing whatever she wanted. My body was more or less there but it felt differently. ... I didn't know for how long we were doing stuff for ... It may be more than two hours. Then we had to stop and have a little something to eat because it had been a long time. After we'd eaten, I was just sitting on the floor at her feet and I was just, she was just looking after me, you know. Feeding me, whatever. I was wrapped up in a blanket and I was completely [doesn't find a word]."

Andrea: In her care?

Pat: I was in her care, yeah. And we weren't done. She said: 'We're not done. You know we're not finished. It's obvious that we have some more things to do.' We went into the other room again and she put me into a bag, which was like made of lycra. So, it's very tight and my whole body was enveloped in this very tight thing. And then she put rope around me as well. So I was completely bound hand to foot in this bag and this rope. And then she put some hoods of lycra over my head as well. ... And I could just about breathe. And I couldn't see properly because there's all these things over my head ... I could hear okay. And then she lay down beside me, I was laying flat on the bed and she lay down beside me. She started to talk to me and she said: 'You're gonna go on a journey to a place far away, to find something that you lost.' And she didn't explain what she was talking about, she just said this. And she described that I was walking through the woods and I had these animals with me. I have animals tattooed on me and she'd asked me, why I had these animals, before, you know, another time. And she'd said what animals were important to me. ... She'd said I have a dog with me and a bear and I have an eagle flying over head. And we were going through these woods and that we have to find this tree and we go all the way up to the top of this tree, through the clouds, through to another land. All these things were happening and I was imagining it, I could see it. I couldn't see the room, all I could hear was her voice, like very quiet, very even in my ear, telling me these things. And I was having pictures to go with the story that she was telling me ... certain things that she told me in the story, she didn't explain them but I had visions of them which were more detailed than what she was explaining ... And in the end, you know, she brought me back. ... She released me from the hoods and everything. And I was suddenly aware of the room again. ... And it's like, you know, you could say she was just telling me a story but I was experiencing this story in my body. I was feeling that I was walking, that all these things were happening to me and yet I was immobilized. ... That's about the most intense experience of any kind that's happened to me. Sure it was guided, somebody else was taking me there in a very real way, in a kind of shamanic journey or something. I still feel that I've been changed by that. (Que. P.: 4–6)

Apart from the fact that Pat's elaborations clearly indicate that the conventional borderlines of time and space were transcended during this 'scene' and that she experienced the 'play' as healing and thus as transformative, she further compares this experience with shaman rituals which obviously have a long tradition in different cultures as elaborated on in the first sections of this chapter.

Anthony's response relates his physical sensations in consensual 'SM' to meditation experiences: "... I was willing to let go of the physical body and go more internal. The feelings I can relate all this to is when I was exploring meditation" (Que.3: 2). During an interview Anthony refers more explicitly to personal transformation through consensual 'SM': "basically I found that since I'm having S/M-sex I've become more assertive, in terms of how I relate to people in the wider world. I'm not aggressive but more assertive" (Interview-file 3: 5). The consensual 'SM' 'plays' altered Anthony's perception of and relationship to 'self' and in turn his interaction with others. Dean remarked: "My S/M experiences certainly were significant in as much as I realized that there are many facets to my sexuality, but I can't say that they have actually changed me" (Que. a: 2), Diabolo notices changes in himself through these experiences in the context of consensual 'SM': "I broke the myth of 'normality' in myself and others.

I feel more relaxed and flexible about myself and life in general, and less inclined to dichotomies. Although my interest is limited (by the standards of my friends) to a het-sub orientation, somehow I feel more open to a 'female' side of me since my involvement in S/M" (Que. D.: 1). Here, once again the 'transcendence' of dichotomies is explicitly mentioned which apparently is often effected by and resulting from consensual 'play' and related 'transcendental states'.

Henry's response begins with a general perspective, in terms of how his engagement with consensual 'SM' has changed his relationship towards himself and 'significant others' [his wife that he's still married to, his children and his 'Lady' with whom he has now lived for ten years.]. Although he wanted to be honest, he feared social sanctions and rejection, living in the 'closet', thus forced to live a lie and two very separate lives turned out to be a very high price. Henry also mentions that his attitude towards life is transformed through the practice of consensual 'SM' as well as through these 'undescribable experiences' during heavy 'play'. Henry: "...I'm very, very good at seeing the other person's point of view. Ehm, I play devil's advocate to my own partner and she says: 'You're always against me.' And I say: 'No, I'm not. I promise you, I even think the same way as you do about this. My opinion is the same as yours, but we both ought to be aware of the other person's opinion, ...' And I will always do that and she gets quite angry sometimes, 'cause I play devil's advocate as it's called."

> *Andrea:* So you always see not only yourself but the whole environment?
> *Henry:* That's right, yes, yeah. I do very much indeed. (Que. H., a))

This answer can be related and comes close to Foucault's notion of 'care of the self' that describes a continuously reflective attitude that becomes the foundation for a personal yet always contextual and relational ethics. Foucault once expressed this existential attitude to the 'self': "Make freedom your foundation, through the mastery of yourself" (Foucault in Rabinow 1997: 301).

Tom, who aims for 'feeling like a child again' relates differently to himself and life in general after the 'transcendental' experiences he had: "..., it's like being a child, watching fireworks for the first time...we all take so much for granted, don't we? It's not only that. That's a story cut short, it's not just like that. It makes me more sensitive and it makes me more caring after" (Que. T.: 3).

Mike states that he feels lastingly different since he had these experiences: "I feel much more relaxed and self confident, knowing that I can exercise the self control to open up and allow body to go through the physical punishment" (Que.M.: 1). This is also true for Ella as she notes that since she obtained these experiences: "...I have become more confident and happy and my relationship with my partner has become closer" (Que.E.: 2).

George states similarly that the connection of consensual 'SM' with these 'undescribable experiences' has had positive effects on him: "I think I feel stronger within myself. More willing to do what I wanted, and more willing to accept risks of not getting what I wanted without feeling hurt or depressed. Happier" (Que. G.: 1).

These diverse answers illustrate the potential of consensual 'SM' for some practitioners to be a transformative 'bodily practice' that allows for 'transcendence'. This effectively enriches and 'enchants' the human beings involved within 'play' that the context of a 'disenchanted world' (Ritzer 1999).

"In and through a transcendent experience a person becomes more and more aware, and – given the right conditions – more responsible, active and capable of fulfilling the creative potential. This makes a person more free. She or he is more able to know, choose and act on the values that are relevant" (Maxwell and Tschudin 1990: 42).

The results of the questionnaire indicate that the majority of 'bottoms' do experience states that can be described as 'transcendental'. Another crucial point within this context is the potential for personal/political change (e.g. in relation to 'gender', 'age', subject/object position, etc.) which appears to be increased through the 'bodily practices' of consensual 'SM' that provided the framework for these 'transcendental experiences'.

6.2.9   Conclusion

The purpose of the questionnaire was to find out if Michel Foucault's notion of 'transcendence' through the experience of consensual 'SM' would prove to be a valid shared motivation and/or experience of other practitioners of consensual 'SM'. This appears to be the case for some practitioners even though none of the interviewees could relate to this abstract term, the experiences reported appear to indicate that 'transcendental experiences' are part of the sensations searched for in consensual 'SM', even though never as an a priori motivation but only *after* the 'discovery' of them, in other words, as a 'gained motivation'.

As only two of the interviewees did not hand back the questionnaire and all the other practitioners of consensual 'SM' that were interviewed, could, in one way or the other, relate to the topic of unusual/transcendental experiences through these 'bodily practices', I think it is possible to conclude that, at times, the practice of consensual 'SM' appears to include experiences like this. Furthermore, it is quite striking that the two people who could not relate at all to these experiences and the people, who did not have very intense or variant experiences, expressed within the answers of the questionnaire, tend to be exclusively 'tops'. It appears as if the 'bottom'-space provides more of a basis for the experience of transcendental phenomena. This observation is crucial as it underlines that the practice of consensual 'SM' is an interrelational 'bodily practice' which offers 'bottoms', 'subs' and 'slaves' the possibility to experience 'transcendental states' as they are enabled to let go of the control of the 'internal supervisor'.

People appear to seek out different 'scenes' and different degrees of sensation in order to match their interest and needs. For some consensual 'SM' serves mainly as a tool to heighten sensual and 'sexual' experience or as a release of pressure or guilt feelings, while for others the achievement of 'transcendental states' appears to be a core motivation.

As all 'transcendental experiences' are subjectively experienced and perceived, so are the conditions that allow for these events to happen. As an example of the reflection on these conditions I quote Pat's comments on her understanding of necessary a priori conditions: "I think that it, it has to do with the person and it has to do with the kind of 'scene' you're having as well. It has to be a heavy physical 'scene' involved, I have to get to a certain place both in pain and in submission. It never has happened with just a physical 'scene' and it has never happened with just a light 'scene'. It's never happened except when I've gone a long way. Pushing my limits – it only happens then" (Interview-file 1: 21).

The answers given further clearly showed that most practitioners of consensual 'SM', who have had 'transcendental experiences', are able to manipulate their responses to potentially painful stimuli in the ritualistic setting of a 'scene'. "There is now considerable scientific evidence that humans can alter their responses to potentially painful stimuli. ... Many clinical and experimental studies have shown that pain can be diminished, and in some cases eliminated, by hypnotic, psychotherapeutic, meditative, or other exercises. Modern studies of pain control support the contention to be found in all sacred traditions that suffering can be overcome through certain virtues and disciplines" (Tart 1975: 87). In 'Health Psychology' Sarafino (1998), for example, deals with varying biophysical interaction processes and also covers the area of pain-management. Sarafino describes in his work behavioural, cognitive as well as physical stimulation therapies that are now sometimes used within conventional medical settings for pain-management and pain-control.

The ability to control 'bodily reaction', to 'channel' pain etc. has apart from an increase in 'bodily' chemicals, consequences for the awareness that the individuals who engage in this 'bodily practice', have of themselves as well as of others. The occurrence of 'altered states of consciousness' through intense experiences that engage the 'lived body' to such a degree that they might represent 'peak-experiences' and provide space for transformations of perception. Maslow saw 'peak-experiences' as the highest form of 'embodiment' allowing for "..., moments of harmony with oneself and between [human beings], ..." (Spurling 1977: 133) and connected these experiences to an increase of self-awareness. As reflected in most of the responses to the questionnaire, individuals who engage in consensual 'SM', stated that they gained in self-assertiveness and also felt an increase in their ease with themselves.

In this context it is relevant to refer to Horn et al.'s (2005) emphasis on the importance of pursuing research into the spiritual aspects of embodied 'health' in the context of professional care: "(.), the dimension of embodied spirituality has implications beyond the narrow scope of sexuality/spirituality research. It also addresses the broader dimensions of body/spirit integration, ... Professionals who are entrusted with the care of others (medical professionals, psychotherapists, pastoral caregivers, and so on) have an ethical imperative to 'do no harm'. Without an understanding of the nature and process of integrating body, mind and spirit, or of the client's level of embodiment, it would be difficult to determine whether the interventions used with a patient or client would facilitate movement towards integration or disintegration and whether they would facilitate healing or contribute to the continuation (and possibly exacerbation) of *dis*ease" (Horn et al. 2005: 97 and 98).

Merleau-Ponty saw human existence as the realization of a "...fusion between inner and outer..." (Merleau-Ponty in Spurling 1977: 133) both of which are inseparable from each other. The context given in consensual 'SM' 'body practices', provides what Merleau-Ponty called 'phenomenal space', especially for 'players' who prefer 'bottom space'. In contrast to 'perception in the natural attitude', occurring in 'objective space', in which categories of (clock-) time and space govern the 'lived body', the 'phenomenal space' enables the human being to perceive in a profoundly different way. Huxley (1959) illustrated Merleau-Ponty's notion of 'pre-objective perception' that occur in 'phenomenal space' well: "...the mind does its experiencing in terms of intensity of experience, profundity of significance, relations within a pattern... Not, of course that the category of space had been abolished. ... Space was still there, but it had lost its predominance. The mind was primarily concerned, not with measures and locations, but with being and meaning" (Huxley 1959: 19). 'Pre-objective perception' that occurs potentially in these intense experiences in 'phenomenal space' is the space in which according to Merleau-Ponty the patterning of relations between meaning and organization takes place.

Foucault believed in the merits of 'limit-experiences' because of the loss of all security which is present within a 'limit-experience', the 'self' would be lost and a reorientation of it, in a 'lawless situation' would thus open up new possibilities. In connection to the notion of 'limit-experience', Foucault saw in consensual 'SM' a 'social experiment' which explores radical 'politics' of the 'self'. These 'bodily practices', in Foucault's opinion, are a way to discover 'new forms of life', because one's thinking (about the 'self' and its orientation through organizing, limiting and hierarchical categories) would get ruptured and shattered through the suffering-pleasure obtained in this special 'limit-experience'.

"..., as Maslow put it, someone who has had peak experiences has 'become more a real person'. There is no need any more to hide anything. ... An experience that is true, will be true throughout life. Its character is personal and also universal. It is practical and also symbolic" (Maxwell and Tschudin 1990: 41).

Within much of feminist thought the category of 'transcendence' is understood to be 'gendered' and its 'gender' is supposed to be 'male'. For example, in 'The Lust to Kill' by Cameron and Fraser (1987), the 'cultural organizing categories' of 'transcendence' and 'aesthetic standard' are presented as originating from romantic and existential movements that are, in this view, responsible for the stressing of the importance and significance of the gaze. "Remember Sade's sexual universe in which the objects of desire must be consumed totally, in which 'all passions require victims'. For Sade and his existentialist followers the erotic is transgressive and transgression is erotic" (Cameron and Fraser 1987: 153). This perspective leads them to a view of Dennis Nilsen, the 'necrophile', as the impersonation of the figure of the 'transgressor'. In Cameron and Fraser's view, there seems to be an interdependent axis of murder, 'transcendence' and an ultimate act of self-affirmation.

The quest for transcendence, human beings struggle for (relative) freedom from determining constraints by means of the conscious act of will, Cameron and Frazer see eroticized by Sade: "Sexual acts and desires that transgress social or religious norms are redefined as inherently forms of transcendence, thus becoming a source of both power and pleasure, and paving the way for that male sadism which becomes, at its most extreme, the lust to kill" (Cameron and Fraser 1987: 169). These authors are thus clearly sceptical of the view that the 'self' can transcend its objectified condition by acts of will. They further point to the 'gender' of traditional understandings of 'transcendence': "... Sade could not take the step of making his fictional game a true 'anarchy of the sexes', so we find in existentialist thought a similar obfuscation of the actual gender of those people who transcend the social and material conditions of life" (Cameron and Fraser 1987: 62).

'Transcendence' in existentialism (e.g. Sartre, Beauvoir), is 'transcendence' towards free subjecthood but as being a subject is predominantly associated and socially sanctioned as 'male', the 'transcendence' of the 'feminine' appears to be the goal for existentialism according to Cameron and Fraser.

Michel Foucault considered 'transcendence' to be a potential available in all human beings but he also rejected an 'unqualified glorification of transgression' as found in de Sade, and noted: "The libertine's nostalgia for a 'society of blood', was, in the last analysis a 'retro-version'" (Foucault in Miller 1994: 244). As already mentioned Foucault's understanding of 'transcendence' in the context of consensual 'SM' explicitly includes and is interdependent with the 'body' and can therefore not be seen as an endeavour to overcome the 'feminine'. Another understanding of 'transcendence' that is not 'gendered' and that embraces the body is thus required.

Martha Nussbaum (in Kerr 1997) offers a different possibility to under-stand 'transcendence', one which is not originating in 'the Augustinian idea of original sin', where according to her reading, ideas about 'transcendence' of human limits are often to be located. Nussbaum attempts to provide a more humane framework of transcendence (here read mainly as 'ascent of love'), one that does not alienate human beings from their 'bodily human-ity' as Nietzsche had pointed out with regards to 'teleological patterns of desire' which he saw as invented and maintained by Christian religion. Apart from the threat of nihilism that Nietzsche had proposed in connec-tion to the demise of religion, Nussbaum found it to be crucial to rid her ver-sion of transcendence from the disgust of the 'body' (especially the 'female body') which is fundamental to most traditional notions of transcendence.

"Classical Greece, medieval Christianity, the Romantic movement-each era has its own paradigm of the ascent of love, its own method of dealing with the natural longing to transcend finite humanity, yet each diminishes and distorts our characteristically human way of being" (Kerr 1997: 4).

Nussbaum thus favours a concept of 'internal transcendence', one that avoids the dangers and unavoidable frustrations of aspirations to 'extra-human transcendence' which certainly matches Foucault's as well as fem-inist interests. The struggle to transcend the limits of our human condition is for Nussbaum still important but as this should not lead to a rejection of our 'embodied condition', she finds it crucial to conceptualize transcend-ence in a more fluid manner. 'Transcending' human finitude for Nussbaum is thus to be understood as a: "...delicate and always flexible balancing act between the claims of excellence, which lead us to push outward, and the necessity of the human context, which pushes us back in" (Nussbaum in Kerr 1997: 21). This understanding of 'transcendence' that still allows for contextuality and fluidity also appears to resemble a lot of the attitudes towards the achievement of 'unusual experiences' that the practitioners of consensual 'SM' have voiced. Nussbaum even uses a comparison that has striking parallels to some of the interviewees' descriptions of the 'struggle within' and its contextual changes. Nussbaum illustrates her understanding of 'internal transcendence' by comparison to the 'paradox of the athlete': "It is the paradox of a struggle for victory in which complete 'victory' would be disaster and emptiness – or, at any rate, a life so different from our own that we could no longer find ourselves and our valued activities in it" (Nussbaum in Kerr 1997: 21). The goal of 'transcendence' in this understanding, as well as the sense of achievement derived from it, is thus interdependent with our specific 'bodily limits' and the situational context which was also explicitly pointed out by several interviewees as well. As contextuality and fluidity do not exclude either 'femininity' or the body, this understanding of 'tran-scendence' is open for all human beings and not 'gendered'. The longing for and practical experience of 'transcendence' that is one of the potential broader meanings of consensual 'SM' and that might also account for some people's interest in these 'bodily practices' has been documented in this chapter. On the basis of a comparative as well as empirical analysis, the experience and understanding of 'transcendence' within the new Scene of consensual 'SM' can only be appreciated as contextual and relational and thus escapes readings such as Cameron and Frazer's (1987). The final chapter of this work engages in the provision of alternative readings of consensual 'SM' that are based on the empirical data presented in Chapter 3 and then related to Foucault's contextual and relational notion of the 'care of the self' (in e.g. Rabinow 1997).

7
Alternative Readings of Consensual 'SM'

This piece of work has demonstrated, through the deconstruction of some of the major organizing, 'naturalized' (thus depolitized) and 'normalizing' concepts of 'truth' about 'body', 'sexuality', 'perversion' and 'pain' that serve to stabilize the social construction of 'Sadomasochism', that these are reductionist concepts and do not capture the dimensions of 'lived bodies'. As these limiting and deterministic concepts continue to be internalized by many and remain predominant within the public sphere as well as part of many expert discourses and practices (e.g. psychologists, psychiatrists, sexologists, teachers and last but not least legal professionals), they are a crucial part of contemporary 'conditions of domination'. This is particularly obvious when the individual and social harms (facilitated and 'legitimated' by such normalizing 'truth' conceptions) that were generated by the entire Operation Spanner, its subsequent proceedings, judgments and the disappointing decision of the European Court of Human Rights, are considered. These harms stand in no comparable relationship to the ascribed harms of the consensual 'SM' that had to stand trial.

Contemporary consumer culture oriented understandings and representations of for example the 'body' and 'sexuality' (see Chapters 2 and 5) generate widespread harms, do not offer meaningful alternatives to the positivist, deterministic and value-laden discourses of modern *scientia sexualis* (Foucault 1990) and have been rejected by most of my interviewees (see Chapter 3). In comparison to these discourses, the richness of meaning as well as the complexity of existential interaction and communication (both verbal and non-verbal) that characterized the empirical world of consensual 'SM' in London (see Chapter 3), makes the engagement in these 'bodily practices' understandable and allows for a more sophisticated reading. While this work does not claim to give an objective account (as this is only an unobtainable ideal of 'rationality'), the following sections will, on the basis of the understandings gained so far, try to provide an alternative reading of the 'bodily practices' of consensual 'SM'.

Jana Sawicki's conception of a 'politics of difference' does not offer a universal theory and it does not embrace a 'borderless', relativistic pluralism, instead, it provides an ethically comparative tool that appreciates the ambiguities of difference but evaluates: "On the basis of specific theoretical analyses of particular struggles, one can make generalizations, identify patterns in relations of power and thereby identify the relative effectiveness or ineffectiveness, safety or danger of particular practices" (Sawicki 1991: 32).

As the 'conditions of domination' immanent to society have been shown to be personally and politically subjugating (Ch.4 and Ch.5), the practice of consensual 'SM' will, in the following discussion, be understood as a potential 'practice of freedom' and contrasted to the notion of 'liberation'.

The results of this research on consensual 'SM' make a reading of these 'bodily practices' as 'practices of resistance' possible. The 'bodily practices' of consensual 'SM' often appear to be able to assume the status of 'practices of resistance' both on an ideological level, in terms of offering alternative narratives of dissent, as well as on the level of the 'bodily practices' themselves. Moreover, in conclusion this final chapter will attempt to explore the relevance of Foucault's notion of the 'care of the self' (1992; also in Rabinow 1997) within the context of these 'bodily practices'.

7.1   Consensual 'SM'-'body practice' as a potential 'practice of resistance'

The potential of consensual 'SM' as a 'practice of resistance' I consider to be located not only within the innovative and non-genital 'bodily practices' which challenge traditional, modern understandings of 'sexuality' that are genitally fixed but also in the appropriation of traditional modes of 'power' (representations, narratives as well as 'body practices'). The appropriation of traditional representations and 'bodily practices' that were part of the subjection of human beings, through their transformation into games that transform them into 'tools' and 'toys' for the achievement of consensual pleasures, can thus be interpreted as representing 'practices of freedom' in the Foucauldian sense of the term.

> Freedom can be found, he said – but always in a context. Power puts into play a dynamic of constant struggle. There is no escaping it. But there is freedom in knowing the game is yours to play. Don't look to authorities: the truth is in your self. Don't be scared. Trust your self. Don't be afraid of living. And don't be afraid of dying. Have courage. Do what you feel you must: desire, create, transcend – you can win the game. (Foucault to Horvitz in Miller 1994: 352f)

Consensual 'SM' 'body practices' can thus be understood as a response of appropriation which through sensuous experiences and potential 'transcendental experiences' allows insight into the instability of constructions of power and of 'identity' and thus into potentials for change. Practitioners of consensual 'SM' further appear to have a greater potential to realize the 'self' as a 'strategical possibility' (Foucault in Halperin 1995: 73) instead of the modern deterministic understanding of 'self' as a fixed unity. The experiential re-inscription of the political, as well as the understanding, experience and use of the 'self' as a strategical possibility that are experienced within much of the new Scene of consensual 'SM' and 'Fetishism' in London, offer constructive responses to the challenges of 'postmodernity' that Seidman (1994) described as characterized by: "... ambiguity, uncertainty, contingency, and social fluidity that many of us may find psychologically and sociologically challenging" (Seidman 1994: 258).

In a similar manner, consensual 'SM' can be seen as a 'practice of resistance' in terms of 'gender' since this social construction loses its culturally inscribed meaning within the 'new' Scene. In it, the current code of conduct does not prescribe mere role reversals (like e.g. the 'old' Scene did) but promotes 'switching' which disconnects 'gender' and 'sex' from the 'body' as well as from certain forms of 'gendered' 'body usage'. The argument in favour of 'SM'-practice for some lesbian feminists that often rests on the presumption that 'gendered' culturally coded unequal power relationships are inherently oppressive and will not present a problem in a consensual 'SM'-relationship between women as it: "... is potentially liberating because it is chosen" (Jonel in Linden et al. 1982: 36) is therefore reductionistic and inherently oppressive itself. Jeffreys (2003) condemnation of the harmful impact of a 'powerful gay male culture' is similarly deterministic and her subsequent analysis is far too undifferentiated. The possibility of choice is explicitly denied to relationships between men as well as between men and women, thus assuming that the conditions of inequality, set by for example, patriarchy, entirely determine 'lived bodies'.

I would like to suggest that the 'bodily practices', their informal framework and reinforcement of rules on the Scene of consensual 'SM' as observed in London does provide a space for 'counterpractices'. It disconnects the fundamental philosophical pattern of the Western world which tied 'sexuality' to 'subjectivity' and 'truth' which in effect permanently shaped and limited human beings' relationships to themselves and each other. In the Scene and particularly in 'play' these patterns lose their limiting and often socially determining impact. These 'bodily practices' allow 'lived bodies' to experiment within the spaces of subject and object position that they are usually assigned to by the apparatuses of domination.

Gay and lesbian as well as queer activists and scholars have been prolific in deconstructing naturalizing and depoliticizing 'common sense' and so-called 'scientific' connections that were traditionally made between 'sex', 'gender identity', 'gender'-roles, 'sexuality' and the meaning attached to the 'sexual' realm (e.g. Kirsch 2000; Warner 1999). Alongside with queer theorists my concern was always to problematize the tendency of processes of inclusion into the mainstream to project, regulate and 'police' the maintenance of a dualistic conception of normative and thus stifling 'hetero' or 'homosexual' 'sexuality' as well as the continued blending out of different changing and shifting 'genders' and 'sexualities'.

While I agree with the critique levelled at some queer theorizing as being too detached from the material background of the casting of representations, concepts of 'self' etc. (e.g. Weeks et al. 2001), I believe that the grounding of social research in the actual 'lived realities' of research subjects and a relating of their concerns to specific 'historical fields', does go some way towards remedying these flaws.

Judith Butler (1987) offered an analysis of Foucault's work as undermining the hegemony of the binary opposition through suggesting a dialectic that lacked a subject as well as a teleology. Through his proposal of writing a 'history of bodies', unitary concepts within feminist thought are thus as well dismissed (Butler 1990). 'Gender' for Butler functions as an apparatus of production that establishes the sexes in its turn. In opposition to much of feminist thought in which 'gender' is seen as the socio-cultural inscription of biologically 'sexed' bodies, Butler understands 'sex' itself produced by the means of socio-cultural discourses which allows for flexibility and change. In rejection of 'liberal pluralist' notions of an 'emancipatory sexuality' that exists in the absence of law, Butler promotes the political strategy of performances of disruption that work against the consolidation of the discourses of 'subjection'.

In consensual 'SM' the 'parodic redeployment of power' (Butler 1990) is thus a potential for subversions of inscribed identity as these are only feasible, according to Butler, within practices that function constitutive to identity.

Dissident 'bodily practices' that either undermine and/or transcend traditional dualism of for example, male (active) and female (passive) as well as conceptions of absolute power and powerlessness have the potential of disruption. The weakening of the dominating discourses of subjection by performances of diverse 'genders' and 'sexualities', will, according to Butler reveal the constructed 'nature' of 'gendered sexuality' and the 'sexualized gendered body'. To my mind the same holds true for consensual 'SM' 'bodily practices' of the 'new' Scene in which also, especially in 'switching', the experience of the interdependence and fluidity of power disrupt the socio-cultural representations of power(lessness) as static.

Halperin also views freedom and resistance as being contained in power itself. For him potential counter-practices lie in 'creative appropriation and resignification', 'appropriation and theatricalization' as well as in 'exposure and demystification' (Halperin 1995: 48–51).

The explicit and very visual codification of dress and adornment that severed the means of role definition and the signalling of 'sexual' interests find often application in the 'SM'-Scene. But unlike for example, 'butch' and 'femme' the distinctions elaborated and offered within consensual 'SM' are not connected to 'gender':

> ..., the Top-Active/Bottom-Passive distinction offers a signaling system which, unlike 'I am a male'/'I am a female', actually *means* something in the sense that it indicates sexual orientation and provides clues for an appropriate behavioural response..., Top-Active/Bottom-Passive signals and roles offer the possibility of structuring sexual relations in ways which respect feminist values-implying, 'Yes, I recognize that sex is a power game, but, no, I do not recognize any intrinsic relationship between maleness and power. (Polhemus and Randall 1994: 148)

The shifting of metaphors in these 'bodily practices' changes the meaning, the plot and in effect the interpretation of the enacted content.

This process of destructuring and restructuring of dominant discourses and metaphors, makes a subversion of the dominating code of these discourses of domination possible.

> Increasingly today we have to recognise that sexuality is as much about self-making and self-invention as it is about dominant forms of regulation. ... For many of us today it is the resistance, or to put it in another way, the forms of agency that shape personal life and collective identities, that needs expression as much as the structures of power and domination. (Weeks and Holland 1996: 6)

Thus the code of conduct, rules and acquired sense of 'sexual' ethics based on reflexivity and empathy that characterize the 'new Scene' of consensual 'SM' offer a crucial contribution to the debates on 'late modern' and/ or 'postmodern intimacies' (Plummer in Browning et al. 1999 and Plummer 2003).

7.2   Beyond de Sade

In Foucault's eyes de Sade can be understood as the designer of an eroticism proper to disciplinary society in contrast to the practice of consensual 'SM' in contemporary times. "The body in Sade is still strongly organic, anchored in this hierarchy, the difference being of course that the hierarchy is not organized, as in the old fable from the head, but from sex" (Foucault in Lotringer 1996: 187). The so 'designed' eroticism matches the society that de Sade lived to see emerge: "...a regulated, anatomical, hierarchical society whose time is carefully distributed, its spaces partitioned, characterized by obedience and surveillance" (Foucault in Lotringer 1996: 189). De Sade's eroticism has therefore no function in the project of resistance or innovation and thus Foucault proposed: "We must invent with the body, with its elements, surfaces, volumes, and thicknesses, a non-disciplinary eroticism: that of a body in a volatile and diffused state, with its chance encounters and unplanned pleasures" (Foucault in Lotringer 1996: 189).

Michel Foucault had pointed out the distinctive and very different features between power and 'domination' in society and consensual 'SM'. Consensual 'SM' he saw as a strategic relation for the creation of pleasure, and on the other hand, he described domination within society's power structures as serving the purpose of personal and political subjugation. At first glance, the fact that consensual 'SM' borrows images and symbols of everyday cultures of power, it appears to obey and serve the conventions of power. But the use of these conventional 'power-fetishes' is very different and might seem paradoxical.

What strikes me with regard to S/M is how it differs from social power. What characterizes power is the fact that it is a strategic relation that has been stabilized through institutions. So the mobility in power relations is limited, and there are strongholds that are very, very difficult to suppress because they have been institutionalized and are now very pervasive in courts, codes and so on. All that means that the strategic relations of people are made rigid. (Foucault in Halperin 1995: 86)

Whereas the power relations within society subordinate the individual and groups of individuals and ascribe them fixed, rigidly structured and hierarchically ordered power positions, the 'bodily practices' of consensual 'SM', or in Foucault's terms, the S/M game, subordinates these traditionally stable positions of power (or power differentials) to the purpose of the fluid and interdependent production of pleasure.

"The relations of power are perhaps among the best hidden things in the social body" (Foucault in Kritzman 1990: 118). Another crucial point of difference between power in society and within the context of consensual 'SM' is the necessity of secrecy. "... power is tolerable only on condition that it mask a substantial part of itself. Its success is proportional to its ability to hide its own mechanisms. Would power be accepted if it were entirely cynical? For it, secrecy is not in the nature of an abuse; it is indispensable to its operation" (Foucault 1990: 86). Foucault's statement that the mechanisms of power work best while being hidden suggests that through their demystification and exposure within consensual 'SM'-'play' these mechanisms are (at least temporarily) hindered in their operations.

The sphere of 'play' is always distinct from everyday life although some people actually formed contracts that extended their 'play-sphere' into day-to-day routines but even in these situations the thus constructed power inequalities are consensually used to obtain mutual pleasures. Polhemus and Randall also consider the most striking difference between de Sade's eroticism and consensual 'SM'-'body practices' as understood and practiced by Califia to be their reciprocity and interaction. "...dynamic reciprocity lies at the heart of S/M and it structures all of its philosophy and actions..., such reciprocity couldn't exist without mutual concern and respect. And it is these three fundamental tenets of the S/M Scene-reciprocity, concern and respect-which make the stereotyped public perception of such activities so erroneous" (Polhemus and Randall 1994: 113/114). Coercion as for example effected through the conditions of domination within society exclude consensuality and thus constitute direct and/or indirect violence. Consensual 'SM' based on reciprocity should therefore not be termed violence.

> "..., the S/M game is very interesting because it is a strategic relation, but it is always fluid...roles can be reversed....Or, even when the roles are stabilized, you know very well that it is always a game. Either the rules are transgressed, or there is an agreement, either explicit or tacit, that makes [the participants] aware of certain boundaries....I wouldn't say that it is a reproduction, inside the erotic relationship, of the structure of power." (Foucault in Halperin 1995: 86)

A mere reproduction of society's power structures could be found in the many cases of domestic violence in which individuals often identify with internalized ascribed positions and roles of societal power which their attached strategic advantages, even if this involves the physical and emotional subjugation of the other individual[s] to this non-reciprocal power slope. In the case of social power structures the aim of subjugation lies beyond the individual in an ideal of overpowerment, whereas in consensual 'SM' there "(.) is an acting out of power structures by a strategic game that is able to give sexual pleasure or bodily pleasure" (Foucault in Halperin 1995: 86).

A Foucauldian understanding of resistance through 'practices of freedom' implies the challenging of traditional modes of empowering knowledge as well as the traditional modes of authorizing and legitimizing power. In my opinion the theory and practice of consensual 'SM' does just this and therefore might be seen as one possible 'practice of freedom'. Consensual 'SM' practice often interferes with and breaks down monopolies of professional expertise (e.g. in school, doctor practice and torture 'scenes'). It most definitely breaks with the public/private administration of the body and its pleasures and, of major importance, consensual 'SM' allows and even requires a different set of power relations which alters the understanding of the dynamics of personal and political struggle for the individual as well as the groups of practitioners. Thus, Foucault's understanding of power as a 'dynamic situation' is manifest in consensual 'SM': "Resistance to power takes place from within power; ... What escapes from relations of power – and something always does escape, according to Foucault – does not escape from the reach of power to a place outside power, but represents the limit of power, its reversal or rebound. *The aim of an oppositional politics is therefore not liberation but resistance"* (Halperin 1995: 17).

7.3 'Practices of freedom' versus 'liberation'

As Foucault always remained critical towards the notion of liberation and considered it mainly to be an a priori for 'practices of freedom', drawing a parallel to Chancer's term of 'limits' needs precaution. Foucault suggested that: "Liberation paves the way for new power relationships" (Foucault in Halperin 1995: 17). A recollection of the empirical data presented in Chapter 3 in connection with repressive strategies of dominating power within 'liberating' movements shows that this suggestion by Foucault is valid. In pointing out the fundamental difference between 'liberation' as a process and necessary political strategy but insufficient in itself, he said in relation to 'sexuality': "...does the expression 'let us liberate our sexuality' have a meaning? Isn't the problem rather to try to decide the practices of freedom through which we could determine what is sexual pleasure and what are our erotic, loving, passionate relationships with others?" (Foucault in Bernauer and Rasmussen 1984: 114).

While the limited and finally limiting use of liberation movements for the possibility of freedom is emphasized by Foucault he underlined nevertheless: "..., it is clear that a number of liberations were required vis-a-vis male power, that liberation was necessary from an oppressive morality. ... Liberation paves the way for new power relationships, which must be controlled by practices of freedom" (Foucault in Lotringer 1996: 434).

Within the Scene that developed around the 'bodily practices' of consensual 'SM' an ethical code of conduct prevents claims of authority and ensures that the principle of the acceptance of diversity is learned by most members which leads to a nearly automatic rejection of absolute values and of the notion of morality as such. The Scene code of 'equal validity' does not imply that differences do not exist and are not expressed but that these differences are not excluded. Diabolo gave an example of this notion within the Scene: "... I'm not homophobic. But on the other hand I find gay relations unattractive, you know and if any man makes approaches to me I'm really disgusted and sickened by it. But then, you know, equal validity, you know. So, there's two things happening, aren't there? There's public space equal validity, respect and what have you but your own orientation which is necessarily discriminatory and subjective and limited" (Interview-file D.: 8).

Instead of a judgmental and absolutist position in favour or against 'sexuality' Weeks suggests: "... that sex only attains meaning in social relations, which implies that we can only make appropriate choices around sexuality by understanding its social and political context. This involves a decisive move away from the morality of 'acts' which has dominated sexual theorizing for hundreds of years and in the direction of a new relational perspective which takes into account context and meanings" (Weeks 1986: 81). In my opinion this matches Foucault's notion of 'resistance versus liberation', whereby Foucault delegitimates 'traditional' liberal authorities who abused their power in defining the political on behalf of absolute beliefs via a critique of the formation of expertise that is utilized to create a basis for claims of authority.

The previous sections illustrate that consensual 'Sadomasochism' constructed as a threat to 'freedom' is conditioned by the requirements of the dominant, reductionist cultural order, which ultimately holds the rights for the representation and dissemination of cultural material. The critique of consensual 'SM' both of conservative bodies as well as of radical feminists that it reproduces and therefore stabilizes societal power relationships is reductionist and lacks a deeper understanding of the phenomenon. Consensual power games that are still labelled as 'SM' do serve different purposes, they "... [are] a process of invention. S/M is *the use* of a strategic relationship as a source of pleasure ..." (Halperin 1995: 86).

7.4   The need for ethics versus morality and the 'care of the self' within consensual 'SM'

> I do not think that a society can exist without power relations, if by that one means the strategies by which individuals try to direct and control the conduct of others. The problem, then, is not to try to dissolve them in the utopia of completely transparent communication but to acquire the rules of law, the management techniques, and also the morality, the *ethos*, the practice of the self, that will allow us to play these games of power with as little domination as possible.
>
> (Foucault in Rabinow 1997: 298)

The various sections of this work that dealt with the 'subjugated knowledges' of consensual 'SM' practitioners illustrated that the aim of many Scene-members seems to be just that, although this goal was a rather implicit one. The 'bodily practices' of consensual 'SM' provide the 'players' with the possibility to appropriate strategies of power play as well as 'technologies of government', usually serving to effect states of domination and the establishment of authority, for themselves in order to produce individual states of 'bodily pleasure'.

Foucault pointed to the need for a new form of ethics that would be aiming at as little domination as possible and that would centre around the relationship one has to one's 'self' in interrelation to other(s).

> I do not believe that the only possible point of resistance to political power-understood, of course, as a state of domination-lies in the relationship of

the self to the self. I am saying that 'governmentality' implies the relation-ship of the self to itself, and I intend this concept of 'governmentality' to cover the whole range of practices that constitute, define, organize, and instrumentalize the strategies that individuals in their freedom can use in dealing with each other. Those who try to control, determine, and limit the freedom of others are themselves free individuals who have at their disposal certain instruments they can use to govern others. Thus, the basis for all this is freedom, the relationship of the self to itself and the relationship to the other. (Foucault in Rabinow 1997: 300)

This more contextual relationship to the 'self' is a crucial element that reap-peared again and again within the context of consensual 'SM' and is repre-sented explicitly in the 'golden rule' of the Scene: "A good 'top' has to be a 'bottom' first." This concept implicitly states that only once an individual has experienced his/her own limits, in other words, has established a pro-found knowledge and 'care of self', only then will it be able to respectfully deal with the other and avoid to limit the 'Other's' freedom. This kind of ethic is "... fundamentally empathetic and proxemical. History may promote a moral (political) attitude, but space will favour an aesthetics and exude an ethics" (Maffesoli 1993: 15). This notion matches Foucault's notion of 'gov-ernment of self'.

Bauman stated: "The ethical paradox of the postmodern condition is that it restores to agents the fullness of moral choice and responsibility while simultaneously depriving them of the comfort of the universal guidance that modern self-confidence once promised" (Bauman 1992: xxii).

This 'lack of universal guidance' has not only an impact on mainstream society but also effected the 'SM' Scene which changed as illustrated in Chapter 3 from a regulated space of reversed power relationships with impli-cit role-expectations towards a space of relative de-regulation. However, the new Scene in London developed beside the informal but collectively re-enforced general guide-line of 'equal validity' also its rule of 'consen-suality' which both provide a fundamental possibility of choice in 'bodily practices', in contrast to society *not determined by socially constructed roles*. Although it could be argued that specific elements of 'role'-performance etc. might be internalized, the 'return to the spectacle' within the context of these 'bodily practices' promotes 'role-distance' through explicit contrac-tual obligations that are fundamentally based on direct responsibilities.

In 'Discipline and Punish' Michel Foucault described the formation of the 'disciplinary society' as being embedded in a move from a 'society of spec-tacle' to a 'society of surveillance' (1975). The functioning of the Panopticon represents the mechanism of power that is needed for this transformation reduced to its ideal form. This 'house of certainty', alike Western society's capitalistic consumer culture in which human beings are constantly on dis-play, leaves the individual permanently "subjected to a field of visibility"

(Foucault 1975: 202). In effect the individual assumes responsibility and "(.) inscribes in himself the power relation in which he simultaneously plays both roles; he becomes the principle of his own subjection" (ibid.). In consensual 'SM' there is in contrast a return to the spectacle, to direct as opposed to assumed responsibilities and a preference for contractual obligations. Whereas 'the disciplines' guarantee the non-reversible subordination of people, the contractual obligations entered in consensual 'SM' are temporary and agreed upon power relations. These power relations are thus open for change, for experiments within the realms of power that are not serving the aim of 'normalization'.

Maffesoli (1996) stated that there exists a close connection between what he termed the 'aesthetic matrix' and the 'ethical experience'. Within the new Scene in London the rules of abstract morality are rejected and individually specific and contextual ethics are promoted. The hegemonic discourses and regulations of a governmentality that aims at the production of 'docile bodies' is thus rejected and replaced with an ethical attitude towards the 'self' which in turn applies to the thus changed relationship to 'Other'.

Again this relates to Diprose's (2002) notion of 'corporeal generosity' as she argues that the ambiguity of bodily existence can be interpreted as the productive opening of new possibilities of existence. This model of 'intercorporeal generosity' implies a contextual 'care of the self'.

Foucault saw the 'self' as a strategical possibility, the individual, voluntary care of this 'self' thus has the potential to become an alternative to morality. "In the classical Greek world, after all, the purpose of self-fashioning was not to discover one's 'true self' but to work on one's self so as to transform it into a vehicle of personal autonomy and social preeminence. Self-regulation was a specific strategy for gaining power both over oneself and over others;..." (Halperin 1995: 74). The ancient philosophical view of the 'self' was different from contemporary understandings: "...it is the space within each human being where he or she encounters the not-self, the beyond" (Halperin 1995: 75).

While I am aware of the critique that was levelled at Foucault's representation of Ancient Greek notions of 'personhood' that were interdependent with slavery and the oppression of women (duBois 2003), I remain convinced that Foucault certainly was not unaware of these problematic interrelationships. Throughout his later works Foucault concentrated on the formulation of a contextual ethics and his explorations of the notion of 'care of self' should perhaps better be reflected upon in relation to his engagement with and understanding of consensual 'SM'.

"Slave bodies,...could remind free persons of their own vulnerability to enslavement" (duBois 2003: 102) in the context of the conditions of domination' of institutionalized slavery within Ancient Greece. In contrast, consensual 'SM's' code of conduct and especially the 'Golden Rule' of 'A good top has to be a bottom first' even requires the acquisition of 'skin knowledge'

(Howes 2005) of vulnerability. This does not merely imply reflexivity but an 'attuning to', an openness to the other [human and non-human] that makes the 'care of self' a process of becoming affectable in context. This stands certainly in deep contrast to the exploitation and de-humanization of slaves.

In Foucault's opinion the 'art of existence' was a practice of 'self'-regulation.

"...an ethical practice that consisted in freely imposing on the form of one's life a distinctive shape and individual style, and thereby transforming oneself in accordance with one's own conception of beauty or value" (Halperin 1995: 69).

The guiding principle of this 'art of existence' is the 'Care of the Self' and in Foucault's eyes, the methods of self-cultivation resulting from this care might not only lead to self-mastery but also to self-sufficiency and happiness. The 'self' then becomes a strategical possibility ready for individual conversion.

In this context it is helpful to refer once again back to the political philosopher Golding for whom the 'wonderland' of the 'clit-club' and the practices of consensual 'SM' are characterized by the paradoxical mixture of excess and denial, a 'sampling'-process of "...the that of life itself, in all its precarious imbalances and delicacies" (Golding in Kroker 1993: 149). "We are the thieves who play with and against. [the] law, who traverse it (if lucky), who get caught in it (if not). And in so doing, create, disrupt, invent, duplicate, a 'home-land' identity, an 'exiled' identity, situated somewhere between the 'that' of techne and the 'not' of its other" (Golding in Kroker 1993: 149/150).

7.5 Concluding reflections on consensual 'SM'

..., postmodernity can be seen as restoring to the world what modernity, presumptuously, had taken away; as a *re-enchantment* of the world that modernity tried hard to *dis-enchant*. It is the modern artifice that has been dismantled; the modern conceit of meaning – legislating reason that has been exposed, condemned and put to shame. It is that artifice and that reason, the reason of the artifice, that stands accused in the court of postmodernity. The war against mystery and magic was for modernity the war of liberation leading to the declaration of reason's independence.

(Bauman 1992: x)

Apart from the major catastrophes that this 'government' of pure reason and the interconnected notion of progress brought about (e.g. world-climate changes, continuing warfares and poverty etc.), people themselves have become increasingly aware of the 'limits of progress and reason' and of the disenchantment of modernity and consumer culture.

As elaborated in this piece of work the 'bodily practices' of consensual 'SM' are in many ways re-enchanting the 'life-world' of its practitioners. The 'body' and 'sexuality', stripped of any meaning but competitive consumption and 'body image', gain new experiential meanings in consensual 'SM'. The same holds true for 'pain' as the 'art of suffering' can be re-discovered and learned in this context. Through the 'desexualization of pleasure' as well as the necessity of the learning of the 'care of the self' in the 'scenes' that are played in consensual 'SM', rigid categories of separation are broken down and communication (verbal/non-verbal) is made possible. The concept of 'skin knowledge' (Howes 2005) lends itself here perfectly as it underlines the importance of this dimension of 'being' and 'pleasure' that increasingly is substituted by mechanized ways of knowing ('electronic skins') and in this way consensual 'SM' practices can be seen as a way of exploring and celebrating the 'sensing and sensual body'.

The continued semi-criminalization and pathologization of consensual 'SM' thus does not only further all the negative effects of stigmatization and uninformed stereotyping but also limits existential areas of human freedom. The experiences of re-enchantment, of 're-sensualization' and self-actualization as well as the fulfilment of apparently existing desires for spiritual or religious experiences through the 'bodily practices' of consensual 'SM' are aims that should be recognized as existentially important especially in contemporary technologized capitalist-consumer cultures. The realm of the 'sexual' and its representations within the public sphere of consumerism threatens meaning: "The diminishment of psychological horizon is a diminishment of the dimension of space in human consciousness, and that diminishment characteristically is experienced as a radical paradox: the ease of travel makes getting there less meaningful" (McFarland 1996: 112).

Parallel to this erosion of spatial meaning McFarland (1996) notes the difficulty to have actual relationships with other people. As consensual 'SM' also demonstrates and is fundamentally based on the requirements of responsibility and self-responsibility it has a potential to ease feelings of alienation, meaninglessness as well as isolation. "The liberalisation of heterosexuality in the context of the transition from 'sex as production' to 'sex as consumption' is more illusion than reality. The choices that are for some the indicators of freedom are in fact a more subtle form of regulation through the myth of individual autonomy inherent in consumer choice" (Hawkes 1996: 115).

The commodification of 'sexuality' and 'sexual desire' thus has fatal costs: "The 'real sensual qualities' are obscured by objectified mechanistic manipulation, in which the real sensuality is not just assumed but occluded" (Hawkes 1996: 122). Levy noted referring to her notion of 'raunch culture', that it: "... is not essentially progressive, it is essentially commercial" (Levy 2005: 29) and with reference to the 'self'-confessed 'non-sexual' Paris Hilton she elaborates: "... Hilton looks excited when she is posing for the camera, bored when she is engaged in actual sex. (...) She is the perfect sexual celebrity for this moment, because our interest is in the appearance of sexiness, not the existence of sexual pleasure" (Levy 2005: 30).

As illustrated in Chapter 3 the 'bodily practices' of consensual 'SM', in contrast, directly focus on sensual experiences. Sadly though it seems that the use of one's own body is only legitimate if it serves the goal of adjustment to a 'consumer realm normality'.

"... Foucault politicizes both truth and the body: he reconstitutes knowledge and sexuality as sides of contestation, thereby opening up new opportunities for both scholarly and political intervention" (Halperin 1995: 42).

The political implications of this perspective are that human beings, instead of being reduced to objects of expert-gazes and discourses, should become the subjects of expert discourses on 'sexualities' and 'bodies'. The authorization of subjective experiences and the legitimization of life-reports as 'knowledge' would end the pathologization, criminalization as well as the moralizing discourses by psychiatrists, sexologists, social scientists etc. that so far shaped mainstream understandings of 'sexualities'.

Social constructions work as instruments of separation and hinder understanding and communication. As such they do not further critical thought that is the basis of a 'politics of difference' (Sawicki 1991) and a potential often achieved through the 'bodily practices' of consensual 'SM' on a practical level.

In 'Truth and Eros: Foucault, Lacan, and the question of ethics', Rajchman explains the notion of the 'concern for oneself' in the late Foucault: "... the eros of this experience of critical thought would not be a sacrificial or renunciatory one; it would not be perfectionist, salvationist or progressivist; and it would not assume the form of inducing people to accept principles or rules known independently of their experience of themselves" (Rajchman 1991: 10). The experimental games of consensual 'SM' allow for the discovery of new intensities, the diverse dimensions and potentials of 'lived bodies', as well as requiring the development of contextual ethics. As a consequence, they have the potential to bring about a 'political spirituality' on a practical level which would involve "... questioning through which people might start to depart from the historical limits of their identifications, ..." (Rajchman 1991: 108).

Within the framework of consensual 'SM', 'the care of the self' as well as for the 'Other' is fundamentally important for the development of a good 'play'. The exploration of one's own limits and a high sense of self-responsibility are required and learned through experiential games, apart from the development of empathy that can usually only develop with time and experience. The code of conduct and practices of consensual 'SM' seem to be able to foster an experience-oriented approach to ethics as the conscious practice of freedom. In this context people seem to have been able to develop an ethics that is fundamentally based on the 'other's' freedom which allows for fluidity and change as well as for dialogue to prevail, as opposed to moral approaches which lead inevitably to exclusions and conditions of domination. Sawicki's (1991) notion of a 'politics of difference', includes the suggestion to see differences as resources and in my opinion this piece of work, based on reflections of field-experiences and subjugated knowledges, has illustrated that the 'bodily practices' of consensual 'SM' and their practitioners have a lot of resources to offer. They do not only provide an example of an *ars erotica* but further provide examples for a framework of 'sexual ethics' that is not exclusionary but that is open for the diversity of 'life world' as it is contextual, relational and consensual. It is further a framework that is interdependent with an awareness of the consequences of actions, both on a theoretical- reflexive as well as on an existential 'embodied' level.

Bibliography

Aas, K. F. (2006) ' "The Body Does Not Lie": Identity, Risk and Trust in Technoculture', in *Crime, Media, Culture*, 2 (2): pp. 143–158, Sage.

Agamben, G. (2004) 'Bodies without Words: Against the Biopolitical Tatoo', in *German Law Journal*, 5 (2): pp. 168–9.

Agamben, G. (2005) *State of Exception*, University of Chicago Press, Chicago and London.

Agamben, G. (2007) 'The Coming Community', in *Theory Out of Bounds*, 1, University of Minnesota Press, Minneapolis.

Agnew, R. and Peters, A. (1986) 'The Techniques of Neutralisation: An Analysis of Predisposing and Situational Factors', in *Criminal Justice and Behavior* (13): pp. 81–97.

Anthony, E. (1995) *Thy Rod and Staff*, Brown and Company, UK.

Apter, E. (1991) *Feminizing the Fetish: Psychoanalysis and Narrative Obsession in Turn-of-the-Century France*, Cornell University Press, Ithaca, NY and London.

Ardill, S. and O'Sullivan, S. (1986) 'Upsetting an Applecart: Difference, Desire and Lesbian Sadomasochism', in Feminist Review, 23: pp. 31–57.

Ardill, S. and O'Sullivan, S. (2005) 'Upsetting an Applecart: Difference, Desire and Lesbian Sadomasochism', in *Feminist Review*, 80 (1): pp. 98–126.

Arnould, E. J. and Thompson, C. J. (2005) 'Consumer Culture Theory (CCT): Twenty Years of Research', in *Journal of Consumer Research*, 31 (March): pp. 868–882.

Asthana, A. (2007) 'Call to Ban All School Exams for under-16s', *The Observer*, 10 June: p. 1.

Attwood, F. (2002) 'Reading Porn: The Paradigm Shift in Pornography Research', in *Sexualities*, 5 (1): pp. 91–105.

Attwood, F. (2005) 'Fashion and Passion: Marketing Sex to Women', in *Sexualities*, 8 (4): pp. 392–406.

Bacchi, C. L. and Beasley, C. (2000) 'Citizen Bodies: Embodying Citizens – a Feminist Analysis', in *International Feminist Journal of Politics*, 2 (3): pp. 337–358.

Bacchi, C. L. and Beasley, C. (2002) 'Citizen Bodies: Is Embodied Citizenship a Contradiction in Terms?', in *Critical Social Policy*, 22: pp. 324–352.

Badgett, M. L. (2001) *Money, Myths, and Change*, University of Chicago Press, Chicago.

Bakthin, M. M. (1968) *Rabelais and His World*, MIT Press, Cambridge, MA.

Bastian, D. (2002) *Chainmale*, Daedalus, Los Angeles.

Bateson, J. R. (1972) *Steps to an Ecology of Mind*, Ballantine, New York.

Bauman, Z. (1992) *Intimations of Postmodernity*, Routledge, London and New York.

Bauman, Z. (2001) *Community: Seeking Safety in an Insecure World*, Polity, Cambridge.

Baumeister, R. F. (1991) *Escaping the Self: Alcoholism, Spirituality, Masochism and Other Flights from the Burden of Selfhood*, Basic Books, New York.

Beasley, C. (2005) *Gender & Sexuality*, Sage, London, Thousand Oaks, CA and New Delhi.

Beck, U. (1994) *Risk Society – Towards a New Modernity*, Sage, London, Thousand Oaks, CA and New Delhi.

Becker, H. S. (1960) 'Notes on the Concept of Commitment', in *American Journal of Sociology*, 66: pp. 32–40.

Becker, H. S. (1963) *Outsiders: Studies in the Sociology of Deviance*, Free Press, New York.

Beckmann, A. (2001a) 'Deconstructing Myths: The Social Construction of "Sadomasochism" versus "Subjugated Knowledges" of Practitioners of Consensual "SM"', in *Journal of Criminal Justice and Popular Culture*, 8 (2): pp. 66–95, University at Albany, New York.

Beckmann, A. (2001b) 'Researching Consensual "Sadomasochism", Perspectives on Power, Rights and Responsibilities – the Case of "Disability"', in *Social Policy Review*, (13): pp. 89–106, The Policy Press, Bristol.

Beckmann, A. (2004) 'Sexual Rights and Sexual Responsibilities in Consensual "SM"', in Cowling, M. and Reynolds, P. (eds) *Making Sense of Sexual Consent*, Ashgate, Aldershot and Burlington, VT.

Beckmann, A. (2005) 'Representing "Healthy" and "Sexual" Bodies: The Media, "Disability" and Consensual "SM"', in King, M. and Watson, K. (eds) *Representing Health: Discourses of Health and Illness in the Media*, Palgrave Macmillan, Houndmills, Basingstoke, Hampshire and New York.

Beckmann, A. and Cooper, C. (2004) '"Globalisation", the New Managerialism and Education: Rethinking the Purpose of Education in Britain', in *The Journal for Critical Education Policy Studies*, 2 (September): p. 2.

Beckmann, A. and Cooper, C. (2005) 'Conditions of Domination: Reflections on Harms Generated by the British State Education System', in *British Journal of Sociology of Education*, 26 (4): pp. 475–489.

Behr, R. (2008) 'Sex: Having It All', in *The Observer*, 26 October.

Bell, D. (1975) 'Toward the Great Instauration: Reflections on Culture and Religion in a Postindustrial Age', in *Social Research*, 42 (3), New York.

Bell, R. (2007) 'Love in the Time of Phone Porn', in *the guardian education*, 30 January.

Bell, R. (2008) 'I Was Seen as an Object, Not a Person', in *The Guardian*, 19 March, p. 18.

Benedict, R. (1968) *Patterns of Culture*, New American Library, New York.

Berger, P. L. and Luckmann, T. (1966) *The Social Construction of Reality*, Doubleday, Garden City, New York.

Bernauer, J. W. W. (1992) *Michel Foucault's Force of Flight: Towards an Ethic for Thought*, Brill Academic Publishers, Boston, MA.

Bernauer, J. and Rasmussen, D. (eds) (1984) *The Final Foucault*, The MIT Press, Cambridge, MA and London.

Bernstein, B. (1990) *Class, Codes and Control: The Structuring of Pedagogic Discourse*, Routledge, London.

Biernacki, P. and Waldorf, D. (1981) 'Snowball Sampling: Problems and Techniques of Chain Referral Sampling', in *Sociological Methods and Research*, 10 (2): pp. 141–163.

Bindel, J. (2004) Report for the Child and Woman Abuse Studies Unit at London Metropolitan University in August 2004, 'Profitable Exploits: Lapdancing in the UK', Available at http://www.rapecrisisscotland.org.uk/documents/ profitable%20exploits.pdf

Binnie, J. (2008) 'Locating Economics within Sexuality Studies', in *Sexualities*, 11 (1/2): pp. 100–103.

Blackburn, R. (1995) *The Psychology of Criminal Conduct*, John Wiley & Sons, Chichester, New York, Brisbane, Toronto and Singapore.

Blackman, L. and Walkerdine, V. (2001) *Mass Hysteria: Critical Psychology and Media Studies*, Palgrave Macmillan, Basingstoke and New York.

Bleier, R. (1984) *Science and Gender*, Pergamon Press, New York and Oxford.

Blumer, H. (1969/1986) *Symbolic Interactionism: Perspective and Method*, University of California Press, CA.

Bordo, S. (1995) *Unbearable Weight: Feminism, Western Culture and the Body*, University of California Press, London.

Boseley, S. (2002) 'Eternal Youth Available at Your Local Chemist's', in *The Guardian*, 25 May, p. 7.

Bouchard, D. (ed.) (1963/1977) *A Preface to Transgression in Michel Foucault, Language, Counter-Memory, Practice: Selected Essays and Interviews*, Cornell University Press, Ithaca, NY.

Bourdieu, P. (1998) *Acts of Resistance: Against the Tyranny of the Market*, The New York Press, New York.

Bourke, J. (2005) *Fear: A Cultural History*, Virago, London.

Boyne, R. (1990) *Foucault and Derrida – the Other Side of Reason*, Unwin Hyman, London, Boston, MA, Sydney and Wellington.

Brake, M. (ed.) (1982) *Human Sexual Relations*, Penguin, Suffolk.

Braun, V. (2005) 'In Search of (Better) Sexual Pleasure: Female Genital "Cosmetic" Surgery', in *Sexualities*, 8 (2005): pp. 407–424.

Brennan, T. (1989) *Between Feminism and Psychoanalysis*, Routledge, London and New York.

Brennan, T. (2004) *The Transmission of Affect*, Cornell University Press, Ithaca, NY.

Bretherton, I. (1984) *Symbolic Play*, Academic Press, New York.

Browning, G., Abigail Halcli, A. and Frank Webster, F. (eds) (2003) *Understanding Contemporary Society: Theories of the Present*, Sage, London.

Browning, G. K., Halcli, A. and Webster, F. (eds) (1999) *Understanding Contemporary Society: Understanding the Present*, Sage, London.

Bryman, A. (1988) *Quantity and Quality in Social Research*, Routledge, USA and Canada.

Bunton, R., Nettleton, S. and Burrows, R. (eds) (1995) *The Sociology of Health Promotion*, Routledge, London and New York.

Burgess, R. G. (1990) *Investigating Society*, Longmans, London.

Burkitt, I. (1991) *Social Selves*, Sage, London, Newbury Park and New Delhi.

Butler, J. (1990) *Gender Trouble*, Routledge, London and New York.

Butler, J. (1993) *Bodies That Matter*, Routledge, London and New York.

Butler, J. (2004) *Precarious Life*, Verso, London.

Butler, J. (2005) *Giving an account of Oneself*, Fordham University Press, New York.

Butler, J. (2005) *Undoing Gender*, Routledge, London and New York.

Caillois, R. (1950) *L'homme et le sacre*, Gallimard, Paris.

Califia, P. (1988) *The Lesbian S/M Safety Manual*, Alyson Books, New York.

Califia, P. (1994) *Sensuous Magic: A Guide for Adventurous Lovers*, Masquerade Books, USA.

Califia-Rice, Patrick. (2001) *Sensuous Magic: A Guide for Adventurous Couples*, 2nd ed., Cleis Press, San Francisco.

Califia-Rice, P. (interview) http://www.technodyke.com/features/patcalifa3.asp [accessed 15.10.08].

Califia, P. and Sweeney, R. (1996) *The Second Coming: A Leather Dyke Reader*, Alyson Books, New York.

Cameron, D. and Fraser, E. (1987) *The Lust to Kill*, Polity Press, Cambridge: Polity and New York: NYU Press.

Chancer, L. S. (1994) *Sadomasochism in Everyday Life: The Dynamics of Power and Powerlessness*, Rutgers University Press, New Brunswick, NJ.

Chisholm, D. (1995) 'The "Cunning Lingua" of Desire: Bodies-Language and Perverse Performativity', in Grosz, E. and Probyn, E. (eds) *Sexy Bodies: The Strange Carnalities of Feminism*, Routledge, New York.

Chomsky, N. (2005) *Imperial Ambitions*, Hamish Hamilton, London.

Christie, N. (1993) *Crime Control as Industry*, Routledge, London and New York.

Church Gibson, P. (ed.) (2004) *More Dirty Looks*, British Film Institute, London.

Church Gibson, P. and Gibson, R. (eds) (1993) *Dirty Looks: Women, Pornography, Power*, British Film Institute.

Ciclitira, K. (2004) 'Pornography, Women, and Feminism: Between Pleasure and Politics', in *Sexualities*, 7 (3): pp. 281–301.

Clarke, L. (2006) *Worst Cases: Terror and Catastrophe in the Popular Imagination*, The University of Chicago Press, Chicago.

Cohen, S. (1992) *Visions of Social Control*, Polity Press, Cambridge.

Cooper, A. (1998) *Surfing into the New Millennium*, in Cyberpsychology and Behavior, (1): pp. 181–187.

Couliano, I. P. (1991) *Out of this World*, Shambhala Publications, Boston, MA and London.

Cowan, L. (1982) *Masochism: A Jungian View*, Spring Publications, Dallas, TX.

Cowling, M. and Reynolds, P. (2004) *Making Sense of Sexual Consent*, Ashgate, Aldershot and Burlington, VT.

Cross, P. A. and Matheson, K. (2006) 'Sadomasochism: Powerful Pleasures', in *Journal of Homosexuality*, 50 (2/3).

Cullen, F. T. and Burton, V. S. (eds) (1994) *Contemporary Criminological Theory*, Dartmouth, Aldershot, Hong Kong, Singapore and Sydney.

Cunningham, S. and Lavalette, M. (2004) ' "Active Citizens" or "Irresponsible" Truants? School Student Strikes against the War', in *Critical Social Policy*, 24 (2), May.

Curtis, P. (2008) 'Minister Calls for School Guidelines to Tackle Exploitation of Young Girls', in *The Guardian*, 6 December, p. 17.

Daily Mail (1996) *Torture Gang Take Britain to Court*, 19 October, p. 16.

de Beauvoir, S. (1974) *The Second Sex*, Vintage Books, New York.

de Haan, W. (1992) 'Universalismus und Relativismus in der kritischen Kriminologie', in "Krim J.", 1/1992, in Scheerer, S. (ed.) `Materialien zum Kurs-Geschichte der Kriminologie', Universitaet Hamburg.

Deleuze, G. (1989) ' *"Masochism" – Coldness and Cruelty*; incl. *"Venus in Furs"* ' by Leopold von Sacher-Masoch[1870], Zone Books, New York. Derrida, J. (1978) *Writing and Difference*, Routledge, London.

Diamond, I. and Quinby, L. (eds) (1988) *Feminism & Foucault*, Northeastern University Press, Boston, MA.

Dickenson, A. H. (2002) 'Gate Control Theory of Pain Stands the Test of Time', in *British Journal of Anaesthesia*, 88 (6): pp. 755–757.

Diprose, R. (2002) *Corporeal Generosity*, SUNY Press, Albany, NY.

Ditton, J. (1979) *Controlology: Beyond the New Criminology*, Macmillan Press, London.

Dominguez, I. (1994) *Beneath the Skins*, Daedalus, Los Angeles.

Douglas, M. (1966) *Purity and Danger*, Routledge, New York and London.

DSM-IV-TR of the American Psychiatric Association, 4th ed. (2000) American Psychiatric Publishing, Inc.

duBois, P. (1991) *Torture and Truth*, Routledge, New York and London.

duBois, P. (2003) *Slaves and Other Objects*, The University of Chicago Press, Chicago.

Durkheim, E. (1965, ori. 1915) *The Elementary Forms of the Religious Life: A Study in Religious Sociology*, Macmillan, New York.

Dworkin, A. (1987) *Intercourse*, Secker & Warburg, London.

Eden, I. (2007) 'Inappropriate Behaviour: Adult Venues and Licensing in London', report for Lilith Project, available at http://www.eaves4women.co.uk/Lilith_Project/ Documents/Reports/Inappropriate_Behaviour_2007.pdf

Elchardus, M. (2002) *De Dramademocratie*, Lannoo, Tielt.

Eliade, M. (1978) *A History of Religious Ideas*, (Vol. 1), The University of Chicago Press, Chicago.

Ellis, H. (2007) *Studies in the Psychology of Sex*, BiblioBazaar, LLC.

Ellwood, R. S., Jr (1980) *Mysticism and Religion*, Prentice Hall, Englewood Cliffs, NJ.

European Court of Human Rights in Strasbourg ([1997] Cr App Rep 44).

Falk, P. (1994) *The Consuming Body*, Sage, London.

Fausto-Sterling, A. (2005) 'The Bare Bones of Sex Part One: Sex and Gender', in *Signs*, 30 (2): pp. 1491–1517.

Favazza, A. R. (1996) *Bodies under Siege: Self-mutilation and Body Modification in Culture and Psychiatry*, The Johns Hopkins University Press, Baltimore, MD.

Featherstone, M. (1993) *Consumer Culture and Postmodernism*, Sage, London, Newbury Park, CA and New Delhi.

Featherstone, M., Hepworth, M. and Turner, B. S. (1991) *The Body: Social Process and Cultural Theory*, Sage, London, Thousand Oaks, CA and New Delhi.

Feinberg, J. (1987) *The Moral Limits of the Criminal Law Volume 1: Harm to Others*, Oxford University Press, Oxford.

Foot, M. (2005) 'A Triumph of Hearsay and Hysteria', in *The Guardian*, 5 April, p. 20.

Foucault, M. (1971) *The Order of Things*, Vintage Books, New York.

Foucault, M. (1975) *Discipline and Punish*, Penguin, London.

Foucault, M. (1979–1990) *The History of Sexuality*, Vol. 1–3, Penguin, London.

Freud, S. (1919) *A Child Is Being Beaten: A Contribution to the Study of the Origin of Sexual Perversions*, edited by Ethel Spector Person (1997), Yale University Press, London.

Furedi, F. (2002) *Culture of Fear*, Continuum, London.

Galbraith, J. K. (1983) *The Anatomy of Power*, Hamish Hamilton, London.

Garfinkel, H. (1967) *Studies in Ethnomethodology*, Prentice Hall, Englewood Cliffs, NJ.

Garfinkel, H. (1972) 'Conditions of Successful Degradation Ceremonies', in Manis, J. and Meltzer, B. (eds) *Symbolic Interactionism*, Allyn and Bacon, New York.

Giddens, A. (1990) *The Consequences of Modernity*, Polity Press, Cambridge.

Giddens, A. (1991) *Modernity and Self-identity. Self and Society in the Late Modern Age*, Polity Press, Cambridge.

Gilligan, C. (1983) *In a Different Voice*, Harvard University Press, Cambridge.

Glaser, B. G. and Strauss, A. (1967) *Discovery of Grounded Theory. Strategies for Qualitative Research*, Sociology Press, Mill Valley, CA.

Glaser, D. (1978) *Crime in Our Changing Society*, Holt, Rinehart and Winston, New York.

Gluckman, A. and Reed, B. (1997) *Homo Economics: Capitalism, Communism and Lesbian and Gay Life*, Routledge, New York.

Goffman, E. (1967) *The Presentation of Self in Everyday Life*, Doubleday, New York.

Goffman, E. (1972) *Interaction Ritual*, Penguin, London.

Golding, S. (1993) 'The Excess: An Added Remark on Sex, Rubber, Ethics, and Other Impurities', in *New Formations*, Spring (19): pp. 23–28.

Gordon, O. (2008) 'Beauty Salons Give Makeovers to Six-Year-Olds', in *The Observer*, 15 June: pp. 14, 15.

Grabham, E. (2007) 'Citizen Bodies, Intersex Citizenship', in *Sexualities*, 10 (29): pp. 29–48.

Green, P. and Ward, T. (2004) *State Crime: Governments, Violence and Corruption*, Pluto Press, London.

Grof, S. (1985) *Beyond the Brain*, SUNY Press, New York.

Grosz, E. and Probyn, E. (eds) (1995) *Sexy Bodies*, Routledge, London and New York.

Halberstam, J. (1998) *Female Masculinity*, Duke University Press, Durham, N.C.

Halperin, D. M. (1995) *Saint=Foucault – towards a Gay Hagiography*, Oxford University Press, New York and Oxford.

Hamm, M. S. (2004) 'Apocalyptic Violence: The Seduction of Terrorist Subcultures', in *Theoretical Criminology*, 8 (3): pp. 323–339.

Hardy, S. (2008) 'The Pornography of Reality', in *Sexualities*, 11 (1/2): pp. 60–63.

Hawkes, G. (1996) *A Sociology of Sex and Sexuality*, Open University Press, Buckingham, PA.

Hearn, J. (2008) 'Sexualities Future, Present, Past...towards Transsectionalities', in *Sexualities*, 11: pp. 37–45.

Hennessy, R. (2000) *Profit and Pleasure: Sexual Identities in Late Capitalism*, Routledge, New York and Oxon, UK.

Hersh, S. M. (2005) *Chain of Command*, Penguin, London.

Hess, H. (1986) 'Kriminalitaet als Alltagsmythos.Ein Plaedoyer dafuer, Kriminologie als Ideologiekritik zu betreiben', in *Kriminologisches Journal*, 1.Beiheft: p. 24ff.

Hess, H. (1993) 'Desorganisierte Kriminalität', in Kampmeyer, E. and Neumeyer, J. (eds) *Neue Unsicherheit. Eine kritische Bestandsaufnahme*, SPAK, München: pp. 95–101.

Hill, A. (2008) ' "Streetwise" British Teenagers Are Ignorant about Sex, Survey Reveals', in *The Observer*, 7 September: p. 10.

Hitchens, C. (2008) 'Believe Me, It's Torture', in *Vanity Fair*, August.

Hoinville, G. and Jowell, R. (1987) *Survey Research Practice*, Heinemann, London.

Holland, J. and Adkins, L. (1996) *Sex, Sensibility and the Gendered Body*, Macmillan, Basingstoke.

Horn, M. J., Piedmont, R. L., Fialkowski, G. M., Wicks, R. J. and Hunt, M. E. (2005) 'Sexuality and Spirituality: The Embodied Spirituality Scale', in *Theology and Sexuality*, Sage, 12 (1): pp. 81–101.

Horney, K. (1937) *The Neurotic Personality of Our Time*, WW Norton, New York.

Howells, K. (ed.) (1984) *The Psychology of Sexual Diversity*, Basil Blackwell, Oxford.

Howes, D. (2005) 'Skinscapes: Embodiment, Culture and Environment', in Classen, C. (ed.) *The Book of Touch*, Berg, Oxford.

Hulsman, L. H. C. (1986) 'Critical Criminology and the Concept of Crime', in *Contemporary Crisis*, 10: pp. 63–80.

Hunt, A. and Wickham, G. (1994) *Foucault and Law: Towards a Sociology of Law as Governance*, Pluto Press, London.

Hussein, J. and Fatoohi, L. (1998) 'The Deliberately Caused Bodily Damage Phenomenon as Exceptional Human Experience', in *Journal of Religion & Psychical Research*; January, 21 (1): p. 14.

Huxley, A. (1959) *The Doors of Perception*, Penguin, Harmondsworth.

Illich, I. (1977) *Limits to Medicine*, Marion Boyars, London.

Irigaray, L. (1993) *An Ethics of Sexual Difference*, Cornell University Press, New York.

Jackson, S. and Scott, S. (eds) (1996) *Feminism and Sexuality*, Edinburgh University Press, Edinburgh.

Jamieson, J. and McEvoy, K. (2005) 'State Crime by Proxy and Juridical Othering', in *British Journal of Criminology*, 45 (4): pp. 504–527.

Jaspers, K. (1951) *Way to Wisdom*, Victor Gollancz, London.

Jeffreys, S. (1991) *Anticlimax*, New York University Press, New York.

Jeffreys, S. (1993) *The Lesbian Heresy: A Feminist Perspective on the Lesbian Sexual Revolution*, The Womens Press, London.

Jeffreys, S. (2003) *Unpacking Queer Politics: A Lesbian Feminist Perspective*, Polity Press, Bristol.
Johnson, T. (2000) *Gay Spirituality: The Role of Gay Identity in the Transformation of Human Consciousness*, Alyson Books, Los Angeles.
Jones, J. W. (1991) *'Contemporary Psychoanalysis and Religion' – Transference and Transcendence*, Yale University Press, New Haven, CT and London.
Jones, M. (2008) *Skintight*, Berg, Oxford and New York.
Kalthoff, H. (2005) 'Practices of Calculation', in *Theory, Culture & Society*, 22 (2): pp. 69–97, Sage, London, Thousand Oaks, CA and New Delhi.
Katz, B. (1982) *Herbert Marcuse and the Art of Liberation*, Verso Editions, London.
Katz, J. (1987) *Seductions of Crime: Moral and Sensual Attractions of Doing Evil*, Basic Books, New York.
Kent, G. and Dalgleish, M. (1986) *Psychology and Medical Care*, Bailliere Tindall, London, Toronto.
Kerr, F. (1997) *Immortal Longings*, SPCK, London.
Kershaw, A. (1992) 'Love Hurts', in *Guardian Weekend*, 28 November: p. 12.
Kimmel, M. S. (2004) *The Gendered Society*, Oxford University Press, Oxford and New York.
Kinsey, A. C. (1948) *Sexual Behavior in the Human Male*, W. B. Saunders Co., Philadelphia.
Kinsey, A. C. (1953) *Sexual Behavior in the Human Female* W. B. Saunders Co., Philadelphia.
Kirsch, M. (2000) *Queer Theory and Social Change*, Routledge, London and New York.
Knott, J. R. (1993) *Discourses of Martyrdom in English Literature*, Cambridge University Press, Cambridge.
Krafft-Ebing, R. (von) (ori. 1886/2006) *Psychopathia Sexualis*, Kessinger, LLC, Whitefish, Montana.
Kristeva, J. (1982) *Powers of Horror: An Essay on Abjection*, Columbia University Press, New York.
Kritzman, L. D. (ed.) (1990) *Michel Foucault-Politics-Philosophy-Culture; Interviews and Other Writings 1977–1984*, Routledge, New York and London.
Kroker, A. and Kroker, M. (1993) *The Last Sex*, Macmillan, Basingstoke.
Kuehl, J. (1981) 'Ascribed Behaviour', in *Kriminologisches Journal*, 13.Jahrgang, Issue 3.
La Barre, W. (1972) *Ghost Dance*, Delta, New York.
Lacan, J. (1998) *The Seminar of Jacques Lacan: On Feminine Sexuality, the Limits of Love and Knowledge*, Norton, New York.
Langdridge, D. and Barker, M. (eds) (2007) *Safe, Sane and Consensual*, Palgrave Macmillan, Basingstoke and New York.
Langdridge, D. and Butt, T. (2004) 'A Hermeneutic Phenomenological Investigation of the Construction of Sadomasochism Identities', in *Sexualities*, 7 (1): pp. 31–53, Sage, London, Thousand Oaks, CA and New Delhi.
Leary, T., Metzner, R., Karma-Glin-Pa Bar Do Thos Grol and Alpert, R. (1964) *The Psychedelic Experience*, Citadel Underground Press, Carol, US.
Lee, R. M. (1993) *Doing Research on Sensitive Topics*, Sage, London.
Lemert, E. M. (ed.) (1967) *Human Deviance, Social Problems and Social Control*, Prentice Hall, New Jersey.
Levy, A. (2005) *Female Chauvinist Pigs*, Free Press, New York, London, Toronto and Sydney.
Linden, R., Pagano, R., Russell, D. R., Star, D. and Leigh, S. (eds) (1982) *Against Sadomasochism: A Radical Feminist Analysis*, Frog In The Well, California, San Francisco.

Lotringer, S. (ed.) (1996) *Foucault Live*, Semiotext(e), New York.

Luhmann, N. (1986) *Love as Passion: The Codification of Intimacy*, Polity Press, Cambridge.

MacKinnon, C. (1987) *Feminism Unmodified: Discourses on Life and Law*, Harvard University Press, Cambridge.

MacKnee, C. M. (2002) 'Profound Sexual and Spiritual Encounters among Practicing Christians: A Phenomenological Analysis', in *Journal of Psychology and Theology*, (30): pp. 234–244.

Maffesoli, M. (1996) *The Time of the Tribes*, Sage, London.

Malinowski, B. (1963) *Sex, Culture and Myth*, Rupert Hart-Davis, London.

Marcuse, H. (1964) *One Dimensional Man*, Beacon, Boston, MA.

Marcuse, H. (1970) *Five Lectures*, Beacon, Boston, MA.

Maslow, A. (1970, 2nd ed. ori. 1954) *Motivation and Personality*, Harper, New York.

Mason, J. and Fattore, T. (eds) (2005) *Children Taken Seriously*, Jessica Kingsley Publishers, London.

Mathiesen, T. (1997) *Theoretical Criminology*, Sage, London, Thousand Oaks, CA and New Delhi.

Matsueda, R. L. (1992) 'Reflected Appraisals, Parental Labeling, and Delinquency: Specifying a Symbolic Interactionist Theory', *The American Journal of Sociology*, 97 (6): pp. 1577–1611.

Matza, D. (1964) *Delinquency and Drift*, John Wiley & Sons, New York.

Matza, D. (1969) *Becoming Deviant*, Prentice Hall, Englewood Cliffs, NJ.

Matza, D. and Sykes, G. (1961) 'Juvenile Delinquency and Subterranean Values', in *American Sociological Review*, 28: pp. 712–720.

Mauss, M. (1979) *Sociology and Psychology*, Routledge and Kegan Paul, London, Boston, MA and Henley.

Maxwell, M. and Tschudin, V. (eds) (1990) *Seeing the Invisible*, Arkana, Penguin, London.

May, T. (1993) *Social Research*, Open University Press, Maidenhead.

May, T. (2003) *Social Research*, Open University Press, Maidenhead.

McEwen, C. and O'Sullivan, S. (eds) (1988) *Out the Other Side*, Virago Press, London.

McFarland, T. (1996) *Paradoxes of Freedom*, Clarendon Press, Oxford.

McSmith, A. (2008) '£60.000 for Mosley's Pain', in *The Independent*, Friday, 25 July.

Mead, M. (1962) *Male and Female*, Pelican, London.

Melossi, D. (1994) 'The "Economy" of Illegalities: Normal Crimes and Social Control in Comparative Analysis', in Nelken, D. (ed.) *The Futures of Criminology*, Sage, London.

Melzack, R. (1977) *The Puzzle of Pain*, Basic Books Inc., New York.

Melzack, R. and Torgerson, W. R. (1971) 'The Language of Pain', in *Anaesthesiology*, 34: pp. 50–59.

Merck, M. (1993) *Perversions: Deviant Readings*, Routledge, New York.

Merleau-Ponty, M. (1968) *The Visible and the Invisible*, Northwestern University Press, Evanston, IL.

Merton, R. K. (1968) *Social Theory and Social Structure*, Free Press, New York.

Miller, J. (1994) *The Passion of Michel Foucault*, Flamingo, London.

Monbiot, G. (2005) 'Protest Is Criminalised and the Huffers and Puffers Say Nothing', *The Guardian*, 4 October: p. 27.

Money, J. and Keyes, R. W. (1993) *The Armed Robbery Orgasm: A Lovemap Autobiography of Masochism*, Prometheus Books, Amherst, NY.

Morris, S. (1991) *The Culture of Pain*, University of California Press, Berkley.

Morrison, W. (2006) *Criminology, Civilisation and the New World Order*, Routledge, Cavendish and Oxon.

Moser, C. (2001) 'Paraphilia: Another Confused Sexological Concept', in P. J. Kleinplatz (ed.) *New Directions in Sex Therapy: Innovations and Alternatives*, pp. 91–108, Brunner-Routledge, Philadelphia. Also available at http://tempik.webzdarma.cz/literatura/parmoser/

Moser, C. A. and Kalton, G. (1979) *Survey Methods in Social Investigation*, Heinemann, London.

Moser, C. and Kleinplatz, P. J. (2005) 'DSM-IV-TR and the Paraphilias: An Argument for Removal', in *Journal of Psychology and Human Sexuality*, 17 (3/4): pp. 91–109.

Murphy, T. (1997) 'Feminism on Flesh', in *Law and Critique*, VIII (1): pp. 37–59.

Murray, T. E. and Murrell, T. R. (1989) *The Language of Sadomasochism: A Glossary and Linguistic Analysis*, Greenwood Press, New York.

Murray-Swank, N. A., Pargament, K. I. and Mahoney, A. (2005) 'At the Crossroads of Sexuality and Spirituality: The Sanctification of Sex by College Students', in *The International Journal for the Psychology of Religion*, (15): pp. 199–219.

Naffine, N. (1997) *Feminism and Criminology*, Polity Press, Cambridge.

Nietzsche, F. (1954) *Thus Spoke Zarathustra*, Vintage Books, New York.

Nietzsche, F. (1967) *The Will to Power*, Vintage Books, New York.

Paasonen, S., Nikunen, K. and Saarenmaa, L. (2007) *Pornification: Sex and Sexuality in Media Culture*, Berg, Oxford and New York.

Payne, S. L. (1973) *The Art of Asking Questions*, Princeton University Press, New Jersey.

Peters, E. (1985) *Torture*, Basil Blackwell, Oxford and New York.

Pfohl, S. (1993) 'Male Mas(s)ochism and Cybernetics,' abridged version of 'Venus in Microsoft,' Chapter 14 in Arthur and Marilouise Kroker (eds), *The Last Sex*, New York: St Martin's Press, 1993: pp. 184–197.

Pfohl, S. (1993) 'Venus in Microsoft: Male Mas(s)ochism and Cybernetics,' in *Canadian Journal of Political and Social Theory*, 16 (1–3): pp. 82–123.

Pidd, H. (2008) 'Punishment That Was Not a Crime: Why Mosley Won in the High Court', in *The Guardian*, Friday, 25 July: p. 4.

Plummer, K. (1975) *Sexual Stigma: An Interactionist Account*, Routledge and Kegan Paul, London and Boston, MA.

Plummer, K. (1995) *Telling Sexual Stories. Power, Change and Social Worlds*, Routledge, London.

Plummer, K. (2003) *Intimate Citizenship: Private Decisions and Public Dialogues*, McGill-Queen's University Press, Montreal and Kingston.

Polhemus, T. and Randall, H. (1994) *Rituals of Love*, Picador, London and Basingstoke.

Quart, A. (2003) *Branded the Buying and Selling of Teenagers*, Arrow Books, London.

R.v.Brown-case ([1993] 2 WLR 556; [1993] 2 All ER 75; 1994] 1 AC 212.

Rabinow, P. (ed.) (1997) *The Essential Works of Michel Foucault 1954–1984*, Vol. 1, New Press, New York .

Radin, M. J. (1996) *Contested Commodities*, Harvard University Press, Cambridge, MA.

Radner, H. (2008) 'Compulsory Sexuality and the Desiring Woman', in *Sexualities*, 11 (1/2): pp. 94–99.

Raisborough, J. (2002) 'Feminist Theory – a Question of Difference', in Marsh, I. (ed.) *Theory and Practice in Sociology*, Prentice Hall, London.

Rajchman, J. (1991) *Truth and Eros: Foucault, Lacan, and the Question of Ethics*, Routledge, London.

Raymond, J. G. (1989) 'Putting the Politics Back into Lesbianism', in *Women's Studies International Forum*, 12 (2): pp. 149–156.

Rich, A. (1980) *On Lies, Secrets and Silence*, Virago, London.

Rich, A. (1986) *Your Native Land, Your Life*, Norton, New York.

Richardson, M. (1994) *Georges Bataille*, Routledge, London.

Ricoeur, P. (1988) *Time and Narrative*, University of Chicago Press, Chicago.

Ritzer, G. (1999) *Enchanting a Disenchanted World: Revolutionizing the Means of Consumption*, Pine Forge Press, Thousand Oaks, CA.

Robertson, M. and Amnesty International (1984) *Torture in the Eighties*, The Pitman Press, London and Bath.

Rogers, C. (1951) *Client-Centered Therapy: Its Current Practice, Implications and Theory*, Constable, London.

Roughgarden, J. (2004) *Evolution's Rainbow: Diversity, Gender and Sexuality in Nature and People*, University of California Press, Berkley.

Rousseau, J. J. (1782/1953) *Confessions*, Penguin Classics, London.

Rubin, G. (1984) 'Thinking Sex: Notes for a Radical Theory of the Politics of Sexuality', in Vance, C. (ed.) *Pleasure and Danger*, Routledge and Kegan Paul, London.

Rubin, G. (1994) 'Thinking Sex: Notes for a Radical Theory of the Politics of Sexuality', reprinted in Abelove, H., Barale, M. A. and Halperin, D. M. (eds), *The Lesbian and Gay Studies Reader*, Routledge, New York.

Russell, D. E. (1998) *Dangerous Relationships. Pornography, Misogyny and Rape*, Sage, London.

Sallis, J. (1988) 'Dionysus – in Excess Of Metaphysics', in Krell, D. F. and Wood, D. (eds) *Exceedingly Nietzsche: Aspects Of Contemporary Nietzsche Interpretation*, Routledge, London.

Sampson, E. (1993) *Celebrating the Other*, Harvester Wheatsheaf, New York, London, Toronto, Sydney, Tokyo and Singapore.

Saner, E. (2008) 'Crime and Punishment', in *The Guardian*, 9 July: pp. 5–7.

Sarafino, E. P. (1998) *Health Psychology*, John Wiley & Sons, Hoboken, NJ.

Sawicki, J. (1991) *Disciplining Foucault*, Routledge, Chapman and Hall, Boca Raton, FL.

Scarry, E. (1985) *The Body in Pain: The Making and Unmaking of the World*, Oxford University Press, New York.

Scharfetter, C. (1980) *General Psychopathology*, Cambridge University Press, Cambridge, London and New York.

Schatzmann, J. and Strauss, A. (1973) *Field Research: Strategies for a Natural Sociology*, Prentice Hall, New Jersey.

Schinkel, W. (2004) 'The Will to Violence', in *Theoretical Criminology*, 8 (1): pp. 5–31.

Schrag, O. O. (1971) *An Introduction to the Philosophy of Karl Jaspers*, Duquesne University Press, Pittsburgh, PA.

Scott, G. R. (1938) *The History of Corporal Punishment: A Survey of Flagellation in Its Historical, Anthropological and Sociological Aspects*, Torchstream books, London.

Segal, L. (1994) *Straight Sex*, Virago, London.

Segal, L. and McIntosh, M. (eds) (1992) *Sex Exposed*, Virago, London.

Seidman, S. (1994) *Contested Knowledge: Social Theory in the Postmodern Era*, Blackwell, Oxford.

'Sex Uncovered Poll: Homosexuality' http://www.guardian.co.uk/lifeandstyle/2008/oct/26/relationships

Shaffir, W. B. and Stebbins, R. A. (1991) *Experiencing Fieldwork*, Sage, Newbury Park, CA.

Shah, H. and Rutherford, J. (2006) 'This Vision of a Good Society Can Lift the Nation Out of Social Recession', *The Guardian*, 20 September: p. 28.

Shilling, C. (1993) *The Body and Social Theory*, Sage, London, Thousand Oaks, CA and New Delhi.

Shilling, C. (2003) *The Body and Social Theory*, 2nd ed., Sage, London, Thousand Oaks, CA and New Delhi.

Shilling, C. (2008) *Changing Bodies*, Sage, Los Angeles, London, New Delhi and Singapore.

Smart, B. (2003) *Economy, Culture and Society: A Sociological Critique of Neo-liberalism*, Open University Press, Buckingham and Philadelphia.

Smart, C. (1995) *Law, Crime and Sexuality*, Sage, London, Thousand Oaks, CA and New Delhi.

Snitow, A., Stansell, C. and Thompson, S. (eds) (1983) *Powers of Desire – the Politics of Sexuality*, Monthly Review Press, New York.

Solomon, D. (ed.) (1964) *LSD – the Consciousness-Expanding Drug*, G. P. Putnam's Sons, New York.

Spengler, A. (1977) *Manifest Sadomasochism of Males: Results of an Empirical Study. Archives of Sexual Behavior*, 6: pp. 441–456.

Spurling, L. (1977) *Phenomenology and the Social World*, Routledge and Kegan Paul, London, Henley and Boston, MA.

Staal, F. (1975) *Exploring Mysticism*, University of California Press, Berkeley and London.

Stanley, C. (1995) 'Teenage Kicks: Urban Narratives of Dissent not Deviance', in *Crime, Law and Social Change*, 23: pp. 91–119, Kluwer Academic Publications, Netherlands.

Stanton, D. (ed.) (1992) *Discourses of Sexuality*, University of Michigan Press, Michigan.

Starkloff, C. F. (1974) *The People of the Centre – American Indian Religion and Christianity*, The Seabury Press, New York.

Staub, E. (2003) *The Psychology of Good and Evil: Why Children, Adults, and Groups Help and Harm Others*, Cambridge University Press, Cambridge.

Stychin, C. F. (2003) *Governing Sexuality: The Changing Politics of Citizenship and Law Reform*, Hart Publishing, Oxford.

Stover, E. and Nightingale, E. O. (eds) (1985) *The Breaking of Bodies and Minds*, W.H.Freeman and Company, San Francisco.

Stratton, J. (1996) *The Desirable Body: Cultural Fetishism and the Erotics of Consumption*, Manchester University Press, Manchester.

Sumner, C. (ed.) (1990) *Censure, Politics and Criminal Justice*, Open University Press, Milton Keynes.

Superson, A. M. (2005) 'Feminist Philosophy in the Analytic Tradition', in *Hypatia*, 20 (4), Fall 2005: pp. 1–9.

Sutherland, E. (1974) *Criminology*, J.B. Lippincott Company, Philadelphia.

Sykes, G. and Matza, D. (1957) 'Techniques of Neutralisation: A Theory of Delinquency', in *American Sociological Review*, (22): pp. 664–673.

Synnott, A. (1993) *The Body Social*, Routledge, London and New York.

Szasz, T. (1972/1995) *The Myth of Mental Illness*, Paladin, New York.

Tart, C. T. (1975) *States of Consciousness*, E. P. Dutton & Co., New York.

Taylor, G. W. (1997) 'The Discursive Construction and Regulation of Dissident Sexualities: The Case of SM', in Ussher, J. D. (ed.) (1997) *Body Talk: The Material and Discursive Regulation of Sexuality, Madness and Reproduction*, Routledge, London.

Taylor, G. W. and Ussher, J. (2001) 'Making Sense of S&M: A Discourse Analytic Account', in *Sexualities*, 4 (3): pp. 293–314.

Theweleit, K. (1978) *Männerphantasien 1+2*, Stroemfeld Verlag, Frankfurt am Main.

Thompson, B. (1994) *Sadomasochism*, Cassell, New York and London.

Thompson, M. (1991) *Leatherfolk*, Alyson Publications, Boston, MA.

Tombs, S. and Hillyard, P. (2004) 'Towards a Political Economy of Harm: States, Corporations and the Production of Inequality', in Hillyard, P., Pantazis, C.,

Tombs, S. and Gordon, D. (eds) *Beyond Criminology: Taking Harms Seriously*, Pluto Press, London.

Townsend, L. (1993) *Leatherman's Handbook II*, Carlyle Communications, New York.

Trigg, R. (1970) *Pain and Emotion*, Clarendon Press, Oxford.

Turner, B. (1996) *The Body and Society: Explorations in Social Theory*, 2nd ed., Sage, London and Thousand Oaks, CA.

Turner, B. S. (2008) *The Body and Society*, Blackwell, Oxford.

Tyler, M. (2004) 'Managing between the Sheets: Lifestyle Magazines and the Management of Sexuality in Everyday Life', in *Sexualities*, 7 (1): pp. 81–106, Sage, London, Thousand Oaks, CA and New Delhi.

Vale, V. and Juno, A. (eds) (1989) *Modern Primitives* (Re/Search 12), Re/Search Publications, San Francisco.

Valier, C. (1994) *Seductive Methaphor: In Pursuit of Excess. Sadomasochism and Dissemination*, unpublished Master thesis, University of Cambridge.

Van den Hoonaard, W. C. (1997) *Working with Sensitizing Concepts: Analytical Field Research*, Sage, Thousand Oaks, CA.

Van Swaaningen, R. (2005) 'Public Safety and the Management of Fear', in *Theoretical Criminology*, 9 (3): pp. 289–305, Sage, London, Thousand Oaks, CA and New Delhi.

Vance, C. S. (ed.) (1984) *Pleasure and Danger: Toward a Politics of Sexuality*, Routledge and Kegan Paul, Boston, MA.

Visker, R. (1995) *Michel Foucault: Genealogy as Critique*, Verso, London.

Wade, J. (2000) 'Mapping the Courses of Heavenly Bodies: The Varieties of Transcendent Sexual Experience', in *Journal of Transpersonal Psychology*, 32: pp. 103–122.

Warner, M. (1999) *The Trouble with Normal: Sex, Politics, and the Ethics of Queer Life*, Harvard University Press, Cambridge, MA.

Weber, M. (1948/1965) *The Sociology of Religion*, Methuen, London.

Weeks, J. (1986) *Sexuality*, Tavistock, New York.

Weeks, J. (1995) *Invented Moralities: Sexual Values in an Age of Uncertainty*, Polity Press, Cambridge.

Weeks, J. (2003) *Sexuality*, Routledge, London and New York.

Weeks, J. and Holland, J. (1996) *Sexual Cultures – Communities, Values and Intimacy*, Macmillan, Basingstoke and London.

Weeks, J., Donovan, C. and Heaphy, B. (2001) *Same Sex Intimacies: Families of Choice and Other Life Experiments*, Routledge, London.

Weinberg, T. and Kamel, G. W. (1983) *S and M: Studies in Sadomasochism*, Prometheus Books, Buffalo, NY.

Welton, D. (ed.) (1998) *Body and Flesh*, Blackwell Publishers, Oxford.

Westhaver, R. (2005) ' "Coming Out of Your Skin": Circuit Parties, Pleasure and the Subject', in *Sexualities*, 8 (3): pp. 347–374, Sage, London, Thousand Oaks, CA and New Delhi.

Wilkins, L. (1964) *Social Deviance*, Prentice Hall, London.

Wilkinson, R. G. (2005) *The Impact of Inequality: How to Make Sick Societies Healthier*, Routledge, Abingdon.

Wilkinson, S. and Kitzinger, C. (1993) *Heterosexuality*, Sage, London.

Windybank, S. (1992) *Wild Sex*, Virgin Books, London.

Winnicott, D. W. (1971) *Playing and Reality*, Tavistock, London.

Wolf, N. (2003) 'In the End, Porn Doesn't Whet Men's Appetites – It Turns Them Off the Real Thing', in *NY Magazine*, October 20: p. 1.

Woodward, K. (ed.) (1997) *Identity and Difference*, Sage, London.
Woodward, T. (ed.) (1993) *The Best of Skin Two*, Richard Kasak Book, USA.
Wulff, D. M. (1997) *Psychology of Religion*, 2nd ed., John Wiley & Sons, New York.

Other Sources

Aitkenhead, D. (2003) 'Netporn' http://www.guardian.co.uk/theobserver/2003/mar/
   30/features.review7, accessed 12.11.2008.
The Independent, 20.2.97: 5.
The Observer, 20.4.2008, NHS cases of childabuse.
The Scotsman, March 96: 14.
The Times, 12.3.93: 21.
The Times, 20.2.97: 12.
Times Law Reports, 12.3.93: 42.

Index

Unitary 'truth', 151
universalizing strategy of psychology, 34
'unruly bodies', 16, 77
unstructured non-directive
  interviews, 63
Utilitarian calculus of pleasure and
  pain, 141

'valorization of the victim', 49
van Swaaningen, R., 158
'vanilla-sex', 86, 87, 117, 169, 194
'victimless crimes', 78

violence, 4, 8, 30, 31f, 35, 56, 62, 79, 80,
  115, 125ff, 131, 141, 145ff, 151, 156f,
  159f, 234

Warner, M., 230
Weeks, J., 1, 2, 47, 51, 53, 80, 87,
  231f, 235f
Welton, D., 1, 9, 15, 24f, 36, 54, 140,
  161f, 165f
Woodward, 112, 160
woundhealing in domestic violence and
  torture etc. vs in consensual 'SM', 56ff